Cases in Strategic Marketing Management:

Business Strategies in Latin America

Guillermo D'Andrea
Instituto de Altos Estudios Empresariales

John A. Quelch
London Business School

Prentice
Hall

Upper Saddle River, New Jersey

Library of Congress Cataloging-in-Publication Data

D'Andrea, Guillermo J.

    Cases in strategic marketing management : business strategies in Latin America/
Guillermo J. D'Andrea, John A. Quelch.

       p. cm.

    Includes index.

    ISBN 0-13-089490-7

    1. Marketing—Latin America—Management—Case studies. I. Quelch, John A. II. Title.

HF1416.6.L38 D36 2000

658.8'02—dc21   99-086112

VP/Editorial Director: James C. Boyd
Senior Editors: Leah Johnson and Bruce Kaplan
Editorial Assistant: Rebecca Calvert
Assistant Editor: Anthony Palmiotto
Senior Marketing Manager: Shannon Moore
Director of Production: Michael Weinstein
Manager, Production: Gail Steier de Acevedo
Production Coordinator: Kelly Warsak
Permissions Coordinator: Suzanne Grappi
Media Project Manager: Cindy Harford
Manufacturing Buyer: Natacha St. Hill Moore
Associate Director, Manufacturing: Vincent Scelta
Cover Designer: Bruce Kenselaar
Full Service Composition: Carlisle Communications, Ltd.

Printed in the United States of America.

10 9 8 7 6 5 4 3 2 1
ISBN 0-13-089490-7

CONTENTS

Foreword

Latin America is a continent of huge contrasts. Latin America is also a continent seeking sustainable growth. The 1990s introduced a series of sharp changes that affected the face of business on the continent. The openness, deregulation, and privatization of the regional economies led to a new competitive and international scene. Monopolies rapidly disappeared because of the openness of domestic markets. Chile, Mexico, Venezuela, Argentina, Colombia, and Brazil opened their economies, and both local and multinational companies suddenly found their markets threatened.

Consumers quickly became allies of the open and competitive markets. They welcomed the entry of less expensive and more modern products from foreign countries. For example, Colombian steel consumers wanted Venezuelan steel, which is comparable in quality to Colombian steel and much less expensive. Before the opening of markets, however, Columbians were not able to import Venezuelan steel due to market restrictions.

The State started to withdraw rapidly from operating sectors it had monopolized for decades and began to focus on arbitrating, regulating, and promoting private business. Telecommunications, previously considered a state-owned sector, has opened multiple opportunities due to deregulation. The case of Impsat reflects this situation including the opportunities and difficulties that this dynamic presents.

Restructuring of companies, and a better focus of markets, products, and strategy are occurring, just as happened in the United States and Europe during the 1980s.

These trends have a major consequence for companies: they must become market oriented. The change from protected and unstable markets—where it was possible to limit quantity in order to maintain prices—to open markets with an unlimited volume of modern and low cost products, introduces the new factor of competition. Companies have to win over their customers to gain their loyalty.

With growing and protected economies, marketing activity was limited to advertising and selling. Changes implemented by the government in the 1990s have brought in new foreign competitors, along with opening the region's economies. Joint ventures with foreign companies and acquisition of local companies became a quick way to enter these new markets. Some companies chose to open their ownership possibilities, listing their common stock not only in their own countries but also in the more developed financial markets where they can obtain a greater flow of investment capital.

The priority now is to manufacture and market updated products at competitive prices. This means that companies have to consider added value, market segmentation, positioning of the company and its products, operating niches, and effective distribution operations and post-sale service. Management becomes more complex, and new opportunities emerge in a region that is struggling to rapidly modernize its economies.

In this new economic context, a professional middle class, with more education and buying power is emerging. This class of people is exhibiting an increasingly rational behavior: they are becoming intelligent consumers. Product innovation, information systems applied to marketing, managing the business chain, and franchising are growing trends that lead to new ways of communication, such as direct marketing.

A significant number of companies in the region are family owned, leading to typical problems of achieving a high level of professional management. Former protectionism that encouraged economic growth and industrial development reduced the competitiveness of the sectors. Political and economic instability and inflation caused the immediate demand for goods, thus reducing the importance of more sophisticated marketing practices.

Effective management in the new economic climate requires a passion for quality and careful follow through, which can lead to competitive advantages.

Increasing competition and growing globalization lead to the necessity of being more market oriented than ever before. For decades, companies were focused on producing more of the same goods, for lower costs, but these savings were not necessarily reflected in lower prices. Now, companies need to fit into the global context through innovation, in which the major challenge is in the selling stage. Winning and keeping markets is a challenge well beyond product standardization and competitive pricing. Adding value, market segmentation, identification and effective operation of market niches, careful attention to distribution and service—these are the challenges for companies in Latin America.

New skills are needed to cope with the complex selection of products, technologies, markets, partners, and financial means. This complexity opens a whole range of options, with opportunities and discoveries that challenge a new breed of entrepreneur.

In this book, we want to reflect the impact of these developments in the practice of marketing. Our experience teaching marketing to executives and consulting to companies in several Latin American countries has shown us the need to adapt the marketing framework in order to apply its concepts effectively in the changing regional reality at the start of the new millennium.

The cases and business stories illustrate the challenges and some of the solutions devised to overcome them. There are few books devoted to clarifying the management of marketing in Latin America—interesting as it may be for practitioners, students, and academics, both in the region as well as those who want to learn more about how the business environment is changing in Latin America.

We would like to extend our special thanks to our colleagues and research assistants who generously contributed the cases and articles. Professor Jorge Gutiérrez Villarreal from IPADE (Mexico), Professor Carlos Guillermo Sequeira from INCAE (Costa Rica), and Professor Jon Martinez from Universidad Adolfo Ibañez (Chile) generously agreed to let us use their cases. In Buenos Aires, Sergio Postigo assisted with the research that is the basis for notes appearing in some chapters, especially the brief stories of Latin American companies.

Leah Johnson was key to "getting things done," and so was Terry Routley, who showed impressive amounts of patience and commitment. To all of them, we give our gratitude.

CHAPTER

1

MARKETING IN THE CHANGING LATIN AMERICAN ENVIRONMENT

THE CHANGING MODEL

Latin America is recovering from its lost decade. Big changes in the macroeconomic models have brought about changes in the operation of the markets in the Latin American region that are reflected by both the increase of competition and the strong awakening of national economies vying to take their place in the global marketplace. The political and economic instability that for decades characterized this region with its periods of growth followed by deep recessions appears to be giving way to an environment that is more politically stable, deregulated, and open to international competition.

The pervading conviction that these countries are overrun with drugs, debt, devaluations, and dictators is changing. These negative perceptions contributed to the loss of almost one-third of this region's share in the gross world product during the 1980s, in spite of its abundant and diverse natural resources and large potential markets. Most countries of Latin America are finally carrying out true reforms, even though the opportunity, sequence, and speed of these changes differ among the various nations.

It is difficult to establish with any accuracy the moment when the change in the Latin American markets began. During the 1970s, under General Pinochet's government, the privatization and liberalization of Chilean commerce occurred, led by a group of young economists from the University of Chicago. Other milestones included the cessation of Mexico's repayments in 1982, and in the early 1990s, Argentina managed to beat its hyperinflation and cause Brazil serious worry about the stability of prices.

Even though all have been decisive factors, Chile has taken the lead in the economic race. Its market reform has had its difficult moments—especially in 1982—but these reforms appear to have been placed on solid ground, with a rate of savings close to that of Asia, considerable budgetary surplus, and a solid and stable financial sector. The results seem to confirm it: a decade of high growth, diversified exports, and the most comprehensive capital market of the region.

The remaining Latin American countries emerged from the debt crises of the 1980s with much difficulty. The sudden collapse of external financing dramatically reduced

1

investments leading to an increase in taxes and an increase in tariffs to discourage imports. The quick solutions met with little success. They tried to curb inflation by controlling prices and salaries but, without addressing the real problem, governments tended to be wasteful in their spending. These failures, pitted against the obvious fact that the reform in Chile was working, and that the new generation of economists were educated principally at North American universities, generated a new consensus that Latin America needed to extensively reformulate the role of government. A new, large-scale, comprehensive strategy aimed to reduce tariffs, deregulate the financial sector, and bring about large budgetary cuts supported by privatization programs. These efforts were combined with a resolute attack to reduce inflation, producing varying results from country to country.

In Argentina, the inflation of 1989 was the most serious economic factor, discrediting the capability of the government to manage its fiscal policy. An exchange system was introduced to anchor the peso to the dollar, eliminating all monetary freedom. In Brazil, the population had grown accustomed to living with inflation, which is why the Plan Real was directed to deregulate the economy. In both cases the results were similar: The government no longer absorbed all the financial resources and the population was able to make plans beyond the following day, for the first time in decades.

These serious—and apparently successful—initiatives of introducing fiscal reform into the larger Latin American countries coincided with extensive changes at the international level. The Brady Plan, after decades, was a creditable initiative to deal with the debts of the commercial banks of this region by allowing these indebted reformers to reduce their debts by converting them into long-term bonds. Changes in the capital market of the world's wealthy countries also contributed. The regulatory reform of the North American stock market simplified the issue of stocks abroad on behalf of companies in developing countries, with a great increase in the number of institutional investors who, between 1988 and 1993, increased their assets from $7.5 to $13 billion (U.S. dollars). At the beginning of the 1990s, a drop in the U.S. interest rates encouraged investors to look for higher profits in the emerging markets.

Wealthy Latin Americans, who had invested their savings abroad to protect themselves from inflation and unpredictable governments, began to bring their capital back home, even though this money was not necessarily any more stable at home than abroad. The elite of Latin America are sophisticated investors and they more quickly perceive the vulnerability of their own respective countries: The disaster in Mexico at the beginning of 1994 possibly originated because of the fleeing of Mexican capital. Foreigners also have begun to invest heavily in the region. Between 1990 and 1994, they deposited almost $70 billion (U.S. dollars) in direct investments in companies that they perceive to have great potential under these recently restructured economies. In the same period, portfolio profit takers invested $50 billion in stock and $45 billion in bonds.

The flow of money into this region totally changed the financial outlook of the area. After paying $114 billion (U.S. dollars) to foreign creditors between 1983 and 1989, Latin America received almost double that amount between 1990 and 1994, with Mexico topping off the list, receiving $100 billion. This affluence lessened the pain of economic reform, helping to increase the value of many Latin American exchange rates, but the same easy access to money sources also helped to exaggerate the extent of these financial reforms. The leaders of Latin America—always conscious of their political image—used these flourishing markets of stocks and bonds to prove the success of their economic strategies.

The increase in interest rates in the United States in early 1994 helped to make Latin American investments less attractive, when the institutional investors noticed that the most reliable assets in their own country began to offer better profits. Returns on bonds increased dramatically, slowing new stock issue; and stock markets suffered a prolonged drop in prices, showing a lack of clear direction. Flaws also began to appear in the economic structure of the region.

Mexico was almost back to where it began. Because the government wanted to win the election, it made the situation very difficult for the ruling party (the PRI) to undertake any steps toward austerity that might suggest recession. Meanwhile, investors' concern about political assassinations and popular rebellions grew. Argentina managed to maintain its exchange rate in this situation, but it could not improve its large budgetary deficit in 1994. Brazil had barely begun its own fiscal reform, but in general the region managed to maintain an important growth ratio.

BPI% Growth							
	1994	*1995*	*1996*	*1997*	*1998*	*1999*	*2000 (Est.)*
Latin America	5.4	0.9	3.5	4.4	2.1	0.7	4.0
Argentina	7.4	(4.6)	4.4	7.6	3.6	(3.4)	3.0
Brazil	5.8	4.1	2.9	3.4	(0.1)	0.8	3.0
Mexico	4.5	(6.2)	5.1	6.5	4.9	4.0	5.0

Safe from the prolonged scourge of inflation, Latin Americans got on the wave of consumerism, buying all kinds of products that they had desired for so long. Short-term investing continued to dominate, the fragile banking system of the region never quite managing to guide savings to more long-term investments. Soon they became aware that the money had not been invested well and that there still remained certain unresolved aspects of reform that required further thought. Legal standards in many countries had to be modernized to offer better guarantees of equality and independent justice. Education required a long-term investment to bring subjects and teachers up to date to better educate the population and alleviate the rates of illiteracy still too high in some countries. The systems of health and social services also were not strong enough to offer the necessary sense of comfort and well-being to a growing labor force, which in a democratic environment demands rights with a louder voice.

LATIN AMERICA: A NEW GLOBAL COMPETITOR

Latin America is returning to the world economic map. In addition to previous economic alliances, such as Aladi, the Andino Pact, the Economic Community of Central America, CariCom of the Caribbean countries, and NAFTA, a new alliance emerges. It is called Mercosur, and it offers great promise to this region of 300 million people, who speak two languages, have common cultural roots, and are self-sufficient in energy matters and convergent politics. To the four original members comes Chile, with the incorporation of Bolivia and the addition of Peru not too distant in the future. Venezuela, Colombia, and Ecuador will not be excluded from this integration process. Chile is proving that distance is not an obstacle, and Argentina is straightening up its economy and fighting for a better government and better training for its businesspeople. These two countries lead the region. According to the annual survey of the Foro Mundial Ecónomico, at the end of 1996, Brazil led the group of nations rich in natural resources such as India, South Africa, Indonesia, Venezuela, and Russia. Mexico is fighting to recover itself, and Colombia and Venezuela are still presenting doubts, according to the executives surveyed.

The last 20 years have seen many dramatic changes in the region. Democracy and a greater economic stability brought on a reduction in inflation and economic growth toward the end of the 1980s. In the 1990s, the opening up and deregulation of the economies, and a growing wave of privatization, have brought about new opportunities for local and international companies, attracting foreign investment, as in the case of tourism. The Spanish chain, Sol Meliá, invested $1 billion in Cancún, Puerta Vallarta, and Baja California; Ixtapa Marina is a development of $640 million. Investments were also directed toward the Dominican Republic, the Virgin Islands, and Puerto La Cruz in Venezuela. Valle Nevado in Chile received $300 million. Buenos Aires is recycling its port, and together with Santiago, these two cities saw the arrival of the Hyatt Hotel chain and the remodeling of hotels in the Sheraton and Kempinski chains.

The Regional Scene

The consequences for the economy of the region have been many. After decades of product scarcity—when consumers could buy only those products companies decided to sell them—markets have now become oversupplied. Customers who are discovering their power and are influenced by the recession, which brought adjustments to the economy, behaved more rationally. Companies also are discovering the value of their loyal customers. This growing professional middle class demands better products and services, as these consumers begin to travel more, regionally, comparing and incorporating products they discover in their travels. The change in orientation of companies, which before looked to the products but now looks to the consumer, demands that family enterprises show a new professionalism. This new look will enable them to compete with the new international competitors and regional entrepreneurs such as Chilean Guillermo Carey, who went from being president of Ladeco to building hotels in association with Novotel; or Juan Navarro, who acquires companies with his Exxel Group in Argentina. Regional businesses are growing in number. The largest publisher of the region, Lord Cochrane of the Chilean Edwards family, formed a joint venture in Brazil with the O Globo group, in Colombia, with Carvajal Publiguías and Ditempo, and in Argentina they now distribute through Bertrán.

Current technological advancements flaunt the comparative advantages of the region. For example, trees grow in 8- to 20-year cycles in this region, as compared with 40-year cycles of the Northern Hemisphere, making lumber production increasingly lucrative. The abundant fishing industry is exploited and reaches even the most sophisticated of markets, such as the Japanese, thanks to Salmond Gourmet Choice and Five Stars of Chile. Exporklore of Ecuador exports its lobsters to Italy, Spain, and France. Lerner, the second largest world producer of gelatin, exports to thirty-five countries from its plants in Brazil and Argentina. Leather is the foundation of the shoe industries in Brazil and the Caribbean. The Colombian leather industry exports 65% of its production to the United States and 10% to the European Union. Israeli capital is invested in Mexico to produce the Haas avocado pear, ranked first in world consumption. Local companies such as David del Curto promote the distribution of Chilean fruit in Europe. Exports of mangos and other tropical fruits from Venezuela are growing, as is the palmetto production in Colombia and Brazil, where producers are taught to harvest better yields by taking advantage of the off-season. Chilean wine competes with those of New Zealand, Australia, and South Africa and its wine industry has seen the arrival of foreigners: Los Vascos has signed an agreement with Chateau Lafitte of Bordeaux, Miguel Torres of Spain is settling into the country, Hampton Inv. of the United Kingdom has acquired part of Viña Undurraga, and Franciscan Estates of California has acquired 50% of Errazuriz Panquehue. From Uruguay, Paylana and Dancotex export fine cashmere woven cloth to manufacturers in Hong Kong, Eastern Europe, and Mexico. But even with the advantages of location, other companies such as Emzo of M. del Plata export packaging machines to such demanding clients as Nabisco, Unilever, Colgate, Bayer, Johnson & Johnson, and Nestlé with a price premium. In a like manner, Siderca, of the Techint Group, has a 30% share of the world market for steel tubing.

National Markets or a Regional Market?

In this context, management is becoming more and more regional than national, and individual careers and mobility will be proven true in this region. In 1992, Mavesa of Venezuela bought a 29% share of Procter and Gamble in that country and exchanged brands and lines of production with Cargill, managing a 52% share in the mayonnaise, mustard, vinegar, and sauce market. They expanded into Colombia, where through an agreement with Nacional de Chocolates, they gained access to 80,000 market outlets, getting a larger share of the market formerly in the hands of Corn Products. They also imported cookies and chocolate drinks to Venezuela. An agreement with Sungene of California allowed them to better their production of sesame seeds for oil, exporting 25% of their sales of $200 million to India and Central America.

The increase in global competition is creating pressure to better the quality of products: New or updated products are appearing, and the standards of exportation are improving the domestic products. As long as the public remains uninformed, they will have a strong loyalty to brand names with local brands winning out. With a freeing up of the markets, prices and margins will decrease, which will push to reduce manufacturing costs in specialized factories. New products will be introduced according to regional standards and will be distributed regionally. The life cycle of products will converge and new Latin American products and brands will appear (e.g., Topper shoes, Corona beer, and Sadia turkey).

These new products will be advertised regionally, through services such as those that CNN and MTV offer for Latin America and through TNT which reaches 800,000 subscribers in twenty-seven different countries with trilingual programming in English, Spanish, and Portuguese. The Fox Channel is following in the same direction. Home Box Office of Time Warner and Omnivisión of Venezuela arrive with HBO Olé to supply 300 chains of cable networks to compete with CineCanal, a result of a merger between United International Pictures and MVS of Mexico. Also from Mexico, Multivisión offers movies in Spanish 24 hours a day to cable chains in Latin America and the Caribbean.

Perhaps most revealing is what the Mexican chain Televisa has managed to do. It entered Venezuela through Venevisión, Peru through Compañía Peruana de Radiodifusión, in Chile it created Megavisión, and in Argentina and the United States it operates Galavisión-Univisión. With the Univisa chain, it operates in San Francisco, Los Angeles, Fresno, Phoenix, Albuquerque, Dallas, San Antonio, Miami, and New York, directing itself toward the Spanish-speaking audience with programs in Spanish. Through PanAmSat it operates three satellites with which its news channel, ECO, covers forty-five countries. With its radio operations and the 120 million issues of eighty titles published by the America Group in Miami, its sales reach $6 billion (U.S. dollars).

Regional competition will bring on a fierce fight for regional participation. It will increase the power of modern distribution chains, which already feel the presence of foreigners such as Wal-Mart who is facing off its predecessor Carrefour in Brazil and Argentina. The growth in self-service is opening up opportunities to establish new concepts, for example, the hard discount of chains such as Aldi, Lidl, or Día of Promodes of France, and the appearance of clubs that buy and sell by mail.

A few difficulties remain to overcome, including the small investments in science and technology. The region also must eliminate corruption, curb the still powerful bureaucracy, secure political stability, lower still too high import tariffs, and avoid the appearance of new and more subtle forms of protectionism. *The Wall Street Journal* has criticized that intraregional commerce has grown in response to a moderate increase in trade with other regions. But more than showing the formation of a new closed trade bloc such as the European Union, NAFTA, or that of Southeast Asia, it reflects a strengthening of the region to help it face a more competitive world.

EL MERCOSUR

In spite of existing differences in the political and economic evolution of Latin American countries and a history of failure in matters concerning regional commerce (such as the Associación de Integración Latinoamericana, the Mercado Común Andino, and the Mercado Común de América Central), the Latin American nations have signed several trade (bilateral and multilateral) investment agreements. In the Treaty of Asunción, signed in March 1991, the most ambitious of these treaties, the presidents of Argentina, Brazil, Paraguay, and Uruguay bound their nations to the creation of the Zone of Free Trade of the Cono Sur (Mercosur) that would gradually eliminate all trade barriers. It represents a serious initiative to create a large consumer market and assume a larger role in the world economy. Other countries in South America (Chile, Bolivia, Venezuela, and Peru) have approached Mercosur and have begun negotiations for their participation. It is expected to create a common market to be formed in 2006, but since 1991, the regional trade has tripled in economic value. With a population exceeding 200 million people, it constitutes one of the most important economic blocs in the world today.

The European Union is the most important partner for the Mercosur, absorbing 26% of its exports while 18% goes to the United States, 5% to Japan, and 51% to the rest of the world. Its bilateral trade is shaped as follows:

Mercosur	*EU*	*US*	*Japan*
Exports	26%	18%	5%
Imports	25%	22%	5%

The European Union also leads in direct foreign investment with 47%–42% comes from the United States and 11% from Japan. Most of the investment is directed to telecommunications, air transportation, automobiles, tourism, and financial services industries. Regarding cooperation to regional development, 75% comes from Europe. On December 15, 1995, an agreement between the European Union and Mercosur was signed in Madrid which aimed at creating a free trade area between the two economic blocs before the year 2005. It is based on three main principles: a systematic political dialogue; a schedule for progressive trade liberalization; and economic rules to support integration including scientific, entrepreneurial, technological, transportation, and energy cooperation. The integration encompasses a GDP of $6.9 trillion (U.S. dollars), with $660 billion in imports, $638 billion in exports, and a consumer base of 600 million people.

Regarding NAFTA, there have been negotiations for establishing a "Four plus Three" agreement between Mercosur and NAFTA member countries, but formal relationships exist only between Mercosur and the United States, and this agreement has not been active. The countries from both blocs are now actively working for the creation of the American Free Trade Area, a project that the Mercosur countries have supported since the Miami American Summit Meeting in December 1994.

The idea of hemispheric integration has not been abandoned. The integration of other Latin American countries into Mercosur—creating SAFTA (South America Free Trade Agreement)—seems to be the logical next phase to increase its members' competitiveness.

Managerial Consequences

Trading in this more competitive and regional environment requires different skills than those that facilitate the growth of local companies. It demands the ability to quickly adapt oneself to a different way of doing business. The free markets have become the general rule in the region. At the same time, the multinational companies that enter into these regional markets should be able to adapt themselves to situations that evolve quickly, toward practices that serve to bring companies together rather than dwell on initial differences that are particular to each country.

The lack of capital to finance the growth of companies creates problems especially for small and medium-size companies. These companies have less access to financial resources and are more vulnerable to the presence of competitors and foreign products.

The marketing executive should be accustomed to a changing environment, to governmental interventions—only sometimes advantageous—and to inflations that erode the value of money so quickly that one soon develops an attitude of "save yourself while you can." These changes to a more stable and competitive environment oblige managers to master the prudent administration of their business, and not simply the tools of commerce. Managers must also focus on stock, where returns on investments show measurable results not waste, to stay abreast of the competitive field. Strategic alliances with foreign or regional companies offer managers unique opportunities to gain insight into how other businesses operate, to gain access to Latin American markets and the associated technology, and to benefit from the knowledge and experience of other partners.

In summary, the chance to take up a competitive position in this complex but promising region—where the first on the scene will have the best choice of partners, countries, and products—demands that management, in general, and marketing specialists, in particular, ask a series of questions before compromising their company's resources.

- What goals should one set?
- In what countries should one invest and in what order? and how quickly?

- What products and services should one offer? What similarities or differences exist among the varying markets?
- What form of participation should the company take?
- What marketing tactics should the company employ?
- How should products and services be distributed, taking into account the level of concentration and the degree of development of the channels?
- What advertising should be done in proportion to each country?
- What pricing policies apply?
- How should a company organize the specific agendas of the region?

BUSINESS OBJECTIVES

Multinational and local investors can differ in their strategic objectives. The multinationals have four basic goals.

1. To supply the internal open markets with products and technology that they develop in the region or have been developed elsewhere.
2. To have the advantage of being first on the scene over other global competitors in internal protected markets or to reduce the initial leadership of competitors already on the scene.
3. To secure reliable and competitive supply sources, at the same time improving the global sales and manufacturing base of the company. This applies to traditional commodities (i.e., oil, copper, bananas), nontraditional merchandise (i.e., lobster, hazel nuts, macadamia nuts, concentrated lemon juice), and little proven manufacturing methods (i.e., manufacturing of electronic components, garments).
4. To improve the competitive position of the company through the combination of worldwide profits with competitive and comparative advantages.

Meanwhile, the local investors have two main goals.

1. To improve their competitive position in their local markets and to defend themselves from foreign competitors about to enter the market.
2. To supply the foreign market while they gain access not only to export profits (i.e., tax credits and subsidy credits), but also to the strong foreign currency or foreign tax credits.

Local investors can perhaps also invest abroad (e.g., Cemex and Vitro from Mexico, Petroven from Venezuela, and CMPC and Cochrane from Chile) to improve their global and local competitive position, thus meeting some of the same objectives as the multinationals.

SELECTING LOCATIONS

Foreign investors should seek to understand how countries operate on an individual basis, and how each country fits into the regional picture.

Regional Grouping

The common but mistaken tendency is to see Latin America as a homogeneous bloc of countries. Although the countries can be grouped in several ways, the differences are still evident at virtually all levels. These differences can make a country more or less attractive to investors. It is useful, therefore, to group the countries according to certain criteria, as presented in Exhibit 1.

Level of Development

Three groups use the criteria from Exhibit 2. The first consists of the three countries of the Cono Sur: Argentina, Chile, and Uruguay, which have the same high standard of living. Demographically, these countries also are different from the rest of Latin

	EXHIBIT 1 Summary of the Groups		
Country	*Level of Development*	*Economic Performance*	*Liberalization of the Economy*
Argentina	High	Good	Open
Bolivia	Low	Good	Open
Brazil	Average	Average	Trying to Open
Chile	High	Good	Open
Colombia	Average	Good	Open
Costa Rica	High-Average	Good	Open
Ecuador	Low	Average	Trying to Open
Mexico	Average	Good	Open
Paraguay	Average-Low	Good	Open
Peru	Low	Poor	Trying to Open
Uruguay	High	Average	Trying to Open
Venezuela	Average	Average	Trying to Open

	EXHIBIT 2 Demography and Development of Selected Countries in Latin America					
Population				*Level of Development*		
	1998 Inhabitants (millions)	*Annual Growth Rate 90–98*	*% of Urban Population*	*Life Expectancy 90–98*	*Infant Mortality 90–98*	*Adult Literacy[1]*
Argentina	35.6	1.3	88	71.8	23.2	96.2
Bolivia	7.5	2.2	52	59.3	75.1	80.1
Brazil	163.7	1.4	78	66.3	57.7	83.3
Chili	14.6	1.5	84	74.4	14	95.2
Colombia	40	1.91	73	69.2	37	91.3
Costa Rica	3	2.4	54	76.3	13.7	93.1
Ecuador	11.5	2.2	57	68.8	49.7	89.1
Mexico	94.3	1.73	73	71.5	34	89.6
Paraguay	4.3	2.7	48	70	38.1	90.1
Peru	24.4	1.74	71	66	64.4	88.7
Uruguay	3	0.6	86	72.4	20	96.3
Venezuela	22.8	2.15	86	71.8	23.2	91.1

[1]The illiteracy rate was taken for persons 15 years old or older.

Sources: United Nations, Banco Mundial, BID, CEPAL.

EXHIBIT 3	Economic Performance of Selected Latin American Countries					
	GDP				**Inflation**	
	1998 GDP Total[1] **(billions)**	**GDP per capita**[1] **1998**	**% rate of Annual Growth**[2] **1990–97**		**Annual % rate 1990–98**	**1998**
Argentina	325	8,950	5.4		19.3	0.9
Bolivia	5,126	708	4.0		10.55	
Brazil	820	4,790	3.4		289	3.2
Chile	77	4,820	8.3		10.9	5.1
Colombia	95	2,180	4.4		18.7	22.7
Costa Rica	5,375	1,606	3.7		21.25	
Ecuador	15,970	1,423	3.4		24.1	
Mexico	348.6	3,700	2.2		19.7	15.9
Paraguay	6,190	1,282	2.9		14.4	
Peru	63.7	2,610	6.2		48.3	7.2
Uruguay	8,366	2,641	3.8		39.75	
Venezuela	79.3	3,480	2.2		49.9	35.8

[1]The data on the total and per capita GDP is figured at constant market prices, based on 1980.
[2]The calculation of the annual growth rate of the GDP is done based on constant market prices, 1990 base.

America in that they have fewer black or indigenous inhabitants, more European descendants, relatively low ratios of population growth, and more than 80% of the population concentrated in urban areas. In terms of health conditions and education, Costa Rica also could be included in this group, even though it is significantly different in geographic proximity and demographic composition.

The second group includes Brazil, Colombia, Mexico, Venezuela, and, considering only levels of health and education, Paraguay. These five countries are somewhat lower on the scale of development and all show similar patterns of population growth and urban concentration. Nevertheless, they differ greatly in terms of language, size, and standard of living.

The third group includes Bolivia, Ecuador, and Peru which are relatively alike in geographic and demographic characteristics. Paraguay also could enter this grouping based on these criteria. This group shows the lowest levels of development in the region.

This type of grouping gives better results than using only the GDP per capita, the classification most widely used (see column 2 of Exhibit 1). The GDP index would suggest six levels: (1) Argentina and Uruguay; (2) Brazil, Mexico, and Venezuela; (3) Chile and Costa Rica; (4) Peru and Colombia; (5) Paraguay and Ecuador; and (6) Bolivia.

Economic Performance

The countries also could be classified into three economic groups: high performance, average performance, and low performance. The high-performance group includes Argentina, Bolivia, Chile, Costa Rica, Colombia, Mexico, and Paraguay. Each of these countries shows moderate to steady growth, relatively low inflation, strong exports, and a foreign debt that is shrinking or at least under control. The countries of average performance are Ecuador, Uruguay, and Venezuela. These countries show mixed

EXHIBIT 3 (cont.)

Investments		Foreign Commerce		External Debt	
Coefficient of Fixed Gross Investments[3] 1992–1994	1994 Net Direct Foreign Investment (billions)	1998 Export (billions)	1998 Imports (billions)	1998 Debt Total (billions)	Annual % Rate of Debt Variation 1993–1995
8.9	1,200	26.2	30.4	123.2	15.0
−4.8	128	1,042	1,215	4,523	9.5
4.9	2,035	53.0	61.4	193.7	4.6
5.2	796	17.0	18.9	31.4	5.3
20.6	1,515	10.7	15.4	31.8	5.3
1.5	298	2,750	2,954	3,794	−0.4
−0.8	531	4,358	4,095	13,934	1.3
1.2	10,973	110.4	1,120	149.7	12.5
0.0	180	1,966	3,667	1,328	4.5
11.1	2,326	6.8	8.6	30.5	10.3
5.2	155	2,117	2,682	4,825	6.3
−15.2	239	22.7	8.9	35.5	3.3

[3]The coefficient of the net fixed investment equals the growth rate percentage of investment as a percentage of the GDP.

Sources: United Nations, World Bank, IDB, CEPAL, The Economist.

results, but generally have only average prospects. Finally, Brazil and Peru show low economic performance.

Political and Economic Liberalization

There are four possible combinations based on political and economic measures. The most developed nations are open both politically and economically. Since the 1950s, the majority of the governments of Latin America have followed protectionist political and economic measures, even though some countries (Costa Rica) were then open politically. Chile was the first, in the mid-1970s, to implement open economic policies even within politically protectionist measures. Since the mid-1980s, most Latin American governments have changed, first in more open political policies and then in more open economic policies. At the end of the 1980s, Chile integrated its economic freedom into its new political openness. In 1992, Argentina adopted an aggressive program of economic deregulation and privatization of public services. Brazil is following a similar, yet more gradual program, as is Peru.

Although the open political systems have been strengthened throughout the entire region, the economic liberalization has not been brought about in the same manner. It is not surprising that the countries with the best economic performance are also the ones with more liberal and market-oriented economies. Argentina, Bolivia, Chile, Costa Rica, Colombia, Mexico, and Paraguay have relatively open economies with successful results as proof. A large problem that investors encounter when establishing operations in the majority of these countries is the lack of experience that the government has in dealing with this new openness.

Some companies have developed their own ways of grouping the countries. For example, a board director of Citibank of Chile explains,

The same as Citibank, we don't use the map to classify the countries. Instead we use other criteria. For example, countries in Latin America with debt problems can be placed into two groups: "convergent" countries with effective solutions, as in the case of Chile, Uruguay, Colombia, and Mexico; and countries without performance like Peru, Argentina, and Brazil. Citibank, the same as others, tries to differentiate between past performance and future promise.

Even though the criteria of the groupings is generally useful, investors who are only interested in specific products or industries should consider the countries individually. For example, investors interested in raising lobsters will recognize the infrastructure, specialization, and experience that Ecuador has as a source of competitive global advantage. Ecuador, then, will be more attractive than other countries that have better scores in the groupings.

Careful Evaluation of the Country

Investors should understand the unique characteristics of each country. This information is easily available from different sources including the regional directors, the U.S. and host country governments, banks, research centers, multilateral agencies, and specialized publications (*Business Latin American, LDC Debt Report, Latin Trade,* and *América Economía*). The first analysis will prepare the investors to visit those countries that offer the most attractive opportunities, that is, those that are compatible with the speciality, resources, values, and objectives of the investor.

PRODUCT SELECTION

What product categories will offer the most attractive business opportunities? The degree of attraction, of course, depends on the resources and goals of the investor. Agribusiness, directed equally to internal and foreign markets, offers opportunities to develop, sustain, and improve global advantage, as the export of flowers, out-of-season fruits, and vegetables already demonstrate. Wood, paper, and pulp products also are at this point, as are renewable and nonrenewable commodities, which offer great potential once the world economy recovers from its current slump.

All durable and nondurable consumer goods will offer important investment possibilities once internal markets are opened, if the economic reform continues. In several countries of Latin America, especially in Brazil, the middle class is already growing rapidly. Many people can, for the first time, buy the consumer goods they have always been desiring. In Brazil, only one-fourth of the homes with electricity have washing machines. In addition, the median age in many Latin American countries is low (18.4 years in Mexico compared with 32.7 years in the United States). Thus, a large percentage of the population is now entering the age of highest consumption, a factor that will surely affect the demand for goods.

Telecommunications has only recently been initiated into Latin America. Many state-owned telecommunications companies have been privatized. Foreign companies can see enormous potential: Only 6% of the population has a telephone connection compared with 71% in the United States, 45% in Europe, and 16% in Asia. There are more telephones in France than in all of Latin America. AT&T and Motorola are already capitalizing on that fact: AT&T sold fiber-optic equipment to Telmex (the Mexican telephone company) at a value of $130 million (U.S. dollars) and Motorola has just received the license for distribution of cellular telephones in the northern section of Mexico. Similar opportunities will arise as more public services become privatized.

Another flourishing business in Latin America is tourism. The region has beautiful beaches, underwater diving spots, archeological expeditions, and an exceptional climate. The proximity of the region to the United States and Canada virtually assures a constant flow of North American tourists. The Caribbean Islands alone received more than 17 million visitors in 1989. Mexico, where tourism employs one of every twelve Mexicans and where income from that sector is second only to that of oil, considers this industry to be the most promising source of economic growth. The investment opportunities available are hotels, shopping malls, ski resorts, and airlines.

Some countries have already attained satisfactory investments in tourism. The Spanish group Sol-Meliá is investing $1 billion (U.S. dollars) for the construction of six hotels in Mexico; Marriott and Cementos Mexicanos have formed a joint venture to invest $500 million more in that same country; and the huge project of transforming the old port of Buenos Aires into hotels and shopping malls attracted more than $500 million from foreign investors.

The pharmaceutical industry is soon to open up. In Brazil, a commission appointed by the government is developing a new copyright code and it is hoped that other countries will follow. This reform that protects copyrights could cause "major changes in investments and formation of corporations" in the pharmaceutical industry, says R.A. Cage, vice president of Eli Lilly.

Other opportunities exist in the computer, automobile, footwear, and garment industries, even though restrictions in some countries still apply. Nevertheless, their sheer size boasts their potential. For example, the region's computer hardware market already exceeds $6 billion annually and the software market (in spite of the lack of adequate protection) is at $1 billion with an annual growth of more than 10%.

INVESTMENT PARTICIPATION

There are several ways to invest in the Latin American market, ranging from contractual agreements to direct investments. In this section we analyze some of the most important alternatives.

Exporting

Foreign companies can export directly or indirectly. Indirect exporting means that one uses an export management company based in the region, an export trading agency, or an export agent who takes charge of exporting the products of the investor. This intermediary can be paid on a commission basis for services rendered or payment could be titular, buying merchandise with discounts and reselling it in Latin America. The short-term advantage of this strategy is that it already uses existing channels of commercialization and international distribution, thus avoiding the expense of having to establish them. However, if a company eventually wants to be involved in the Latin American market, this strategy may not be the most sensible or effective when dealing with long-term costs.

The exporting company also can assume the direct responsibility for the commercialization of its products in Latin America, either selling directly to the consumer or finding a local representative to sell its products in the country. The choice between the two methods often depends on financial capacity, the level of import barriers, and the amount of risk or loss that the foreign company is willing to assume.

Strategic Alliances

For investors who know nothing about Latin America, alliances with local producers or distributors may be the best way to enter into the market. An alliance allows investors to share the risks and to increase strongholds with their companies experienced in the region. The most common types of cooperative agreements in the region have been joint ventures, licenses, franchises, mutual distribution agreements, and subcontracting.

Generally, governments support joint ventures (JV) and sometimes offer incentives for them. Joint ventures bring in not only foreign capital, but also technology and experience. Foreign companies benefit from cheap labor, abundant raw materials, access to new exporting markets, and local experience. It is hoped that joint venture activity increases in the near future for the following three reasons: (1) While it increases the competition for western investments and increases competition among global industries, it will be progressively reducing the controls over foreign investments. (2) As western companies look for the advantage of being the first investors, a joint venture with a company can speed up the fight among global competitors for similar business. (3) Because regulations regarding joint ventures are more favorable, companies currently exporting on an operation base that is set up only through transaction or licensing might look to better their ties and form new joint ventures. With time, hopefully some of these joint ventures will turn into subsidiaries of unlimited holdings.

Successful joint ventures make sense for both partners, as is illustrated by the case of Cadbury Schweppes, who signed a joint venture with Sanbra in preparation of its launching of Schweppes tonic water in Brazil. Sanbra distributes the tonic water in the Brazilian market for nonalcoholic beverages, which is third in the world after the United States and Mexico. "Without the help of an experienced partner, we would not have felt comfortable," says John Neilson, vice president of marketing for Cadbury International. "But we had faith that Sanbra was on our side and we managed to make headway in spite of the volatile Brazilian economy." Sanbra, for its own part, added products with higher margins to its existing distribution system, improving its efficiency and increasing its importance as a provider of nonalcoholic beverages.

Other companies prefer to sign long-term licensing contracts. These are a good alternative for small or midsize companies that lack the experience, capital, and security to risk direct investments abroad. Nevertheless, licensing contracts have their risks. The lack of control on the part of the one who grants the license can cause severe problems if the products are of low quality and harm the company name, or if the "filtration" of the products into other countries at lower prices deteriorates the relations with other partners in the venture.

Franchising in Latin America is still in the development stage. Perhaps Brazil has the greatest development in this area. In less than 3 years, McDonald's, Kentucky Fried Chicken, Pizza Hut, and Benetton have established operations in Chile. Mexico has concluded contracts with Arby's, McDonald's, Baskin Robbins, Holiday Inn, Alpha Graphics, and Athlete's Foot. The majority of the contracts are brand franchises, which allow the possessor of the franchise to grant subfranchises and also to open their own businesses.

Other companies have signed joint distribution contracts through which they agree to distribute the products of both companies in their own territories, which is what happened between Digital Equipment Corporation (computer hardware) and Sonda (software) to form the joint venture.

Firms also can subcontract to existing companies so that they can offer them operations and services. Even nonprofit organizations can use this strategy. For example, the United Nations Development Program subcontracted to Fundación Chile, a nonprofit organization with proven experience in the transfer of foreign technology, with the goal that it would give technical assistance to Argentina, Bolivia, Ecuador, El Salvador, and Guatemala.

Assembly Plants on Deposit

For years, American companies have operated assembly plants just across the border, called *maquiladoras* (cross-border assembly plants). They export components to Mexico and then, later, import the finished product, paying only a reduced customs tax, if any, on the added value. In many cases, a twin plant in the United States manufactures the components. The proximity of the two plants allows for close supervision by a manager who can direct both plants. In February 1990, more than 1,800 companies were operating *maquiladoras,* employing more than 500,000 workers. This represents a 20% increase when compared with 1989, a growth rate that seems to have continued into the beginnings of 1991. Japanese and Korean companies, like their American counterparts, are now operating cross-border assembly plants.

Originally there were only a few *maquiladoras* for agricultural use; however, recent changes in ownership rules and a new relaxed attitude toward foreign investment have pushed the development of the promising food-processing industry in Mexico. Agribusiness now represents the most rapidly growing segment of the $3 billion (U.S. dollars) annually coming from cross-border plants, with agricultural products at a wholesale value that totals $100 million (growing from only $20 million at the beginning of 1989). A firm based in California grows onions in Mexico from imported seeds and then exports onion powder and onion flakes for distribution in the United States. Such agreements can be beneficial to both parties. The consumers in the United States get good products at a reasonable price while Mexicans are able to find jobs without having to cross the border. Businesses in the United States use this method to compete with the low costs of foreign competition.

Acquisitions

Acquiring a company already in operation is a relatively cost-efficient way of entering into the Latin American market. This method can be particularly attractive, because the heavy devaluations in the majority of the countries give excellent returns in terms of the local currency when buying these companies. The experts believe that the recent crisis has created a buyers' market in Latin America. Procter & Gamble took advantage of these factors in the 1980s. Instead of establishing subsidiaries on its own, it acquired Industria Phebo in Brazil, Mammi in Venezuela, Inextra in Colombia, and Laboratorios Geka in Chile.

The swapping of debt capitalization has made investments more attractive. Investors buy the government notes of debt with large discounts in secondary markets and then exchange these notes for local currency (or state assets) at much higher rates. The investor gets an excellent price and the government cancels part of its debt at favorable rates. This method is especially satisfactory for privatization measures.

The use of debt capitalization "swaps" in privatization (in billions of U.S. dollars)			
	1989	*1990*	*1991 (Est.)*
Argentina	1.00	2.90	2.00
Brazil	0.88	1.50	1.80
Mexico	2.24	2.85	3.25

Source: Instituto Internacional de Finanzas, Fostering Foreign Direct Investment in Latin America, Washington D.C., 1990.

In the last two years, the foreign multinationals have acquired or are in the process of acquiring the government telecommunications companies of Chile, Argentina, Uruguay, Mexico, and Brazil through debt capitalization "swaps." The U.S. Bell Atlantic and Spain's Telefónica acquired 60% of ENTEL of Argentina paying only $750 million (U.S. dollars) for the equivalent of $5 billion of Argentina's external debt. The consortium formed by Scott Paper, Citibank, and the Chilean subsidiary Royal Dutch Shell invested $350 million (U.S. dollars) in the Chilean industry of paper and pulp manufacturing. Swift, the Argentine subsidiary of Campbell Soup used debt capitalization swaps to reduce the $41 million cost of constructing a new meat packaging plant.

Totally New Investments

To set up a totally new company from its conception is perhaps the most risky and the most difficult way to start operations in Latin America. The bureaucracy and protectionism in many of the countries, and the unique characteristics of the markets, make it difficult to begin a new business without a local network of contacts who can provide knowledge of the local commercialization practices, consumer behavior, and relationships with the government. This method would be best for those companies who are familiar with Latin America or who already operate in the region.

CONCLUSION

The climate of political and economic change that is running throughout Latin America is as real as the one affecting Eastern Europe, although less publicized. The commercial agreements, the tariff reductions, and the privatization promise a more competitive business environment and growing opportunities for foreign multinationals. Former President Bush's Americas Initiative, the constitution of the Area de Libre Comercio de las Americas, the admission of Mexico into the North American Free Commerce Zone, and the formation of Mercosur and its future expansion all reinforce the need for the multinationals of North America, Asia, and Europe—with their headquarters and their focus in the Northern Hemisphere—to look south and to include Latin America in their strategic planning. The makeup of the regional market with more than 300 million inhabitants, two languages (Spanish and Portuguese), common historical roots, and convergence in regard to political stability and economic alignment offers investors a unique opportunity.

2

THE INTERNATIONALIZATION OF LATIN AMERICAN MARKETS

COUNTRIES OF OPPORTUNITY

Many factors have helped to open up the Latin American markets: large foreign debts, foreign demand interested in obtaining quality products and the willingness to pay for them, and the need to attain the technology available abroad. The most dynamic companies have already begun to make contacts abroad as a key strategy for their survival. Strategic alliances, international sourcing, and foreign investment are some of the strategies followed.

Alliances with companies from developed countries are increasing in order to reach marketing agreements, use technology, or supply products. Licensing agreements and joint ventures also allow companies to simultaneously gain greater presence in the richest markets. Other types of alliances being developed among companies in the region allow them to compete abroad. For example, Brahma, Brazil's leading beer producer, joined with Lodrina of Argentina to combine the production of Argentine barley with Brazilian technology to better compete at the international level.

Other opportunities arise from the search of global companies for quality products at the best price without regard to the geographical location of the supplier. From car engines to data processing, many companies are dedicated to producing the goods that those companies prefer not to produce.

In the early 1990s, American investors, who were already established in Asia with plants of manufactured products, began to look toward Latin America and the Caribbean. The driving factors for this shift in outlook included the increasing cost of Asian labor, the growth of the area's industrialization, and the uncertainty over Hong Kong's status after 1997 when it would no longer be part of the British Empire and would become incorporated into the People's Republic of China. Other causes were the rebelliousness of Japan's Liberal Democratic Party considered as a submission to pressure from Washington, and Indian Prime Minister V.P. Singh's lack of clarity in regard to foreign investments in a country with an impressive industrial infrastructure. Dissatisfaction also was growing in the United States where, although flooded with Asian products, they were still facing restraints for entry of American products into Asia. In a similar way, anti–North American feelings were growing in Asia because of commercial reasons.

This search for new business horizons went unnoticed by many, because of media news about the emergence of the European Union in 1992 and the annexation of Central European countries after the fall of the Berlin Wall. However, Hong Kong businesses silently started to establish operations in the Bahamas, Jamaica, Argentina, and Chile. The textile industry alone offered from 50,000 to 75,000 plants as opposed to only 16,000 in the United States and 8,000 in Mexico. Thus, Brazil became the first exporter of women's shoes to the United States, making some American businesspeople a little nervous; and the Dominican Republic became the sixth major exporter of garments. The manner of doing business and commercial perception in the garment sector of Argentina, Brazil, and Chile was very European in nature. Besides, Latin America was nearer, therefore reducing both the time and cost of maritime transportation. The region also demonstrated a good operating capacity, especially in the garment and shoe industries.

As businesspeople searched for (1) low-cost locations to set up their plants (e.g., for garment manufacturing), (2) local markets with certain appeal, and (3) the possibility of exporting to the United States, they began to discover opportunities in Argentina, Chile, Colombia, and Brazil. The Caribbean, Chile, and Argentina became more interesting than Mexico and Brazil, countries which up until this time had received the bulk of direct investment in this region.

Pending Tasks

Not all economic fronts have progressed in a similar fashion in every country of the region; but its growth should persuade us to look beyond our borders and realize that Latin America is the logical destination for companies of the region. This region has the same language, a common historical origin, and is a short distance away. But it has not always been so when it comes to the forming of joint ventures. In 1974, Jorge Delano, president of Vencerámica of Venezuela, decided to create Ecuatoriana de Sanidad with an investment of $2.5 million.

INTERNATIONAL EXPANSION

Until recently, most Latin American products in the global-level market were bulk. They were basic products with low processing and relatively secure export markets, suffering a steady downward trend in prices. The current opening up of economies has presented a new level of competitiveness that has forced many companies in the region to improve their products and services, reaching a point at which they are able to compete with foreigners, not only in their own domestic markets, but also in the markets where those imported products originated. Thus, the strategy of added value has become an increasingly popular idea among competing companies. Adding intelligence to products, including those with a high content of natural resources, is fundamental as values of in-bulk resources decrease. Vale do Rio Doce is a Brazilian company that illustrates this course of action.

Vale do Rio Doce

Vale do Rio Doce was founded in 1949 as a company of mixed capital (45% in the hands of 60,000 shareholders and 55% owned by the Brazilian government). The company grew under the leadership of Eliezer Batista, minister of mines in 1960 and president of his own private steel company.

In the 1960s the company surprised everyone with its construction of a port at Tubarao with a ship capacity of up to 100,000 tons. At that time, the biggest ships received in Brazil reached only 35,000 tons. Even though there were no big port facilities in any part of the world, this company knew that the only way their products could enter Japan was through a revolution in maritime transportation, which began with the arrival of tank ships. From the beginning, this company sought a shipping company and the creation of a competitive value chain covering operations, marketing, logistics, and port facilities.

In 1990, with 24,000 employees and sales totaling $2.072 billion, Vale do Rio Doce had the highest profits of any Brazilian company with $734 million. It diversified in almost all possible mining-related specialties, forest project services, and had its own transportation network that combined railways, ports, ships, and foreign investments. It owned 50% of California Steel Industries, which is an American company that formed a joint venture with Japan's Kawasaki Steeland (a ferromanganese plant in Dunkirk, France, in partnership with France's Usincor-Sacilor, the world's second largest steel company) by that time.

Looking for a stronger presence in Europe, Vale do Rio Doce established its international marketing company—Rio Doce International. Based in Brussels, it accounted for 25% of the world iron export market in 1990. The company's strategy was then oriented toward diversification. Through association with its customers, it created Nibrasco, Hispanobras, and Itabrasco, iron pellet facilities devoted to the markets of Japan, Spain, and Italy. It also created Cenibra, a cellulose and paper plant, 49% of which was owned by its Japanese customers.

Their presence abroad allowed Vale do Rio Doce not only to control the marketing network in its final stages, but also to have firsthand information about market evolution and technological developments. Thus, they were among the first to adopt fiber optics for its railway network signals and e-mail to network its subsidiaries and associated companies. Vale do Rio Doce has two railways, one running 400 kilometers to the Tubarao port and another of 900 kilometers connecting the Carajás Basin with its own port of San Luis de Maranhao at the head of the Amazon River. These routes offer transportation to third parties such as Fiat, who uses them to dispatch its automobiles from Belo Horizonte instead of sending them by truck to the seaports.

The next problem Vale had to face was debt. The completion of the Carajás project, including railway tracks, required an investment of $3 billion, leaving a debt of $2 billion in 1987 (most of it in yen, German marks, and Swiss francs that fluctuated according to the U.S. dollar) and a domestic debt of $1 billion. Facing this, the "competitive network" was almost useless and for the first time in 31 years the company showed a considerable loss of $191 million. Wilson Brummer, now company president but at that time finance director, was in charge of the financial restructuring, stretching out the debt profile, protecting it against the fluctuation of the dollar, and establishing a retirement incentive program that saved $100 million. He raised $300 million in foreign funds through financial debenture, not convertible into shares but with profit sharing. He also raised another $280 million through certificates of indebtedness with future gold options or cash reserves at 8% and $200 million in commercial security bonds on future exports. Perhaps the most important move was the direct debt repurchase advantage of the large discount on Brazilian debt. The financial success of Rio Doce has not affected the original mining mission of the company, which contributes an important percentage of profits, but it has added instead another key dimension to the business.

With a manageable debt, the future outlook of the company is promising, having made some great investments: doubling aluminum production for finished products by association with Japanese companies, establishing a cellulose and paper plant with Suzanco paper company, doubling the production of Cenibra, tripling gold production and introducing the production of titanium, nickel, and copper. The change from raw materials to industrialization has meant a sales increase from $3 billion to $5 billion. Company personnel are making long-term bets on the company, with lower-level wages above current market rates and higher-level wages below current rates, thus giving continuity to the administration.

FREE TRADE AREAS

The free trade areas have generated new export businesses such as the Dominican Republic's fourteen zones that supply most of the country's exports, becoming the most dynamic at the end of the 1980s and absorbing 10% of U.S. purchases to the Caribbean. These areas offer very low salaries, for example, $0.60 per hour for assembly workers. Some offer labor selection and hiring services, personnel administration, on-site custom facilities and agents, wage and payroll services, banking, and also housing and school search for foreign executives and their families. The most modern areas have a private hospital and full-time physicians, including a gynecologist, as 75% of the labor force are women. A broad range of products is assembled or manufactured including garments, footwear, jewelry, electronic components, manufactured goods, pharmaceutical products, data processing, and computer-aided graphic design. Political stability and its proximity to the American market add to the appeal of the 2 million workers available at a competitive cost.

The "twin-plant" connection is a strong ingredient for profits through agreements with plants in Puerto Rico or in the United States, which can opt for a 100% (U.S.) or 90% (Puerto Rico) tax exemption. By combining the hourly labor cost of $8 in Puerto Rico with $2 in the Dominican Republic, a "combined cost" of $4 is reached compared with $18 labor cost in the United States.

Garment manufacturing has attracted Asian companies suffering from the limited quotas to enter the American market. Pharmaceutical and health companies are setting up twin plants. Twenty firms, including Westinghouse, employ thousands of workers and their exports of electronic equipment are steadily increasing. Footwear companies do the sewing in the Dominican Republic, cementing the soles in Puerto Rico (within North American commercial barriers), and then export the finished products to the United States, achieving quality similar to that of Southeast Asia with only a third of the dispatch time. AMR Caribbean Data Services, established in 1987, is an affiliate of American Airlines and employs about 700 workers who, working in three shifts, enter data for airline and insurance companies.

Mercosur

In 1990 before the signing of the Mercosur agreements, Brazilian companies had already been established in Uruguay and were enjoying the benefits of South American integration. Tintas Renner was constructing a paint plant and Brahma, together with

Malterias Pampa of Argentina, purchased Malterias Uruguay. The agreement between Uruguay and Brazil (PEC) exempted 2,000 products from levies and Cauce with Argentina, establishing tariff preferences, immediately increased the exchange. But investors had to face the following obstacles: the enormous amount of paperwork caused by government bureaucracies, a myriad of contradicting rules and decrees, and the risk of searching for shelter under state protection. The patriarchal generation of the 1940s and 1950s was clearing the way for new progress.

Ciquiñe Companhia Petroquímica found out about the Argentine projects and decided to move quickly. It set up Ciquiñe Uruguay in Pando, 30 kilometers from Montevideo, to preserve the chance for a high-potential market, like that of Argentina, for alcohol, one of its main products. With an investment of $1.2 million, it secured the Uruguayan market, the entry into Argentina without tariffs, the raw materials processing in Brazil, and its reentry into that country without tariffs. Its partner, Dacarto, engaged in the plastics business, invested $400,000 to sell its production of $3 million to Brazil with freight prices less expensive than from its branches in Sao Paolo or Bahía, and also targeting the Chilean and Argentine markets.

The emergence of commercial blocs is a typical phenomenon of the 1990s in Latin America along with previously unknown trade freedom within the region. Slowly, but systematically, countries are forming economic blocs and companies are adapting the strategies to this new environment that opens up unimaginable business opportunities.

TEN KEYS FOR EXPORT COMPANIES

Exports of some Argentine traditional products have fallen lately. The famous "meat of the Pampas" does not enter the European Union except under Hilton Quota, and cooked meat that overcomes health barriers is placed with difficulty. Fruits such as oranges and grapefruit have been replaced by those of Brazilian origin. The explanation of a low exchange rate works for many, but it still does not explain why exports of compressed air tubing, wool thread, steel pipes, packaging machines, sport shoes, and denim fabric continue to thrive. The confusion grows if we consider the idea that these products are not based on comparative advantages that have traditionally backed exports, nor are they whole sectors like meat or fruit which push exports, but rather are specific companies that maintain the export activity. So the question is what helps a company to develop its export capacity, especially in a nonbenefited sector? Besides the rules of quality, continuity, and reliability, we have observed ten other points that allow export companies to gain advantage.

1. Competitive advantages should be the main priority to sustain operations abroad. Comparative advantages, if any, can help in the early stages, but competitive advantages ensure a long-term defendable position. The international competitive position must be determined by the company and also the strategy that it will follow: opportunistic, striving, unstable, or sustainable.

2. Strong management commitment over the long run and managerial quality are indispensable for the internationalization of a company. The obstacles and barriers, both internal and external, are innumerable and can discourage some from setting up a small-volume operation, in which strong customer demands are high and profitability may be low. Without the support of an "internal champion" with sufficient leadership, exporting will be no more than a marginal activity, providing some social prestige. At the operating level, demanding customers, long distances, low profitability, low volume, and constant travelling make this job unpopular.

3. Local leadership is highly recommended before starting export operations. In exporting, problems are amplified by distance. Therefore, it is necessary to develop within the organization a solid knowledge of those key factors of business that will help to put out the "fires" brought on by distance. Avoiding interferences in operative and management resources requires an organization capable of taking care of and solving local problems so as not to affect exports. It is not about dominating the sector in which the company competes, but rather dominating those key factors related to the company's business. Problems can then be solved locally, not at a distance of 7,000 kilometers, or after a 10-hour flight, or in another language.

4. The point of no return occurs when foreign operations start to have an important role in the sales and earnings volume, and then find it hard to retreat and absorb volume-keeping profitability at the local level. If one exports only 5% of sales the effect on volume is almost imperceptible, but it is radically different if one exports 60%. Each company, according to its internal features, competitive position, and sector conditions, must determine the threshold from which there is no backing down. This analysis should be done at the point when exports reach 25% of sales, especially when the internal market does not grow at the same rate as that of total sales.

5. Market selection is key, not only due to its impact on volume but also as a learning tool for the company. Markets that are close and small—even though less attractive and challenging—are good for the initial stages because they teach the company how to solve typical export problems. Larger, more distant, and more competitive markets are more advisable for the second stage when the company is more trained in international issues and the kinks have worked out so as not to discourage buyers who are usually cautious when beginning to deal with a new, unknown supplier from a country about which they know little except their traditional products. Meats, fruit, and grain are familiar to them, but as yet, there is no image established for such products as wine, marmalade, biscuits, iron and steel products, software, or satellite communications services. In those cases, it will be necessary to overcome that natural disadvantage, as experienced 30 years ago with Japanese audio products and cars, or more recently with wines from Spain and Chile, and the Brazilian arms industry.

6. Product adaptation is essential. Adapting a product to fit the market with assistance from the destination market is a more complex, but simpler solution to this classic problem. As much as a company tries to generate a differentiated product with competitive advantages in its destination market, the original product will seldom remain untouched without some change in its design or, at least, its packaging. Understanding this need for adaptation is best done by those who are familiar with the market, generally the local distributors in the destination country.

7. Entry strategies for moving into the market must be evaluated. Market penetration can be accomplished using representatives with or without exclusivity, distributors, or production licenses, or establishing one's own assembly or production abroad. The list implies different levels of commitment, from furnishing orders originated abroad, to setting up production facilities at the destination market. International commitment implies different levels of requirements determined by the scope of the project; therefore, the choice of entry strategy must be appraised from the possibility of giving the proper response to the demands of each alternative. At the low end of the spectrum, the product will be sent and money received. At the other end, equipment, know-how, technicians, and managers will be sent, apart from the products and parts. The complexity unquestionably increases as the commitment abroad grows. Knowing the internal structure of the company and its ability to respond to demand is critical when choosing markets and entry strategies. Understanding which alternatives will provide better learning for improving a company's capabilities, within acceptable risk levels, is usually a good guide when selecting market and entry strategies. Exporting is the first step of the internationalization process. As with any other organizational process, it strongly impacts the company environment. Foreseeing this, three essential developments must occur: new visions, communications processes, and shared values.

8. New perspectives are needed to develop within the company a strategic business vision and at the international level a strategic sector vision. Executives must see business through a new, broader outlook at an international level, thus changing the way they usually do business in order to be more appealing to new global outlets.

9. The internal communications processes must be improved to achieve international efficiency. The requirements of operating abroad add demands to the usual procedures of doing business in the domestic market. The typical disagreements between operations and marketing areas are inexcusable when trying to respond to foreign demand, which is why the company's information processes must be fined-tuned to the market.

10. A new attitude of shared values encourages the exchange of knowledge and information abroad. It is necessary to develop a clear idea of the importance of external operations, especially at the beginning when impact on volume and profitability is low. The objective must be to create an export environment within an organization which traditionally dealt with the domestic market. Exporting sets in motion a process of internationalization within the company that leads toward international expansion. Assigning licenses, finding commercial support in other markets, and establishing facilities for product distribution or operations abroad—all in relationship to companies in the destination countries—are only different stages in the long process that constitutes the international business challenge of global markets. Latin America should be among the participants in this wide international development of businesses.

CASES

2-1   INTERNATIONAL MARKETING MANAGERS (A): SUSANA ELESPURU

In an 18-year career with Procter & Gamble (P&G), Susana Elespuru had advanced from a brand assistant in P&G Peru to vice president and general manager overseeing Bolivia, Ecuador and Peru. Married with two children, she wondered whether she would have to leave Peru to advance further in the company.

BACKGROUND AND EARLY CAREER

Susana Elespuru was born in Peru, attended a private English-language school in Lima, and went on to Dartmouth on a Fulbright Scholarship as a member of the second co-ed class in the college's history. The only Latin American in her class, she double majored in geology and French literature, spent one semester studying in France, and graduated magna cum laude in 1977. On her choice of majors, Susana commented: "I realized I wasn't interested in hard core science. I didn't have the patience to sit at a lab bench. I wanted to make things happen."

After graduating, Susana spent one year in Spain as a field exploration geologist with Phelps Dodge. She was moved frequently from one project to another; the diversity of projects and locations was appealing initially but the frequent moves made for a difficult social life. In 1978 she returned to Peru.

Susana spotted a job advertisement in one of Lima's Sunday newspapers. The ad did not specify the job function or name the recruiter but described a set of personality characteristics and a working environment that appealed to Susana. She applied and began work as a market research assistant with Procter & Gamble in July 1978. Susana commented: "I remember looking at the consumer products on display in the offices I interviewed in. I was intrigued."

Eight months later, Jorge Montoya, then P&G's general manager in Peru (and now P&G's Latin American president), offered Susana a chance to transfer to the Advertising department as a brand assistant. A friend of Susana's applied for and obtained the market research position she vacated.

Susana's first assignment was on Ace, the leading brand of laundry detergent in Peru. Soon, she became the brand assistant on Zest soap, then in test market. After it was launched, she took on a similar role for another new product, Salvo dishwashing powder. Susana commented:

In a small, rapidly expanding subsidiary with many new products being launched, I benefited from being able to

Professor John A. Quelch prepared this case as the basis for class discussion rather than to illustrate either effective or ineffective handling of an administrative situation.

work on many brands in many categories in a relatively short period of time. At the same time, my market research background helped me add value, especially in testing and designing the launch programs for new brands.

After two years at P&G, I finally had time to do my two months of sales training out in the field but, half way through, the brand manager on Salvo resigned. Salvo had, by then, been launched and I became the assistant brand manager. Two weeks later the Peruvian government reduced sales taxes and I remember having to convince our sales force to pass price decreases through to the trade with the benefit of only one month's sales training!

BRAND MANAGER

One year later, in 1981, Susana was promoted to brand manager in charge of both Salvo and Camay soap. Using creative sampling promotions new to the Peruvian market, she tripled Salvo's market share in 14 months. She also launched a new advertising campaign on Camay after market research showed the existing 10-year-old copy strategy to be outdated in the eyes of women consumers.

In 1982, Susana was appointed brand manager in charge of the national launch of Pampers diapers. She retained responsibility for Camay. The Pampers launch required that current and future mothers, pediatricians and hospitals all had to be educated about the merits of the new disposable diaper category. Establishing the product in the market was further complicated by an annual inflation rate in Peru of 200% which required Susana to manage frequent price increases on imported Pampers.

After successfully launching Pampers, Susana transferred to P&G world headquarters in January 1984. She first worked as an assistant brand manager on a new product later launched as Crest Tartar Control Toothpaste. Nine months later she was appointed brand manager on Pepto-Bismol. This over-the-counter pharmaceutical brand represented the sixth product category on which she had worked in her seven years with P&G. She developed a marketing program for Pepto-Bismol that especially targeted Hispanic consumers in the United States and hired a separate advertising agency to execute it; at the time, this was only the second initiative of its kind within P&G. The result was an impressive increase in Pepto-Bismol trial among Hispanic consumers.

Susana commented on her time in Cincinnati:

> It was like going to Mecca. What impressed me most was the thoroughness of product development at P&G. I especially enjoyed the contact with the scientists in the product development department.
>
> However, I saw not only the good but also the bad and the ugly. The period I was in Cincinnati was a tough time for the company—Pampers, Crest and Tide all lost market share. The bureaucracy was suffocating—over 10 iterations on one brand budget! In marketing you have to work with your heart, not just your head. When the company's plans changed, it was a little disappointing to me to see all my files on the proposed launch of a new brand of toothpaste end up on the desk of the Crest brand group.

RETURN TO PERU

In January 1986, Susana returned to Peru as associate advertising manager, reporting to a new country general manager but someone whom Susana knew from her previous stint in Lima. She found two tough challenges awaiting her:

> First, the brand groups had lost touch with the importance of advertising copy. They were too heavily influenced by a

particularly charismatic brand manager who loved to run spectacular promotion events. Role models are so important in developing young managers. I had to try to become the brand managers' role model.

Second, the country, governed by President Alan Garcia, was in the grip of hyperinflation (up to 100% per month) with price controls. The economy was seemingly booming but it was a subsidized supply-driven economy, a house built on sand. In production and marketing, we had to prepare ourselves for the inevitable crash.

On Monday, September 4, 1988, Susana Elespuru was appointed the first woman country manager in P&G history. The next day, the Peruvian economy and the value of the currency collapsed. Susana described the challenges:

Consumer demand fell precipitously as prices soared. The trade had six weeks of inventory on hand at normal sales rates; this quickly became 12 weeks worth of inventory so the trade stopped buying from us. Yet we had contracts with our raw material suppliers and they had to be paid. I remember them lining up in the street outside our offices to get their money. Of course, the prices on P&G imported as opposed to locally-made products became untenable, given the collapse of the currency. Our employees—like all Peruvians—were very scared; somehow we were able to find the money to increase their salaries by up to 100% per month, lagging the inflation rate but not too badly. During my first year on the job, I felt more like a finance manager than a marketing manager. And how could we expect to obtain help from Caracas or Cincinnati—we were a distant outpost, it was not obvious how to deal with extreme hyperinflation (which reached almost 7000% in the worst years), and it was up to us to solve our own problems.

There were two important lessons I learned from this experience. First, no company, however strong it may seem, is immune from the external environment. Second, when times are not so good, there is a tremendous opportunity to gain market share, especially if you're a larger company with the resources to invest in building consumer value. After the crash, our first reaction was to cancel all our media advertising but, 30 days later, we went back on the air. Our sustained investment in building brand equities has paid off in higher market shares.

ADDITIONAL RESPONSIBILITIES

Since 1990, the scope of Susana's responsibilities has progressively expanded. In 1990, she was named general manager (as opposed to country manager) of Peru and a member of P&G's worldwide operations committee. In 1992, she became general manager responsible for Ecuador and Bolivia as well as Peru. In 1994, she was additionally appointed a vice president of Procter & Gamble (worldwide). In all these roles, she reported to Jorge Montoya, president of P&G Latin America, who was based at regional headquarters in Caracas, Venezuela. During this period, she gained experience integrating the Peruvian operations of an acquired multinational (Richardson-Vicks) and led several P&G regional task forces.

In the five years since 1988, under Susana's leadership, P&G sales volume in Peru doubled. P&G's 400 employees in Peru were all local nationals. These included 100 managers and support staff at Lima headquarters and 34 full-time salespeople. The full-time sales force was supplemented by about 100 independent salespeople who purchased goods from P&G's distributors to resell to small outlets nationwide.

The small Ecuadorian and Bolivian markets were run from Lima without their own country managers. A small marketing team, based in Lima, oversaw field sales efforts in Ecuador and Bolivia and worked with the local distributors.

The business climate facing Susana in 1994 was very different from the one that she had faced in 1988. Hyperinflation continued through 1990 but the election in that year of President Alberto Fujimori was followed by tight monetary controls and a measure of economic stability. Susana commented:

> Peru's 23 million consumers represent an increasingly attractive target. We anticipate more multinational brands trying to enter or reestablish themselves in this market. But we intend to capitalize on the fact that P&G has been here all along, through thick and thin, relentlessly building our brand equities. Economic growth in Peru means that a greater percentage of people can afford to start using our products—we must educate them to category usage and attract them to our brands, but, at the same time, we must deliver product improvements to those consumers already using our brands. The market is becoming more competitive and more demanding than ever before.
>
> Interestingly, the increased interest in Peru and in Latin America in general coincided with Ed Arzt (CEO of P&G) transforming P&G from being a U.S. company with international operations into a global corporation. That means we are often asked to adopt global marketing programs and the challenge is to make them suitable in the Peruvian market or adapt them appropriately.
>
> I believe we have to take the best Cincinnati has to offer and adapt their marketing programs to our local needs. For instance, we haven't pushed compact detergents in Peru because many of our consumers can only afford to buy a small 250-gram package at any one time; if we condensed this volume, we'd end up with a package of detergent the size

of a tea bag! For the same reason, 70% of all shampoo is sold in individual sachets in Peru. We would never have gone from having no shampoo brand in 1990 to having the three leading brands (Pert Plus, Pantene and Head & Shoulders) today if we hadn't invested in special production lines to make single sachets.

REFLECTIONS ON GENERAL MANAGEMENT

Susana was a strong believer in management by OGSM (objectives, goals, strategies, measures). She developed goals over a three-year horizon and required all her functional heads to develop annual rolling plans which had to be coordinated through a team effort into a corporate plan. This corporate plan was communicated throughout the organization. Each individual employee was motivated in part by seeing how his/her activities fitted into the overall plan. Susana required a monthly letter from each functional head to verify progress towards the previously agreed-upon goals. In addition, every quarter, she met offsite for two days with the functional heads as a team to check on progress, especially on important and urgent projects, to ensure accountability, and to anticipate unexpected problems.

Susana described her time allocation as follows:

Developing, reviewing and monitoring functional and corporate plans:	35%
Reviewing and advising on functional operating issues:	30%
Attending external meetings with government officials, industry associations, consultants, suppliers and customers:	15%
Attending internal meetings relating to Ecuador and Bolivia and to P&G Latin America, and visiting Cincinnati:	20%

Susana noted that the time allocation of general managers varied according to personal style, the tasks at hand, and the quality and expertise of the functional heads:

When the economy was less stable, I was spending much more time than I am now dealing with government officials. Also, a good half of the time I spent on functional issues related to finance. Now, I'm able to spend much more time on marketing. However, the general manager's role is not to be more of a functional expert than the functional head. Rather, it's to ensure that all the functional plans fit into the best overall business equation.

Susana viewed coaching and mentoring as critical to the general manager's role:

I had the benefit of great coaching so I'm particularly sensitive to its importance. Marketing people often make good coaches because they recognize that not everyone's needs are the same. Some employees require and enjoy frequent coaching, others don't. Some require gentle encouragement, others require a good kick. I'm a great believer in three things. First, any coaching has to be genuinely given from the heart to be effective. Second, a great deal of good coaching can occur in team meetings in which people from different functions coach each other. Third, a good coach always asks his or her employees to evaluate the coaching that they're receiving.

Good coaching produces happy, productive managers, lower job turnover and less time spent on training new people in the basics. It's a great investment. My belief in coaching is one reason I think local nationals usually make better general managers of foreign subsidiaries of MNCs—they know the local culture and can adjust their coaching style to each local employee more successfully.

Recruiting was an equally important way in which Susana believed she could shape the organization:

People who are successful in this business in the marketing arena have a great deal of leadership, very good analytical skills to sort through complex data, strategic thinking to develop the right business plan for each brand, creativity for problem solving and innovative thinking. For productive team work, solid interpersonal skills and effective communication are essential.

I look for people who are creative but who also want to get things done—as members of a team as much as individuals. It's great to be creative, impatient and to want to challenge the status quo. But there are just so many ideas that any one organization can handle. ■

2-2 RHEEM-SAIAR

Our international strategy has clearly produced results. We have moved beyond the stage of slow and sporadic sales to achieve continuity of distribution in certain markets. Nevertheless, we are confronting new problems. The situation we are facing in Australia is of great concern. With regard to the United States, we must decide right away on one of the companies through which to begin distribution. Evaluating the advantages and disadvantages of each of them is difficult. Further, we have to decide on what to do about Hometech in Chile, and I am sure these decisions will have an impact on how we will go about our export plans. I would like to evaluate the possible consequences before we decide each case.

With these words Saiar SA's Fernando Zapiola welcomed José Flores in his office. They had been worried for some time about the scope taken by the export business they started some years ago. Their competitor in Australia had recently threatened to enter the Argentine market if Saiar continued to promote its products in Australia—a prospect that brought the company's situation to a breaking point.

INTRODUCTION

Saiar SA was the container division of the Garovaglio & Zorraquin (G&Z) Group. G&Z also held investments in other businesses through various companies in the petrochemical industry with Ipako, Petroken and Polisur, and in the mining industry with Cerro Castillo. The G&Z Group also controlled farming and animal husbandry installations.

Besides Saiar SA, G&Z also owned Textilyute (the Textiles Division that specialized in polypropylene material for bags and carpets) and Electronica Iguzu (the Household Goods Division). Other divisions of G&Z's portfolio of interests included Administration and Finance, which assisted the other divisions, and the International Division, started in 1989.

The Household Goods Division was devoted to the manufacture and sale of water heaters and gas space heaters. Household Goods was the leader in the domestic market with 50% market share in the water heater market and annual sales of about 30 million pesos. Internationally, it had commercial relationships in Australia and the United States, as well as subsidiaries in Chile and Brazil.

THE COMPANY'S HISTORY

In 1947, Rheem Manufacturing and G&Z formed a joint venture for the manufacture of metal cans. In the following years, the company, whose name was Saiar— Sociedad Anonima Independiente de Aceros Rheem—devoted itself to the introduction of 20-liter metal pails in Argentina. The pails were used in the chemical, agrochemical and oil industries, and Saiar eventually became the leading metal pails company in Argentina.

In 1962 Saiar decided to invest in the development and introduction of the first water heater tanks. The objective of Saiar and Rheem, the leading world maker of this product, was to develop the market in Argentina, where only older, more primitive "automatic pilot" water heaters were in use.

Twenty years later, and through Saiar's efforts, a substantial market for water heater tanks had developed. Of the products used to heat water for domestic consumption in 1982, 40% were automatic pilot water heaters and 60% were water heater tanks. In the latter market, Saiar faced two important competitors, Orbis and Longvie,

This case was prepared by Serio Postigo, Master Degree Candidate, Instituto de Altos Estudios Empresariales (IAE), Universidad Austral, Buenos Aires, in association with Juan Florin and under the supervision of Professor Guillermo D'Andrea. This case study has been prepared to be used as a base for discussion and does not illustrate the effective or ineffective handling or an administrative situation.

who between them held a 20% market share.

In the early 1980s Rheem International sold its interests in the Argentine market, partly to keep with its worldwide divestment policy and partly in response to the Argentine economy's severe recession. Rheem had lost market share in the last years because the water heaters, despite their high quality, had became too expensive for Argentine consumers.

In 1988, it became clear to Saiar that it needed to diversify into other products and markets, because maintaining a presence in only one product category and in only one market seemed too expensive and risky.

The sales manager in charge of the Argentinean market started the first phase of export development. He succeeded in starting operations in Bolivia, Peru, Chile, Cuba and Paraguay, reaching total sales of $127,646 in 1989 (1989's domestic sales totaled approximately $20 million).

Also in 1989, Saiar took on a new direction under the leadership of new general director Fernando Zapiola. Mr. Zapiola was a hands-on director with sound knowledge of the company's management and its history. Young and dynamic, he had a clear vision of what he called, "the importance of exporting as a means of improving the company's competitiveness."

In a 1989 planning meeting, Mr. Zapiola told his executive team "We are not taking advantage of the product technology that made us a market leader. We must identify and develop new markets for our products, as the domestic market will not afford us long-term growth."

The gloomy long-term growth prospects in Argentina were due to the country's persistent economic instability. Throughout most of the 1980s, the domestic market declined drastically as a result of the economy's frequent ups and downs. Because the company was heavily dependent on this market, its situation worsened with the economy. Mr. Zapiola and his team of executives felt that if they could develop export markets and maintain a steady flow of commercial exchange, the company's financial situation would stabilize, and its medium-range planning goals would be met.

Mr. José Flores was hired and given the objectives of screening markets and highlighting commercial opportunities outside of Latin America. Mr. Flores visited potential markets such as Australia, New Zealand, Europe, the United States and South Africa over a period of six months, after which he made the following comments:

The first decision we made was to identify markets by visiting them, and not by gathering information through the Chamber of Foreign Commerce or the Commercial Attachés. The latter strategy is more popular because it doesn't involve the cost of traveling or the use of managers' time, but it is also less effective.

We made the decision to travel because we think that's the way to get a feel for which of the proposals have real chances of success.

For three to six months we were traveling, interviewing, preparing schedules and exploring markets, with a lot of frustration due not only to the large number of useless contacts we made, but also to our realizing that most of the products we made were not suitable in some of the markets.

THE PRODUCTS

Water Heater Tanks

Water heater tanks, used both in the commercial and residential market, have the property of heating water by accumulation, keeping large amounts of water warm at desired temperatures. Their capacity ranges from 60 to 150 liters (Exhibit 1).

EXHIBIT 1   The Rheem-Saiar Water Heater Tank

Nuevo termotanque 190 lts. Alta Potencia.

Otro gran producto RHEEM SAIAR que viene a cubrir, con abundante agua caliente, todas sus demandas de confort.

El único termotanque que aúna en un sólo producto la máxima capacidad, 190 lts., con la más moderna tecnología industrial.

Además de las aplicaciones convencionales, el nuevo termotanque RHEEM SAIAR de 190 lts. amplía su uso a:

▲ Llenado en 10 minutos de una bañera de hidromasaje de hasta 200 lts.

▲ Familias numerosas. Propiedades con más de un baño.

▲ Confiterías. Bares. Restaurantes. Vestuarios. Pequeñas Industrias y escuelas.

RHEEM SAIAR
Líder tecnológico; desde hace muchos inviernos.

REGALO LANZAMIENTO
Hasta el 31 de Julio, con cada termotanque 190 lts Alta Potencia, Rheem Saiar le regala a su elección un taladro eléctrico marca Skil o una agenda electrónica Texas Instruments
APROVECHE AHORA

Rheem **SAIAR**
CALOR IMPERTURBABLE

The advantage of an automatic water heater unit is that it heats water instantly. The flow of hot water changes according to the number of outlets open at the same time, producing a variable water temperature at the moment the water heater is used.

A water heater is made of a tank, a burner, a thermostat. The tank is lined internally with enamel to prevent corrosion and externally with a polyurethane insulation.

Saiar's water heaters were housed in a thermoplastic container with two top panels of polyurethane. These features were seen as some of the most important advantages, as the products were sold in household goods stores. The water heaters' aesthetic appeal, combined with proper presentation and merchandising—in the store window or in the entryway—were important in generating sales.

In Argentina, Saiar targeted three segments: retail stores that sold to consumers, housing construction professionals, and contractors. All products were sold with a one-year warranty. Customers' technical problems were handled by the Technical Service and Assessment Department. This department stayed in regular contact with customers, giving them advice on how to install, operate, and make technical adjustments to the equipment.

Sales were seasonal, with the peak sales season from March to October.

Space Heaters

Space heaters typically use gas (natural or propane) or electric power to provide heat to indoor areas that are either not served or are poorly served by a central heating system (Exhibit 2).

Saiar's space heater units used gas, and featured thermostat-controlled air flow that could regulate the temperature of the environment by means of an adjustable flame.

The space heaters in use at the time in the domestic market did not rely on such a mechanism, which meant that the flame, and therefore the temperature, had to be controlled manually. Certain manually controlled units came with a remote control mechanism.

The fact that Saiar's product had "thermostat-controlled air flow" meant that it took in clean air from the outside, used it for combustion, and then expelled toxic gasses back to the outside. This thermostat-controlled air flow technology was developed in France and was licensed-in through an agreement under which Saiar paid set fees in exchange for permission to manufacture and sell in Latin America.

EXPORT SALES

Saiar started its operations with bordering countries since those markets were less sophisticated. Saiar's products were well received, despite the poor commercial reputation of Argentinean businessmen. Saiar also made some sales in Panama, Cuba and Trinidad but sales volume in those areas was not significant and strong commercial relationships were difficult to develop. Exhibit 3 shows export sales in those years.

In a December 1989 board meeting, Flores explored other possible markets:

Based on the market research conducted outside the continent, we have concluded that a potential market for space heaters exists in the United States. South Africa has very high tariff barriers and there is no possibility of exporting to Europe, at least not with space heaters, as we imported the technology from there and the degree of development of the product is very different. Finally,

EXHIBIT 2 The Space Heater

Termoestabilizador Rheem

Si la temperatura baja, la llama aumenta.
Si la temperatura sube, la llama disminuye.

Regulación Automática de Temperatura

Menor consumo

Servicio al Cliente

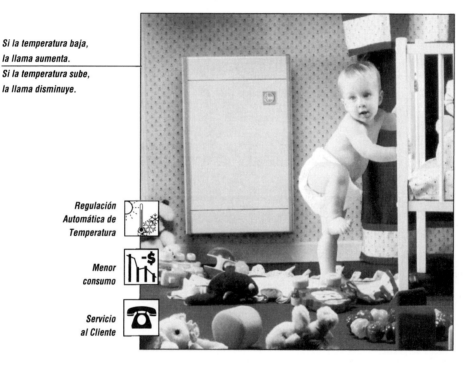

El nuevo Termoestabilizador Ambiental Rheem es el único que posee un termostato que regula la llama de acuerdo con la temperatura del ambiente: si la temperatura baja, la llama aumenta; si la temperatura sube, la llama disminuye.

Un sistema de calefacción a gas que reúne cualidades superiores tanto en confort como en seguridad y economía. Un sistema con la más alta tecnología, que usted y su familia no pueden dejar de disfrutar.

EXHIBIT 3 Export Sales (FOB) in Units and U.S. Dollars

Product	1988/89		1989/90		1990/91	
	Units	Value	Units	Value	Units	Value
Gas Heater	106	$13,793	196	$27,586	611	$83,528
Electric Heater	213	$31,114	710	$60,424	477	$34,466
Plastic Pails	16,702	$28,742	44,540	$79,152	75,340	$102,122
Metal Pails	11,000	$24,920	35,810	$77,849	63,920	$134,022
Stabilizers	n/a		n/a		189	$22,018
Containers	n/a		500	$5,000	3,390	$44,643
Accessories	14,390		179,383		96,153	

Export Sales (FOB) by Country (1988–1991)

	Gas Heater Tanks	Electric Heater Tanks	Plastic Pails	Metal Pails	Stabilizers	Containers	Accessor.
Units							
Australia	320						
Chile	407	8	104,500	110,730	164	3,790	
Others	186	1,392	32,100		25	100	
Total	913	1,400	136,600	110,730	189	3,890	
Dollars							
Australia	32,000						1,748
Chile	62,221	764	184,677	236,791	18,984	48,557	206,453
Others	30,685	125,241	25,340		3,304	1,086	249,158
Total	124,908	126,005	210,017	236,791	22,018	49,643	289,926

Other export countries include Cuba, Bolivia, Paraguay, Peru, Trinidad & T., Uruguay.

Australia remains, with an interesting market potential.

Exhibit 4 summarizes the business development reports for these markets.

THE ENTRY INTO THE AUSTRALIAN MARKET

Having determined from its market analysis that good sales opportunities existed in Australia, Saiar decided to enter the Australian market. It was not an easy task since Australia had the most rigorous quality control standards in the world. This meant that the first step consisted of redesigning the product.

Saiar formed a commercial relationship with a barely known Australian businessman with good connections to the important gas companies, who was a space heater distributor, and who a year ago had started negotiations with Saiar in Argentina in order to import its products into his country.

From the end of 1989 to the end of 1990, Saiar did all the necessary testing to have the product approved by the National Regulatory Agency of Australia. During that time Saiar continued to gather and process information on the new market.

Among other things, Saiar's management discovered that at the time, Rheem

EXHIBIT 4 Business Development Report

SAIAR SA
DIVISION OF FOREIGN TRADE
AREA, REST OF THE WORLD

1. OBJECTIVES AND RESULTS 1989
1.1 Objectives
- To concentrate efforts on Europe, USA, Australia/New Zealand and South Africa
- To investigate and develop open markets for our product line
- To further develop distribution
- To present a business plan in December

1.2 Activities Completed
- Trips to The Netherlands, Italy, France, and England, South Africa, Australia and New Zealand
- Participation in EUROLATINA and EXPOARAB
- Visits to INTERCLIMA and K89

1.3 General Conclusions
- Foundations for attaining success in the market objectives
  - QUALITY that results in better profit margins
  - TECHNOLOGICAL BACKING and or local volume in order to assure supply and technical support
  - FLEXIBILITY in adapting products to markets
  - A PRICE lower than that of the competition
- NONE OF OUR PRODUCTS FULFILL THE REQUIREMENTS
- MEDIUM RANGE ACTIONS
  - Work for the improvement of quality and flexibility
  - Develop the local market and seek external technological support
  - Development of new products for the local market and for export

2. MEDIUM RANGE PLANS
2.1 Bulky
- Improvements in design and construction
  - LABORDATA (Achieved)
  - NEL (Goal)
- Acquisition of production technology and investment in the product line
  - MULOX, HOLMESWORTH
- Representation of systems of loading and unloading as support to local and nearby market development
  - BAGFILLA OVERSEAS
- Development of the local market
  - Cabot
  - Polisur/Indupa/Monsanto
  - Induner
  - Industrias de Maiz/Molinos
  - Cerro Castillo
  - Conaprole/Sancor
  - Pioneer/Cargill
- Investigation of the North American Market

2.2 Home Appliances
- Approval of hot water tanks in Australia and the USA
- Launching of a line of heating elements in Australia and the USA
- Development and adaptation of a hot water heater for the North American and Mexican markets
- Sale of Martiri kitchens in the USA
- Development of a trademark for export

EXHIBIT 4 (cont.)

2.3 Others
- SP METAL (Leer Van Development by third parties)
- REDES PARA EL AGRO [FARMING NETWORKS]
- AGAPOL BACKING/ALFOMBRAS [Carpets]

3. ANALYSIS BY MARKET/COUNTRY

3.1 South Africa
- Very protected market
- Rheem South Africa
  - Anglo American
  - Hot water tanks and bulky
- Tufbag—Bulky
- Alnet—Networks
- Traders who operate in other African countries
- Opportunities
  - Backing
  - BCF
  - Hot water tanks and heating elements

3.2 Australia
- Market for water heaters
  - 350,000 total hot water users
  - 170,000 gas hot water tanks
  - Rheem Market Share: 90%
  - Tariff: 15%
- Approval
- International Gas Corporation
  - Distributors of Charotequx et Maury
  - 10,000 hot water tanks domestically and 40,000 abroad
  - EMERGE heating elements
  - AUER heating elements
  - Very good relationship with the gas company
- Agents who are working with our products
  - Sanwa, Polesy
- Opportunities
  - Backing (32%)
  - Carpets
  - Fiber/BCF (2%)
  - Heating elements

3.3 USA
- Advanced gas technologies
  - Heating elements, hot water heaters, kitchens
- Bulky—Potential direct sales to users

3.4 Europe
- AUER—Hot water tanks
- Bulky—Possible distributor in the UK with direct sales to users

Australia—a leader in Australia's manufacturing industry—dominated the country with a 95% share in the water heater market. Its product, however, was overpriced and unattractive. Rheem Australia relied on its strength as a leader, but because it had only one product to sell, its relations with channel intermediaries were poor.

The remaining 5% of the market was shared by importers who marketed these products as much to consumers as to intermediaries. The intermediaries were gas companies who sold domestic and imported products to consumers and contractors, who also bought from importers. Forty percent of all water heaters were sold through these gas companies. The salespeople working for these gas companies received a commission based on the price of the product sold and another commission on the volume of gas consumed by the item.

Saiar advertised mainly in the specialized trade press under the distributor's brand name Cassis using images of the product.

Sales were estimated at approximately 1,500 water heaters per year which represented 3% of the market. Because of its functional and modern design, Saiar's product was readily accepted by consumers and contractors. Soon, however, customers began registering complaints about the product: condensation problems, water loss and other difficulties. Saiar quickly responded to the complaints.

Between 1988 and 1991 Saiar sold 320 gas water heaters in Australia. Rheem Australia, however, had taken notice of this progress and reacted in several ways. It filed a legal accusation charging Saiar with plagiarism of its operating manuals, and it also advised Saiar to simply take its product off the market.

Because Rheem Australia was the main market leader, its relationships with the gas companies were excellent. Taking advantage of those strong ties, executives from Rheem telephoned periodically to complain that they had bought Cassis water heaters which had serious quality problems.

At the end of 1992 sales grew slowly but solidly, even though the Australian economy suffered from a severe recession. That recession caused a drop-off in sales for 1992 of about 50% of the gas market. Flores explained to the case's authors:

Sales of our water heaters were not immune to [the recession] so we started to think of ideas to spur growth again in the Australian market. The best idea was to build, in association with the distributor, an assembly plant in Australia for our products. A quick estimate showed we could save half of the shipping costs, which added up to $50 (Exhibit 5).

Besides, with this new project we could manufacture a water heater different from the one we were making in Argentina, one that would be better adapted to the Australian market. It was not profitable to make this new product in Argentina due to the fact that its new design and larger size increased shipping costs a lot. On the other hand, we believed, this new product could allow us to penetrate further the Australian market.

The project required an estimated investment of about $1.5 million with project sales of $8 million in five years—about 7% of Australia's water heater market.

While Saiar's management evaluated the company's prospects in Australia, Saiar received a letter (Exhibit 6) from Rheem Australia threatening to enter the Argentinean market if Saiar proceeded to manufacture in Australia.

EXHIBIT 5 Project J.V. Australia

1. Australian Market
2. Objectives
3. Initial Stage

1. MARKET

Hot Water Market	Units: 500,000
	Value: $200,000,000
Heating Tanks Market Share	90%
Heating Tanks Rheem Market Share	95%
Gas Water Heater Tanks	200,000 units at $90,000,000
Project Target	
Market Share	7% of Hot Water Market
Period	8 years

2. OBJECTIVES OF THE PROJECT

  a. To establish ourselves in the Australian hot water market
  b. To achieve a penetration of 7% in 8 years
  c. To have a platform for launching other products

2.1 FORM OF ENTRY

  a. Establishing a Joint Venture (J.V.) with:
    • A local distributor (ICG) who contributes the approved product, local management, and the know-how of distribution, sales, and service.
    • A third foreign partner who contributes the technology products and venture capital (e.g., Rheem USA, Vaillant).
  b. Beginning the assembly of outside water tanks in Australia with tanks and parts provided by SAIAR. Assembly will be accomplished initially by means of third parties.

3. INITIAL STAGE

  a. To begin the manufacture and sale on a small scale during the first six months (July–Dec. 1992)

Total Sales	$500,000
Billing-In	$100,000
Local Bank Financing	$150,000
Financing with SAIAR Tanks	$46,000

  b. To continue negotiations with Rheem and Vaillant in order to interest them in the J.V.
  c. To concretize the J.V. at the end of 1992 in order to begin the massive sales stage, with adequate structure and financial support.
  d. Options for beginning the second stage
    • Saiar financing
    • Australian Manufacturer (St. George)
    • Australian venture capital

EXHIBIT 6 Rheem Letter

SABH
APPLIANCE GROUP

26 May 1992
Mr. Luis Fernandez

SAIAR
Av. de Mayo 701, Piso 17°
(1084) Buenos Aires
Argentina
Facsimile: (0541) 331 7299

Dear Luis:

There are a couple of things that have transpired here in Australia since your visit. This has raised some concern in South Australia Brewing Holdings' mind about the prospect of a relationship, which we discussed back in February.

Firstly we believe that Mr. Jose Flores has recently visited Australia but did not make contact with us. We also understand that part of the reason for Mr. Flores' visit was to establish a final assembly plant for the Cassis branded gas water heater using cylinders and components imported from SAIAR. Clearly we would view this as an unwelcome and unfriendly move which would negate any prospects of a future relationship.

If it was to eventuate, we would quickly move to discontinue any arrangements that have been put in place regarding the Tipper Tie business which formed part of your discussions with Brian Porter.

Since your visit we have received Justice Department approval to purchase another water heating company in the USA, Mor-Flo. The combination of the Bradford-White business and the Mor-Flo business will make us the largest manufacturer of mains pressure water heaters in the US and worldwide. Off this substantial US base we would consider taking a similar position in Argentina to that which we believe you are planning in Australia to offset any potential erosion of our Australian business.

This is a serious issue and I would appreciate you reviewing it with your people in the water heater business and advising us of your intentions before we take any further steps.

Yours sincerely,

Bruce W. Kemp

Bruce W. Kemp
Executive General Manager

BWK:JLD

THE UNITED STATES MARKET

Based on the research completed in 1989, management of Saiar decided to enter the United States market in 1991. In February of that year, Saiar contacted a consulting company in Los Angeles. Its objectives were to develop a plan to obtain technical approval of the product and to design a commercial strategy.

Technical Approval

Saiar decided to present the largest model of the product sold in the Argentinean market to the American Gas Association (AGA). The AGA regulates the design of products that use gas and controls their safety by granting (or denying) official approval.

Saiar's intention was to gain from the AGA a realistic technical diagnosis of the changes that the product needed. Saiar hoped to begin selling by August or September, before the winter season. It took only two months—until April of 1992—to receive technical approval from the AGA.

Commercial Strategy

Saiar decided to do a direct mail campaign to contractors and distributors, providing them with information about the products and asking their opinions with regard to product advantages, customers' expectations, product name suggestions, and the like.

Based on the results of the direct mail campaign, Saiar organized a trip to the United States for July and August of 1991, with the objective of visiting potential contractors and distributors.

Two candidates that appeared interested in working with the company came from the direct mail campaign, and one candidate was referred by a third party.

Market Conditions

The size of the U.S. space heater market was about 250,000 units per year—a huge market when contrasted to that of Argentina. By this standard, an 80% market share in Argentina would translate only to a small niche market in the United States.

Of the total market, the segment of thermostat-controlled air flow space heaters was 30,000 units per year and had excellent growth potential since consumers were purchasing them to replace manually controlled space heaters.

Additionally, the importance of personal safety and environmental concerns in the United States had led to strict laws in some states prohibiting the use of space heaters without thermostat-controlled air flow mechanisms. California was one such state, and since it provides a leadership role with regard to innovations and consumer trends, Saiar was excited about the future market for thermostat-controlled air flow space heaters in the rest of the country.

Saiar faced only one potential competitor, though the competitor's product was designed in 1950 and unlike Saiar's products, appeared dated and outmoded.

THE CANDIDATES

After spending almost a month in the United States, traveling through eight states, and visiting 25 national and regional prospective distributors, Saiar identified three potential national distributors who were interested in selling its products in the United States.

Controlled Energy (CE)

CE was a small, 10-year-old organization to which the addition of space heaters to the company's existing range of products would have a significant impact. CE promised to sell 2,000 units in the first year.

Due to the fact that it was a small company, dealing with CE would mean more control for Saiar, in exchange for small commercial volume and little aggressiveness in the market. Nevertheless, it offered a learning opportunity. As the manager of Saiar's International Division put it, "It would cost us more, but we would learn more."

Molitor

Molitor was a Japanese company that sold high-technology kerosene space heaters at a rate of about 5,000 per year. These heaters had the advantages of odorless exhaust and temperature control. Molitor responded enthusiastically to the sample sent by Saiar and saw great potential in adding the space heater to its product line.

DESA

DESA was a manufacturer and market leader of manually controlled space heaters, selling 150,000 units per year. The company was very interested in marketing the Saiar product as a means of broadening its line of heaters.

Working with DESA would mean learning less about market trends and having less control over the product, since Saiar's heaters would form part of DESA's line of products, but it would provide an important commercial stimulus.

DESA proposed to start with about 1,000 units per year. They also accepted lower margins in order to better facilitate market entry.

THE CHILEAN MARKET

In 1989 the channels and distribution structure in Chile was similar to that of other markets (e.g., Australia), with private gas companies marketing their product line. The Chilean market for water heaters in 1989 was in the same state of development as that of Argentina in the 1960s. That is, only automatic pilot water heaters existed and space heaters with thermostat-controlled air flow were unknown. Jose Flores told the case authors, "We had the impression that we had already seen that movie; we relied on the know-how of earlier market development." The problem, he added, was that Chilean "consumers had a negative concept of the water heater. [They thought] water heaters could not supply enough water." At one point there were plans in Chile to mandate the use of electric water heaters, but their excessively high rate of energy consumption had made such plans untenable.

Custom duties on Saiar's products were 15%, and all products needed approval from the Chilean regulatory agency. Each shipment entering the country had to be checked by testing a sample.

The Chilean makers of the water heaters were almost all small shop operations. Their design was antiquated and their prices were in the neighborhood of $600—substantially higher than the $250 price of Saiar's heaters.

An important segment of the space heater market was the paraffin and/or kerosene space heater, and an even more important segment was the catalytic space heater. Catalytic heaters use a very small amount of gas, they allow very little heat to escape, they maintain a steady temperature, and due to their low temperature, flameless combustion oxidation, catalytic space heaters are generally very safe. Chile had originally imported them from Spain, though by 1988 the Chilean makers of them were well established. Another important reason for their popularity was the absence of natural gas lines in Chile's buildings. Natural gas lines, as they commonly exist in other countries, were only installed in the southern part of Chile, though construction projects to extend the natural gas line system from Argentina to Santiago were in progress.

A major problem in Santiago was the city's thin and heavily polluted air. Every day, the city's pollution index was announced along with the temperature. Regulations were in place that used a license plate serial system to limit vehicle traffic. Even schools were closed at times because of the dangerous level of environmental contamination.

THE ENTRY INTO THE CHILEAN MARKET

Before 1988, Saiar had consistent sales in Chile's Punta Arenas region. In 1988, the company decided to participate in Santiago's International Trade Fair (FISA)—a very important industrial trade show in Latin America. Participating in FISA enabled Saiar to identify several promising contacts.

As the Chilean market became more interesting to Saiar, its management also considered setting up an office there. In order to complete a market analysis, Saiar hired an engineer who had close contacts in the gas companies. He arrived at the following conclusions:

a. Automatic pilot water heaters constituted 95% of Chile's water heater market.

b. There was no market for water heater tanks, and therefore no established distribution network.

c. There was no supplier of thermostat-controlled air flow space heaters.

d. Chile's residents were acutely aware of the country's pollution problems.

e. There was a project underway to develop more natural gas lines.

f. The country had the best economic situation of any Latin American country. Both macro- and microeconomic growth prospects were good.

g. Saiar would have to reeducate consumers regarding its current products, both space heaters and water heaters.

h. Two potential market segments for Saiar products were new construction projects and recently built residences.

THE SAIAR STRATEGY IN CHILE

Based on those conclusions and with the objective of starting a base of operations in Chile, Saiar decided to divide the market into segments. The criteria used were population growth and the potential development of a larger natural gas line system.

"What we wanted was to control the distribution of the product in Chile, not do the distribution ourselves. That way, we could protect the brand name and the product from being mishandled," said Roberto Deleo, the Saiar executive responsible for the Chilean market entry.

The trademark rights to the brand name were given, but the technology was not patented as it was already well known throughout the world.

Saiar developed a five-year plan starting in 1990. Both the water heaters and space heaters needed to be modified for the new market.

At the end of 1989, Saiar founded a company named Hometech SA in which Saiar held a 99% stock ownership. Other than two Argentine managers, the company was staffed entirely with Chilean employees. A commercial manager was hired from the local university as were a gas technician and some administrative personnel. The main characteristics of the work group were its flexibility and very low operating costs.

Chile's most important gas companies supported Saiar, not only because they liked the product, but also because they realized that the more gas space heaters they sold, the more gas the population would consume.

Operations were initially modest, though they improved substantially when Hometech began marketing thermostat-controlled air flow space heaters along with the water heaters. A Hometech manager commented:

In 1990, we sold more water heaters in Chile than we did in Argentina the first year [415 units, $758,449]. Everything improved when we added the space heater to our commercial package, since people did not have a negative preconception of this product the way they did with water heaters.

We launched an advertising campaign for the space heaters called "Clean Air," because we were concerned about the importance of pollution in Chile. Our product takes in and expels the air with minimum pollution and that makes a strong impression on customers.

Saiar received few complaints, and those were due largely to defects in installation and not to the quality of the product itself. The company went so far as to offer a complete installation service in which Hometech paid all installation expenses—masonry and others—guaranteeing good working conditions of the equipment. The results for 1991 follow:

a. The number of water heaters sold was much less than Saiar had forecasted.

b. The advertising campaign cost $80,000.

c. Accumulated loss was $67,000 (Exhibit 7).

EXHIBIT 7   HOMETECH S.A

Balance as of December 30, 1990

Assets		Liabilities	
Liquid Assets		**Current Liabilities**	
Cash	10,000	Suppliers	24,080
Inventory	16,274,325	Foreign Creditors	22,388,859
I.V.A. (sales tax)	4,438,600	SAIAR Loan	3,129,259
Cash Dollar Account	2,164,823	Accounts Payable	273,170
Provisory Tax	107,372	Lease Payments	374,821
Customers	7,704,114	Bank	998,325
Shareholders	3,820,500		
Total Cash Assets	34,519,734	Total Liabilities	27,188,514
Fixed Assets		**Owners' Equity**	
Tools	417,253	Capital	34,546,000
Furniture and Ins.	985,996		
Leased Furn and Ins.	2,291,682	Cash Liability	27,188,514
Accum. Depreciation	(84,160)		
Total Fixed Assets	3,610,771	Loss	(23,604,009)
Total Assets	38,130,505	Total Equity	38,130,505

Operating Statement
As of December 30, 1990

Operating Income		
Sales		8,722,716
Various		137,915
Operating Expenses		
Sales Costs		(6,370,632)
Profit Margin		2,489,999
Administration and Sales Expenditures		
General Expenditures	1,702,874	
Rent	1,098,567	
Salary and Payroll Taxes	2,428,240	
Advertising and Promotion	6,970,927	
Honoraria	285,105	
Travel Expenses	329,189	
Losses from Previous Fiscal Year	12,677,997	(25,492,899)
Non-operating Expenses—Monetary Adjustment		(60,109)
Losses as of 30 December 1990		23,604,009

d. Saiar continued to provide a subsidy to Hometech which it had begun doing at the time Hometech was formed.

e. The commercial manager of Hometech was the main domestic distributor of catalytic space heaters.

THE BOARD MEETING

Faced with such a somber picture, the Board of Directors of Saiar met to decide on what to do with Hometech.

They had recently received a firm offer from an important national distributor of catalytic space heaters in Chile. The offer included taking over exclusive distribution of all Saiar products.

This Chilean firm was part of a financial group headed by a gas company and was the country's most important distributor of catalytic space heaters. They had large distribution and service networks at the national level, and the company enjoyed a good customer service reputation in Chile.

The firm eventually bought 30% of Hometech in an agreement that took into account market valuation, minimum sales volume, and established growth. ∎

2-3 GRUPO TELEVISA S.A. DE C.V.

As the senior executives of Univisa met in Los Angeles in early 1993 to discuss the company's future strategy, they were keenly aware of the growing Spanish-speaking population in the U.S. which they were determined to entertain, educate, and inform. Univisa was the North American subsidiary of Grupo Televisa S.A. de C.V., the largest media company in Mexico and the world's leading producer of Spanish-language television programming and Spanish-language magazines. Grupo Televisa's long-term goal was to be the leading media provider of entertainment and information to every one of the 350 million Spanish-speaking people in the world.

In pursuit of this goal, Televisa had already achieved media dominance in Mexico where 60% of all advertising was placed with Televisa's television networks, radio stations, magazines, and outdoor advertising company. Increasingly, Televisa was expanding its interests in the Americas and Spain through acquisitions, joint ventures, and strategic alliances. In 1991, Televisa reacquired the U.S. Univision television network which the company had had to sell in 1986. The new U.S. holding company was named Univisa. The top management was determined to restore Univisa to profitability and to provide outstanding media services to the 38 million Spanish-speaking people in the United States.

COMPANY BACKGROUND

In the late 1920s, Emilio Azcarraga became the Mexican distributor for the Victor talking machine, an early version of the phono-

Research Associate Jonathan J. Ginns prepared this case from public sources under the supervision of Professor John A. Quelch as the basis for class discussion rather than to illustrate either effective or ineffective handling of an administrative situation. Certain names and data have been disguised.

graph. Effective advertising of the product over the radio was limited by poor audio quality. As a result, Azcarraga decided to invest in radio stations, improve transmission quality, and develop live talent for broadcasts. In the 1950s, the company expanded into television; Telesistema Mexicano was incorporated in 1957 with three stations in Mexico City. Over the following 35 years, the company expanded its interests and became the dominant media company in Mexico.

Televisa incurred annual losses between 1988 and 1990 on increasing revenues which approached $750 million by 1990. The losses were partly a result of Televisa voluntarily following Mexican government price controls, which prevented advertising rates being raised, and partly a result of investments in the development of a 24-hour Spanish-language news channel called ECO. Early in 1991 the company was reorganized, and revenues, adjusting for inflation, rose 22%. Floating 20% of the equity injected $845 million in new capital, though the Azcarraga family still controlled 63% of the outstanding shares. As indicated in Table A, Televisa's sales, operating margins, and net profits were all improving by 1992.

TABLE A	Grupo Televisa Financial Performance, 1990–1992 (billions of pesos)		
	1990	*1991*	*1992E*
Net sales	2,321	2,832	4,253
Operating margin (before interest, depreciation, and taxes)	185	641	1,256
Net profit (loss)	(103)	542	704

Note: First two columns in pesos valued as of December 31, 1992.
Third column in pesos with an estimated valuation as of December 31, 1993.
3,000 pesos = US$1.00.

Source: Company records and analysts' estimates.

Most analysts expected the 1992 growth rate in sales and profits to continue for at least two to three years. Others, however, were concerned that Televisa's centralized management might stifle division-based initiatives and that Televisa had recently committed to more joint ventures and acquisitions than top management had time to monitor.

TELEVISA IN MEXICO

In 1991, Televisa derived 90% of its revenues in Mexico, as indicated in Exhibit 1. Almost 80% of domestic revenues came from the sale of advertising time on Televisa's four broadcast television channels. Revenues from cable television, radio stations, music recording and distribution, magazine publishing, and other activities accounted for the remaining revenues.

Television

As indicated in Exhibit 2, Televisa owned one Mexico City channel and three national television networks, one of which reached 96% of the 15 million Mexican households with television sets.[1] Televisa's channels dominated the viewer ratings; Televisa aired almost all of the 50 most-watched programs in 1992 and produced all of the top 25. In 1992, Televisa transmitted over 30,000 hours of national television programming in Mexico, 70% of which was produced by Televisa in its 17 studios.[2] Exhibit 3 summarizes the mix of programming produced in 1992. Televisa broadcasts reached consumers through 224 television stations, of which only 55 were not wholly owned; these received fees from Televisa for carrying one or more channels and for carrying national advertising sold by Televisa.

---

[1] About 85% of Mexican households had television sets.
[2] Televisa also ran acting schools from which many of the actors and actresses who appeared in its programs graduated.

EXHIBIT 1 Grupo Televisa Sales Mix (billions of pesos)[a]				
	1991	*(%)*	*Domestic*	*International*
Total Revenues	2,832	100.0%	2,556	276
Television	2,123	75.0	1,937	186
Cable	158	5.6	158	—
Radio	100	3.5	100	—
Music	138	4.9	99	39
Other	313	11.1	262	51
Television	2,123	75.0	1,937	186
Domestic television advertising	1,858	65.6	1,858	—
Videocassettes	95	3.4	65	30
Other revenues	14	.5	14	—
International programming sales	84	3.0	—	84
Advertising (Galavision)	54	1.9	—	54
U.S. (advertising)	13	.5	—	13
U.S. cable subscriber fees (Galavision)	5	.2	—	5
Cable	158	5.6	158	—
Basic system subscriber fees	67	2.4	67	—
Premium channel sales commissions	5	0.2	5	—
Advertising	34	1.2	34	—
Cabling and installation	21	0.7	21	—
Other revenues	31	1.1	31	—
Radio	100	3.5	100	—
Advertising	42	1.5	42	—
Campaigns	42	1.5	42	—
Other	16	.5	16	—
Music	138	4.9	99	39
Sales of records and CDs	112	4.0	73	39
Other revenues and royalties	26	0.9	26	—
Other	313	11.1	262	51
Publishing	64	2.3	63	1
Dubbing and duplicating services	43	1.5	1	42
Film production	65	2.3	57	8
Special events	69	2.4	69	—
Outdoor advertising	62	2.2	62	—
Other	10	.4	10	—

[a] 3,000 pesos = US$1.

Source: Company records.

EXHIBIT 2 Televisa's Mexican Television Networks, 1991

Channel	Television Households Reached	Share of Viewing Audience in Mexico City	Total Affiliated Stations (wholly owned)[a]	Hours of Advertising Time Sold	Advertising Capacity Utilization[b]	Prime-time Advertising Capacity Utilization[c]	Estimated Percentage of Televisa TV Advertising Revenues
2	14.4 MM (96%)	52%	147 (135)	576	53%	75%	55%
4	4.1 MM (27%)	7	33 (11)[d]	415	11	76	18
5	10.4 MM (69%)	21	31 (22)	439	31	63	25
9	4.1 MM (27%)	13	1 (1)	8	25	20	2

[a]Other affiliated stations were either majority owned by Televisa, minority owned by Televisa, or wholly independent.

[b]Includes advertising time assigned by law for government public service announcements and bonus time assigned to advertisers. Most "free" bonus time was believed to be assigned on the less-popular Channels 4 and 9.

[c]Prime-time hours were 5:00 P.M. to midnight on Channel 2 and 7:00 P.M. to midnight on the other three channels.

47

EXHIBIT 3	Mix of Television Programming Produced and Broadcast by Televisa for Its Four Mexican Channels, 1992	
ECO		30%
News (other than ECO)		10
Sports		10
Cultural		9
Music		7
Telenovelas		8
Game shows		3
Children's shows		5
Situation comedies		2
Drama		1
Telemarketing		15

Televisa's four channels offered a variety of programming. Channel 2, the "channel of the stars," was the most-watched channel in Mexico. It offered a round-the-clock mix of first-run Spanish-language programs, including telenovelas (soap operas), talk shows, game shows, and variety shows—including Sabado Gigante, the most watched Spanish language television show in the world. From 1991, Channel 4 began to target a more educated, higher-income audience with sports, serious movies, and the ECO news service modeled after CNN, which had cost Televisa $200 million to develop between 1988 and 1991. Channel 4's share of audience dropped by five percentage points following the format change to ECO, but most was recaptured by Channels 2 and 5. Channel 5 offered foreign programs dubbed in Spanish during the day, including cartoons and children's shows, and evening programming targeted at younger urban audiences that included *Miami Vice* and *Magnum PI*. Channel 9 changed its format in 1991 from commercial-free cultural programming to mainly Channel 2 reruns with advertising.

The Mexican government owned four competing channels, two of which were broadcast nationwide via 244 owned and af-filiated television stations. These four channels combined held only an 8% audience share but, due to their government owner-ship, they attracted close to 20% of total Mexican television advertising. To counter the media dominance of Televisa, the Mexican government in 1991 offered a license for a ninth channel in Mexico City and also planned to privatize a package of government-controlled media including two television networks, 168 television stations, the *El Nacional* daily newspaper, and the COTSA movie theater chain. Expected proceeds were $500 million, and bidding consortia were said to include Turner Broadcasting and Fox Television. Advertising on the privatized channels was expected to drop once the government affiliation ended but recover later as the new owners attracted larger audiences through more appealing programming.

Televisa sold advertising on all four of its channels. Partly because 70% of Mexico's 85 million people had little disposable income, Televisa advertising costs per thousand (CPM) in Mexico averaged $2.40—only 22% the average CPM in the United States—and advertising expenditures as a percentage of gross national product were 0.6% in Mexico, compared with 2.9% in the United States.[3] Yet, annual gross domestic product growth of 4% between 1988 and 1991, government deregulation of the economy and privatization of public sector enterprises, and the fact that 64% of the Mexican population was under 24 years old in 1991, meant Mexico was viewed as a promising market, especially for multinational companies. Eight of Televisa's top ten advertisers were multinationals.

Televisa's major advertisers typically participated in an advance purchase

---

[3]Comparable television advertising costs per thousand (CPM) in 1991 were $20 in Spain, $11 in the United States, $6 in Venezuela, $3 in Argentina, and $2.70 in Brazil.

arrangement known as the French Plan. In late October and early November each year, advertisers committed to advertising budgets that they would spend with Televisa (across all media) during the following year. In return for advance cash deposits of their budgeted expenditures, Televisa granted advertisers bonus television and radio advertising based on their total commitments and their percentage increases in spending over the prior year. Televisa guaranteed the advertising rates in effect at the time the cash deposits were received so French Plan advertisers were not affected by rate increases during the following year.

About 80% of Televisa's Mexican television advertising revenues were received in advance under the plan. This facilitated Televisa's financial planning and cash flow, especially since 45% of all television advertising was aired in the last four months of the year. In 1992, about 300 advertisers participated in the French Plan. Televisa's top 25 advertisers accounted for 45% of national television advertising sales, but no single advertiser accounted for more than 5%. More than 150 Televisa salespeople negotiated sales of media time directly with advertisers; advertising agencies were not employed as intermediaries.

In the late 1980s, Televisa aimed to increase television advertising revenues through rate increases that matched inflation, even at the risk of less advertising being sold, rather than through offering discounted advertising rates to sell unused commercial time. On April 1, 1991, for example, Televisa's television advertising rates were increased 40%, matching the inflation rate during the previous twelve months. Industry experts believed Televisa's domestic television advertising revenues would increase by 20% per year after inflation between 1992 and 1995.

The Mexican government did not set advertising rates but did regulate television advertising. No more than 18% of total tele-

vision broadcast time could be devoted to advertising, and no more than 50% of commercials broadcast in a given day could air between 8:00 P.M. and midnight. No more than six advertising breaks with a maximum length of two minutes each were permitted each hour. The Mexican government reserved the right to use 12½% of the available broadcast time each day (with no carry-forward) for government programming; 70% of the available time was used by the government through August 1991 and 61% through August 1992.

Cable Television

Televisa's Cablevision subsidiary offered basic, premium, and pay-per-view services, principally in Mexico City.[4] The basic service included the eight Mexico City broadcast channels plus eleven others—five from the United States, and six that were locally programmed by Cablevision using a combination of original programs, movies from the Televisa film library, and programs licensed from third parties. Advertising time could be sold only on cable channels that carried at least 20% Mexican-produced programming. By the end of 1992, Cablevision had installed 4,836 km of cable, signed up 193,400 subscribers, and achieved approximately 40% penetration of homes passed. At that time, there were about 100 cable systems operating in Mexico serving 900,000 subscribers. Cablevision had applications pending with the government for 52 nonexclusive 15-year cable television franchises. In 1992, 22% of Cablevision's revenues came from advertising as opposed to subscriber fees, compared with 3% for typical U.S. cable system operators. Televisa cable television revenues were expected to grow at over 30% per year. Potential profits were somewhat limited by the existence of a competitor,

---

[4]Mexico City and the surrounding suburbs accounted for 19% of the Mexican population, but generated 50% of the gross domestic product.

Multivision, which had signed up about 180,000 subscribers in Mexico City since being launched in 1989.

Radio

Televisa owned and operated 10 radio stations, listed in Exhibit 4, that used a variety of programming formats to appeal to different target audiences. The stations with the most powerful signals—six of which (including the flagship XEW-AM) broadcast in Mexico City—had a wide geographical coverage. Between them, the 10 stations reached half the Mexican population. Televisa's audience share was much lower in radio than in television; there were about 1,000 radio stations licensed to operate in Mexico, including 58 in Mexico City alone. However, in Mexico City, Televisa's three FM stations ranked second, third, and fourth in audience share and one of its three AM stations ranked third in 1991. To the extent competition permitted, Televisa had been increasing its radio advertising rates faster than the rate of inflation; as in the television business, total time sold fell, but revenues increased.

Publishing

Televisa was one of the leading publishers of general-interest and entertainment magazines in Mexico. Its two main magazines were *Eres* and *Somos*. *Eres* was a biweekly magazine targeted at teenagers, with a circulation of 500,000 copies per issue. *Somos*, which targeted the 20-to-40 age group, was the fourth-largest magazine with a biweekly circulation of 100,000. The magazines retailed for $1.50 and $1.70 per issue with Televisa retaining around 60% of the newsstand price. Advertising accounted for 30% of revenues. Advertising in the two magazines was available as part of Televisa's multimedia French Plan. Both magazines often promoted Televisa television programs and celebrities.

Music Recording and Distribution

Televisa owned three record labels, including Discos y Cintas Melody which ranked third in unit sales in Mexico in 1991. The profitability of these activities was reduced by widespread unlawful duplication of recordings and by termination of a distribution agreement with EMI Records at the

EXHIBIT 4 Grupo Televisa Mexican Radio Stations, 1992					
Station	*Location*	*Power (Watts)*	*Number of Stations in Market*	*Rank in Market*[a]	*Approximate Population Coverage by Signal*
XEW-AM	Mexico City	250,000	33 (AM)	3	31,200,000
XEX-AM	Mexico City	100,000	33 (AM)	17	27,700,000
XEQ-AM	Mexico City	50,000	33 (AM)	6	23,400,000
XEW-FM	Mexico City	100,000	25 (FM)	4	20,000,000
XEX-FM	Mexico City	100,000	25 (FM)	2	20,000,000
XEQ-FM	Mexico City	100,000	25 (FM)	3	20,000,000
XEWK-AM	Guadalajara	50,000	24 (AM)	1	3,000,000
XEWA-AM	San Luis Potosi	150,000	9 (AM)	1	7,000,000
XEWA-AM[b]	Monterey	500	23 (AM)	NA	3,500,000
XEWB-AM	Vera Cruz	50,000	9 (AM)	NA	3,700,000

[a]IRNA rank based on January-August 1991 average ratings.
[b]XEWA-AM was a repeater station of XEWA in San Luis Potosi.
Source: Adapted from IRNA statistics.

end of 1990. Televisa had recently closed some of its music-recording facilities and, instead, subcontracted a part of its production to third parties.

Other

Televisa's other interests in Mexico accounted for around 11% of 1991 domestic revenues. They included:

Feature Film Production and Distribution Televisa was a leading Mexican feature film producer. In 1991, Televisa produced 8 of the 35 feature films produced in Mexico, 2 of which ranked among the top 10 in box office receipts. Mexican films cost comparatively little to make; Televisa's average cost per film was about $400,000 in 1991. Televisa's film library included over 160 Spanish-language titles in 1992, 120 of them produced or co-produced by the company. Televisa also acted as the exclusive Mexican distributor of feature films produced by Warner Brothers, Touchstone Pictures, and Walt Disney Studios.

Videocassette Duplication Through acquisition, Televisa owned two videocassette duplicating plants in Mexico and Spain. In 1991, as part of the corporate reorganization, Televisa had divested itself of Videovisa which sold and distributed prerecorded videocassettes.

Program Dubbing Televisa was responsible for 72% of all Spanish-language program dubbing in Latin America in 1990. Half of this dubbing was for programs shown on Televisa channels, the other half for third parties.

Nationwide Paging In February 1992, Televisa took a 51% stake in Skytel, a paging system that could reach half the Mexican population in 18 cities. By the end of 1992, Skytel was reported to have about 24,000 subscribers.

Outdoor Advertising Televisa owned 37% of Vendor S.A., Mexico's largest billboard advertising company. Vendor controlled over 5,000 billboards, 30% of which were located in Mexico City.

Sports Televisa owned Azteca stadium in Mexico City; it also owned two of the three first-division soccer teams that played there, including the top-rated team America. Televisa further added to the range of sports programming available for broadcast on its channels by promoting bullfights, wrestling tournaments, and other events.

Consumer Products Distribution In 1991, Televisa established two joint ventures with Mexican partners to distribute U.S. consumer products in Mexico. Televisa received advertising spending commitments and a percentage of sales from the products represented; in return, the manufacturers received strong distribution support and preferential advertising rates on Televisa channels. By 1992, five consumer products were being represented.

INTERNATIONAL EXPANSION

Televisa's most important source of international revenues was from licensing the rebroadcast of its programs to other television networks throughout the world. In many countries, deregulation of broadcasting and new cable and satellite television technologies resulted in more channels being established to serve consumers. These new channels required programming, which Televisa—with a library that, in 1991, included 87,000 half-hour shows alone—was eager and able to provide. Because Televisa's production costs were estimated to be only one-quarter of those in the United States, the company could license its programs at very competitive prices.[5] Except for minor selling and administrative costs, licensing revenues dropped directly to the bottom line since

---

[5]Televisa's per-hour cost of production for telenovelas (soap operas) was thought to be around $40,000.

fixed production costs had already been incurred in developing the licensed programs for the domestic market. In 1991, Televisa licensed 36,361 hours of programs of all types for rebroadcast in 52 countries—22% more hours than were licensed in 1990. Table B breaks down 1990 licensed programming sales by geographical region. Only 6% of these sales were to stations not broadcasting in Spanish; this included a growing market for dubbed telenovelas in the former Communist countries of Eastern Europe.

In addition to licensing rebroadcast of individual programs, Televisa also sought to broadcast its programs in other countries at the same time as they were seen in Mexico. Channel 2, for example, was broadcast via satellite under the Galavision name to 45 countries, mainly in Central and South America and the Caribbean; the signal was picked up by local cable companies and individual satellite dishes. Channel 2 was also transmitted to Spanish owners of satellite dishes, many of them installed free by Televisa in communities and apartment complexes in exchange for demographic audience data. By early 1992, Channel 2 programming could be accessed via 3,300 satellite dishes by 1.4 million (or 13%–14%) of Spain's television households. Overall, 20%–30% of Channel 2 revenues in 1992 were estimated to be derived from international feeds. As the distribution of Televisa programming expanded beyond Mexico, Televisa was able to justify increases in its advertising rates. Though the premiums that multinational advertisers were prepared to pay for the extra reach varied, several were interested in pan-regional advertising buys covering all of Latin America.

To meet its strategic objective of becoming the dominant media company serving the Spanish-speaking world, Televisa increasingly developed its own programming with international markets in mind. The ECO 24-hour news program, for example, was designed to reach an international upscale Spanish-speaking audience. With 210 correspondents in 53 countries, ECO earned international recognition for its coverage of the Gulf War and the failed coup in the Soviet Union in 1991. By 1992, it was aired in 45 countries.

To publicize further its international strategy and test the capabilities of potential partners, Televisa oversaw and substantially produced 700 hours of programming to celebrate the 500th anniversary of Columbus's voyage. Developed in collaboration with broadcasters in 19 Spanish-speaking countries, these programs were aired in 45 countries on the so-called "Network of the Americas" between April and October 1992.

Televisa planned to expand its affiliations with local television stations throughout Latin America. Televisa not only provided international feeds of its Mexican channel and ECO news service but also tailored these feeds to the needs of each country market, adjusting for time-zone differences and adding or deleting advertising spots. To cement its relationships, for example with a private television channel in Argentina, Televisa planned to produce or co-produce programs with its Latin American affiliates for broadcast on their local stations.

In October 1991, Televisa entered into a 60/40 co-distribution joint venture with

TABLE B	Total Programming Hours Licensed by Region, 1990
South America	13,832
Central America	7,208
Caribbean Nations	2,891
United States, Canada and Mexico[a]	2,645
Europe	1,775
Asia and Australia	1,340
Africa	151
Total	29,842

[a]This figure does not include Galavision contracts.

Source: Grupo Televisa.

Venevision, Venezuela's largest media company and the second-largest producer of Spanish-language programming in the world. The two companies agreed to jointly distribute each other's programming throughout Latin America and to pursue cable television opportunities in the Spanish-speaking world. The Venevision joint venture did not preclude relationships with other television broadcasters in other nations. Televisa was enthusiastic about further co-distribution and co-production joint ventures in Latin America.

Televisa also pursued international growth through equity stakes and acquisitions. In December 1991, Televisa acquired, for $7 million, 49% of Megavision S.A., a leading privately owned Chilean broadcaster. The purchase gave Televisa an opportunity to participate in a rapidly growing media market and a further vehicle through which Televisa could distribute its programming. After replacing American-dubbed programming with Televisa novelas, Megavision advanced from fifth to second place in prime time audience ratings among Chilean television channels. In addition to the Megavision equity stake, Televisa acquired 76% of Compania Peruana de Radio Difusion for $7.7 million; this company owned 10 television stations and 2 radio stations and reached 75% of the Peruvian population. Such acquisitions expanded Televisa's presence in Latin America. However, international equity stakes were sometimes hard to complete due to government sensitivities about foreign ownership of broadcast media.

Finally, Televisa pursued international acquisitions in publishing as well as in electronic media. In 1991, the company acquired Grupo America from Miami-based American Publishing Group for $130 million. The acquisition included 80 Spanish-language magazines, comics, and romance novel series with combined annual circulation of over 120 million copies, as well as several distribution companies that Grupo America owned in Latin American countries. Sixty percent of Grupo America's sales were in Mexico where, aided by about 1,300 distributors, it commanded an 80% share of magazine distribution. As a result of the acquisition, Televisa became the largest Spanish-language publisher in the world and planned to extend *Eres* and *Somos* sales through the newly acquired distribution network.

Televisa was increasingly encountering U.S. companies that were also seeking to expand internationally. In 1991, Turner Broadcasting launched CNN Latin America and TNT Latin America. By 1992, the former was available to 700,000 cable television subscribers in 15 countries. The latter was the first trilingual network (in Portuguese as well as Spanish and English) and was accessible to 800,000 cable television subscribers in 27 countries. In 1992, MTV announced the launch of a Latin American service in October 1993, with a mix of U.S. and Latin American music to be presented by Latin disc jockeys.

TELEVISA IN THE UNITED STATES

In 1955, Grupo Televisa bought Channel 41, a San Antonio, Texas, UHF station with a low audience share and poor audio quality. The company successfully expanded the station's audience by using the same formula as it used in Mexico: scouted talent and live broadcasts. Soon, Televisa began to broadcast its signal from Mexico to affiliate stations in the Southwestern United States which carried Televisa's programming along with other broadcasts. Success in the Southwest led to the acquisition of stations in Florida and New York. With these additions, the company formed the Spanish International Communications Company (SICC). In 1972, SICC became the Spanish International Network (SIN). In each new market it entered, Televisa repeated its formula of live broadcasts, local Spanish-speaking talent, and rebroadcasts of programming produced in Mexico.

In 1977, Televisa established Galavision to enter the growing U.S. cable television market. Galavision carried Channel 2 Spanish-language programming from Mexico and was transmitted through U.S. cable operators who paid Televisa a modest fee per cable subscriber for the right to do so. Unlike SIN which had sold individual programs to broadcasters, Galavision offered a network with continuous Spanish-language programming. Televisa also arranged for advertisers to be able to make network buys of commercial time on all stations carrying Galavision whereas, through SIN, they had had to buy time separately on each local station.

In 1986, Grupo Televisa sold SIN and its stations to Hallmark Inc. for $600 million, partly to comply with U.S. Federal Communications Commission (FCC) regulations regarding foreign ownership of broadcast licenses.[6] While Televisa was technically in compliance with these regulations, which permitted foreign ownership of no more than 20% of a company that had an FCC broadcast license and 25% of a holding company controlling a license, an FCC administrative judge found that the close business relationships between Televisa's owners and their SIN partners amounted to excessive foreign control. Galavision, a relatively small operation, was not included in the Hallmark purchase. Subsequently, Galavision programming was made available to UHF and VHF television stations as well as to cable operators.

Hallmark renamed the network Univision, with headquarters in Miami. It consisted of nine full-power Spanish-language television stations located in Los Angeles, San Francisco, Fresno, Phoenix, Albuquerque, Dallas, San Antonio, Miami, and New York, and four low-power stations in other smaller Southwestern and California markets.

Under Hallmark's control, Univision continued to buy nearly half of its programming from Televisa. Under the terms of the acquisition, Univision had an option on half of the first-run programs Televisa distributed in the United States. Univision was therefore able to cherry-pick the most popular Televisa shows, leaving the remainder for Galavision. Univision paid Televisa fees based on the advertising sales revenue generated for the programming, the number of hours of Televisa programming shown, and the time periods in which the programs were shown. Univision expanded from 6% to 45% the programming produced in its own facilities in the United States, and purchased the rest from other Latin American television producers, such as Chile's Megavision and Argentina's Channel Argentina. Hallmark saw Univision as the centerpiece of a broader effort to market products to Hispanics. However, these expectations were not realized and, while Univision's revenues doubled to over $200 million between 1986 and 1991, interest on the debt burden assumed to acquire the company plus escalating operating costs limited profitability. Costs rose as Univision increased the percentage of its programming produced in the United States. These programming costs were only partly offset by foreign sales of Univision programming; under Hallmark's control, Univision programming was sold to broadcasters in 15 countries.

In 1992, Televisa was able to reenter the U.S. market by buying back Univision's network and stations from Hallmark for $550 million as part of a joint venture with Hollywood producer Jerrold Perecchio and Venevision, a Venezuelan television company. Under the terms of the deal announced in April and finalized in December, Televisa and Venevision each acquired 12½% ownership of the broadcast stations

---

[6]Of the $600 million, the value of SIN excluding the stations was estimated at $286 million.

and a 25% interest in the network. They both had the opportunity to increase their stakes should future FCC regulations allow. The consortium also acquired *Mas,* the largest circulation Spanish-language magazine in the United States. After the deal closed, Galavision became a cable-only network. As many as possible of Galavision's VHF- and UHF-affiliated stations were to be incorporated in the Univision broadcast network though some would doubtless have to be dropped due to duplicate coverage of the same geographical markets.

In January 1993, Televisa extended its U.S. interests further by purchasing for $200 million a 50% interest in PanAmSat which operated a single, privately owned satellite. Although in competition with the 17 satellites operated by the Intelsat consortium, PanAmSat was the principal satellite serving Latin America. The capital injected promised to help PanAmSat launch three more satellites by 1995, thereby enabling PanAmSat to offer broadcasters global reach of their signals. Televisa planned to use PanAmSat satellites to transmit more of its programming both to Europe and worldwide; to gather more quickly news reports from correspondents around the world for use on the ECO

network; and to persuade the Mexican government to lower the transmission costs it required Televisa to pay for using Intelsat and its own two Morelos satellites.

HISPANIC MARKETING IN THE UNITED STATES

Demographics

In 1992 there were 25 million Spanish-speaking residents and 13 million unregistered Spanish-speaking immigrants in the United States out of a total population of 255 million.[7] Their average age was only 17 years—10 years below the national average. The U.S. Hispanic population was expected to grow between 1990 and 2000 by 41%, versus 3% for the non-Hispanic population. On this basis, the United States would be the fifth-largest Spanish-speaking country in the Americas by the year 2000. As indicated in Table C, the U.S. Hispanic population was concentrated in California, Florida, New York, Texas, and Puerto Rico; this facilitated

---

[7]There were five persons in the average Hispanic household. There were about 7 million Hispanic households in the United States.

TABLE C Top Ten U.S. Cities in Hispanic Population and Hispanic Media Expenditures, 1990 (in $ millions)

	Total Population	*Hispanic Population*		*Hispanic Media Expenditures*	*Hispanic Media Expenditures per Thousand*
Los Angeles	14,531,429	6,080,304	(42%)	$139.5 MM	$22.94
New York	18,087,251	2,737,098	(15%)	89.5	32.20
Houston	3,711,043	1,300,038	(35%)	19.4	14.92
Chicago	8,065,633	1,284,147	(16%)	30.5	23.75
Miami	3,192,582	1,014,356	(32%)	92.0	90.73
San Francisco	6,253,311	1,008,310	(16%)	26.2	25.99
San Antonio	1,302,099	987,080	(76%)	19.7	20.59
McAllen/Brownsville, Texas	1,097,142	415,998	(38%)	NA	NA
Albuquerque, New Mexico	480,577	351,616	(73%)	NA	NA
El Paso, Texas	591,210	341,954	(58%)	9.4	27.49

Source: Adapted from U.S. Census Bureau, *Hispanic Business,* and *Advertising Age.*

efficient target marketing by advertisers seeking to appeal to Hispanics.

The U.S. Hispanic population was not homogeneous. First, it could be broken down into five groups which differed in their cultural values, accents, and expenditure patterns: Mexicans (62%) living mainly in California and the Southwest; Central/South Americans (14%); Puerto Ricans (11%) living mainly in New York; Cubans (5%) living mainly in Miami; and all others (8%).

U.S. Hispanics could also be segmented on the basis of preferred language, which was often related to the number of years their families had been in the country. First- and second-generation Hispanics were more likely to speak Spanish exclusively, while subsequent generations were more likely to be bilingual and to be exposed to English as well as Spanish media. Many Hispanic immigrants assimilated slowly into the so-called mainstream of U.S. culture, partly because of population concentrations and government-mandated bilingual education. A recent study concluded: "The majority of the U.S. Hispanic population appears to be more comfortable in a Spanish-speaking environment."[8] Exhibit 5 provides data on the language preferences of U.S. Hispanics.

While U.S. Hispanic households earned on average only 77% of the amount non-Hispanic households earned, they spent 83% of the amount non-Hispanic households spent. Hispanic households spent more on food and children's clothing than non-Hispanic Americans. They bought a higher proportion of brand name (versus private-label and generic) merchandise than the average U.S. household, and first-generation U.S. Hispanics were often loyal to U.S. brands they had first experienced in their home countries. Thus, for many manufacturers, the U.S. Hispanic market represented an important opportunity. (Hispanic expenditures by product category are reported in Exhibit 6.)

Advertising to Hispanics

Though at least 10% of the U.S. population was Hispanic, U.S. advertisers spent only 1% of their budgets in Hispanic media. In 1990, expenditures in Spanish-language media were $628 million, of which 23% went to national television, 21% to local television, and 32% to radio.[9] Though 68% of major marketers reportedly planned to run Spanish-language advertising in 1992, up from 58% in 1991, only Procter & Gamble (which spent $30 million in 1990) and Colgate-Palmolive Co. spent a proportion of their advertising budgets that came close to reflecting the percentages of sales they derived from Hispanics.

---

[8]Data Resources Inc., *Hispanic Consumer Maketing,* p. 7.

[9]Expenditures in national Hispanic television advertising were expected to rise from $143 million to $177 million in 1992.

EXHIBIT 5   Language and Media Preferences of U.S. Hispanics

- 51% speak Spanish only; 20% speak Spanish predominantly with some English; 26% speak Spanish and English equally; 3% speak English exclusively.
- 55% prefer television and radio programs in Spanish; 20% find Spanish and English programs equally preferable; 19% prefer English programs.
- U.S. Hispanics on average watch 14 hours of Spanish-language television and listen to 11 hours of Spanish-language radio per week.
- 68% of U.S. Hispanics do not read Spanish-language magazines and 53% do not read Spanish-language newspapers.

Source: Adapted from Market Segment Research study, Miami, 1992.

EXHIBIT 6 Hispanic Population, Income, and Expenditures in the United States, 1990–2000 (current dollars)

	1990	*1991*	*1992E*	*2000E*
Households:				
Total U.S. (millions)	93.3	94.3		
Hispanic (millions)	6.0	6.2		
Hispanic % of total	6.4	6.6	6.8	8.1
Disposable income:				
Total U.S. ($ billions)	4,058.5	4,218.4		
Hispanic ($ billions)	206.9	220.2		
Hispanic % of total	5.1	5.2	5.4	6.7
Consumer spending:				
Total U.S. ($ billions)	3,742.6	3,889.1		
Hispanic ($ billions)	192.7	205.1		
Hispanic % of total	5.4	5.5	5.6	7.0
Hispanic % of Total Spending				
Autos and parts	5.0	5.1	5.3	6.6
Furniture and appliances	4.7	4.8	5.0	6.3
Food and beverages	6.4	6.5	6.7	8.5
Clothing and shoes	6.5	6.6	6.8	8.6
Gasoline and oil	5.4	5.6	5.7	7.2
Other nondurable goods	4.4	4.5	4.6	5.8
Housing	6.5	6.6	6.8	8.6
Electricity	6.5	6.6	6.8	8.6
Transportation services	5.0	5.1	5.3	6.6
Medical services	3.6	3.7	3.8	4.8

Source: Adapted from *The Hispanic Consumer Market Report,* June 1992.

There were several explanations for the shortfall. First, some marketers saw the development of customized Hispanic advertising programs, including the purchase of time and space in Spanish-language media, as adding unnecessary complexity to their national marketing programs. Second, though there were several advertising agencies specializing in Hispanic communications, the mainstream advertising agencies lacked bilingual, bicultural experts and often assigned junior personnel to Hispanic advertising projects. Third, audience measurement data needed to compute the cost effectiveness of advertising in Hispanic media were considered unreliable, though this problem was mitigated in late 1992 when A.C. Nielsen began selling a national Hispanic viewing report based on people meters placed in 800 Hispanic households.[10]

Some Hispanic advertisers, including Coca-Cola and PepsiCo, found that they could simply translate their familiar slogans into Spanish though they developed commercial executions with Hispanic actors. Others developed customized campaigns. Chevrolet, for example, targeted Hispanic consumers with a family-oriented value message instead of its mainstream "Heartbeat of America" campaign.

---

[10]People meters were monitoring devices attached to household television sets that recorded when a set was on and the channel to which it was tuned.

SPANISH-LANGUAGE TELEVISION IN THE UNITED STATES

There were three Spanish-language networks broadcasting in the United States in 1992: Univision, bought back from Hallmark by Televisa and an investor group late in the year and renamed Univisa; Telemundo, owned since 1987 by financier Saul Steinberg; and Galavision, owned by Televisa. (Exhibit 7 compares the audience reach of the three networks via VHF/UHF broadcasters and cable system operators.)

In 1992, there were 11,086 cable systems in the United States serving 57.2 million (61.5%) television households. Of these, 714 carried at least one Spanish-language network. Over 85% of these systems broadcast two or more Spanish-language networks. Almost all of them offered one of these networks as part of the basic package, though there was increasing competition among programming suppliers to be included in cable systems' basic packages. The Spanish-language networks received a modest fee from cable system operators for each of their subscribers with a Spanish surname.

Univision was the most watched Spanish-language network among Hispanic households in 1992 during 92% of weekly programming hours. As shown in Table D, eight of the ten top-rated Spanish-language programs were shown on Univision. The network broadcast more news and sports than its competitors, but was especially popular for the prime-time entertainment and variety shows like Sabado Gigante and Siempre en Domingo which it licensed from Televisa and which appealed to all age groups.

Telemundo reached over 80% of the U.S. Hispanic population. It bought about 70% of its programming from non-Mexican Latin American media companies, the remainder being U.S.-produced shows, some of them dubbed. Telemundo targeted younger viewers by broadcasting programs such as the MTV Video Music Awards with Spanish-language voiceovers. Telemundo was thought to appeal more to Caribbean and Cuban Hispanics. Telemundo had only two shows among the ten highest-rated Spanish-language programs in the United States during the spring season of 1992. Following the late 1992 repurchase of Univision by Televisa, a number of top Univision executives were recruited by Telemundo. Telemundo also tried to take advantage of the Univision ownership transition by offering advertisers program sponsorship and barter syndication deals.[11]

---

[11]Under barter syndication, an advertiser received the advertising time associated with a program in return for purchasing the right to broadcast it in a particular market.

EXHIBIT 7 Comparative Audience Data for Three U.S. Spanish-language Networks, 1992			
	Galavision	*Telemundo*	*Univision*
Number of markets covered	50	46	119
Number of cable systems carrying	334	376	609
Number of Spanish-speaking households subscribing to these cable systems	1,200,000	1,200,000	1,625,000
Number of UHF/VHF stations carrying	7 UHF	16 UHF	19 UHF
these networks	2 VHF	16 VHF	19 VHF
Number of Spanish-speaking households served by these UHF/VHF stations	1,400,000	4,500,000	4,650,000
Average prime-time audience (households)[a]	133,000	950,000	1,200,000

[a]Average national audience, Spring 1992, for a program segment half-hour.

Source: Adapted from Strategy Research Corporation, May 1992.

TABLE D	Top 10 Rated Spanish-language Programs, Spring 1992		
Rank	*Program*	*Network*	*Rating*
1	Sabado Gigante	Univision	48
2	Siempre en Domingo	Univision	38
3	Muchachitas	Univision	36
4	Muy Especial	Univision	34
5	Cine Millonario	Telemundo	32
6	Noticiero-1	Univision	29
7	Christina	Univision	27
8	Fama y Fortuna	Univision	23
9	El Desprecio	Univision	21
10	Marielena	Telemundo	19

Note: Rating indicates the percentage of Hispanic households that received the program.

Source: Strategy Research Corporation.

Galavision was broadcast by cable operators in 20 states and on nine VHF and UHF television stations in the Southwest and California (including Channel 22, the third-most popular station in Los Angeles). Galavision broadcast only Spanish-language programming, almost all of which was produced in Grupo Televisa's Mexican studios. The network added more children's programming in 1991. Although Galavision aimed for national coverage and tried to avoid regional slang and cultural bias, its popularity was greatest among Hispanics of Mexican origin. In 1992, Galavision was available to 1.2 million cable television subscribers and to 43% of Hispanic U.S. households. Having bought back Univision in late 1992, Univisa executives were planning to convert Galavision into a cable-only network and to reallocate most of its nine affiliated stations to the Univisa network.

In 1992, between 9:00 A.M. and midnight, Univision's average share of Hispanic households viewing Spanish-language television was 56%, Telemundo's 36%, and Galavision's 9%. In many heavily Hispanic markets, the three English-language networks (ABC, CBS, NBC), which typi-

cally commanded 55% of the U.S. prime-time audience, were regularly beaten by one or more of the Hispanic networks, as indicated in Exhibit 8. However, as indicated in Exhibit 9, local advertising rates in heavily Hispanic markets reflected costs per thousand households reached that were significantly lower than those for the three main English-language networks.

EXHIBIT 8	Spring 1992 Prime-time Ratings Summary: National Composite (7:00–10:00 p.m., Monday through Friday)	
Station	*Number of Households*	*Rating Percentage*
ABC	153,000	2
CBS	155,000	2
NBC	148,000	2
Telemundo	1,033,000	15
Univision	2,341,000	35
Galavision	451,000	7
Fox	124,000	2
Spanish-speaking households using TV	4,196,000	60

Source: Adapted from Strategy Research Corporation, May 1992.

EXHIBIT 9	Comparative Advertising Costs for 30-Second Prime-time Advertisement, December 1992	
	National	*Local*[a]
Univision	$ 13,000	$ 800
Telemundo	8,125	500
Galavision	4,700	300
ABC	192,000	9,000
NBC	190,000	9,500
CBS	180,000	8,500

[a]Miami metropolitan area taken as local sample.

Source: Adapted from Strategy Research Corporation, May 1992.

CONCLUSION

Following the reacquisition of Univision, the top managers of Univisa wondered what strategies they should pursue to boost the revenues and profits of the company. Several of them would shortly be flying to Mexico City for a Grupo Televisa board meeting chaired by Emilio Azcarraga that would review the company's entire growth strategy for the 1990s with particular emphasis on international expansion. ■

3

PRODUCT LEADERSHIP

New products present consumers with a mix of confusion and curiosity because of their lack of knowledge about them. Consumption in today's marketplace makes consumers more demanding yet more cautious, as they plan both their purchases and their budgets.

Growth brings economic obstacles which are perhaps difficult to solve. In a market that has limited ability to finance a company's development, companies face the dilemma of having to choose whether to apply their scarce resources to business operations or to commercial development. This choice of investment often leads to a restriction on competitive advantage.

Many Latin American companies have grown and flourished through strategies of closed and protected economies, which also keep them apart from international treaties that govern trade. The case of Astra, an international sports shoes company, demonstrates the difficulties that this concept implies for multinational companies that start to become interested in marketing their product in the region, in this particular case, in Venezuela (see the Astra Sports, Inc. case study at the end of this chapter).

INNOVATION AS A CRITICAL FACTOR

In developing markets, opportunities often repeat themselves, but require innovative formulas to take advantage of them and to overcome difficulties that usually characterize early development stages. The lack of financial resources requires the use of innovative strategies, as in the case of Hoteles Royal of Colombia. Economic reforms also create many opportunities. The emergence of a new middle class in Chile opened up new business opportunities such as those in the cemetery-park sector. Business knowledge allowed some Chilean businesspeople to take advantage of this sector's deregulation in Uruguay.

Hoteles Royal

An innovative financial scheme and excellence in service were the key factors in the successful entry of a construction firm into the hotel business. In 1991, in the midst of the war against drug traffickers, The Royal Hotel of Colombia began to construct La Boheme, a five-star hotel in the Zona Rosa district of Colombia's capital. During its first quarter of operations, La Boheme reached an 80% occupancy rate. With a revolutionary financing scheme, which will later be copied by other businesses and other countries, the industry shows a real boom.

In 1989, the construction company in charge of the World Trade Center decided to enter the hotel business by capitalizing on the facility's famous name. The Bogotá Royal, a 143-room luxury hotel, was the first link in this chain. In 1993, the chain had three hotels and plans for continued expansion. The financing system was both simple and innovative: Small investors purchased a room in the future hotel (in the case of La Boheme at a price of $100,000), transferring the administration of said purchase to Royal. The income was distributed among the partners, with Price Waterhouse as auditor, and showed an annual profitability of 45% in the case of La Boheme. "The investor has the security of real estate with hotel profitability," stated the manager of the hotel, Arturo Garcia.

The amount of customer relations work doubled, as the hotel balanced the job of keeping both the investors and the customers happy. Concerning the latter, success was based on excellence of service. Customers received hot towels and their favorite drink. The bilingual personnel kept card references on the preferences and habits of each guest so as to better serve them when they returned. Since violence in the country has scared away many tourists, Royal began to target business travelers, providing such amenities as rooms with three phones, a fax machine, a desk with a calculator, and a safety deposit box. Each Tuesday, guests were invited to a cocktail party in the gardens, which provided an opportunity for informal conversations that many times led to new businesses.

The success was rapidly acknowledged and copied in Venezuela and Ecuador, generating the saturation principle in the marketplace that would anticipate lower growth in the future. In 1993, there were a total of 890 rooms at five-star hotels with 500 more expected in 1995, in addition to the traditional chains such as Marriot and Hilton who have also announced plans for expansion (see Exhibit 1).

The total amount of rooms (1,340 + 890 = 2,230 rooms) threatened investors with diminishing benefits due to reduced occupation rates, from 75% to 50%. The onslaught of inexperienced hotel entrepreneurs who started projects without adequate managers

EXHIBIT 1 Opening of New Hotels in Bogotá, 1993–1995		
Hotel Chain	*No. of Rooms*	*Date of Completion*
Casa Medina	32	August 1993
De la Ville	32	August 1993
Molly Penny	25	August 1993
Cosmos 100	100	December 1993
Suites Jones	105	December 1993
Dann Excelsior	180	January 1994
New Orleans	100	January 1994
Portal 82	41	January 1994
HIT	224	December 1994
Saint Michel	70	August 1995
Hacienda Sta. Bárbara	230	December 1995
Holiday Inn	200	December 1995
Total	1,340	

also hurt the industry. Experts considered that continuous innovation would have to be the key to maintaining the profitability of chains.

Parque del Sendero Cemetery

Parque del Sendero is another example of innovation that contributed to changing the habits of the population of Santiago, Chile, at least in regard to cemeteries. In 1989, the company began to promote the area as a cemetery-park, and within a year the cemetery was full. "I cannot say that it is really for strolling, but it is not the macabre example of a traditional cemetery," affirmed Luis Felipe Navarro, general manager of Inmobiliaria Parques y Jardines, and owner and operator of the cemetery, in an interview with *América Economía.* Another executive of the sector indicated that "it is the typical product for this ecologically-minded and aseptic generation."

In the early 1980s, traditional cemeteries started filling up and some companies bought open land to convert them into cemetery-parks. To its original investment of $1 million, which recorded sales of $700,000 per year, Parque del Sendero added 7 hectares of land.

In addition to this innovative proposal, companies initiated new sales and service tactics. They offered discounts of 30% on "advanced" sales (at least 2 years before use of plots). If a family member died before the 2 years, however, the family had to pay full price. About 70% of the sales were conducted in this manner, and the rest came from "emergency" burials. To provide the best service, companies maintained contact with funeral homes who, in turn, closely followed movements in clinics and hospitals. Each referral brought a commission of $115. The information system was so effective that it sometimes led to embarrassing mistakes such as when they offered services to the next of kin before that person had been informed of the family member's death.

The cemetery-park rates differed according to districts, landscape, and population density of the nearby area. Companies offered a 5-year interest rate similar to the real estate market granted by banks, which took the responsibility for collection. The rates also differed based on the relationship between the plot owner and the deceased: The price was lower for sons and spouses and higher for parents and brothers. This encouraged buyers, mostly professionals, to purchase several plots.

The effect on the real estate market in the area has been peculiar. At first, neighbors complained and the surrounding land lowered in value, but then the situation reversed, and the property increased in value. Parques y Jardines bought its first land in western Santiago for $3 per square meter and additional land for $14 in 1992. Generally the cemetery-parks are located in agricultural areas, but in the rezoning process for industrialization or urbanization in northern Santiago, where the first cemetery-park, Parque de Recuerdo, is located, many new industries are springing up. In the west, Parque del Sendero is only 1,500 meters from an outlet mall frequented by middle-class shoppers. In Puente Alto, to the south, Parque de Prado is situated next to a new middle-class suburb which was generated by the economic model and consumer credit.

As demand soon exceeded supply, some parks expanded in adjacent areas whereas others preferred to look for new markets. Isacruz, owner of Parque de Prado, stayed in the provinces near major cities and established a string of cemeteries throughout the country, with monthly sales of $1 million. Parque de Recuerdo, on the other hand, preferred other markets and chose Uruguay. As in Chile, the problem was lack of available land due to sector regulations. For more than 20 years, it had been impossible to get a permit to establish a cemetery-park in Montevideo. In 1991, a total of 30,000 people were interested in paying $6,000 each for the 100 plots offered by the largest public cemetery of Montevideo. Then the city authorities modified regulations to allow private cemeteries. Four of the 15 investors that offered bids were granted a permit. Mater Tera and Colinas Verdes invested $2 million and $1.6 million, respectively, in the San José district. In Canelones, site of Parque de Recuerdo, a joint venture with local capital invested $3 million; and in Los Fresnos, offering a wide range of services in its 14 hectares and 2,000 constructed meters, an investment totals $4 million.

The parcels, all having the same measurements, cost $3,500 and are financed by the Banco de Montevideo, whose major owner is Deutsche Bank. Los Fresnos offers cremation, corpse reduction (preferred by 27% of the market research respondents), and vigil rooms. Los Fresnos also targeted sales to the Uruguayan community in Argentina. Sometimes these people wish to be buried in their native land, as the cemetery is close to Carrasco International Airport in Montevideo.

CASES

3-1 ARCOR CHOCOLATES

"We cannot remain in the fine chocolate market with our current products. I want you to define whether we are pulling out of this sector or staying in it. If so, how should we do it?" Mr. Flaglio Pagani, president of Arcor S.A., used these words to address Mr. Enrique D'Alessandro, communications manager, and Mr. Ricardo Bruno, product manager, at the beginning of 1990.

"We face specialized competition having high quality products and people barely know us in Buenos Aires. Besides, our image is not helping, either," Enrique pointed out. They had started analyzing this segment months before. "We'll bring you our proposal next week," Ricardo promised. The time had come to choose among the alternatives posed by the marketing team.

THE COMPANY

In 1924, Amos Pagani, a baker from Udine, Italy, opened his bakery at Arroyito, a small town in the Córdoba province about 70 miles from the provincial capital in central Argentina. Diversification induced him to add cookies and later candy to his product line. In 1946, his second son, Fulvio, joined his father's business while finishing his last year in high school. They were approached by a group of businessmen interested in acquiring the original machine to produce candy. After looking over Amos' sales or-

ganization, they offered the Paganis the opportunity to participate in the company they were setting up in Sastre, Santa Fé, to manufacture cookies, chocolates, and candy. Immediately, Pagani suggested they increase production to 5,000 kilos daily to reduce costs instead of diversifying further. However, his proposal was rejected by his partners. Instead, they agreed to buy out his cardboard box supplier, who upon trying to buy new machinery for his growing carton plant, received an offer for the whole plant.

In 1951, Fulvio, then 22 years old, along with a group of friends from the company—Brizio and Seveso Maranzana, and his own brothers Renzo and Elio—started to build the 30,000 square foot plant to produce the 5,000 kilos of candy daily. Following a vision of integration, a truly pioneering concept for the times, he sought expansion by establishing several centers in the interior of the country, constantly improving productivity and resourcing to vertical integration for manufacturing all necessary materials.

This not only increased profit margins, but also ensured supplies at a time when Argentine industry was only starting to develop in certain sectors.

"We reached a certain candy production volume on the basis of very effective competition. We had to work with a 10% margin. We realized that, if we produced our own raw materials, we could handle a 30% or 40% margin. Instead of increasing our candy production, we decided we should aim at certain raw materials. Thus, in 1956, we set up our first glucose," explained Mr. Fulvio Pagani. In 1958, they were producing 60,000 kilos of candy daily.

Prof. Guillermo D'Andrea of the Instituto de Altos Estudios Empresariales prepared this case as a basis for class discussion, rather than to illustrate effective or ineffective handling of an administrative situation. Its reproduction is prohibited without the total or partial written permission of IAE.

The 1970s was a time for consolidation. This stage continued into the 1980s. To the new food and candy plants, they added factories for plastic wrap, glucose, fructose, tin containers, ice-cream production, flexible materials, packaging machines, and cardboard. They had a total of 25 plants employing 8,700 people. As an expansion, they installed Van Dam Industries in Uruguay, producing 6,000 kilos daily for the Cowboy, Blowup, and Mentho Plus brands. In Paraguay, they launched Arcopar, which has become a monopoly producing 8,000 daily kilos. In 1980, they acquired Nechar, a Brazilian food manufacturer, and became the first candy exporter with a volume of $27 million. Exhibit 1 shows sales share per division.

On December 29, 1990, Mr. Fulvio Pagani died in a car accident. He left behind a business philosophy and structure to ensure leadership. Mr. Hugo D'Alessandro succeeded him as chairman. He proceeded to build a chocolate factory at Colonia Caroya and afterwards bought Aguila Saint, an old competitor in the segment.

Arcor won a leading position in the Argentine candy market, holding a 70% share. It leads the chocolate segment with a 36% participation. Its sales of $300 million include a variety of 400 other products, such as jam and preserves, flexible materials, paper and cardboard, corn, flour products, and agriculture. "We have goods for all the segments and our distribution chain reaches all the candy stores in the country, from Ushuaia in the southernmost tip of Tierra del Fuego to La Quiaca on the Bolivian border," explained D'Alessandro. The company produced more than 100,000 tons of candies and chocolates, distributing them to more than 170,000 points of sale, including supermarkets, self-service stores, and 600 wholesalers.

Its main competitors were Nestlé and Suchard in the chocolate segment. Two large local companies dominated the cookie market. Bagley had 33% of the markets and Terrabusi held 24% with sales of $300 million. Arcor aims at mass production in all segments. The subsequent acquisitions of Aguila Saint and Noel complied with this objective. "Mass products mean a large market share and the best possible quality," D'Alessandro pointed out. In chewing gums, Arcor had a 28% market share, competing against Stani, recently acquired by the British holding Cadbury-Schweppes. In marmalades, it led the market, followed by the BenvenutoHnos., both reaching 50% of the segment. Arcor was also the main producer of quince jam and it was the number two national producer of corn oil, sauces, canned tomatoes, and tomato paste.

Communication investment totaled $5 million in 1990. "We don't like to throw money away," D'Alessandro added. In 1990, a strong industrial change was underway. The company was trying to become more competitive and efficient. Technological improvements were implemented in an attempt to produce higher quality at lower costs and to penetrate overseas and domestic markets aggressively. Management was looking for higher product contribution, lower costs, and more productivity, seizing its competitive advantages—mainly the fact that it was the only candy manufacturer with exclusive distribution.

EXHIBIT 1 Sales Shares per Division	
Division	*Sales %*
Candies	24
Chocolates	17
James and Preserves	10
Flexible Materials	10
Paper and Cardboard	9
Corn	9
Arcor Brazil	9
Products with Flour	7
Agriculture	5

THE CHOCOLATE MARKET

In 1990, the chocolate market had a volume of 32,000 tons, 2,240 tons of which were sold in the fine chocolate market. Exhibit 2 shows the evolution during the decade. This market was sensitive to the changing domestic economic situation. It had different segments according to product type: fine, airy, bar, filled, and special for children (see Exhibit 3). If the economy grew, imported products were expected to bring more competitiveness to the first segment, an outcome of the open import policy promoted by the government.

The sector was led by Suchard with its brands of Milka and Toberone, bearing 29% and 36% of the market, respectively, at $11 per kilo. Milka had the leading image. Saint came in second, reaching an 11% market share with its brands Aguila D'or and Classique in three varieties. Its image concentrated on high-quality semisweet chocolate. Both had strong business support.

Arcor held 10% of the fine chocolate market and four varieties: milk; milk and almonds; milk, almonds, and raisins; and milk and walnuts—at an average price of $5 per kilo. The remaining 14% was divided among other manufacturers such as Georgalos with a fine bar and Noel with its Italian line in three varieties.

Market trends indicated that teenagers and children value fashion, fun, and fantasy. There was a lack of specific chocolates targeting the adult segment. See Exhibit 4. Exhibit 5 shows the requirements for fine chocolate.

Demand rose as a consequence of the increase in real salary and the economic stability and growth. Supply grew with innovative launches from existing brands and imported products. Renown brand products displayed high quality and price, sophisticated packaging, and new flavors.

A new sociopolitical context posed a wider acceptance of foreign companies and products and, at the same time, a loss of trust in domestic business. State protection demand was constantly decreasing and a new value was placed on companies showing concern for their employees and higher profitability objectives. Consumers expected companies to show more responsibility, creativity, competitiveness, a capacity to run risks, and adjust to the new market needs.

Distribution was carried out by wholesalers, but supermarkets were growing in

EXHIBIT 2	Chocolate Sales (in tons)
1980	46,000
1981	50,000
1982	39,000
1983	47,000
1984	48,000
1985	51,000
1990	32,000

Source: A.C. Nielsen

EXHIBIT 3	Historical Market Share per Chocolate Type (%)						
	1980	*1981*	*1982*	*1983*	*1984*	*1985*	*1990*
Fine	9	10	7	6	10	10	7
Airy	23	18	23	19	22	22	14
Bars	59	59	54	47	43	41	55
Children's	8	7	15	18	12	13	14
Filled	1	6	7	10	13	14	10

EXHIBIT 4 Chocolate Market Definition and Composition

Brand	Target	Communication Presence
Aguila D'Or	Adults	Low
Toblerone	Adults	Low
Suflair/Aero	Adults	Low
Suchard	Children/Adults	Low
Milka	Family/Children	Strong
Tofi/Shot	Teenagers	Strong

EXHIBIT 5 Requirements for Fine Chocolate

Product:
Optimum flavor
Soft
High-quality raw materials
Few aromatic chemicals
Novel ingredients

Price:
High

Packaging:
Very good design
Colorful—bright
Elongated
70–80 gr.
Embossed shapes
High-quality printing

"Specialized" business support

Source: Company's surveys.

their sales share and there was an increasing demand from retail channels. The struggle for the limited kiosk space—100,000 kiosks in the entire country—was a permanent challenge.

ARCOR CHOCOLATES

Arcor distributed mainly in the interior of the country where it was the market leader. It was highly competitive in lower prices with candy, marmalades, children's chocolate bars, and cheap chocolates.

It had little penetration in Buenos Aires where 35% of the country's total population was concentrated. Its massive circulation was low and its image was associated with cheap products of medium and low quality.

In the chocolate segment, Arcor's image was practically nonexistent, as 95% of Arcor chocolates belonged to the low-price segment.

A NEW CHOCOLATE

In the beginning of 1991, Ricardo Bruni was faced with four alternatives to launch Arcor into the fine chocolate segment.

The first alternative was to change to the Bon-o-Bon brand, a type of chocolate bonbon which was already very successful. It had an excellent image and recognition based on appealing and modern packaging, its original round shape, and a valued component mix. In fact, Bon-o-Bon was the only product among Arcor's line that, due to its prestigious image, could compete with imported goods. Actually, consumers associated this bonbon with imported chocolates, especially with a similar high-quality Brazilian bonbon which came in several varieties and became a typical souvenir for Argentines traveling to the neighboring country.

The second option was to update the Arcor brand, thus associating the product to the company. Up until then, its image was more connected to children and mass chocolates than to its capacity as manufacturer since it was not a specialist.

A third choice was to take advantage of the Godet brand used to sell semisweet chocolate. Although it had the image of an old brand for mass chocolates, it certainly had recollection. Brand recollection was a basic factor for this kind of product. In this environment, Enrique D'Alessandro wondered if it would not be wise to introduce a new brand. It would be necessary to outline a positioning, which could be fictional or rational. The considerations were many: to launch one or more varieties, filled or not, large or small sizes, or both. Could Arcor enter the high-priced segment or would it be better to profit from its strong popularity with housewives who bought cheaper products? What kind of share would be acceptable? What would be the distribution objective and the communication campaign?

Finally, there was always the possibility of not going into this market. Indeed, it was no small challenge. According to surveys, consumers still remembered prior failures, and facing off Suchard, Cadbury, and Nestlé in the capital district was a serious affair. Suchard invested $2.3 million in advertising alone on Milka, the embodiment of chocolate itself. Moreover, this investment would surely be increased to adjust to the growing market. The market was becoming more sophisticated as international competitors handled new and more advanced technologies. ■

3-2 ALGODONERA DEL PLATA

As he drove back home by the AU-2 route toward Buenos Aires, José Sánchez reviewed the past months of hard work, since he had been appointed marketing manager of Algodonera del Plata. The challenge had turned out to be an excellent opportunity to put in practice all his knowledge, and the plans already implemented promised encouraging results. However, the dialogue he had just held with Eduardo Gennaro, president of the company, had left him deeply worried. Would it be necessary to advance slower? Or was Eduardo backing down on the promises he had made earlier? In that case, where did he stand? Had it been a good decision to leave his former job in Davor to come to this company at last, or would he be better off searching for a more serious and professional company?

THE COMPANY

Algodonera del Plata was founded in 1940, in Buenos Aires, by Dante Gennaro, an Italian immigrant who had worked in the textile industry in Italy. From the beginning, his major concern was to give the market a product of the best possible quality. This desire gradually pushed his second obsession: the manufacturing technology.

With this philosophy, Dante managed to promote his brand of sports products, under the name Cottone. The line mainly included cotton sweatsuits used by sportsmen and by children and young people for their gym classes at school.

This case has been prepared by Professor Guillermo D'Andrea of the Instituto de Altos Estudios Empresariales, as a basis for class discussion rather than to illustrate effective or ineffective handling of an specific situation.

THE SWEATSUIT

Around 1984, fashion development made the sweatsuit a favorite garment, compared with wool sweaters which had been used until that time. The closed collar Scottish Shetland sweaters, or those softer V-necked sweaters, were replaced by the sweatshirt. Young people adopted this garment quickly, because the cotton fabric was soft but still warm and also less expensive. Children preferred the fabric because it didn't "itch," and mothers liked the fabric because their children left the sweatshirts on and thus stayed warm. Besides, it was easy to wash and required no special care, as opposed to wool clothes which stretched if they were mishandled. Sweatsuits presented other advantages in the fashion field: They could be cut in many different shapes, creating clothes of diverse looks, and easily allow a wide range of printing and embroidery, so they could be printed with drawings and inscriptions.

American universities had adopted sweatsuits years ago, printing on them the colors, names, and emblems of each school. These were sold to students and visitors as souvenirs. Soon young people were wearing sweatsuits with inscriptions of universities, cartoon characters, tourist places, and other varieties of printings.

The cotton sweatsuit consists of two parts: the sweatshirt and the sweatpant. It is generally a thick, comfortable, and warm garment, even though thinner sweatsuits are made for mild climates. The quantity of cotton in the garment determines its weight and, to a good extent, the final quality of its fabric, garment texture, and durability. Manufacturing and dying are two other stages of the process which determine the final quality.

The quality, shown by the thickness of the garment, the firmness of its colors, and its durability, made Cottone sweatsuits the favorites for being warm and longer lasting. For years, blue and white sweatsuits were the most worn and almost the only ones offered in the best sports shops. Dante supervised not only production, but also all marketing aspects of the company, as it grew in size and market prestige.

THE NEW MANAGEMENT

In 1960, Eduardo Gennaro, 20 years old, the only son of Dante's four children, also became interested in continuing the family business. His training took place within the company, where he worked all positions, starting with simpler ones and ending as head of production. Although Eduardo had not attended university, the years in his father's business made him a specialist on the subject. In 1980, Eduardo began to participate in the management of the company. Five years later, when Dante died at the age 83, Eduardo took over full responsibilities as manager of the business, leaving Luis Corral in charge of operations. Luis Corral was a Spanish national who had been trained at Dante's side. The commercial issues were assigned to Susana Rios, a 20-year veteran in sales management for the company. Eduardo also named Ramiro Fonseca, then accountant of the company, to the board of directors with profit sharing.

Since 1980, Eduardo and Ramiro Fonseca had developed nine wholly owned exclusive shops under the Raffael brand. These stores accounted for 25% of gross sales. They were located in popular areas of the Capital City and Greater Buenos Aires: one in a neighborhood with discounted clothing stores (Palermo Viejo, Nuñez, Quilmes, Castelar, San Antonio de Padua, Munro and Morón), and one in the Harrod's stores on the traditional Florida street (see Exhibit 1).

One problematic store location was Harrod's. Over time, its operations in Buenos Aires were declining. It had closed all the floors except the ground level, where it rented spaces to several companies. Har-

EXHIBIT 1 Map of Argentina (Provinces and Capital City)

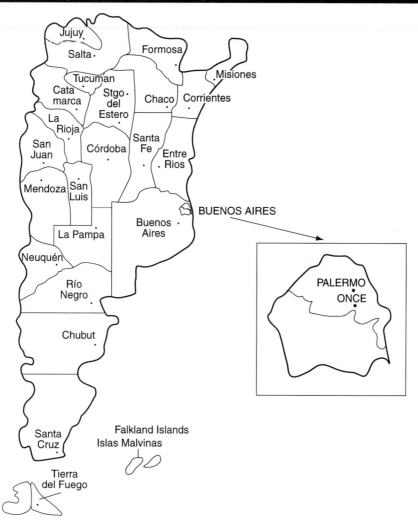

rod's had become a "shopping mall" with small independent stores.

The factory outlet sold another 20%, which included second-quality products at discounted prices, and the remaining sales were in clothing and other types of stores.

Eight salespeople in Capital City and 10 salespeople in areas outside Buenos Aires served 500 retailers. Half of the production volume was sold in the area of Buenos Aires, and the rest in the main cities such as Rosario, Santa Fe, Paraná, Córdoba,

Mendoza, and Río Negro, thus covering most of the large Argentine territory.

Part of the spinning production was done at the Buenos Aires plant, while other operations such as sewing, cutting, dying, and manufacturing were performed in San Juan to take advantage of tax discounts due to the industrial promotion of that province.

The product line consisted of the classics—blue or white—and fashionable designs. The classics were used in gym classes at schools. Fashionable items had premium prices. They were targeted for women and children, based on the idea that the mother would buy it for the child and then would be tempted to buy another one for herself. Sweatsuits had brighter colors, inscriptions, and small embroidered drawings, and were promoted as daily-wear clothing.

Algodonera sold the sweatsuits for $16. Retail prices averaged $35, ranging from $22 to $50, depending on the location. The summer shirts sold at a manufacturer's price of $8.

THE SITUATION IN MARCH 1993

During the ending summer season, 300,000 garments were manufactured. Inventories amounted to 315,000 units at the end of that period, valued conservatively at $2,900,000. Of these, 100,000 garments belonged to the previous winter season. Annual sales were estimated at $6,000,000, and the company employed 200 people. The monthly overheads amounted to $400,000 (Exhibit 2 shows evolution of sales since 1983).

Historically, Aldogonera had always kept high inventories—about 200,000 garments—following an accounting policy that had proved to be beneficial for the company at times of high inflation. A depreciating stock and an updated sale value

generated huge margins that were invested in the financial market. Until 1985, the company had shown a profit for many years. However, the tax policy change in 1985, with the launching of the Plan Austral, called for reappraisals of inventories according to the inflation.

The inventories consisted of four different types of articles:

1. Classics, which were produced in advance for the winter season (63,000 garments)
2. Classics production excess from prior years
3. Fashions of the past year received late for delivery, or collections that had not run well
4. Remaining pieces of incomplete collections, by size and color

The remainders were sold at a discounted price at the factory store. Customers were mainly local people. Garments of the third group were sold to Raffael exclusive stores at discounted prices.

A major concern of the two partners was that the cash deficit rose to $800,000 at the end of the season, and therefore they had to request a second credit line to support the upcoming months. The financing of tax payment delays was still expensive, due to the accounting inflationary adjustment and economic stability which caused no currency devaluation and therefore yielded no benefits per inflation.

Eduardo Gennaro summarized the main conclusions of the managers' meeting held in late March 1993. "We need a really aggressive sales manager. We could increase our sales up to 50% without increasing expenses, except direct costs of raw material. We are in a position to become leaders in sweatsuits for schools and leisure time, selling at convenient prices." Immediately the managers began a job search for the right candidate.

EXHIBIT 2 Volume of Sales 1983–93	
Year	*Volume (in thousands)*
1983	470
1984	479
1985	489
1986	519
1987	419
1988	552
1989	398
1990	460
1991	370
1992	430
1993	400 Estimated

THE ARRIVAL OF JOSÉ SÁNCHEZ

Algodonera hired José Sánchez through an executive search firm. Formerly, José held the position as head of product development at Davor, a company that manufactured informal clothes for young people and teenagers, and showed a consistent growth pattern during the past 10 years. With a bachelor degree in business administration, 30-year-old José started to work in May 1993.

By early June, Sánchez presented his plan to the management of Algodonera. Even though some points were arguable, the management team congratulated him for his quick response and encouraged him to continue with the same energy. His diagnosis overlooked various issues.

Some of the newly manufactured garments would later be rejected by clients for several reasons, late in the season or incomplete orders being the most usual. Nevertheless, the sales department approved the entry of a production order, assuming this risk. Some of the clients expressed that Algodonera was a factory of leftovers.

The variety of items was meant to broaden the product line. Apart from differences in size and color, 21 classic style items and 34 fashion garments were manufactured. The latter, in volumes of 2,000 units, made up the main collection. Sánchez's analysis indicated that 80% of sales accounted for 12% of the items, mainly the classic ones.

Sales were developed by 17 salespeople to 600 clients throughout the country. They were compensated through commissions, ranging from 2% to 4%. Sales performance was quite irregular, as were the field assignments (see Exhibit 3).

Sánchez hired a designer to develop new and more fashionable styles. One of the management proposals was to include some older logos on the garments. They turned out to be too old and unknown, so Algodonera decided to search for new ones and create a Cottone Campus collection. This product line would replace the previous one designed by Susana Rios and reduce the number of models.

Another proposal was to close several Raffael stores and open new ones in areas of better socioeconomic levels, once the collection had been improved. This proposal was later postponed by management. The closing of Harrod's store generated long discussions. Even though managers accepted that Harrod's had lost most of its former attractiveness, it was the only shop in downtown Buenos Aires, and they thought it gave prestige to the brand.

To improve sales in the existing stores, Sánchez proposed various ideas. (Due to the scarcity of resources, promotions would be used to stimulate sales at the retail outlets.) Plans included using photographs, stickers for shop windows, posters, and a changeable marquee. Store selection would be important, because of customer diversity. In Buenos Aires, garments were sold in the best sports stores and middle-level stores.

To increase new sales levels, Sánchez proposed to target new clients in selected areas, so as not to affect those better supplied.

Another alternative considered by the management was to accept the proposal made by the owner of the Raffael store in the discount district at Munro. He proposed to become a partner for the opening of a new store, dedicated to selling only second-quality garments. After deliberations and discussions, management went ahead with this alternative.

A third suggestion of selling to franchised chains in the interior of the country was rejected, because management feared that this could harm the brand image.

Lastly, the management would study the alternative of exporting, although Algodonera had no experience in that activity.

To solve the inventory problem, Sánchez proposed to order stock by class

EXHIBIT 3 Sales Force Breakdown

| Salesperson | Wage or Commission (%) | Sales (1000 Garments) | | $'000 | Area |
		1988	1992	1992	
S. Varela	10	29	17	200	Capital City
M. Loza	2,5	32	11,1	55	Capital City
L. Soprani	4+ travel allowance	9	6	45	Capital City
V. Vinueza	5	32	17	110	North Greater Buenos Aires
M. Duhalde	5	32	14	190	Greater Buenos Aires
N. Freire	4	11	28	170	Greater Buenos Aires
A. Moyano	5	17	17	145	Greater Buenos Aires
Factory Store		87	56		
Raffael Stores		61	40		
I. Srur	4	1	1	12	Tucumán-Santiago Catamarca
D. Becker	5	4	2	26	Northwest
A. Levin	5	11	9	110	Entre Rios
S. Aldrey	4,5	0,7	4	60	Northeast, Santa Fe
D. Nader	4	9	7	43	Cuyo
E. Caretto	5+ tour	35	14	180	Atlantic
C. Nebbia	5	14	12	87	North Buenos Aires
C. Valdeman	6	26	9	190	Córdoba
L. Caubet	7	28	21	270	Rio Negro-Bahia Blanca
S. López	7	24	13	285	Patagonia

Commissions were calculated as a percentage of sales. Salespeople paid their own expenses unless otherwise noted.

criteria. Classic articles would be eliminated from the winter production program, and the rest would be offered to important clients at the provinces, with a 25% discount. Outdated items would be sold to hypermarkets at low prices, either unbranded or under a different brand.

Sánchez started to tour the country, meeting salespeople and clients. He observed big discrepancies: Some stores faired well in retail and customer service, but brand representation was behind his expectations.

At the end of September, after returning from a trip, Sánchez met with Eduardo Gennaro in Gennaro's office. They greeted and then Eduardo posed his concerns.

EDUARDO: I'm worried about how we will incorporate new de-signs into the traditional collection. Our customers are not familiar with this image of the Cottone line, and there may be a possible sales failure. How shall we make this image change? I think the changes you have proposed are generally well directed, but we also have to take into account our people. We have worked with them for a long time and I will not fire them just because we have a couple of bad years. There has to be a less bloody way of improving this situation. What happened with the shops chain we were going to franchise? Inventories are not reduced as it was expected! Our shops are receiving very little attention! Besides, there is still the issue with Susana Rios, and this has to stop right away.

Lately, frictions with Susana Rios were more frequent. The last episode arose when Sánchez proposed to fire some salespeople, beginning with a 69-year-old saleswoman from Tucuman who had 1.5% of total sales and charged a commission of 2%. They had not been in contact with her for months, but this was not unusual.

JOSÉ: But, Eduardo, when we evaluated the situation together three months ago, you agreed that these changes were essential to ensure the company's continuity. I'm only implementing them. Besides, we haven't been able to make important promotions to stimulate sales due to the lack of cash.

EDUARDO: Of course, I remember those meetings very well, and I still think the same way, but I think you are stepping into issues that are not of your concern. You seem to be playing general manager, instead of marketing manager! There is no area in which you do not intend to make changes! I think you must concentrate on specific marketing aspects and leave the rest to me. Let's see if things calm down a little.

With these words, Eduardo ended the meeting. ■

3-3 ASTRA SPORTS INC. (B)

In January 1991, the vice president-Latin America of Astra Sports Inc. and the company's corporate counsel were discussing their options in advance of a meeting with a Venezuelan manufacturer who had for seven years manufactured and marketed athletic shoes under the Astra name.

BACKGROUND

In 1982, Gaviria S.A., a Venezuelan footwear manufacturer, had filed an application to register the Astra brand. Two months later, the application—of which Astra only later became aware—was approved, having gone unchallenged. Astra's general counsel commented on how this same problem had arisen not only in Venezuela, but also in Peru, Guatemala, and Honduras:

In the early 1980s, Astra management had to focus on trying to meet the explosive

---

Professor John A. Quelch prepared this case as the basis for class discussion rather than to illustrate either effective or ineffective handling of an administrative situation.

growth in demand for our products in the U.S. We simply didn't have the resources or experience to get our brands properly registered in all the overseas markets.

Today, there are trademark consulting services that we subscribe to that report filings from all over the world that might infringe our trademarks. We get about twenty notices a week that require further action. But in 1982, these trademark watch services didn't exist.

Venezuela was not a signatory to the major international intellectual property conventions that protected international brands. Trademark piracy was widespread in Venezuela; well-known brands such as Land Rover and Galeries Lafayette had suffered the same fate as Astra.

Under Venezuelan law, Astra had five years after the trademark registration was approved to sue for its cancellation. The case had to be made that Gaviria knew the Astra brand existed outside Venezuela in advance of its application. However, Venezuelan law gave Astra almost no rights of discovery (i.e., requiring Gaviria to reveal internal documents) so no case could be pursued on this basis.

By 1990, the only legal recourse was for Astra to appeal to the Venezuelan government both directly and through the Office of the U.S. Trade Representative to rescind an earlier unjust decision by its own courts. This was considered a "long shot," given the prevalence of trademark preemption in Venezuelan business, since a favorable decision might set a precedent for similar appeals by other international companies whose brands had been preempted. On the other hand, Venezuela had to compete with other countries for foreign direct investment by multinationals, and its reputation as a nonenforcer of intellectual property conventions was an increasingly important impediment.

ASTRA SALES IN VENEZUELA

Between 1983 and 1985, Gaviria made and marketed few "Astra" shoes. By 1986, however, Astra's worldwide brand recognition meant that the brand was known in Venezuela and consumers were willing to pay a premium for it. Astra executives estimated that Gaviria produced 30,000 pairs of Astra athletic shoes in 1986, increasing to 500,000 pairs in 1990. These shoes were of mediocre (but gradually improving) quality, were sold by Gaviria at an average price of $6.50 per pair, and retailed for an average price of $13.00 in Venezuela—$3.00 per pair more than shoes of equivalent quality that did not carry the Astra name. By 1990, Astra executives believed that "Astra" shoes accounted for two-thirds of Gaviria's production and one-quarter of the Venezuelan market for branded athletic footwear, and that 750 employees depended on "Astra" sales for their jobs. Astra was the only brand that Gaviria had preempted in this manner.

Genuine Astra shoes did find their way to some of Venezuela's 16 million consumers through the free trade zone established by the Venezuelan government on the offshore island of Margarita. Since 1983, Astra's Central American distributor in Panama had transshipped Astra shoes to Margarita. Venezuelan citizens were not permitted to purchase goods in Margarita beyond their personal needs, but many did so, reselling the surplus on the mainland. In 1990, 100,000 pairs of genuine Astra shoes were sold to Venezuelans through this channel at an estimated average retail price of $65.00. Astra was unaware of any efforts by Gaviria to curtail its sales through Margarita.

ASTRA LATIN AMERICAN STRATEGY

In 1989, Astra began to place increased emphasis on penetrating international markets. All Astra shoes were manufactured in Asia and fewer than 5% were then shipped to Latin American countries. Many of these countries imposed high tariffs (often between 100% and 300%) on imported footwear to protect their domestic producers. Brazil had a total ban on imported shoes. Astra had considered licensing one or two established shoe manufacturers in the larger Latin American countries to produce some of Astra's designs in return for royalties based on a percentage of sales, but had rejected the idea. Apart from quality control concerns, Astra feared that these manufacturers would simply apply Astra's designs to their existing domestic brands and not put sufficient marketing effort behind the Astra brand. Given the import restrictions and the absence of local manufacturing, Astra found maintaining its trademark registrations to be a constant challenge, especially in countries like Brazil where prospective "free riders" repeatedly claimed Astra was not using its trademark and should, therefore, be denied continued protection.

Astra's Latin American vice president believed that it was essential to protect the Astra brand equity against low-quality imitations. Counterfeits shipped from the Far East through Korean agents in Paraguay and Panama found their way into the major markets of Brazil and Argentina. Genuine Astra shoes were also transshipped in the same manner. In 1990, around 4 million pairs of genuine Astras were believed to have been sold in Latin America. Astra's gross margin per pair averaged $17.50, around 50% of its average selling price. The 4 million pairs represented 6% of branded athletic footwear sales to the 325 million people living in the region and 10% of the sales of international brands. Sales of international brands were growing at 10% per year.[1]

---

[1]One of Astra's international competitors, Adidas, dominated the Latin American market as a result of long-standing agreements with local manufacturers.

THE MEETING

A meeting with Gaviria's chief executive officer and owner was arranged by Astra's local legal advisers in Caracas. The Astra team realized that its bargaining power was weak but decided to develop a framework for computing the price Astra would be prepared to pay to buy back the rights to the Astra brand name from Gaviria.

The Astra team realized that there were other possible "solutions" to the situation in addition to continuing to supply the Venezuelan market via Panama and Margarita island. These included:

1. Appoint Gaviria as a manufacturing subcontractor and provide the necessary technical assistance and manufacturing investment to ensure that Gaviria could make the simpler models in the Astra line to Astra quality standards. Astra might have to invest $1 million and concede an agreement on minimum purchase quantities from Gaviria. A further problem with this option was that Venezuelan law did not allow Astra to enjoin Gaviria from exporting its production to other countries as part of any agreement.

2. Appoint Gaviria as Astra's Venezuelan distributor in exchange for a return of the brand rights and a cessation of unauthorized production. Gaviria had some distribution experience and contacts with the relevant retailers but would not have been Astra's first choice to be its Venezuelan distributor under normal circumstances. However, such an arrangement might enable Gaviria to earn a distribution margin after expenses of around $2.00 per pair, compared with an estimated $1.00 per pair profit on its current production of "Astras." ∎

CHAPTER
4

COMPETING ON PRICE

Decades of inflation present in the region have conditioned consumers' buying habits, making them spend the money before it loses its value. Their habits have changed, however, with the coming of stability, recession, and rising unemployment.

BABYSAN: DIAPERS OF CHILE

Compañía Manufacturera de Papeles y Cartones (CMPC) is the third largest private company in Chile. It produces and exports the majority of Chile's newsprint, it is the number two producer of cellulose, and it leads in toilet paper, napkins, and other related product sales. In the early 1980s, CMPC perceived a broad acceptance of disposable diapers among the higher income levels of the population. Distributed almost exclusively by Procter & Gamble and Johnson & Johnson, both sold expensive diapers to a small percentage of the population. Knowing that disposable diapers were a mass product, CMPC management decided to bet on market development. With a mix of technology and human resources, they generated a successful product at a reasonable price—the adequate disposable diaper for Chilean mothers. Babysan was launched into the market in September 1983 at a price 30% lower than the multinational competition. Supported by an advertising campaign and promotions in maternity facilities that gave free diapers to new mothers, the middle class abandoned the cloth diaper for disposables.

CMPC did not attempt to improve market share, but to develop the market which has grown by 30% per year since 1985. Babysan's sales reached $40 million in 1989. Distribution was another key of its success. The company had its own network that distributed napkins, toilet paper, and other consumer products to innumerable stores and drugstores. These points of sale were appropriate for distributing the diapers in Chile, because they eliminated the middle costs and therefore allowed the greatest price discounts.

Multinational competitors could not offer less quality to create a large market, because CMPC produced the cellulose, the raw material of disposable diapers. The transfer price was the international price of cellulose, as the company was able to export it. This demonstrated that at international prices it was possible to manufacture a reasonably priced product. Babysan became an overwhelming success in the middle-high sectors, and this caused the appearance of the Chilean competitor, Pupy (owner of one of the major supermarket chains and buyer of raw material from CMPC). Babysan and Pupy are numbers one and two in the market while Johnson & Johnson withdrew from the market and Pampers, made by Procter & Gamble, are only imported in small lots to supply the luxury products market.

Based on its production mastery and market leadership, CMPC introduced Babysan Ultra—with ultra-absorbent elements and other additives—aimed at the "boutique" market, which in blind testing conducted for two years resulted in similar quality for the consumers. The next step was to introduce Ladysan, feminine napkins of international quality, based on its distribution capacity and an effective advertising campaign. Johnson & Johnson tried to defend its own product Siempre Libre by offering price discounts and hiring Nydia Caro, a Puerto Rican singer, to do commercials, but it was still seen as an expensive product and was withdrawn from the market in 1989. Ladysan sold $10 million in 1990 with a 60% market share. CMPC began to invest in production facilities in Colombia and Venezuela.

PRINTAFORM: MICROCOMPUTERS IN MEXICO

Jorge Espinosa Mireles founded Printaform in 1961, which has been on the brink of bankruptcy three times. The company started out printing administrative forms and later began to produce calculators, microcomputers, printers, and electronic typewriters. With 350 employees and a few robot-assisted plants in South America, the company sold its line of three compatible computers ranging from a $699 personal computer with 512 kilobytes to a $2,218 hard disk with 40 megabytes. All prices were lower than those of IBM and were without government subsidies. Printaform faced international competition due to the open market policies triggered by the Salinas administration. Even though laws did not allow foreign capital to control more than 49% of a Mexican company in the data processing sector, IBM was granted a license in 1986 to start up operations in the country without a Mexican partner.

Nevertheless, Printaform took advantage of IBM's entry into the market to expand itself, keeping its leadership of 39% in microcomputer sales compared with IBM's 13%. The key was Printaform's price, which was 50% lower than other competing brands. Printaform imported almost all its components from Asia, but with the strategy of keeping ahead of competitors. "IBM sells in Mexico what cannot be sold either in the United States or Europe in two or three years. That is to my advantage. I know what they can introduce here in two years, so I go to Asia and buy the latest technology. I am bringing products to Mexico two years before they do," says Mr. Espinosa.

Although some observers have criticized the quality of Printaform's products, nobody can criticize its price advantage coupled with one of the best distribution networks. In 1989, the company doubled the number of its distribution centers from 6 to 12 with 5,000 sales reps who were everywhere. Conversely, to buy an IBM product it is necessary to turn to a specialized distributor.

The company has begun to export printed forms to the United States and interfaces to Japan. It also has plans to expand South American sales. Through the Argentine company, Autorede, it has contracted with Italy's Olivetti and with Verifone from the United States to transfer technology.

In many cases, the prices in South America are subject to governmental regulations with the objective to avoid fluctuations during lengthy periods of inflation that have characterized the region's economies. Weissberg Gmbh describes the situation faced by the Brazilian branch of a German food manufacturing company in the following case study. These regulations offer alternatives which present advantages, but also complicate beneficial price situations within the region, as reflected in the case of Société Génerale du Papier.

CASES

4-1 WEISSBERG GMBH

At 2:00 a.m. on Sunday, April 7, 1990, Frank Degmann was asleep in his Sao Paulo, Brazil, apartment when the doorbell rang. Degmann was the Dutch-born brand manager for Raysol, one of the leading brands of dishwashing liquid in Brazil. Degmann found two policemen at his door, who wanted to know why the retail price on Raysol at a local supermarket was higher than that permitted under recently introduced government price controls.

COMPANY AND BRAND BACKGROUND

Raysol was marketed by the Brazilian subsidiary of Weissberg, a German consumer goods multinational. Weissberg had had operations in Brazil for 35 years. The wholly owned subsidiary was established in the 1960s following Weissberg's acquisition of a prominent Brazilian soap marketer. By 1990 Weissberg was one of the largest and most visible consumer goods multinationals in Brazil.

Weissberg was organized into three divisions handling various brands of processed foods, detergents, and toiletries. Raysol accounted for around 30% of the detergent division's sales and 10% of total company sales.

Raysol was sold through Weissberg's sales force. Six regional sales managers each supervised around 40 salespeople who called regularly on the most important trade accounts. Because of the fragmentation of the grocery trade in Brazil, Weissberg supplemented its sales force with 240 merchandisers who helped to ensure that the company's brands were in stock and prominently displayed in retail outlets. These merchandisers traveled by bus, called on about 15 shops a day, and often had to pull Weissberg products from a shop's stockroom and place them on the shelves. Both salespeople and merchandisers reported to Weissberg's regional sales managers.

In 1989, retail sales of dishwashing liquids in Brazil amounted to 220,000 tons. Retail sales volume had grown, on average, by 13% per year between 1986 and 1989. Around 78% of Brazilian households used dishwashing liquids in 1989, with annual per capita consumption of 1.5 liters. Since per capita consumption in Western Europe averaged 2.9 liters, analysts believed that there was still substantial growth potential in the Brazilian market. Sales growth of dishwashing liquids depended significantly on economic conditions since consumers could substitute less-expensive hand soaps.

Four brands accounted for almost all retail sales of branded dishwashing liquids: Weissberg's Raysol (21%); Lever's Minerva

---

Professor John A. Quelch prepared this case as the basis for class discussion rather than to illustrate either effective or ineffective handling of an administrative situation. Names and numbers have been disguised.

Plus (30%); the Limpol Brand of the Brazilian company Bombril (21%); and the ODD brand of the Brazilian company Orniex (28%). All four brands were similar in functional performance, range of package sizes, and cost and price structures. Raysol variable costs (including sales commissions and distribution costs) were 75% of net sales (after trade discounts). Raw materials accounted for half of variable costs. Non-variable marketing expenditures were 10% of net sales. Trade margins were 16%. Due to heavier advertising than their competitors, Minerva Plus and Raysol achieved higher unaided brand recall and enjoyed a stronger image with consumers. Raysol, in particular, was believed to have a concentrated formula that provided the consumer good value for the money.

Weissberg's objective for the dishwashing liquid category was to increase the penetration and share of Raysol in the mainstream segment of the market, while trading some consumers up to new higher-margin formulas and packages.

BRAZILIAN PRICE CONTROLS

During the 1980s, the Brazilian economy was plagued by hyperinflation. In the 12 months prior to April 1990, the monthly inflation rate averaged 30%. As a result, changes to manufacturer list prices and retail prices were frequent. Manufacturers focused on pricing ahead of inflation and collecting receivables quickly, often offering incentives like early payment allowances.

Each year from 1987 to 1990, successive trade ministers in the Brazilian government tried unsuccessfully to control inflation by imposing price controls for three- to six-month periods. Whenever price controls ceased or collapsed, a wave of price increases followed and inflation returned at an even higher monthly rate than before as marketers tried to compensate for their margin losses during the control periods.

In December 1989, Fernando Collor de Mello was democratically elected as president of Brazil. Five days before his inauguration, on March 10, 1990, Collor announced a surprise economic reform program to bring inflation under control. The rate of consumer price increases had risen to 80% in February 1990, up from 10% a year earlier. The Collor reform package included the imposition of stringent price controls on a broad spectrum of widely used consumer products.

Under the Collor plan, many raw material prices as well as manufacturer list prices and retail prices were frozen. The items subject to price controls were not announced in advance but included the best-selling items in product categories with high household penetration. The allowable retail prices were published in an official list (called the "Tabela Sunab") which was reproduced in daily newspapers; responsibility for ensuring compliance rested with the manufacturer as well as the retailer. Consumers typically went shopping with the Tabela Sunab in hand and were encouraged to report any cases of overpricing to the police.

Degmann explained how consumer goods marketers responded to price controls:

> Because we never know when price controls may be imposed under a new economic plan, we closely monitor our list prices and retail margins to ensure parity pricing with our face-off competitors at all times. Although grocery retailing is much more fragmented in Brazil than in Europe, our salespeople and merchandisers try to stay close to our retailers to ensure that prices on our brands are in compliance. The major chains—Pão de Açucar and Carrefour— usually present no problem; their own public images are at risk. Compliance problems occur much more frequently in small stores.

Occasionally, the price of a controlled item could be increased during the control period if a manufacturer could demonstrate inflation in input costs. However, only one in four of Weissberg's applications for price increases was accepted between 1988 and 1990. A further challenge was how to obtain supplies of raw materials under price controls when suppliers were often seeking premium payments over the official prices. Weissberg typically held one to two weeks' worth of raw material supplies on hand and could not easily switch suppliers due to stringent quality standards. Multinational companies like Weissberg were wary of engaging in government lobbying or unofficial pricing for fear of negative media publicity. Executives in multinational companies believed that some of their local competitors received preferential treatment when applying for price increases and that they also received inside information that enabled them to raise prices just ahead of the announcement of price controls.

CONTROLLING WORKING CAPITAL

In an inflationary environment, one of Degmann's most important tasks was to control the working capital exposure of his brand. This meant keeping raw material investments to a minimum, collecting accounts receivable quickly, and paying accounts slowly. Weissberg applied an "inflation charge" against each brand manager's profit and loss statement based on how much working capital was tied up in accounts receivable less accounts payable and in raw material and finished product inventories.

Weissberg's policy was to pay raw material suppliers in 16 days and give its trade accounts 28-day payment terms. Astute retailers like Carrefour (which sold 18% of Raysol volume) paid Weissberg on this basis but turned over their inventory of the brand every 7 days and invested their sales revenues on the financial markets for the re-

maining 21 days. To gain further advantage, some larger chains tried to delay payments beyond 28 days. Degmann and his fellow brand managers were not permitted to extend trade terms without top management approval. However, larger chains were gaining share from smaller, less-sophisticated retailers who did not manage their inventories and working capital as well. Because of trade fragmentation and inefficiencies in the distribution system as well as lack of sophistication, the trade stocks held by many retailers were equivalent to six weeks of retail sales.

MARKETING CHALLENGES UNDER PRICE CONTROLS

In the early hours of April 7, Degmann was required by the Sao Paulo police to accompany them to the local police station to provide an explanation. The police had been unable to locate the Brazilian regional sales manager, but his secretary had identified Degmann as the relevant brand manager. After an hour at the police station, Degmann was released on condition that he call back with further information from his office the following day. On Monday morning, Weissberg's head of legal and government affairs debriefed Degmann and took charge of follow-up negotiations with the police.

Ironically, a marketing management meeting had been previously arranged for the afternoon of Monday, April 8, to discuss how Weissberg's marketing plans for its detergent brands should be changed (if at all) as a result of the Collor plan. The following questions were on the agenda:

1. Should advertising budgets be cut to preserve margins, or should they be increased since, as some executives argued, the existence of fixed prices meant that the consumer's focus could be shifted from price to brand attributes?

2. If cuts were made, should they be made evenly across all brands or

should they be disproportionately greater on smaller brands and/or lower margin brands?

3. Should Weissberg go ahead with a consumer promotion planned for late April that offered tiny gold ingots as prizes in a contest open to consumers who submitted entries with Raysol proofs-of-purchase? The brand group had selected gold for prizes because it symbolized the concentration of Raysol's product formula.

4. Should the launch of a premium-priced line extension to the Raysol range, previously scheduled for May, be postponed? Some executives argued that Weissberg should, instead, launch a lower-quality line extension or new brand to obtain an attractive price listing on the Tabella Sunab. It was unclear whether the launch of any line extensions to brands already listed on the Tabela Sunab would require government approval. ■

4-2 SOCIÉTÉ GÉNÉRALE DU PAPIER

Breakfast would be served in thirty minutes. Theo Moussakas, Société Générale du Papier's (SGP) international marketing vice-president for the Latin America division, looked through the windows of his room at the Marriott Hotel in Panama. The view over the Pacific Ocean was splendid. Ships could be seen moving through the Canal toward the Atlantic Ocean which he had crossed the day before to attend a three-day meeting with his Latin American country managers.

Two weeks before, Jean-Paul Cornil, the manager of one of SGP's most promising markets in Latin America, had asked for this breakfast meeting with Moussakas.

Cornil entered the room with his marketing manager, Toni Herrera, and went straight to the point:

We face very tough competition from Kimberly-Clark and Scott Paper in the household products line. For years I have been protecting my share of the market. Now, just as I finally have a price advantage over my competitors, you people from corporate headquarters are taking this opportunity away from me. The overall market is still growing slowly so, if I don't take sales away from the competition, I can't meet your sales expectations. Not all Latin American countries are enjoying the same fast growth as Mexico. You people tend to think of Latin America as one homogeneous market and that is simply not true.

Moussakas had known Cornil for many years as a very controlled person and the agitation he was displaying was not typical.

Visiting Professor Carlos G. Sequeira and Professor John A. Quelch prepared this case as the basis for class discussion rather than to illustrate either effective or ineffective handling of an administrative situation. All names and data are disguised.

As her boss paused to drink some coffee, Toni Herrera intervened with a more measured tone:

We understand that we will be instructed soon to dismantle our household products plant and to ship it to another Latin American country. This plant became fully depreciated last year and therefore, now, for the first time, we are enjoying a rock-bottom unit cost. This allows us to price our products lower than our competitors when we apply SGP's standard pricing formula.

Toni was referring to the standard SGP pricing policy which established a 33% profit margin above unit cost. Country managers had the authority to change the resulting price by 10% in either direction. Beyond a 10% change, headquarters approval was necessary. Herrera commented:

We have been looking for this opportunity for years, and now, when we have it . . . the opportunity just vanishes before our eyes.

As they finished breakfast, Cornil again appealed to Moussakas:

Theo, the plant is in perfect condition, it works well and gives us the level of product technology my market requires. I don't want a new plant, I don't need it. I want to keep my old plant and I'm counting on your help to do this.

SOCIÉTÉ GÉNÉRALE DU PAPIER

With net sales of $4.9 billion and net income of $360 million in 1993, SGP was one of the oldest paper companies in the world, headquartered near Montgolfier in Belgium. The company was a very important player in the European paper industry. However, its involvement outside Europe was considered marginal and opportunistic until 1978 when the International Division (ID) was established.

As of 1993, operations outside of Europe accounted for 20% of sales and 12% of profits. Cornelius Van Der Putten was the first and only ID vice president. Four geographical subdivisions, called "bureaus," reported to Van Der Putten: Africa, Asia, North America and Latin America. Each bureau had two vice presidents, one for marketing and one for manufacturing. Country managers in each bureau were responsible for profit and loss performance in their respective markets. The organization of each bureau required that the country managers report to the bureau's marketing vice president but each country manufacturing manager reported not only to the country manager but also to the bureau's manufacturing vice president. Thus, Jean-Paul Cornil, as country manager, reported to Theo Moussakas, but Cornil's manufacturing manager, Lorenzo Cabral, reported to Sergio Passolini, manufacturing vice president for the Latin America bureau, as well as to Cornil.

Both Moussakas and Passolini had their offices at headquarters in Belgium and reported to Van Der Putten. Exhibit 1 presents a simplified organization chart. At headquarters, it was said that International Marketing interacted more closely with Corporate Finance and Human Resources, while International Manufacturing worked mainly with the office of the Corporate Comptroller. When necessary, Mr. Van Der Putten resolved disputes between the functional heads.

Country managers were compensated through a combination of a fixed salary and a bonus based on the country subsidiary's profit performance. While the international marketing vice presidents were compensated via a fixed salary plus a bonus based on the combined profit performance of the country subsidiaries under their supervision, the international manufacturing vice presidents were compensated with a salary and a bonus based on manufacturing pro-

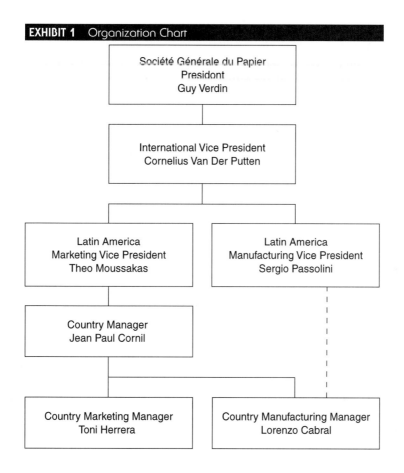

EXHIBIT 1 Organization Chart

Société Générale du Papier
President
Guy Verdin

International Vice President
Cornelius Van Der Putten

Latin America
Marketing Vice President
Theo Moussakas

Latin America
Manufacturing Vice President
Sergio Passolini

Country Manager
Jean Paul Cornil

Country Marketing Manager
Toni Herrera

Country Manufacturing Manager
Lorenzo Cabral

ductivity and the overall company profit margin.

MARKET SITUATION

In Cornil's market, SGP was strongly represented in the industrial segment with dominant positions in products such as wrapping paper, industrial wipers, paper bags and paper office products. Success depended on volume sales and margins were low. The household products business, on the other hand, was very competitive. SGP's market shares trailed those of Kimberly-Clark or Scott Paper in most categories including toilet paper, facial tissues and feminine hygiene pads. In addition, distribution and ad-

vertising expenditures as a percentage of sales were much higher for these products. Nevertheless, SGP's household products line enjoyed higher margins than the industrial products line. The result was periodic price wars among the household products competitors.

THE SOLUTION

When Moussakas understood Cornil's complaint, he promised to find out about the plant changes since that was the first he had heard of it.

During a recess at the three-day meeting, Moussakas met with Vinicio De Souza, the young manager of the latest Latin

American country SGP had entered. He was supposed to receive and set up Cornil's current plant. De Souza had been promoted recently from the Brazil subsidiary where he had been the manufacturing manager. De Souza commented:

> I have no complaints about the idea. I will be acquiring the plant at 70% of what a new one would cost. Cornil's plant can be depreciated once again and I like the idea of a lower depreciation cost. I don't think I need a brand new plant right now, my market is very unsophisticated and I prefer to start manufacturing there using a well-proven process.

At lunch, Theo Moussakas ate in his room with Sergio Passolini to discuss, among other subjects, the issue of Cornil's plant.

PASSOLINI: Well, it was just a very sketchy idea, nothing definitive of course. You know I wouldn't dare give a go-ahead signal without touching base with you Theo. A few weeks ago, De Souza was visiting headquarters as you know. I took him to dinner one night. Christophe (the Corporate Comptroller) was also entertaining a couple of tax lawyers from Latin America and we decided to join the two parties together. During dinner this idea came up.

MOUSSAKAS: What precisely is this idea?

PASSOLINI: A very smart one, you will like it, I bet.

MOUSSAKAS: Well?

PASSOLINI: Its simplicity is amazing and its potential benefits are incredible. Look, Cornil obtained from the tax authorities in his country an accelerated depreciation treatment that provided income tax advantages to his subsidiary. Well, his plant is now fully depreciated and it's one step behind the latest manufacturing technology. On the other hand, De Souza only needs a basic plant. While we were talking about this, our lawyers suggested this tax saving scheme. Listen Theo, we could import and set up a new advanced technology plant for Cornil for around $4 million. Cornil's new plant will start to depreciate and to generate a fresh tax shield for us. Cornil's old plant will go to De Souza who will buy it for $2.5 million dollars. This is roughly 70% of what De Souza would have to pay for a new plant with the same production capacity. So, Cornil's plant, which is no longer providing a depreciation tax shield, will once again do so in De Souza's country.

MOUSSAKAS: Wait a minute. If Cornil sells for $2.5 million, and the plant is carried at zero value on his books, he will need to pay capital gains taxes. So, where is the benefit?

PASSOLINI: That's the beauty of it. Cornil won't sell directly to De Souza. He will sell the plant for something like $300,000 to our off-shore subsidiary in the Cayman Islands, the one created a couple of years ago, you remember? The Cayman Islands is a tax haven. (See Exhibit 2 for a definition.) The old plant will be dismantled and shipped directly from Cornil to De Souza, but the billing will be done first between Cornil and SGP Cayman and then between SGP Cayman and De Souza. Cornil will pay capital gains taxes on the $300,000, De Souza will start to depreciate $2.5 million and thereby generate a tax shield; and the $2.2 million reported by SGP Cayman is free from capital gains taxes.

MOUSSAKAS: Is this legal Sergio?

PASSOLINI: A hundred percent legal. I have checked it twice and will be pleased to do so again.

MOUSSAKAS: Cornil doesn't like the idea.

PASSOLINI: Well, Theo, you know he's retiring in three years, so, he's against anything that affects the short term profitability of his company.[1]

MOUSSAKAS: I'm not sure about that. I do know he wants a cost break so he can try to gain market share from his competitors.

PASSOLINI: Well, I don't think you want our competitors to be the first to deploy the latest manufacturing technology just because Cornil wants to protect his retirement allowance. By the way, his manufacturing manager loves the idea of a new plant.

MOUSSAKAS: Sergio, we won't proceed without you and I agreeing, will we?

PASSOLINI: Of course not. Is two weeks enough time for you to meet with the Corporate Comptroller to look further into this?

EXHIBIT 2 Definition of Tax Haven

A country with a tax-preference laws for foreign companies and individuals. Three classes of jurisdiction are referred to as tax havens. They include those that:

1. Have no relevant taxes (such as Cayman Islands, the Bahamas, Bermuda, Turks and Caicos Islands)
2. Levy taxes only on internal taxable transactions, but no levy or very low taxes on foreign sourced income (such as Hong Kong and Panama)
3. Grant special tax privileges to certain types of companies or operations (such as the Channel Islands, Liechtenstein, and Luxembourg)

The principal functions of tax havens are to 1) avoid or postpone taxes, 2) avoid exchange controls, and 3) act as a shield against confiscation, nationalization, and other forms of expropriation. Note that tax avoidance is not necessarily the same as illegal tax evasion.

Source: Adapted from: "The Portable MBA Desk Reference" by Paul A. Argenti, Editorial Director. John Wiley & Sons, Inc. 1994, pp. 374–375.

---

[1]Passolini was alluding to the way that SGP computed an executive's retirement benefits according to the average compensation of the last three years prior to retirement day.

MOUSSAKAS: Fair enough, but I want people from Human Resources attending the meeting also. And Sergio, about this tax scheme, if you say it's legal, then it's legal, but I wonder how much we should be emphasizing tax avoidance. After all, we do have an image to protect.

THE FACSIMILE

Two days after he returned to his Latin American headquarters office, Theo Moussakas received a fax with the information he had requested from Cornil when they met in Panama. Exhibit 3 summarizes the information contained in Cornil's fax. Moussakas pondered the problem before asking for more elaborate analyses from his staff. ■

EXHIBIT 3   Content of Cornil's Fax

A. SGP's Country Sales by Products and Markets

	Industrial Products	*Household Products*
Industrial Market	86%	24%
Consumer Market	14%	76%

B. Manufacturer Price Index

	SGP	*Kimberly-Clark*	*Scott Paper*	*Johnson & Johnson*	*Others*
Toilet paper	100	108	98	NA	91
Facial tissue	100	97	99	NA	89
Feminine hygiene pads	100	94	NA	109	88
Other	100	96	105	112	94

C. Household Product Market Shares

	SGP	*Kimberly-Clark*	*Scott Paper*	*Johnson & Johnson*	*Others*
Toilet paper	32%[a]	16%	38%[a]	—	14%
Facial tissue	28	43[a]	21	—	8
Feminine hygiene pads	12	39	—	43%[a]	6
Other	13	48	31	—	8

[a]Each company's most important product.

D. Advertising for Household Paper Products

	SGP	*Kimberly-Clark*	*Scott Paper*	*Johnson & Johnson*	*Others*
Share of voice	15%	20%	41%	22%	2%
Top of mind brand recall[a]	23	81	64	32	0

[a]Company's top brand.

EXHIBIT 3 (cont.)

E. *Channel Margin Index (% of manufacturer's selling price, including promotional allowances)*

	SGP	Kimberly-Clark	Scott Paper	Johnson & Johnson	Others
Toilet paper	100	100	98	—	120
Facial tissue	100	108	100	—	112
Feminine hygiene pads	100	110	—	118	122
Other	100	98	120	—	NA

F. *Estimated Unit Cost Index (using current plant)*

	SGP	Kimberly-Clark	Scott Paper	Johnson & Johnson	Others
Household products combined	100	109	112	116	NA

G. *Estimated Unit Cost Index (with new plant)*

	SGP	Kimberly-Clark	Scott Paper	Johnson & Johnson	Others
Household products combined	100	97	100	104	NA

H. *SGP Sales Distribution Channels*

	Supermarkets and Drug Stores[a]	Small Convenience Stores[b]
Household products	43%	57%

[a]Includes all distribution points offering no personal sales assistance.
[b]Includes small stores offering personal sales assistance.

I. *SGP Variable Costs (% of net manufacturer sales)*

	Industrial Products	Household Products
Variable costs	70%	57%

CHAPTER 5

CHANNELS OF DISTRIBUTION

THE EMERGENCE OF MODERN TRADE IN LESS STRUCTURED MARKETS: A GLOBALIZATION PROCESS

The globalization of retailing has been widespread in the last decade for two main reasons:

1. Expansion across borders such as Wal-Mart to Mexico, The Gap to Canada, or Carrefour from France to Spain
2. True internationalization of trade as that of The Gap crossing the ocean toward the United Kingdom or Carrefour expanding operations to South America and Southeast Asia

Three fundamental reasons explain this acceleration of the international commercial activity during the last two years:

1. A strong saturation of their domestic markets by retailers such as Wal-Mart, Toys "R" Us, or Home Depot in the United States, Marks & Spencer in the United Kingdom, C & A in Holland, Carrefour in France, or Jusco in Japan
2. The implementation of regional trade agreements such as NAFTA, the European Union, or Mercosur (Even though these agreements have occurred slowly and have overcome obstacles, they have had a great impact in facilitating the flow of goods and money from one country to another much the same way as they previously moved from one province to another within the same country.)
3. The strong entrepreneurial spirit and sense of opportunity shown by such leading traders as IKEA and Hennes & Mauritz in Sweden, Otto Versand in Germany, and Giordano and Esprit in Hong Kong. (These companies have moved aggressively to adjacent countries, for example, Hennes & Mauritz which now operates 60 stores in Germany selling garments to teenagers and young adults.)

A persistent price deflation and strong competition characterize retail sales in almost all countries. Even the Japanese distribution system, criticized for years as being out of date and inefficient, shows signs of change. The law that regulated large-scale retail trade, which had practically stopped construction of large stores and commercial centers, has been modified. This has, in turn, diminished the number of small retailers and increased that of large ones, shortening the distribution channel, reducing the control of manufacturers over the channel, and therefore leading to more balanced relations. New strategies have appeared that place higher emphasis on economies of scale, develop low cost suppliers, and control goods as well as production and management of low-cost structures. In the search to improve their profitability, Japanese retailers are following different strategies. Ito-Yokado emphasizes innovation whereas Jusco tends to retail formats with excellent operative systems and Uny restructures its costs in order to reduce them.

ECONOMIC SETTING

The economic setting in emerging countries such as Mexico, Argentina, or Brazil in the 1990s offered certain attractive characteristics for the development of new retail businesses, in much the same way as countries in Europe with less structured distribution systems such as Portugal, Greece and Spain, did in the mid-1980s. Democratic regimes are looking for economic stability. Economies growing at a high and sustainable rhythm, with low inflation and a market openness to foreign investment and imported products, are the common denominators. Stabilized salaries and certain levels of unemployment show the need to diminish product prices which creates opportunities for the retail industry. Modern chains bring with them a reduction of prices and they help to introduce new local or imported products. Too many consumers are accustomed to outdated products. For these people, imported products are not only updated, but also of higher technology. Customers welcome the products' entry even though it may indirectly mean a rise in the unemployment level. One beneficial effect of imports is that they force local producers to update their products to keep abreast of their market shares. When markets open up, local companies are suddenly exposed to international competition and in a very short time—sometimes only a few months—they are competing with global products manufactured under the most demanding standards and with the lowest cost.

Modern distribution formats—supermarkets and hypermarkets—not only encourage rapid introduction of these new products, but also help to reduce prices because they are looking both to gain market share over the traditional distribution systems and launch the new products they import. International chains have the ability to enter emerging markets at various stages of development. Carrefour has been in Brazil and Argentina since the 1980s; Wal-Mart entered Latin America in the 1990s; and the German chain, Aldi, is now entering Spain but long after its French competitors Dia por ciento of Promodes.

REGULATORY ENVIRONMENT

Many changes have occurred in the retail environment. Urban planning is now being emphasized, which regulates the possibilities for new sites. It is intended to reduce the country's risk through stricter enforcement of taxation laws, thus facilitating the management of large companies to compete against the smaller traditional stores which usually operate in an informal economy. Changes in legislation referring to capital goods, such as those enacted in Southeast Asia, also open up possibilities for the entry of international dealers. Conversely, old laws are being thrown out, such the antitrust law in Argentina or those that protect small stores in Italy. Both promote the advent of larger stores.

CONSUMERS

As the market environment changes, consumers also modify their habits. Economic growth and stability increases disposable income and the possibilities for planning consumption, even to the point of securing loans for the purchase of large or high-value goods. The initial categories that experience growth are food and cosmetics. Consumers seem fascinated by the new products offered, as if they are in a consumer frenzy trance, wanting to try every new product and delighted with the rising quantity of new formats, packagings, and applications. A feeling of personal updating accompanies the abandonment of traditional brands, and the appearance of new products threatens consumer loyalty to the old ones.

Traditional products and brands are passed over in order to test new offerings introduced by independent importers, licensed distributors, and unauthorized or gray market importers. Only when economic stability proves to be lasting can the original manufacturers organize distribution and communication, taking advantage of the brand development previously accomplished by distributors, as has already happened with many world brands in Taiwan. Therefore, manufacturers face a double challenge with the introduction of new brands—not always of the best quality—and diminishing consumer loyalty to traditional brands when tempted by novelties.

Although the quality of the new products is not always better than that of the old ones, for example, the cheaper fabrics from Southeast Asia, the lower prices and updated products easily attract consumers. As consumers constantly update their consumption, the products' life cycles tend to become shorter. The products first selected are those that imply a personal status and better personal rewards, for example, food. New food products are the first chosen by consumers as a way to improve their lifestyles at a relatively low cost. In this regard, imported products are in a good competitive position, because they are more innovative, have better packaging, and thus reinforce this impulse to buy newly arrived items. As long as available income increases so will retail consumption, which will increase sales in the commercial food industry (hotels, restaurants, and catering).

The balance of power between manufacturers and retailers is tipped in favor of the latter, as they can easily adapt themselves to the changing habits of the consumers. Retailers have this advantage for two reasons: First, they are in closer communication with their customers; and second, they are able to observe the consumers' changing habits first-hand and develop new suppliers to meet these changes. There are plenty of international manufacturers eager to find new markets or to create new local firms to distribute new brands or products, with or without a license.

After a certain period, however, consumers' attitudes experience another change. The length of this first cycle of "impulse" buying depends on the intensity of the open economy process: The more intense this "opening up" of the economy is, the shorter the first cycle becomes. This stage is characterized by more impulsive consumers being impressed by the appearance of new and desired products.

In the second cycle, consumers move toward a more rational attitude. Once new products have been tried in the home, household expenses become more rational and planned with greater care. If the economy is recovering from a long inflationary period, then income stabilization allows for better budgeting. Credit availability appears and monthly installments absorb part of the disposable incomes, emphasizing the need to plan expenses. It appears that the competition of other product categories—appliances, sportswear, or audio equipment—reduces the importance of food expenses, thus changing consumers' habits. Prices of goods decrease, but are not immediately reflected in the price indexes because these show earlier consumer patterns.

RETAILERS

An open and stable business environment accelerates the appearance of large retailers, who choose first to establish themselves in large cities where there are more opportunities for trade. Cities have many sophisticated consumers, experience fast changes in trade laws enactments, and provide easier access to investors.

Emerging markets offer real opportunities for expansion of large retailers, who have already achieved a high share in their original markets, but where further growth is difficult. The simultaneous appearance of numerous large chains makes segmentation necessary, as consumers understand the different types of conveniences offered by retailers. The first hypermarket attracts visitors from all over the city, and then the following one segments the market. Several criteria allow for a differentiated competitive position: geographic area, socioeconomic level, and type of goods and services offered. Competition then becomes fierce and gradually makes possibilities of growth harder.

At this point, large retailers begin to look at less important or smaller cities to direct their future expansions. In Portugal, hypermarkets that once were found in only major cities such as Lisbon have become very competitive in smaller areas such as the Algarve district.

Three Traps for Retailers

The first retail trap involves growth, which is financed by suppliers through longer delivery terms and lower prices or by higher price margins. The larger number of points of sale brings a stronger purchasing power and optimizes logistics and inventories. The excess cash is allocated not only to open new outlets, but also to create investments in the stock markets and guarantee loans that finance new points of sale. In this way, the focus of strategy becomes the growth of outlets financed by suppliers. This emphasis on growth tends to focus large chains on that part of business related to purchasing, somewhat losing sight of consumers' demands and operating efficiency. The consequences of emphasizing purchases, reducing prices, and diversifying suppliers are that product quality may be reduced to secondary brands and may then appeal to an inferior segment.

Another trap for retailers is the temptation to take advantage of strong buying power by opening small, low-priced stores when locations for large areas become more scarce. Management of these stores is different from that of the larger stores. The differences are in product mix (fresh and durable) product range, quality of service, and criteria for store location. Consumers who shop convenience stores and supermarkets also show different habits, purchasing hours, socioeconomic levels, ages, and average purchase amounts.

The third trap for retailers is the replacement of suppliers. As expansion proceeds, competition among chains first focuses on prices, as each claims to have the lowest prices. Price and communications wars are frequent. Prices are sometimes reduced so low that profit margins are nil, causing problems between suppliers and other buyers and ruptures relationships with leading-brand manufacturers. Retailers then may replace their top suppliers with secondary suppliers and thus damage the gondola's (shelf display) appearance. In some product categories, it is difficult to find followers or second suppliers. In developing countries, there are only small numbers of suppliers for products such as soft drinks and beer. The gondolas have such a reputation, then, because they have only one or two brands.

WHOLESALERS

Wholesalers that supply to small stores are often threatened by the large retailers because they lose their clients (the small retailers) in a slow, but sustained way to the competition. Small stores survive only through differentiation and their transformation into self-service stores in areas of less population density or smaller cities. The loss in buying power is balanced by the interest of manufacturers in keeping alternative channels alive, given the growth of purchasing power in the super/hypermarket sector. There are different responses used to face this threat.

The first response is to specialize in institutional channels such as hotels, restaurants, and catering companies (known as Horeca in Europe).

A second possibility is to create purchasing pools among retail groups and avoid the wholesale channel. This not only increases individual buying power, but also helps in its transformation by sharing knowledge and improving manufacturers' opportunities to have more effective promotions at the outlets. This alternative is strengthened by the entry of supermarket chains into minor regional markets.

Wholesale management also becomes modified as it changes from making opportunistic purchases to creating a more accurate management of inventories, and a closer watch of retailer actions. To help in this process, retailers train sales forces (usually independent reps) to get the information out into the field at the same time they carry out their specific sales tasks.

Gathering information about the consumer becomes of greater interest for wholesalers who reorganize both their sales work and their management of purchasing and inventories. Sharing this information with manufacturers strengthens the relationship for a wider collaboration.

MANUFACTURERS

As discussed, changes in consumer habits have added to the increased competition and have lowered prices. Manufacturers that do not follow these changes carefully and work to improve their costs and quality of their products usually blame the retailers for these changes, especially the more modern ones. They lose sight of the fact that such changes originate at the consumer level. Because retailers are naturally closer to the consumer, they are more informed with regard to these changes in purchasing habits and consumer trends.

A closer relationship with retailers keeps the manufacturer from being surprised by these changes in the market. Two tools appear to be of great effectiveness in this regard.

1. Monitoring retailer inventories allows for first-hand information on sales, but also permits a better planning of production and deliveries. Even though this lessens

the negotiating power of both parties, it provides other advantages such as maintaining supply, avoiding inventory breakdowns, losing space in gondolas, and having more accurate category management.

2. Using merchandisers, which manufacturers tend to consider as costly, provides stock and reorder capabilities as well as timely and first-hand information. Gondola management watches profit margins and helps to anticipate price reductions below those agreed upon or recommended, thus controlling products per shelf and per point of sale. Promotions add effectiveness with the possibility of planning them through the individual points of sale and higher precision on their effectiveness. Merchandisers must be trained on the following points: working with the sector store managers, replenishing shelves, and picking up information from the store.

Improving brand value adds value to the retailer and improves the supplier bargaining position. The main tool here is the improvement of products and packaging to add attractiveness for retailers and consumers. Facing the pressure of falling prices, they often concentrate on decreasing profit margins which yields in less resources for research and development and erodes future sales and market share. The defense of profit margins, the promotion of brand value, and the improvement of relationships with channels secure the financing for research and development and market share.

Building relationships with retailers is rather unusual in unstable and developing environments, where demand usually exceeds supply and consumers have neither the possibility of improving consumption nor a broad range of brands and products from which to choose. Under these conditions, retailers must usually wait to be supplied, but as the environment becomes stabilized, consumers will have the time to plan their expenses, strengthen supply by imported products and exceed demand, and balance power shifts in favor of the retailer. Relationships with traders become a major concern in order to keep control of business. Building close relationships with the major chains also helps to guide future development of products and brands.

Manufacturers must carefully follow the changes in consumer habits and one of the consequences of change in less-structured markets is increasing interest to cooperate with channels of distribution.

Being closer to consumers, retailers are in a better position to adapt themselves to changes in consumer habits. But they must also closely follow the manufacturing industry for the introduction of new products which lead to closer relationships between both parties.

In the food industry, two opposite channels of information can be identified. In the first channel, products come from producers of raw materials and move toward the consumer through manufacturers and distribution channels. In the second channel, innovation (or the necessary information) is generated at the consumer level and transmitted from retailers to manufacturers, which in turn pass it on to primary producers in order to meet consumer demands.

CASES

5-1 CUMMINS ENGINE COMPANY, INC.: BLACK FRIDAY

"Almost everybody in America, young and old, remembers where they were when President Kennedy was assassinated. Well, everybody in Venezuela remembers where they were on February 18, 1983, Black Friday," said Lucas Godinez, Cummins Engine's regional manager for Venezuela. He continued:

Ever since Black Friday, when the bolivar was devalued, Cummins has had a real set of problems in Venezuela. We're holding $1.4 million in accounts receivable that's never going to be worth what it was a couple of months ago. The government has prohibited the reexport of the goods, which means they have to stay in the country. Our current master distributor, ACO, owes us one-half of the $1.4 million and to be frank, we've questioned their ability to do the job *without* a financial crisis laid on top. Somehow I've got to figure out how I can protect Cummins' financial interests in Venezuela, while at the same time preserving the Venezuelan distribution and service network. In my spare time, I've got to be very sensitive to the fact that the Venezuelan crisis is just the latest in a string of international difficulties at Cummins. Top management is *very* concerned about our international exposure.

On February 18, 1983, the Venezuelan government had suspended all sales of foreign currency as a result of a steep decline in the country's international monetary reserves. The government decreed a 60-day freeze on prices of all goods and services, effective February 28. Prices would be set at the level effective February 18, 1983; quality, quantity, and sales terms could not be altered. This prevented distributors from raising prices to compensate for the devaluation.

CUMMINS ENGINE COMPANY, INC.

Business

Cummins Engine Company manufactured and sold a diversified line of diesel engines, components, and replacement parts in worldwide markets. The recent financial performance of Cummins is highlighted in Exhibit 1.

The company's principal market was the North American heavy-duty truck industry, where every truck manufacturer offered Cummins engines as standard or optional equipment. Major off-highway customers included construction, mining, agricultural, oil and gas, logging, marine, industrial locomotive, electrical generator, compressor pump and other special-purpose machinery industries.

For the principal markets served by Cummins, 1980–1982 was characterized by a

This case was prepared by Assistant Professor John C. Whitney, Jr., as the basis for class discussion rather than to illustrate either effective or ineffective handling of an administrative situation.

EXHIBIT 1   Cummins Engine Company, Inc.: Black Friday

International Sales, 1980–1982

Net Sales by Marketing Territory[a]
($ millions)

	1980	1981	1982
United States	$1,012	$1,223	$1,022
United Kingdom/Europe	208	193	213
Asia/Far East	116	118	129
Latin America	170	235	88
Canada	122	122	72
Africa/Middle East	39	71	63
	$1,667	$1,962	$1,587

Engines Shipped to Major Markets
(units)

	1980	1981	1982
North American Truck	54,700	59,100	40,200
North American Industrial	22,400	23,900	18,600
International	38,700	40,800	26,200
Total	115,800	123,800	85,000

[a]Net sales to major customers include sales to International Harvester Company of $185.1 million in 1982, $225.7 million in 1981 and $158.0 million in 1980. Sales to Diesel Nacional S.A. (DINA) and DINA-Cummins, S.A. (Mexico) totaled $59.8 million in 1982, $179.9 million in 1981, and $133.8 million in 1980. Devaluations of the Mexican peso during 1982 virtually halted shipments to Mexico, one of the company's principal international markets. In both 1981 and 1980, strong demand for engines and kits in Mexico was the principal factor in increased international shipments.

severe economic decline. In the North American heavy-duty truck market, production in 1982 was 60% below that of 1979. Virtually all of these trucks were powered by diesel engines and little growth was expected. In international markets, engine shipments declined over 35% in 1982, reflecting the worldwide recession.

Latin American Operations

Latin America consisted of three major markets for Cummins: Mexico, Brazil, and all other Latin American countries which, due to the absence of a Cummins' manufacturing facility, became known collectively as the "Export Market." Mexico had been the company's largest market outside the United States, and until 1980 Cummins had a licensing agreement for the manufacture of diesel engines in that country. In October of 1980, following five years of intensive negotiations, Cummins converted the licensing agreement into a joint venture with the Mexican government.

During 1982, the Mexican peso had been devalued several times, leaving Cummins with $18 million in trade receivables. This debt remained outstanding; its collection was in question at the time of the Venezuelan devaluation.

Cummins began business in Brazil in 1970 as a joint venture with a number of Brazilian investors. Although a manufacturing facility was constructed, Cummins had been unable to reach an agreement with any original equipment manufacturer (OEM) who would produce trucks with Cummins engines. Without an OEM customer, Cummins management had made an intense effort to locate a market base in order to make business in Brazil operationally efficient. According to the Cummins area director for Latin America, the Brazilian operation had required constant attention.

The importance of the Export Market (Venezuela, Chile, Colombia, Ecuador, Peru, and Bolivia) rose dramatically in the late 1960s when these countries began to organize themselves. In an effort to create a common market, much like the EEC (European Economic Community), they proposed a strategy to form a major, integrated market which would enable member countries to dictate terms to foreign investors, manage the development of their industries and, in effect, develop a centralized economy. Under the proposed agreement, known as the Andean Pact, a single company would be given the manufacturing assignment for a range of diesel engines for all member countries. In the case of the medium-duty engine market, such an assignment was estimated to create a market equal in size to that of Mexico. Moreover, since Venezuela was the richest and most influential country in the Pact, it was essential that Cummins develop programs to comply with the integration plans of the pact. Until dissension erupted between several member countries, getting a manufacturing facility in the Andean Pact (i.e., outside Mexico and Brazil) had been the number-one priority of the Cummins' vice president–Latin America. Bilateral agreements were signed which might invalidate the goals of the pact, causing Cummins management to question the future of the Andean Pact.

VENEZUELA

The Country

Roughly the size of Texas, Venezuela[1] had a population of 16.5 million (1981 census), per capita income of $3,130,[2] and population growth of 3.4% (Exhibit 2). It had modern seaports, airports and highways, easy access to the Caribbean and Atlantic sea lanes and virtual carte blanche to borrow money on international capital markets.

The Venezuelan economy was heavily dependent on oil, which constituted 90% of total exports and 20% of GNP. The oil boom in the mid-1970s had resulted in free-spending government policies and the creation of many business-related fortunes. However, the subsequent oil glut and general softening of petroleum prices had produced three years of recession by the end of 1981 with only marginal growth projected in the near future. GNP had fallen from a 7% annual growth rate during most of the 1970s to a 1.5% decline in 1982. Unemployment, estimated between 10–12% of the work force of 5 million, remained high for a country accustomed to full employment between 1974–1979. Inflation had jumped from 5.8% in 1978 to 12.3% in 1979 and had remained at 20% thereafter.

Despite the economic slump, there were no major threats to the democratic system in Venezuela. Cummins' management felt the political situation was very stable, although widespread dissatisfaction with the Herrera administration's performance was evident. The current government's five-year, $60 billion investment plan for 1981–1985, a plan that would result in substantial growth in the diesel engine market, was being reevaluated

---

[1]This country description is based upon "Venezuela Trade and Investment Survey" in *The Journal of Commerce,* August 30, 1982.
[2]All numbers are in U.S. dollars unless noted otherwise.

EXHIBIT 2   Cummins Engine Company, Inc.: Black Friday (Map of Venezuela)

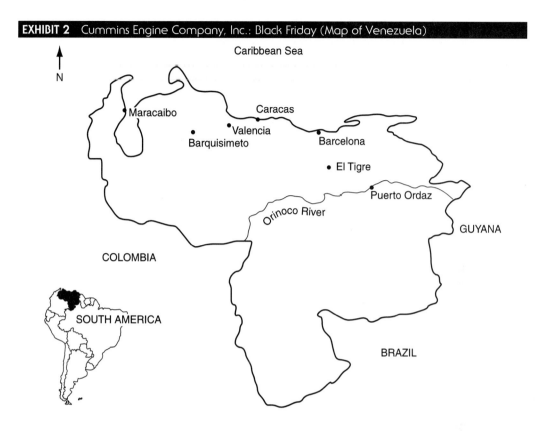

due to the current stagnation of oil prices. Petroleum prices had been expected to provide the lion's share of these funds, while internal taxes and borrowing were to supply the remainder. Although some cuts were expected, the major investment in the country's keystone industry, petroleum, would remain as would large outlays in water, electric power and other heavy industrial equipment. Businesses, confused by sometimes contradictory government policies, were acting with extreme caution with respect to significant new investments.

The Venezuelan Diesel Engine Market

The diesel engine market in Venezuela was segmented into "Automotive," which consisted of engines for on-highway trucks and buses and "Off-Highway," which included engines for the generation of electricity (generator sets), construction, marine, mining and oil and gas markets. The principal factors influencing the sale of diesel engines in these markets included the economy, the government's investment plans, total number of vehicles in the country, the proportion of vehicles requiring diesel fuel engines, and the relative price of diesel fuel to gasoline.

Historically, 80% of diesel engine sales in the automotive market were for heavy-duty trucks (250–350 h.p.), while 20% were sold to the bus market. After peaking in 1978 with 2,500 vehicles, the heavy-duty truck segment had declined to 1,200 vehicles in 1982 with a projected annual growth of 5%. The market was served by five OEMs: Mack (45% unit market share); International Harvester Corporation (23%); Ford (18%); Pegasso (7%); and Fiat (7%). While

Mack, Pegasso, and Fiat manufactured their own diesel engines, IHC and Ford used Cummins engines. However, given the size of the market and limited growth, at least one truck producer was expected to drop out of the market. Mack seemed certain to remain, as were IHC and Fiat according to the Cummins regional office. However, Ford's future in this market was less certain. Recently, Ford had begun to reevaluate its heavy-duty line which, although considered to be a quality product, offered limited sales.

Also experiencing stagnation was the Venezuelan bus market due to the developing subway system and government control of bus fares. Diesel engine sales were expected to peak in 1983 at 510 units and decline thereafter. The bus market in Venezuela was dominated by Encava, a Cummins OEM, which held an 86% market share.

Unlike the heavy-duty truck and bus markets which were completely dieselized, the medium-duty truck (150–210 h.p.) market was 95% gasoline powered. Neither Ford (70% market share of gasoline vehicles) nor General Motors (30% market share of gasoline-powered vehicles) produced a diesel truck in this range, although both were expected to do so by 1983 in anticipation of government mandate. Approximately 5,600 gasoline-powered trucks were forecast for production in 1981 with projected growth of 16% per year. The future market for diesel engines in this market would depend heavily upon the government's decision to mandate dieselization and the annual rate at which OEMs would convert from gasoline to diesel.

Also dependent upon government policy was the off-highway market for diesel engines. The administration's five-year investment plan was expected to create a sizeable market for diesel engines in various markets. However, although most projects had been started, the instability of world oil prices made the future of these projects difficult to predict.

The final markets that generated revenue for diesel engine manufacturers were the repower and parts markets. The spare parts market could be projected from the manufacturer's total engine population in Venezuela, the estimated life of engines and annual expenditures for spare parts per engine. Critical to this market was the availability of an adequate distribution network for servicing. A repower involved the replacement of a current engine (gasoline or diesel) with a new diesel engine. The repower market was dependent upon the availability of service outlets, government incentives to promote dieselization and the relative cost of diesel to gasoline. For reasons previously noted, this market was exceedingly difficult to predict.

Cummins Venezuelan Management

The regional office in Caracas, Venezuela, had experienced several transitions in management, one almost every two years. Lucas Godinez assumed the position of regional manager for Venezuela in June of 1982, approximately eight months before Black Friday. He had joined Cummins in 1981 after receiving his MBA from the Harvard Business School. Having worked for Fleetguard, a subsidiary of Cummins, from 1976–1979 as well as for the summer while at business school, Godinez was familiar with the company and the industry. Moreover, he spoke fluent Spanish and was familiar with the Venezuelan culture. He reported directly to the area director–Latin America who, in turn, reported to the vice president–international.

Distribution of Diesel Engines in Venezuela

In Venezuela, distribution of engines and parts could be classified as either direct or indirect. Direct distribution included sales of engines to local OEMs such as Ford, International Harvester, or Encava (Bluebird buses). Sales were also made to distributors or dealers who sold engines and parts to such end users as owners of pleasure or commercial boats, for repowers of trucks and buses, or for generator sets. In these situations, distribution could either be authorized by the manufacturer or unauthorized. In the latter form, Venezuelan companies purchased engines and parts through companies authorized to distribute in foreign countries but not in Venezuela. Revenue was also produced through indirect sales in which trucks or buses with Cummins engines were shipped into the country by equipment dealers (e.g., Clark Michigan, American Crane, or any of the truck manufacturers) which later required parts, service, or repowering. As a general rule, distributors did not deal directly with OEMs, although they benefited from the increased number of diesel engines in Venezuela and the resulting parts sales, service requirements and repower business.

Most distributors carried several equipment lines although one was generally treated as the primary line. The mix of business between engines, parts, and service varied dramatically between distributors with many older firms viewing service as a necessary evil. This view created serious problems for diesel engine manufacturers in a market where service support was critical. The gross margin for parts averaged 40%, while engines had a margin of 25% to 30%, and service of 15% to 20%. Equally problematic was warranty work which manufacturers reimbursed at standard rates. However, the shortage of skilled labor often resulted in cost overruns for which there was no reimbursement.

Distributor contracts were considered by manufacturers to be lifetime commitments in Venezuela as in many other Latin American countries. Once a contract was signed, dealer protection laws provided considerable help for the local distributor. Foreign manufacturers cancelling these contracts faced significant risks of two types. First, the Venezuelan distributor could bring suit in court and possibly receive a sizeable financial settlement. Second, the manufacturer could actually lose its trademark in Venezuela. Specifically, if the local company could demonstrate that it had been the primary user of the trademark—in effect, the "owner"—the court could grant to the local company the legal ownership of the trademark.

Equipment was sold to authorized distributors by manufacturers at preferred prices (i.e., "D.N." or distributor net). Although a list of suggested retail prices was provided, distributors had considerable discretion in pricing. In view of this lack of leverage, the manufacturer's ability to influence retail prices largely was limited to its negotiating skills.

HISTORY OF CUMMINS' DISTRIBUTION IN VENEZUELA

1956–1979

In 1956 the largest Cummins' distributor in the world, Cummins Sales & Service (Arlington, Texas), formed Cumvenca as a wholly owned subsidiary to act as the Cummins' distributor for Venezuela serving the oil and gas fields out of Maracaibo, Venezuela. Gradually, operations were expanded to cover the service, parts, and engine markets throughout the country. During the 1960s and early 1970s, Cumvenca performed well as the Cummins distributor (which at that time was limited to indirect business given the absence of a Cummins OEM in Venezuela). The total number of diesel engines in Venezuela (referred to as the "engine population") was relatively small and oriented to off-highway—primarily in the oil fields and open pit mines. These end users were extremely concerned with the servicing of their equipment and generally had high parts consumption.

By 1976 Cummins had begun to receive complaints from major end users in

Venezuela that service coverage and parts availability for Cummins' products were deficient. On several occasions, end users either sued or took out full page newspaper ads describing how they had purchased Cummins equipment but were unable to obtain parts or service. By the end of 1979 Cumvenca notified Cummins and the public that it planned to phase out of the Venezuelan market. Cumvenca's decision to pull out of the country had caught Cummins by surprise.

1980

Before Cumvenca officially left the country, the large gap in authorized service was beginning to be filled by a network of independent diesel shops. Though not officially authorized as Cummins distributors, three shops (Sudimat, Junquera, and Dieselval) provided barely adequate service coverage and by the end of 1980, purchased directly from the Cummins MPDC (Miami Parts Distribution Center). By 1982, 80% of Cummins business in Venezuela was direct; 65% to local OEMs (i.e., Ford, IHC and Encava) and 15% to distributors. The remaining 20% of business was indirect. These three independents had been selected temporarily to take over primary representation for Cummins in the parts, service, repower, and warranty markets. Even with limited geographical coverage, it was estimated that they had achieved a 15% service market share for Venezuela and had increased parts market share to 50% by 1981. To defer the lifetime commitment of formal distributor contracts, Cummins reluctantly issued letters of intent as a means to limit its relationship with these independents. These letters referred to the independents as "Distributor Candidates" and allowed them to operate as dealers, noting that any distributorship would be discussed at a future date.

Dieselval   Dieselval was a family business headquartered in Valencia, center of

the automotive industry in Venezuela. The company operated one service shop, employed 30 people and had sales for the year ended June 30, 1981, of Bs. 780.0 thousand ($181,395) and total assets of Bs. 561.8 thousand ($130.561).[3] Dieselval was originally created as the bus service (to include repowers) outlet for its parent company, Encava, which used the Cummins engine. Since its inception, Dieselval had purchased Cummins equipment either from Cumvenca or through unauthorized channels. When Cumvenca announced that it would no longer represent Cummins in Venezuela, Dieselval saw a tremendous opportunity to diversify into the servicing of nonbus engines. By August 1980, Dieselval had established a solid record for having outstanding parts availability, paying close attention to the end user, and providing excellent service for the Cummins product.

Talleres Mecanicos Junquera   (Junquera) Owned by Carlos Junquera, a conservative businessman, this company had sales for the year ended October 31, 1981, of Bs. 4.2 million ($976,744) and total assets of Bs. 1.2 million ($279,070). While employing 26 people, Junquera had provided service for Cummins products for many years in East Caracas (one service shop) as a dealer of Cumvenca. Cummins' regional management considered Junquera to be "good, solid guys who provided good service—but clearly limited to a service shop. From the beginning we always wanted them to link up with someone who had money so they could expand both geographically and into other parts. They just didn't seem to have the ambition or management talent to do so."

Sudimat   Victor Simone, his brother, Sanin, and a third partner were originally

---

[3]Financial statements for Dieselval, Junquera, and Sudimat were unaudited. Publically reported financial statements for family-owned businesses typically did not represent operating reality. For the period 6/30/80–2/18/83, the exchange rate was Bs. 4.3 per dollar.

employees of Cumvenca until 1965, when they concluded that the company's servicing and parts availability were deficient. In June of that year they created their own company, Sudimat, and began to sell and service Cummins products. They built their business around Cummins parts purchased through unauthorized channels with approximately 60% of revenues derived from parts sales, 25% from service, and 15% from equipment sales. By 1982, Sudimat was recognized as one of the strongest competitors in the parts business in Venezuela, having sales for the year ended December 31, 1981, of Bs. 11.6 million ($2,697,674) and total assets of Bs. 5.1 million ($1,186,046). In addition to its headquarters located in East Caracas, the company operated two smaller shops in El Tigre and Puerto Ordaz and employed 21 people. As described by the Cummins area director–Latin America, the Sudimat people were "very street smart . . . if the end user was hiding under a rock, they knew where to lift it and they knew what it would take to sell him."

At the end of his first year at the Harvard Business School, Lucas Godinez worked during the summer for Cummins Engine Company. He reported to the Cummins vice president–international and was to recommend a distribution system for Cummins in Venezuela. At the end of the summer, Lucas recommended that Cummins needed small regional distributors or market specialists, along with a strong Cummins presence to manage the entire Venezuelan market. He felt that Cummins continually would be competing for the attention and resources of any large distributor like a Cumvenca. Further, given the lack of leverage in dealing with a distributor, it would not devote sufficient effort to the development of the diesel market. Moreover, Lucas believed that good market support and Cummins' direct presence was essential to convince the Ministry of Development that Cummins should be assigned a manu-

facturing facility under the Andean Pact. The recommendations were well received by the audience, which included the regional manager, area director, and vice president–Latin America of Cummins.

January–June 1981

In early 1981 the Cummins' regional office was approached by an executive of ACO, a Venezuelan distributor, who proposed that ACO be the Cummins distributor for Venezuela. An executive vice president of Cummins soon traveled to Venezuela to meet with ACO and had concluded by mid year that ACO would be difficult to control. He recommended that ACO not be named the Cummins distributor.

ACO was a major national distributor in Venezuela with sales for the year ended June 30, 1980, of Bs. 145.9 million ($33.93 million), total assets of Bs. 301.9 million ($70.21 million), and 1,370 employees. The company's primary business was automobile dealerships, owning 16 Ford dealerships and selling 17% of the passenger cars manufactured in Venezuela. Being an old, traditional distributor headquartered in Caracas, its parts and service revenues were negligible. The major lines carried exclusively by ACO included John Deere (construction and forestry equipment), Euclid (off-highway trucks), Hyster (fork lifts, front-end loaders), Grove (cranes), and Barber-Greene (heavy loaders, asphalt laying equipment). ACO also represented a number of other manufacturers such as Ford, GM, Toyota, and Fairbanks-Morse (centrifical pumps).

As president of ACO, Harry Mannil was successful in business and very well connected; he knew the president of Venezuela, Venezuelan ministers, dined with all the powerful people and had very close ties with Ford–Venezuela. Also, Harry Mannil had little difficulty interacting with American executives, discussing such topics as his $10 million pre-Columbian art collection which had been exhibited at the Smithsonian Institution in Washington, D.C.

Mannil's management team included Luis Galvez and Peter de Haydu. Galvez, vice president–operations, had joined ACO in the early 1960s as a car salesman at one of the ACO dealerships. His strengths were in finance and administration; Galvez was considered a "good soldier" who had worked his way up the organization. The other top executive of ACO, Peter de Haydu, was a former Wall Street investment banker recruited in late 1980 by Mannil as vice president of finance and strategic planning. It soon became clear that a close personal friendship had developed between Mannil and de Haydu. More important, there was the strong impression—an impression not denied by de Haydu—that he was the chosen successor.

To Peter de Haydu, it was clear that ACO should diversify into diesel engines and that Cummins was being neglected in Venezuela. He wanted the Cummins line not for its traditional 200–400 horsepower line, but for the lower horsepower engines where he saw considerable future growth. At that time, Cummins was preparing to manufacture a lower horsepower engine series for automotive applications. De Haydu saw a clear strategic fit for the Cummins line within ACO and took great pride in the fact that, after such a short time, he had identified such a tremendous opportunity for ACO.

Fourth Quarter 1981

Bob Campbell assumed the position of vice president–international for Cummins in November of 1981 after spending five years managing the company's United Kingdom and European operations. Campbell had dealt with a large European trading company whose considerable financial resources and management talent enabled it to deal with such issues as marketing, financing and distribution. For these reasons, Cummins granted an exclusive distribution contract in the U.K., as it had done in other countries.

After reviewing the situation in Venezuela, Campbell was unconvinced that regional distributors would be able to satisfy Cummins' needs. Campbell remarked,

> I couldn't see who was going to help us develop the Venezuelan diesel market. I couldn't see who was going to deal with the major contractors, who was going to help us with the government as far as dieselization was concerned. I felt there was a need for some "big heavy" and *if* you could control the "big heavy" who had money *and* you could get a separate division with people dedicated to the Cummins line then you knew it was going to be in pretty good shape.

Undoubtedly reinforced by his U.K. experience and the Cummins tradition, Campbell was predisposed to favor a large national distributor as the answer to its problems.

Later that year, Peter de Haydu of ACO made contact with a former classmate who had recently replaced Campbell in the U.K. for Cummins. At his friend's suggestion, de Haydu called Campbell and proposed that ACO be the Cummins distributor for Venezuela. Following an impressive visit to the ACO operations, Campbell was convinced that an arrangement could be reached whereby ACO would start on a limited geographical basis in Maracaibo where the potential for diesel engines was considered to be the greatest. Eventually, Campbell hoped ACO would form a national umbrella while the three independent companies would continue to provide regional coverage. The senior management of ACO was invited to visit Cummins corporate office on December 7, 1981.

In November of that year, an executive briefing book was circulated at Cummins' corporate headquarters stating that the purpose of the visit was "to resolve any issues that have not been agreed upon between

ACO (and Cummins) . . . and to obtain Mannil's personal commitment to having ACO become the Venezuelan distributor for Cummins Engine Company." Venezuela as well as the Andean Pact were seen by Cummins' management as tremendous opportunities; both were devoid of currency and political problems.

Harry Mannil and Peter de Haydu, accompanied by their wives, were given the grand tour of Cummins. Hosted by executive officers, the entire visit was exceedingly pleasant, almost ceremonial. Contract negotiations, which might dampen the friendly atmosphere, were omitted. That ACO would be the Cummins distributor in Venezuela was a foregone conclusion.

January–June 1982

Following the visit to Columbus, however, it became evident to Cummins' management that a number of issues remained unresolved. ACO was adamant about being *the* national distributor for Cummins. It wanted the three independent companies out of the picture. After six months of negotiation, Godinez and the Cummins' area director convinced de Haydu and Mannil that the Cummins proposal would give ACO responsibility for 73% of the Cummins direct engine business in Venezuela, and as such, the independents could actually help ACO by providing the necessary service for the engines they sold. Mannil reluctantly agreed, but noted that "they must definitely be subservient to me, dependent on me and after a limited period of time, I want them out of the picture completely. And to make sure that happens, I want a certain percentage commission on their purchases!" According to those at Cummins familiar with the situation, "by this time it almost seemed as though we *owed* ACO the distributorship. The mindset was one of it being either ACO or nothing!"

In the letter of intent signed in June 1982, it was agreed that ACO would assume total responsibility for *all* Cummins business in the areas of Barcelona, El Tigre, Barquisimeto, and Maracaibo, and sales responsibility (only) for *engines* throughout the country. The three independents, Dieselval, Junquera, and Sudimat, would continue to carry Cummins parts and provide service in their respective areas (Valencia, West and East Caracas) but would pay an additional 5% on any purchases of parts from Cummins (i.e., D.N. plus 5%). ACO would receive this 5% premium as well as a 5% commission on all purchases made by the three companies. ACO further agreed to create and staff a separate business entity devoted exclusively to the Cummins business and to invest $2.337 million in facilities. Lastly, it was noted that a definitive distributor contract would be written by December 1983.

The ACO distributorship was projected to generate sales of $91.8 million for the period 1982–1986 and a contribution of $36.3 million (Exhibit 3) for Cummins. To ACO the distributorship was expected to generate sales of $99.3 million for 1982–1986 (Exhibit 4).

Cummins' top management was pleased with the agreement. As a recognized national organization, ACO brought the prestige, contacts and know-how believed necessary to penetrate two relatively new markets for Cummins: the oil/gas/marine market in the Maracaibo area and the major project market as it related particularly to the Orinoco Tar Belt Region (oil and gas, electricity, housing and transportation). Maracaibo would require the greatest investment by ACO in order to establish operations in the region and to recapture the market from Detroit Diesel. Meanwhile, the three independents could provide service coverage in the major corridor for trucking between Caracas and Valencia. This was critical given that the greatest percentage of the existing engine population and future engine sales were found in the automotive market. In addition, it was estimated that it would take a distributor a

EXHIBIT 3 Cummins Engine Company, Inc.: Black Friday

Projected Contribution to Cummins[a]

Sales ($000)	1982	1983	1984	1985	1986
Parts[b,c]	$ 6,897	$ 8,948	$11,245	$14,307	$17,267
Repowers	724	1,458	2,196	2,994	3,779
Other Direct Engines	2,638	4,064	4,727	4,995	5,557
Total Sales	$10,259	$14,470	$18,168	$22,296	$26,603
Total Gross Contribution[d]	4,113	5,684	7,137	8,835	10,571

[a]All sales are at Distributor Net in constant 1981 dollars. Commissions on purchases made by Sudimat, Dieselval, and Junquera have not been included. Key assumptions made: (1) 5% of the medium-duty truck market would dieselize in 1983; 10% in 1984; 15% in 1985 and 20% in 1986; (2) Ford would use the Cummins engine and retain a 70% market share; (3) according to Cummins management, "very conservative" estimates were made in off-highway users in light of the instability of oil prices; parts sales were estimated to be $800 per engine per year for lower horsepower engines and up to $2,500 for larger engines.
[b]Includes service tools in 1981.
[c]Includes parts sold with repowers.
[d]Assumed a 45% GM for parts and 30% GM for engines and engine repowers. These margins reflect Cummins' sales mix.

EXHIBIT 4 Cummins Engine Company, Inc.: Black Friday

Projects Sales and Net Cash Flow to ACO[,**]*

Sales ($000)	1982	1983	1984	1985	1986
Parts and Service	$ 6,586	$ 9,525	$12,575	$16,144	$20,301
Repowers	444	878	1,336	1,833	2,297
Direct Engines	3,310	5,059	5,885	6,218	6,917
Total Sales	$10,340	$15,462	$19,796	$24,195	$29,515
Net Cash Flow					
Parts and Service	(613)	25	696	1,436	2,525
Repowers	(43)	74	207	327	472
Direct Engines	(300)	(14)	261	356	416
Commissions	189	239	295	378	462
Total Net Cash Flow	(767)	324	1,459	2,497	3,875

[*]Initial Investment in 1981: $2.337 million
 Terminal Value of Equipment in 1986: $4.46 million
[**]These numbers reflected Cummins' assumptions regarding numerous qualitative and quantitative variables which affect revenues and costs. Key assumptions made: (1) ACO would capture 30% of the Cummins parts and market in 1982 and that this would rise to 45% by 1986; (2) ACO would capture 80% of direct engine sales in 1982 and 85% by 1986; (3) ACO would perform 60% of repowers in 1982 and 75% by 1986.

minimum of one year to develop a competent service offering.

According to Victor Simone, the reaction of the three independents "was simple— we felt as though we'd been shafted! That's it—we had devoted ourselves to Cummins and they had abandoned us. Now we were ex-candidates!" Simone knew of the price disadvantage and that ACO received a commission on any of its purchases made through the MPDC. The intentions of ACO were made perfectly clear to Sudimat during a cocktail party when an ACO executive informed one of the Sudimat partners that (with the new pricing arrangement) "we're going to drive you right out of business!"

Sudimat responded quickly. First, Victor Simone sent Cummins a letter stating that he wouldn't be able to compete with such a cost disadvantage, that he would undoubtedly lose market share and that the future of his firm would be in question. Second, he diversified his business by becoming an International Harvester truck dealer with access to IHC engines. There were also rumors that he was laying the groundwork to purchase non-genuine Cummins parts through some other contact should he be cut off by Cummins. Lastly, it was believed that Sudimat was being courted by Isuzu, a competitor of Cummins.

July 1982–January 1983

One of the principal attractions of ACO to Campbell had been its financial capabilities and close ties to Ford. However, ACO continued to drag its feet during the second half of 1982. No investments were made in facilities or service tooling and as a result, ACO was not providing service to Cummins engines. Meanwhile, it had become clear that while de Haydu might be the next successor to Mannil, Galvez had the responsibility for getting the Cummins business going. However, according to Godinez, "Galvez didn't really believe in this 'dieselization crap.' He just didn't see it! He also resented what he saw as Cummins' efforts to push him around—whether it be pricing or the other three independents. Galvez felt that Cummins had no right to tell him how to run his business!"

In September of 1982, ACO concluded that it was unable to locate a capable manager to run a separate operation for the Cummins' business. To solve this problem, Cummins decided to lend ACO Noberto Invernizzi, the Cummins regional manager of Argentina. Having spent 20 years with Cummins, Invernizzi knew the company, its products and the industry backwards and forwards. He had been the marketing director of Brazil and had started up distributorships in Peru and Chile. The understanding with respect to Invernizzi was that (1) ACO would pay his salary; (2) Invernizzi would work for ACO for 18 months, reporting to Luis Galvez; and (3) Invernizzi would be responsible for finding and training his replacement. Furthermore, it was understood that ACO would create and operate a separate operation for the Cummins business under the name of Cumminsa.

Invernizzi visited Venezuela for five weeks in late 1982 to become acquainted with ACO and do some preliminary work. On January 1, 1983, he began work full time, and by the end of the month had completed a business plan for Cummins, and had hired a manager who would be his replacement. According to Godinez, "Noberto really dug right in preparing an implementable plan—it covered facilities, tooling, people, training programs, sales calls, marketing priorities, selling, service— you name it, he covered it." By the time of the devaluation, Invernizzi had been unable to receive any feedback or the approval from Galvez necessary to receive any resource allocation. Galvez had apparently been occupied with his other responsibilities. Although ACO had made sizeable purchases of parts in 1982, all goods remained in inventory, reflecting their lack of service activity. Purchases by ACO and others are reflected in Exhibit 5. This was the situation on "Black Friday."

EXHIBIT 5 Cummins Engine Company, Inc.:Black Friday

Cummins' Sales to Venezuela

	Parts Sales ($000)		
	1980	*1981*	*1982*
Junquera	–	$ 290	$ 400
Dieselval	$ 280	500	600
Sudimat	–	1,100	1,300
ACO	–	–	730
Cumvenca	460	120	–
Dealers	660	540	670
Total Parts Sales	$1,400	$2,550	$3,700

	Engine Sales[a] (Units)		
	1980	*1981*	*1982*
Junquera	–	–	–
Dieselval	–	–	115
Sudimat	5	7	33
ACO	–	–	–
Cumvenca	–	–	–
Dealers	1	–	5
Encava[c]	424[b]	201[b]	263
IHC[c]	591	340	121
Ford[c]	206	317	120
Total Engines Sold	1,227	865	657
Total Engines Sales ($000)	13,497	9,515	6,899
Total Cummins Sales–Venezuela	$14,897	$12,065	$10,599

[a]Includes repowers.
[b]Dieselval and Encava shipments consolidated.
[c]No parts had been sold to Encava, IHC, or Ford.

FEBRUARY 18, 1983— THE DEVALUATION

Receivables Due from Distributors

After its experience with the devaluation of the peso in Mexico, Cummins' top management was convinced that it should take a very proactive role in the collection of its $1.4 million in receivables. Of this amount, $1.2 million was due from ACO, Sudimat, Junquera, and Dieselval.[4] Godinez and Bill Noonan, the international credit manager, believed that Cummins should make it clear to each of the four firms that repayment plans must be agreed upon before discussions about distribution continued. Further, interest (New York floating prime plus 1%) would begin to accrue immediately on all outstanding balances.

The Venezuelan government indicated that, at some future date, companies might be able to purchase dollars at the predevaluation rate (4.3 bolivars per dollar) for repayment of private sector debt. This preferential rate would be permitted for debt

---

[4]$200,000 was due from other equipment dealers.

contracted as of February 20 for "essential" goods. It was unclear when this might happen, or whether Cummins products would be classified as essential goods. Nevertheless, the debts owed to Cummins remained in U.S. dollars.

Dieselval According to Noonan, Dieselval had traditionally been a very conservative firm, very strong financially, and had always paid its debts promptly. Total debt was always minimal. At the time of the devaluation the company owed Cummins $160,000, none of which was past due,[5] for a recent shipment of engines which were still in inventory. Although they didn't have current financial statements for Dieselval, Noonan and Godinez were aware that the company had purchased considerable off-shore funds in U.S. dollars.

Junquera Junquera owed $130,000 for engines it had sold on credit. Of this amount approximately $20,000 was 10–15 days past due. Before any serious discussions began however, Carlos Junquera came in to the regional office one day with a stack of checks ranging from $200–500 and made a partial payment totaling $6,000. According to Godinez, Junquera and his family must have stood in countless lines at banks to scrape together that much money.

Sudimat Sudimat's debt to Cummins for parts shipments had reached $178,000 of which $80,000 was 90 days past due. On several occasions, Noonan had requested information on Sudimat's current financial condition in order to develop a repayment plan. However, Victor Simone was never eager to share financial statements of any kind with Cummins. According to Noonan, "We interpreted this to mean that they were in a very delicate position ... and we couldn't tell how much he owed to others but we thought he

was on the hook to some Panamanian banks." According to Simone, he just needed time. He was confident that he would qualify for the Bs. 4.3 exchange rate. In the meantime, Simone told Cummins that he was about to sell an engine and Cummins could deduct his commission; that Cummins owed him for seven to eight warranty claims, which it should consider a payment; and so forth.

ACO At the time of the devaluation, ACO owed Cummins $730,000 for parts, all of which remained in inventory. Invernizzi and his manager remained the sole employees of Cummins, which had not yet registered to sell Cummins products. Under terms of the letter of intent, these parts had been sold to ACO on 180-day terms, all of which became due in April. According to Noonan,

> Although we knew they'd been buying a lot of U.S. dollars, we had sufficient financial information on them to know that our position was risky. In speaking with banker friends, I began to piece together what we believed to be a realistic financial picture of ACO. They had about $80 million in debt, mostly due to banks and to John Deere. There were a number of things going on between their holding company and their investment company. We realized that if we didn't move quickly, that the money they had would soon disappear.

March 1983

On March 14, 1983, a meeting took place in Caracas in which a Cummins senior vice president, the area director–Latin America and Lucas Godinez met with ACO management to discuss the $730,000 as well as distribution. However, on March 13, Peter de Haydu informed Godinez that he would be unable to attend. No reason was offered. After brief pleasantries, Harry Mannil excused himself from the meeting to take a

---

[5]Cummins' terms of sale were net 30 days (full amount due in 30 days).

phone call and never returned. The meeting then proceeded with Galvez explaining that the present government's ambiguous policy regarding currency coupled with the fact that there was a lame-duck government, made it impossible for ACO to do anything. He said that "the best we can do for you is to freeze everything right here where we are. No promises, no changes. We'll let you know when we think things are changing and then we may get back on this program. That's my only option. Take that or just forget everything!" More specifically: *parts* sales would remain suspended until such time as the future availability of dollars could be determined; no *service* shops would start up during the freeze period, no tools would be brought in nor would service personnel be hired; and all sales efforts and advertising would be terminated.

Godinez decided not to respond to Galvez' proposal on the spot. To buy time he sent Galvez a letter stating that "we consider this issue to be serious enough that we must give it our best consideration. We owe you a good answer... In the meantime, in order to support the end users in Venezuela, we are suspending the commission payment to you on any further purchases made by Sudimat, Dieselval, and Junquera and we are putting them back on our distributor list (i.e., will sell to them at D.N.)."

Current Situation

The government still had not defined which debts would qualify for preferential exchange rates. With elections scheduled in the fall, private sector debt was quickly becoming a political issue with little hope for a speedy resolution. However, it was made clear that once defined, Recadi, the government office for Allocation for Preferential Dollars, would verify the debt and pay the foreign creditor directly. Thus, the hope of qualifying for preferential dollars (Bs. 4.3) provided a strong disincentive to repay debt when the open market rate stood at Bs. 11.0.

In April, Godinez attended a dinner party at the home of Bob Campbell, Cummins' vice president–international marketing. Also present was the area director–Latin America. As the guests were about to leave, Bob Campbell took Godinez aside and told him, "Your number-one job is getting our $1.4 million back. Do that—everything else is second." Then, looking at the area director, he went on to say, "This guy's number-one job is getting the money back—not salvaging distribution, just getting the money back!"

As Godinez drove back to his hotel that evening, Campbell's comments were foremost on his mind. Four options—none of which was a perfect solution—came to mind.

1. *Dump ACO. Go with distributor candidates.* Since it was illegal for foreign corporations (e.g., Cummins) to become a majority stockholder in any Venezuelan company, Cummins would be unable to take possession of the inventory held by ACO and the three distributor candidates. However, Cummins would be able to transfer all inventory from ACO to Dieselval, Junquera, or Sudimat. Once the inventory was transferred, Cummins could either discontinue ACO as its distributor or accept the freeze proposed by ACO.

2. *Pull out of Venezuela. Take legal action to collect debt.* The anticipated departure of Ford from Venezuela and the unlikely future of the Andean Pact were strong reasons to pull out of the country entirely. Cummins could continue to service Encava from its Miami Parts Distribution Center and initiate law suits against ACO, Sudimat, Dieselval, and Junquera to recover all debts.

3. *Salvage all relationships.* Under this option, Cummins would accept the freeze and not require ACO to establish a separate operation for the Cum-

mins' business. Godinez would prepare a repayment plan to recover all
debt from ACO within one year with
interest continuing to accrue at prime,
plus 1%. In view of the financial strain
on ACO, Godinez considered whether
he should continue to pay the salary of
Noberto Invernizzi, in addition to a
service manager for the next year. Pre-
sumably this approach would placate
Dieselval, Sudimat, and Junquera
since Cummins would not be the primary line for ACO. However, Godinez

also realized that senior management's perception of the role of distributors in Venezuela would have to
be changed.

4. *Sever ties with distributor candidates.
Agree to all of ACO's demands.* This
option assumes that ACO's lack of
performance was due to Cummins'
dealings with Junquera, Dieselval, and
Sudimat. In addition, Godinez wondered about the ability of the three
small distributors to survive difficult
economic times ahead. ■

5-2 DAVID DEL CURTO S.A.

In June 1989, Lothar Meier, president of
David Del Curto S.A. (DDC), reflected
on his company's future in the European
Community's (EC) impending integrated
market. Headquartered in Chile, DDC
was the largest private company in the
southern hemisphere dedicated to the export of fresh fruit. Though it exported to
more than 35 countries, its products were
sold mainly in the northern hemisphere to
supply "contraseasonal" (off-season)
needs for fresh fruit.

Lothar Meier wondered whether the
1992 EC market integration program represented a threat or an opportunity to
DDC. In addition, he pondered the decisions he would have to make about the
company's entry strategy in Europe, its

marketing organization, distribution channels, and branding and communications
policies.

COMPANY BACKGROUND

In 1949, David Del Curto Libera emi-
grated from Italy to Chile, where he joined
his uncle Antonio in running a small firm
in the Aconcagua Valley, about 60 miles
north from Santiago. The company exported onions, garlic, melons, almonds,
chestnuts, and walnuts to Argentina.

In 1953, David Del Curto founded his
own firm in the same business. In 1956,
the new company started exporting and
added some leguminous crops such as
lentils, beans, and peas as well as honey to
its product line. During a trip to West Germany, David Del Curto met Lothar Meier,
a young German trained in foreign trade
who worked in the cereals department of
a DDC agent. David Del Curto offered

*Professor Jon I. Martinez of the Universidad Adolfo Ibanez, Santiago, Chile, prepared this case in association with
Professor John A. Quelch as the basis for class discussion rather than to illustrate either effective or ineffective
handling of an administrative situation.*

Meier a job at DDC to promote cereals, and he arrived in Chile in 1958.

In 1958, DDC entered the fresh fruit business and began to export nectarines, peaches, and plums to the U.S. market. However, the firm's main exports were still grains and brans to West Germany and the United Kingdom, animal feeds to Scandinavia, melons to the United States, onions to the United Kingdom, garlic to Brazil, walnuts to Argentina, prunes to Europe, and honey to West Germany. In 1963, DDC became interested in exporting apples and pears and, four years later, bought its first orchard. By then, DDC was the fifth-largest Chilean exporter of fresh fruit.

Increases in its apple, business prompted DDC to build in 1971 the first private fruit plant in Chile for selecting, standardizing quality of, packing, and precooling fruit to ensure resistance to damage during transportation and distribution. Subsequently, the company built six additional fruit plants, three in the 1970s and three in the 1980s.

In 1971, DDC became the third-largest exporter of fresh fruit from Chile, and four years later the first. This rapid growth was due to DDC's leadership in three areas. First, because of David del Curto's knowledge of consumption patterns in foreign markets, the company was able to advise growers on which varieties to plant. It worked with Chilean and foreign agronomists specializing in fruit research to advise growers about plantation planning, soil fumigation, and other modern farming methods.

Second, DDC pioneered in plant engineering. Chilean fruit had not always arrived in good condition in world markets due to improper postharvest storage. David Del Curto persuaded growers that they had to take more responsibility for the appearance and quality of the fruit that they cultivated to combat this problem. Hence, DDC obliged growers to participate in the final outcome of the selling process by accepting their fruit only on consignment, the same system imposed on DDC by its distribution agents.

Third, the company pioneered in opening several new markets for Chilean products, including the Middle East in 1974 and Southeast Asia in 1976. Because DDC understood each country's different consumer preferences and needs, the company was very successful in the European market from the outset.

The Company in 1989

In 1983, David Del Curto died in an air accident. Ownership of the company passed to his family and to Lothar Meier, Manuel Sánchez, and Ramón Guerrero, who had been shareholders since 1978. These executives became president, vice president, and executive director, respectively.

In the 1987–1988 season (from September to August), DDC became the first Chilean firm to break the 10-million-box barrier, exporting a volume of 13.7 million boxes (about 140,000 metric tons) valued at $85.3 million. This volume represented about 15% of Chile's total fresh fruit exports (Exhibit 1 shows company exports and share of Chilean exports from 1980 to 1988). Net profit in 1988 was about $2.5 million, which represented a 16% return on equity (Exhibit 2 shows selected financial indexes). Besides exports, DDC's revenues included $3 million in domestic fruit sales and sales of products and services worth about $7 million to growers.

Though its main activity was the export of fresh fruit, DDC defined itself as an "agroindustrial producer and marketer of fresh fruit, dry fruit and vegetables, with worldwide distribution." Its basic operating cycle consisted of six phases: production, selection, packing, shipping, distribution, and marketing of the fruit. The staff consisted of about 550 permanent employees and over 2,500 temporary workers due to the high seasonality of operations. DDC maintained some 25 to 30 employees in major ports abroad to supervise product unloading and clearance and to coordinate its distribution.

EXHIBIT 1 DAVID DEL CURTO S.A.
Evolution of Company Exports

| Year | Volume | | Value in $000 | Share of Chilean Exports |
	000 Boxes	Tons[a]		
1980	5,157	1,906	$43,897.6	23.7%
1981	7,126	515	54,003.6	28.5
1982	6,628	817	54,043.7	24.01
1983	5,871	384	42,899.2	16.48
1984	7,596	927	55,376.9	17.42
1985	8,808	602	61,745.8	16.83
1986	9,346	454	69,113.9	15.74
1987	9,889	442	76,742.7	13.79
1988	13,651 +	621	85,278.7	15.2

[a]Some dry fruit, such as walnuts, was exported in bags and therefore measured in tons. This column is *in addition* to boxes of fruit.

Source: Company records.

EXHIBIT 2 DAVID DEL CURTO S.A.
Selected Financial Indexes

	1987	1988
Liquidity Ratios		
Current ratio	1.02	1.03
Quick ratio	0.78	0.78
Debt Ratios		
Total debt/equity	4.84	4.83
Long-term debt/equity	67.44%	86.62%
Profitability Ratios		
Gross profit margin	11.77%	11.27%
Net profit margin	3.67	2.65
Return on equity	23.03	16.02
Return on assets	3.79	2.67

Source: Company records.

Only 15% of the fruit the company exported came from its land and land held by the company's owners; the rest was provided by a network of more than 800 independent growers in Chile. DDC maintained one- to five-year contracts with these growers and provided several support services. These services included technical assistance (on fertilization, irrigation, pest and disease control, weed control, growth regulations, prun-ing, thinning, maturity development, and harvest readiness), delivery scheduling, financing, and a computerized service that kept each grower constantly informed about its fruit's progress and the average prices in overseas markets.

DDC's main products were grapes, which represented about 50% of its exports in U.S. dollars and 53% in volume; stone fruits, 19% and 18%, respectively; apples, 18% and 18%; pears, 6% and 5%; and kiwi fruit, 2% and 2%. Exhibit 3 illustrates some of the company's main products. The shares of DDC exports accounted for by various destination markets was as follows:

	1986	1987	1988
United States and Canada	61%	61%	59%
Europe and Scandinavia	22	23	31
Middle East	12	12	7
Far East	4	4	2
South America	1	1	1

More detailed information about DDC's products and markets is presented in Exhibit 4.

EXHIBIT 3 Main Products and Varieties Exported

		U.S.A., East Coast	U.S.A., West Coast	Middle East	Far East	Europe	South America	Total Maritime	Air and Truck	Total
NECTARINES	1987	270,901	143,398	65,434		52,542	744	533,019	47,450	580,469
	1988	376,989	363,907	28,655		85,221		854,772	54,247	912,019
	1989	357,761	508,930	54,008		97,136		1,017,835	79,300	1,097,135
PLUMS	1987	343,645	125,181	55,381		31,212	1,896	557,315	37,911	595,226
	1988	376,115	217,712	2,688		75,105		671,620	28,847	700,467
	1989	441,948	507,483	32,755	10,136	104,527		1,096,849	90,833	1,187,682
PEACHES	1987	159,971	60,136	4,321			416	224,844	35,632	260,476
	1988	237,624	200,507	4,000		1,242		443,373	32,817	476,190
	1989	278,734	343,614	1,404		19,770		643,522	93,265	738,787
APPLES	1987	138,273	65,807	319,175	188,832	944,109	12,458	1,668,654		1,669,278
	1988	108,234	47,138	469,251	41,903	1,167,277	15,948	1,849,751	624	1,849,751
	1989	140,238	150,897	407,310	36,000	1,279,914	23,592	2,037,951		2,037,951
PEARS	1987	114,047	44,286	40,480	32,231	257,679	960	489,653	144	489,797
	1988	240,136	44,906	33,368	8,016	363,922		688,348		688,348
	1989	274,454	121,148	26,331	22,848	511,551		956,332	20	956,352
GRAPES	1987	2,581,922	1,459,671	361,039	65,287	737,873	7,032	5,212,824	74,729	5,287,553
	1988	3,073,236	2,263,876	194,029	81,757	1,572,658		7,185,556	51,538	7,237,094
	1989	2,255,177	2,827,390	76,628	142,734	1,495,225		6,797,154	102,163	6,899,317
CHERRIES	1987	336	336					672	32,271	32,943
	1988	10,368	16,848					27,216	53,280	80,496
	1989	11,872	13,050					24,922	64,935	89,857
APRICOTS	1987	10,544	1,152	3,408				15,104	10,567	25,671
	1988	16,152	11,476	2,848				30,476	12,023	42,499
	1989	21,993	23,074	2,611	1,762			49,440	21,396	70,836
MELONS	1987	39,941	12,270	3,890		930		57,031	2,785	59,816
	1988	4,005	1,335			19,071		24,411		24,411
	1989									
ONIONS	1987	16,218	6,720			55,523		78,461		78,461
	1988	27,646	8,634			128,070		164,950		164,950
	1989	11,280	11,568			129,687		152,535		152,535

EXHIBIT 4 (cont.)

Crop	Year	1	2	3	4	5	6	7	8	9
WATERMELONS	1987					332		332		332
	1988									
	1989									
LEMONS	1987					1,358		1,358		1,358
	1988									
	1989									
KIWIS	1987					8,517		8,517		8,517
	1988	12,960	17,928			278,199		309,087		509,087
	1989	9,072	5,184			334,337		348,593		558,311
GARLIC	1987					3,228		3,228		3,228
	1988		6,052			3,168		10,120	9,718	10,120
	1989		2,112			2,640		4,752		4,752
PERSIMMONS	1987					3,963		3,963		3,963
	1988									
	1989									
ASPARAGUS	1987									
	1988	100						100	29,087	28,087
	1989								41,210	41,310
ARTICHOKES	1987									
	1988	504						504		504
	1989	80						80		80
NUTS	1987									
	1988									
	1989									
RAISINS	1987									
	1988	1,800				6,053		7,853		7,853
	1989	10,800			2,050	20,500		33,350		33,350
PRUNES	1987					100		100		100
	1988									
	1989									
TOTALS	1987	3,675,798	1,918,927	853,128	286,350	2,091,945	23,506	8,849,654	242,113	9,091,767
	1988	4,485,769	1,199,219	734,839	131,676	3,700,686	15,948	12,268,137	263,839	12,531,976
	1989	3,813,509	4,514,450	601,047	215,530	4,000,708	24,592	11,168,836	502,840	13,571,676

The Fresh Fruit Industry in Chile

The fresh fruit industry accounted for over 1% of Chile's total GDP. In addition, it was the second most important generator of foreign currency in Chile, after copper mining. In the 1987–1988 season, fruit exports valued at $680 million represented 10% of total Chilean exports that year. More than $800 million in exports was expected in 1988–1989.

Although Chilean fruit represented only 2.3% of all world trade in fruit, its relative importance was higher for selected products: 16% of grapes, 6.1% of apples, and 4.5% of pears. Chile was a major southern hemisphere supplier to the contraseasonal markets of North America and Europe. During winter and spring in the northern hemisphere, Chile accounted for 80% of world trade in grapes, 92% in peaches and nectarines, 31% in apples, and 23% in pears.

The area planted with fruit in Chile had grown almost three times since 1973, while export volumes had increased more than 20 times. Data on the two main crops illustrating this growth are presented in Table A.

The fruit industry in Chile comprised about 11,000 growers, most of whom sold abroad through nearly 100 exporting firms. Data on the first six, accounting for 57% of exports in volume, are presented in Table B.

All six leading companies competed worldwide and especially in Europe. DDC's main competitors were:

Standard Trading was a wholly-owned subsidiary of the American multinational Castle & Cooke, one of the leaders in the world fruit business. It established operations in Chile in the early 1980s. It marketed in Europe under the Dole brand through a branch network that organized distribution.

United Trading Company was owned by an important Arab consortium with several businesses in Chile. New to the fruit business, it began operations in Chile in the early 1980s. It sold in Europe through distribution

TABLE A Evolution of Planted Surface (in hectares) and Exports (in tons)				
	1973	*1978*	*1983*	*1988*
Grapes: Surface	4,150	10,300	24,100	42,200
Exports	13,600	51,100	149,930	359,900
Apples: Surface	11,290	13,800	18,100	22,500
Exports	24,500	116,100	179,296	347,336

Sources: ODEPA and Associación de Exportadores de Chile A.G.

TABLE B Leading Chilean Fruit Exporters				
	Total Exports[a]	*%*	*Exports to Europe*[a]	*%*
1. David Del Curto S.A.	13,661	15.2	3,694	11.5
2. Standard Trading	11,609	13.5	5,325	16.6
3. United Trading Company	8,050	9.4	2,775	8.6
4. Unifrutti Traders	6,933	8.1	1,799	5.6
5. Frupac Ltda.	5,299	6.2	1,605	5.0
6. Coopefrut Ltda.	3,909	4.5	2,065	6.4

[a]1987–1988 season, in 000 boxes (1 ton = 95–100 boxes).

Sources: Servicio Agrícola Ganadero and Associación de Exportadores de Chile A.G.

agents, and in the United States through a joint venture with Californian partners.

Unifrutti Traders was owned by an Italian family. It marketed fruit throughout Europe but particularly in Italy. It began operations in Chile in 1983. Its subsidiary, Unifrutti of America, distributed to the U.S. market, while elsewhere it marketed through distribution agents.

Frupac was a Chilean firm owned by several growers who joined together in 1979 to export their own fruit. It was the first Chilean company to establish subsidiaries in the United States and Europe to import and market its own fruit. Frupac's operations were international in scope: it owned plantations in Perú, businesses in Argentina, and also marketed Mexican fruit worldwide.

Coopefrut was a cooperative founded in 1964 by Chilean owners that focused on apples. It used two distribution agents in U.S.A. and several in Europe. It had recently established a branch in Europe to import its own fruit and support the marketing activities of its distribution agents.

THE WORLD MARKET FOR FRESH FRUIT

The world production of fresh fruit was about 210 million tons in 1983–1985. The main producers were Brazil, U.S.A., Italy, Israel and Spain in citrus; U.S.S.R., Italy and U.S.A. in stone fruits; U.S.S.R., China,

France and Italy in apples and pears; and Brazil, Philippines, India and Colombia in bananas

World trade in fresh fruit represented about 10% of world production, and almost doubled in volume between 1963 and 1983 as shown in Table C.

Europe was both the main exporter and importer of fresh fruit in the world. It accounted for 30% of world exports and 54% of world imports. The main exporting countries were Spain 9%, U.S.A. 8%, Italy 6% and Ecuador 5%, while U.S.A. 15%, West Germany 14%, France 9% and U.K. 6% were the main importers.

THE EUROPEAN FRESH FRUIT MARKET

Basic Patterns

The per capita consumption of fruit differed markedly across countries in the EC. Table D shows the evolution of consumption (in kilograms per capita) for all fresh fruit except citrus, and for apples, the most heavily consumed fruit.

Consumption patterns in each country were rather stable except in Greece where per-capita fruit consumption had increased significantly. However, there were great differences among countries. For instance, per-capita consumption in West Germany and Greece was more than double that in Ireland and the United Kingdom.

TABLE C World Trade in Fresh Fruit						
	1963		**1973**		**1983**	
	000 Tons	***%***	***000 Tons***	***%***	***000 Tons***	***%***
Bananas	4,088	38.1	6,603	39.4	6,762	33.6
Oranges	2,923	27.3	4,543	27.1	4,994	24.8
Apples	1,588	14.8	2,448	14.6	3,535	17.6
Grapes	720	6.7	896	5.3	1,139	5.7
Other	1,415	13.1	2,310	13.6	3,711	18.3
Total	10,734	100.0	16,800	100.0	20,141	100.0

Source: FAO.

TABLE D	Evolution of Fresh Fruit Consumption in Europe (kilograms per capita)			
	All Fresh Fruit[a]		Apples	
	1973–1974	*1984–1985*	*1973–1974*	*1984–1985*
Belgium/Luxembourg	55	50	24	20
Denmark	42	38	14	19
France	56	55	17	16
Greece	56	77	21	22
Holland	66	64	36	33
Ireland	28	30	10	18
Italy	68	69	15	20
Portugal	NA	37	NA	9
Spain	NA	67	NA	21
United Kingdom	31	38	12	12
West Germany	86	79	22	22
EUROPE	60	60	18	19

[a]Not including citrus
Source: Eurostat.

Total EC production of fresh fruit reached 28.3 million tons in 1985, representing 13.5% of world production. Table E shows the production (in thousand tons) by country of all fruits, production of apples alone, and the percentage of fruit consumed in each country that was home-grown.

The countries that consumed the least fruit were those with the lowest self-supply ratios: Ireland, United Kingdom, and Denmark. The opposite was also true: Italy, Spain, and Greece, with self-supply ratios over 100%, were among the heaviest consumers.

European markets not only differed significantly in consumption per capita, but also in tastes and preferences for varieties, sizes, quality, and color. For instance, U.K. consumers preferred red apples with intense red color, excellent quality, in all varieties and in medium to small sizes. Spaniards preferred streaky varieties, with little color, medium quality, but large in size. For Italians, variety and color were not important features, but they insisted on big apples. Finally, Germans preferred small size, medium color, and were not as exacting on quality. In

general, consumers in Mediterranean countries had stronger preferences regarding size and quality because these countries produced excellent fruit; conversely, consumers in northern Europe were not so demanding since they produced less.

EC imports of all fresh fruit except citrus, and of apples were as follows (in thousands of tons):

	1983	1984	1985	1986
All fresh fruits[a]	1,393	1,573	1,642	1,517
Apples	419	504	475	508

[a]Not including citrus
Source: Eurostat.

Almost all the fruit imported into the EC during winter and spring came from the southern hemisphere. The main suppliers to the EC in 1986 are listed in Table F.

Key Markets

In 1988, the Marketing Unit, Saatchi & Saatchi affiliate, performed a study for the Chilean Association of Fruit Exporters. The study focused on the three main markets for

TABLE E Fresh Fruit Production in Europe: 1985

	All Fresh Fruits[a]	Apples	Self Supply[b]
Belgium/Luxembourg	353	222	61%
Denmark	73	45	38
France	3,433	1,793	89
Greece	2,265	267	125
Holland	439	300	57
Ireland	15	9	15
Italy	6,802	2,014	128
Portugal	419	95	95
Spain	4,188	1,004	116
United Kingdom	494	301	22
West Germany	2,694	1,383	54
EUROPE 12	21,175[b]	7,433	87

[a]Not including citrus
[b]Part of this production was exported or was used for animal feed or in the food-processing industry.
Source: Eurostat.

TABLE F Sources of EC Fruit Imports: 1986 (in thousands of tons)

	Deciduous	Citrus	Subtropical	Other	Total
South Africa	250	299	20	5	504
Chile	205	2	–	–	210
New Zealand	98	–	1	40	139
Argentina	50	86	–	–	136
Brazil	1	73	5	4	83
Uruguay	–	39	–	1	40
Australia	18	3	–	1	22
Total Southern Hemisphere	622	432	26	54	1,134

Source: Eurofruit.

Chilean fruit: West Germany, France and the United Kingdom:

West Germany was the largest European fruit market with an annual consumption of about five million tons. It was a stable and mature market, increasing in value but static in volume. Due to its high per capita consumption (the highest in Europe) and its relatively low self-supply ratio average (54%), West Germany was the largest market for imports, with a well-developed contraseasonal market (approximately 30% of all apples). Its principal contraseasonal sources were: Chile 11%, South Africa 9%, New Zealand 7% and Argentina 3%.

The trade structure was very decentralized. There were many independent stores (125,000), local and regional (rather than national), chains and department stores (about 30,000), purchasing co-ops and "symbol groups" which bought on behalf of individually owned stores. Exhibit 5 diagrams the distribution system for fresh fruit in West Germany.

Both the independents and chains tended to be conservative. The worldwide trend towards retail concentration was developing fairly slowly in West Germany.

There were also many regional differences with suppliers operating for the most part on a regional basis. Hence, a great number of primary wholesalers was needed to supply the West German market.

France was a mature market with an annual consumption of about three million tons. Due to its high self-supply ratio and

EXHIBIT 5 David Del Curto S. A. Channels of Distribution of Fresh Fruit in West Germany

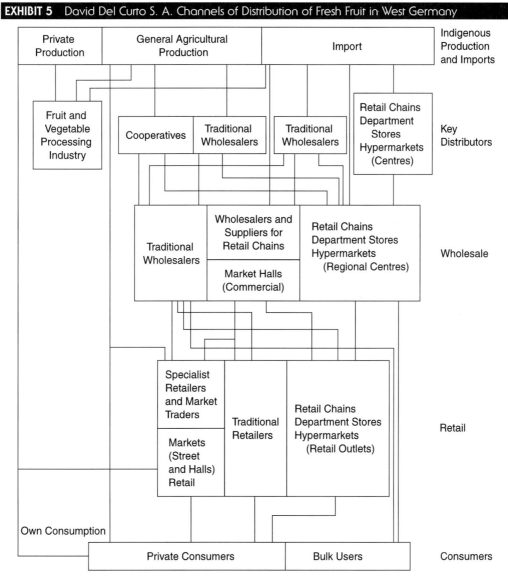

Source: The Marketing Unit.

per-capita consumption a little under the EC average, its import volume was modest, but exports were high. The contraseasonal fruit market was still underdeveloped but growing, while the seasonal market was in slow decline. The apple market was dominated by the home-grown Golden Delicious variety; contraseasonal apple imports accounted for about 15% of consumption. The key contraseasonal suppliers were Chile 35%, Italy 20%, New Zealand 12% and South Africa 11%.

The trade structure was rather fragmented, as indicated in Table G.

The distribution channels for fresh fruit in France are diagrammed in Exhibit 6. France had the most rigidly structured distribution system of any of the key EC markets. It was dominated at one end by a few large chains (hypermarkets/superstores), and, at the other end, by a very large number of small independents selling fruits and vegetables. There were major regional differences between north and south in patterns of fruit consumption and channel structure. There was a gradual shift of share and trade power toward the major chains in the north. However, the rural south was more conservative, dominated by markets and small shopkeepers, and loath to accept imports.

United Kingdom had one of the lowest per-capita consumption levels in the EC. Like France and West Germany, it was a stable, mature market with declining consumption year-to-year, but increasing in value. With a low self-supply ratio, the contraseasonal fruit market in the United Kingdom was still developing, driven by the major chains. Its main contraseasonal suppliers were South Africa 25%, New Zealand 11%, and Chile 7%.

Unlike in the other major markets, the U.K. trade structure for fresh fruit was highly centralized. Grocery retailing was dominated by only ten chains. The retail channels for fresh fruit were as follows:

	Number	Fruit Share
Chains	> 30,000	> 45%
Greengrocers	> 15,000	> 30%
Independents	> 70,000	> 20%

All retailers bought through wholesalers/importers. Innovations were initiated and driven by the chains. The distribution system for fresh fruit in the United Kingdom is diagrammed in Exhibit 7.

Consumer Attitudes, Habits and Trends

According to The Marketing Unit survey, consumer attitudes were basically similar in all three major markets. Consumers bought primarily on the basis of visual appearance. The fruit's country of origin, like Chile or South Africa, was not usually advertised at the point-of-sale and consumers did not generally ask for this information.

The main factors that seemed to determine fruit purchasing were price, quality, varieties, visual appeal, trust in the retail outlet, seasonal habits and fashion (as in the case of kiwi fruit). In some markets, like the U.K., consumers tended to buy with their eyes and had a very low brand awareness of fruit. Branding of fruit was often precluded by the risk of bruising, especially in the case of soft fruit. Consumer recall of brands of fruit was low, though some brands like Cape (South Africa's brand) did have significant consumer awareness. Some analysts believed that branding had a greater benefit in marketing to the trade than to the end consumer.

TABLE G	Retail Channels for Fresh Fruit in France	
	Number	Fruit Share
Markets	9,000	29.4%
Supermarkets	11,000	22.7
General Stores	29,500	14.1
Greengrocers	5,000	11.4
Hypermarkets	550	9.9
Other	NA	12.5

EXHIBIT 6   DAVID DEL CURTO S.A. Channels of Distribution of Fresh Fruit in France)

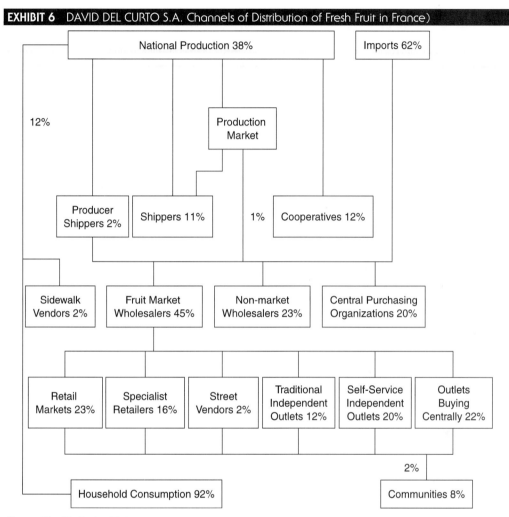

Source: The Marketing Unit.
These descriptions are the standard ones used for the French retail/wholesale markets.

Recently, consumers were showing more interest in exotic fruits, such as kiwi fruit, and better quality and new varieties of staple fruit. This upmarket trend was stronger in countries like the U.K. with a more concentrated trade where the major chains sought to boost their margins on a stable volume of demand.

Sourcing Patterns

Consumers did not determine sourcing patterns. These were decided by the trade.

The key criteria used to select the country of origin and exporter were: availability, consistency of supply throughout the season, quality of produce, price (adjusted for the exchange rate), and service.

CHILEAN FRUIT POSITIONING IN THE ECC MARKET

Chile's share of the EC contraseasonal fruit market grew significantly in the 1980s. It was the leader in West Germany and France with

EXHIBIT 7 DAVID DEL CURTO S.A. Channels of Distribution of Fresh Fruit in France

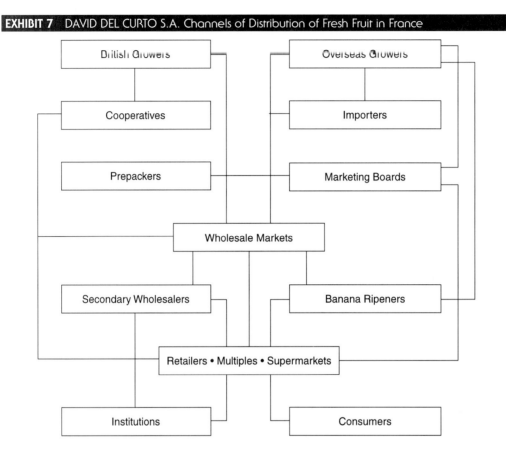

11% and 35% market shares respectively, and third after South Africa and New Zealand (its main competitors) in the U.K. Table H shows the mix of Chilean products in these three key markets.

According to market observers, the key sources of competitive advantage for Chile were: 1) a relatively neutral political profile compared to South Africa; 2) recent rapid increases in overall fruit quality; 3) a longer harvesting season; 4) a speed of delivery which rivaled that of South Africa; and 5) a broad and competitive range of deciduous fruits.

Image

Retail and wholesale perceptions of Chilean fruit quality varied across markets. West German and French distributors con-

sidered Chilean products to be of very good quality. Germans tended to believe that Chilean fruit had "little or no chemical treatment." Chilean exporters were viewed as responsive, particularly by French importers. In the U.K., Chilean fruit was seen as fairly good in quality, but not as good as that from South Africa or New Zealand.

The main criticisms made by the trade about Chilean fruit concerned consistency of quality and consistency of supply. Other problems mentioned by the trade in Europe were the lack of consumer awareness of fruit originating from Chile, the lack of overall coordination among Chilean exporters which led to missed marketing opportunities, and the lack of standardization in packaging.

TABLE H Mix of Chilean Fruits by Volume and Value in Three EC Markets					
	Germany		*France*		*United Kingdom*	
	% Volume	*% Value*	*% Volume*	*% Value*	*% Volume*	*% Value*
Apples	81	72	69	56	58	41
Pears	7	8	15	13	4	3
Grapes	6	12	12	20	27	42
Plums	–	–	1	2	1	2
Peaches	–	1	2	5	1	2
Other	5	7	2	5	10	11

Trade Relations and Marketing

Both South Africa and New Zealand had marketing organizations in West Germany, France and the U.K. These government-controlled organizations were called "marketing boards" ("UNIFRUCO" and A.P.M.B., respectively). The mission of these organizations were to coordinate harvesting, shipping, importing and marketing. The marketing boards distributed the fruit through a "panel" system. Panel appointments were franchises granted to wholesalers by producers to sell fruit on their behalf. Panelists were selected by the marketing boards and were reviewed on a yearly basis. They sold to retail customers on a fixed commission basis which ranged from 5 to 8 percent. The price at which the fruit was sold was set by the central marketing board. Panelists meant that the producers did not have to trade directly.

The marketing board was also in charge of all marketing activities. The main activities were advertising, promotion and branding. For instance, South Africa's board UNIFRUCO created awareness for its brands "Cape" and "Outspan" through advertising (mainly on radio) and promotional material for the point-of-sale (posters, educational leaflets describing the fruit's nutritional value, mobiles, brand logos, brochures, carrier bags, and sometimes badges and T-shirts). In addition, UNIFRUCO advertised in trade magazines.

It was estimated that UNIFRUCO spent on 1987 about $2.1 million in its communications program for the Cape brand in the U.K., West Germany, and France.

Chile did not use a marketing board or panelists and operated in an "uncoordinated" way through distribution agents and importers in all three countries. Chile performed almost no marketing activities, and had very little direct contact with the major retailers. Except for Standard Trading's Dole brand, Chilean fruit was usually unbranded. Finally, Chilean exporters had never attempted to promote their fruit generically in Europe; only a few individual exporters advertised in trade magazines.

IMPLICATIONS OF 1992 FOR THE FRESH FRUIT MARKET

Although the impact of the 1992 market integration program on the fresh fruit market was not yet clear, some changes were expected. The EC Commission was expected to decrease agricultural subsidies because of the enormous cost of the Common Agricultural Policy (CAP). EC authorities were concerned about the continuing rapid growth of the CAP budget, caused by consistent excess production and large stockpiles of certain food products. In 1988, CAP net expenses reached 25.2 billion ECUs,[1]

---

[1] In 1988, one ECU was between US$1.1 and US$1.2.

accounting for 65% of the EC's general budget. About 7% of these expenses subsidized fruit and vegetables.

However, analysts believed that, even if agricultural subsidies were reduced, some measures would have to be taken to protect agriculture, a sector that employed 8.8% of EC workers. There was growing pressure on the Commission from COPA (the European growers association) to restrict imports from southern hemisphere suppliers. The reasons were overproduction of apples (primarily in France and Italy) and the support of other growers of peaches, nectarines, and strawberries. Balanced against this pressure was the Commission's awareness that it had to ensure competitive prices for EC consumers.

These pressures had led to restrictions being imposed on southern hemisphere suppliers in the fresh fruit market, first on apples and then on grapes. The restriction on apples, applied in 1988, consisted of quotas on imports which, as shown in Table I, had grown significantly since 1984.

The producing country most damaged by the quotas was Chile, which, until 1987, had exhibited the greatest growth. Whereas South Africa was assigned a quota of 165,000 tons, Chile's quota was only 130,000; its capacity was 190,000. Finally, South Africa was actually allowed to supply 195,000 tons, but Chilean imports were halted at 142,130. Thousands of tons of product en route to Europe had to be thrown away. Chile had recourse to the General Agreement on Tariffs and Trade (GATT), and one year later the GATT Group of Experts passed judgment favorable to Chile in an unprecedented verdict. For 1989, the EC assigned 188,000 tons to South Africa, and Chile negotiated a voluntary agreement for 168,000.

Fruit imported from outside the EC was charged a standard tariff that ranged between 5% and 22% for all EC countries, depending on type of fruit and variety. Also, tariffs were higher at the beginning and end of the season to protect the sale of EC-grown fruit. For example, tariffs for apples were 8% from January 1 to March 31, 6% from April 1 to July 31, and 14% from August 1 to December 31. It was thought that these tariffs would not be higher, but would remain steady or even go lower. Besides tariffs, other restrictions included quotas, minimum prices, licenses to import some types of fruit, and sanitary regulations. The general trend, even before 1992, was to harmonize and standardize all sanitary regulations in the EC countries. Although these regulations varied from country to country, especially in Italy, the fruit that had passed the tests in whatever European port it had entered was allowed to move to other countries without further controls. Therefore, there already was a free movement of fruit across EC markets.

TABLE I	EC Imports of Apples, 1984–1989 (in thousands of tons)					
	1984	*1985*	*1986*	*1987*	*1988[a]*	*1989[a]*
South Africa	157	147	164	170	195	188
Chile	98	87	151	161	142	168
New Zealand	77	96	97	105	128	135
Argentina	53	64	32	53	79	78
Australia	2	10	6	8	6	11
Total	388	405	451	497	550	580

[a]Quotas

Source: Eurostat.

Consumer preferences after 1992 were difficult to predict. Despite the deep differences in tastes, habits, and patterns of consumption, experts forecast a slow but continuous homogenization of European markets. The free movement of workers, easier travel across countries without border controls, development of pan-European television and other media, and an increasing concentration of distribution were among the factors that argued for further similarities among European consumers.

DDC OPERATIONS IN EUROPE

Markets and Products

DDC sold in all of Western Europe except Portugal. It could not sell in Eastern Europe because of a boycott on Chilean products since the overthrow of Allende's socialist government in 1973. DDC's European sales in 1988 were $17.83 million, which represented 20.9% of total company exports. The 3.7 million boxes exported to Europe in 1988, which accounted for 27.1% of company export sales by volume, had the following initial destination:

Holland and Belgium	22%
United Kingdom	20
West Germany	17
France	13
Italy	12
Sweden, Finland, Denmark, and Norway	11
Other	5

DDC did not know where its fruit was finally consumed. Actual consumption in Holland and Belgium was only 5% of the shipments. The main markets for DDC's fruit were West Germany, the United Kingdom, France, Italy and Scandinavian countries.

The types of fruit DDC exported to Europe in 1988 were grapes (43% of volume), apples (32%), pears (10%), kiwi fruit (8%), and stone fruits (4%).

Distribution

The company used different distribution arrangements in each EC market:

Holland, Belgium, Switzerland, Austria: Distribution Agent 1

United Kingdom and Ireland	: Distribution Agent 2
West Germany	: Distribution Agent 3 and Central Purchasing Org. 1
France	: Distribution Agent 4
Italy and Greece	: Distribution Agent 5
Sweden, Finland, Norway, Denmark	: Central Purchasing Org. 2
Spain	: Importers

For most of the EC markets, DDC used five distribution agents to sell and market its products. They were independent agents paid by commission who sold to various wholesalers and retailers, including most supermarket and hypermarket chains. Additionally, the company sold directly to two central purchasing organizations. One belonged to a West German supermarket chain and the other to the Union of Scandinavian Consumer Cooperatives. Finally, DCC's clients in Spain were three importers and producers of fruit.

The distribution agents worked exclusively for DDC during the contraseason, but represented other firms from Europe and other countries during the rest of the year.

DDC executives met each distribution agent personally twice a season to discuss the distribution strategy and prepare annual orders based on historical trends and expected changes during the next season. In these meetings they also analyzed the total supply situation in Europe: new varieties, countries of origin, qualities, types of packing, new transportation technologies, forecasted prices and volumes, and the mix of varieties to include in future shipments.

Distribution agents also sent weekly market reports by telex or fax which commented on volume sold that week, estimated prices, the general market situation, and future prospects.

Pricing

Due to fruit's perishable nature, its uncertain condition after transportation and changing consumer tastes, fruit prices were highly volatile both seasonally and from year to year. However, early contraseasonal prices were typically much higher because of the insufficient supply at the beginning of the winter, but then fell quickly. Thanks to the quality of its fruit, its prestige as the largest and oldest Chilean supplier, and dependable supply throughout the contraseason, DDC usually obtained prices a little higher than average in the market.

DDC used three methods to sell fruit: firm price, minimum guarantee, and free consignment. DDC employed the first method with Spanish importers, the second with German and Scandinavian central purchasing organizations, and the third with distribution agents. Under free consignment, the exporter delivered the fruit to the destination port distribution agent, who sold it to wholesalers and retailers at the highest possible price. After the sale, the distribution agent presented a "sales account" which detailed sales revenues for each product minus customs fees, duties, handling of fruit in the port, cold-storage, internal transportation, and other expenses.

Agents' commissions were normally 8% of the selling price. DDC's sales to wholesalers and retailers worldwide in 1988 totaled about $150 million. However, its net revenues were only $85.3 million. The difference, about $65 million, was used by distribution agents to pay their commissions (8% of $150 million), distribution expenses, port expenses, duties, and freight and insurance. From net revenues, DDC deducted a commission of 8%, which was standard among Chilean exporters. Other DDC income came from all services and products provided to growers. Exhibit 8 shows a typical cost breakdown on fruit exported to Europe from Chile.

Organization and Control

The company's commercial department consisted of a manager and four executives, as shown in Exhibit 9. Basically, it was structured according to geography. One executive was in charge of the U.S. West Coast market and dry fruit exports; another was responsible for the U.S. East Coast market; the third coordinated the European markets; and the fourth was in charge of South America and air shipments. Apart from managing the whole department, the commercial manager oversaw the Middle and Far East markets.

The executive in charge of the European markets was Rodrigo Falcone, who described his task in this way:

> My objective is to maximize the revenues for the boxes sent to Europe. To accomplish this task, I have to be in close and permanent contact with each distribution agent so as to move the fruit toward the highest priced markets.

Rodrigo Falcone's mission was to coordinate and control all shipments to Europe in order to secure the maximum possible price for the fruit delivered on consignment to distribution agents. First, the fruit was allocated to distribution agents from Chile, and then Rodrigo Falcone reallocated it to agents whose markets offered better prices at any time. This task required almost instantaneous decisions by phone, telex, or fax.

Rodrigo Falcone had no established travel plan; every year was different due to changing market conditions. However, he usually worked in Europe from March to August and in Chile the rest of the year. While in Europe, he worked in different markets, but resided in Hamburg, West

EXHIBIT 8 DAVID DEL CURTO, S.A.
Cost Breakdown of a Typical Export of Apples and Grapes to Europe[a]

		Apples	Grapes
	Selling price to wholesalers or retailers in Europe	100%	100%
minus:	Distribution agent's commission(over selling price)	8%	8%
	Expenses in Europe (discounted by the distribution agent):		
	• Port and distribution expenses (discharge, handling, trucking, storage, etc.)	7–8%	5–6%
	• Duties	5–6%	11–13%
	• Freight and insurance	34–37%	17–20%
equal:	FOB Chile	41–46%	53–59%
minus:	Exporter's commission (8% over FOB price)	3–4%	4–5%
	Expenses in Chile (discounted by the exporter):		
	• Port expenses	0.9%	1.3%
	• Domestic freight	2.0%	1.6%
	• Cooling	2.1%	2.8%
	• Packing service	3.5%	6.7%
	• Packing materials	13.4%	12.5%
equal:	Grower's revenue	15–21%	23–30%

[a]Data from 1987–88 season for Granny Smith apples and Ribier and Thomson Seedless grapes, the varieties most exported to Europe. Costs have been estimated over the following average prices per box: apples $13.5–14.5 (18.2 kilograms) and grapes $8.5–9.5 (5 kilograms).

Source: Casewriter estimates based on information given by several fresh fruit exporters.

EXHIBIT 9 DAVID DEL CURTO S.A. Organization Chart of the Commercial Area

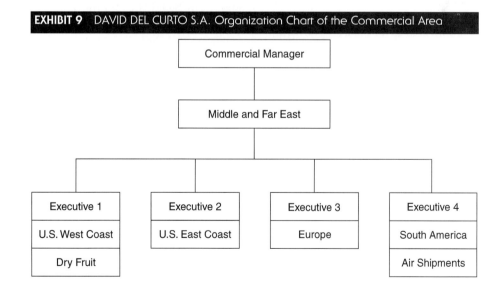

Germany. His operations base was the Central Representation Office for Europe. The company did not own this organization, but used it exclusively during the contraseason. Like distribution agents, the organization worked with both European fruit and products from tropical countries. It had a permanent staff of six or seven people, all West Germans. Its functions were a) to coordinate the logistics: regular shipments, charters, and the reallocation of fruit to different markets; b) to serve as the communications center: telex, fax, and mail; and c) to supervise the financial and administrative activities of DDC's European business: payments, collection, credit lines for ships, and handling of all kinds of formalities, documents and other papers. In sum, the organization focused not on the marketing of the fruit but on the coordination of operations.

Finally, DDC employed a full-time agronomist engineer in Rotterdam, the main port of entry for its fruit in Europe. Other agronomists and technicians traveled from Chile to inspect the fruit's condition on its arrival in Europe. They ensured quality control and monitored the effectiveness of different experimental packing techniques.

Branding and Communications

DDC's fruit in Europe neither carried its own brand nor that of any distribution agent. Only a few supermarket chains used displays that included boxes with the logo "Del Curto-Chile"; normally these retailers did not brand their fruit. Merchandising activities were performed by neither DDC nor distribution agents. From time to time, chains offered special promotions of DDC products.

The company did not advertise its products to the final consumer; however, it did place some full color institutional or image advertisements targeted at the trade in specialized magazines such as "Fruchthandel" from West Germany and "Eurofruit" from the United Kingdom. These were bi monthly publications sold by subscription to importers, distributors, wholesalers, supermarket chains, and exporters throughout the world. The distribution agents neither advertised nor promoted DDC's fruit, but only advertised their own firms' capabilities.

REVIEWING THE EUROPEAN STRATEGY

In mid-June 1989, Lothar Meier wondered whether the trends and expected changes in the EC fresh fruit market would necessitate modifying his company's strategy.

Organization

His first concern was the suitability of DDC's organization and distribution in Europe. There were at least three alternatives: first, to continue with the current way of doing business in Europe; second, to create a subsidiary that could import, distribute, and market its own fruit; and third, to foster the creation of a marketing board for all Chilean fruit, like the ones run by South Africa, New Zealand, and Israel. This last alternative was not considered by Lothar Meier, but was a possibility suggested by some market observers.

Of the six main Chilean exporters, four had European sales subsidiaries or operated through their parent companies' European networks. DDC had previously rejected the idea of a sales office to import, distribute, or market its fruit in Europe. Lothar Meier concurred with the opinion of Rodrigo Falcone, the executive in charge in Europe:

If we had a sales branch in Europe, we would need at least 15 employees to manage our current volume, and this would reduce our flexibility. For instance, if the dollar goes up much, if there is a significant fall in demand, or the export of some product into the EC market is suddenly forbidden, we can divert our fruit to the USA and deliver less in Europe. If we did do this, we couldn't justify the fixed expenses of a subsidiary in Europe. Instead, by being the major private exporter from the southern hemisphere, DDC has the capacity to work with the best distribution agents in each country. After almost 30 years in this business, the company knows all the distribution agents in Europe and works with the best ones. That our main competitors constantly offer them opportunities to join their organizations demonstrates their quality.

Lothar Meier added:

Besides being a matter of flexibility, it's a matter of cost. If we operate in the European market for just six months a year, we cannot absorb the overhead expenses for the whole year. With our current organization and distribution system we keep our costs low.

Asked about running the sales office all year long and handling fruit of the northern hemisphere in the seasonal market, Lothar Meier stated that instead of continuing to grow in volume and embarking on new ventures, the company should consolidate its current activities.

The third alternative, to promote the creation of a marketing board with other Chilean exporters to coordinate the harvesting, shipping, importing, distribution, and marketing of Chilean fruit in the EC market, was suggested by The Marketing Unit to the Chilean Association of Fruit Exporters as a result of its study (see Exhibit 10).

Some of the large Chilean exporters were opposed to the marketing board idea. They believed that the central planning and coordination provided by such a

board could not compensate for the flexibility and rapid response time that they enjoyed as independent entrepreneurs. To some the faster growth of Chilean exports compared with those from South Africa and New Zealand proved the superiority of the independent or uncoordinated approach. Lothar Meier agreed with this position. He believed that marketing boards had often failed because of inefficiency and the high costs of production and transportation.

Distribution

As previously mentioned, DDC operated directly with the central purchasing organizations of two major supermarket or cooperative chains in West Germany and Sweden. Asked about extending these arrangements to other large chains in Europe and forming joint ventures or strategic alliances, Lothar Meier answered:

We can't do so much. Our company receives many proposals from important chains. As they are big retailers they want to buy in the country of origin, to have a link there. Currently, we reach all important chains across Europe through our distribution agents. To serve the chains directly, we would need a huge staff. We can't do all the business in the world. We are specialists in a part of the distribution channel.

Branding and Promotion

Finally, Lothar Meier wondered about making a greater marketing effort to increase consumer awareness and loyalty toward Chilean fruit and, in particular, toward DDC's fruit. Two crucial subjects were branding and communications.

On these issues, Lothar Meier commented:

Advertising to create awareness and loyalty in this business is expensive and

EXHIBIT 10 DAVID DEL CURTO S.A.
Excerpts from Marketing Unit Report

Chile has no marketing organization on site in Europe.

- For Chile, the importers are the trade interface
- Therefore there is negligible coordination
- Activities in Europe are fragmented, opportunistic

This flexibility and opportunism has served Chile well:

- It has been an appropriate strategy during periods of open access to EC markets and buoyant EC economies
- Chilean exports to Europe have grown dramatically, due to:
  - Increases in availability
  - Incentives to importers including dating
  - Exchange rates favorable to European currencies

But are flexibility and opportunism right for the new climate?

The New Climate in Europe

1. The EC is closing ranks (and frontiers) against southern hemisphere fruit suppliers. Chile has been singled out for close attention. Chile must expect rigidly applied limitations in the future.
2. Exchange rates expected to continue to move in favor of European currencies at least until the end of 1989.
3. The scope for further cost-effective direct incentives to importers is limited. Investment in marketplace impacts at the point-of-sale is likely to represent the most profitable use of support funds.

The Market Now Demands a Strategic Rather Than a Tactical Approach

Such strategy requires:

- Systematic marketing planning for each major outlet
- Development of close trade relationships
- Ability to guarantee supply
- Point-of-sale merchandising support

A Marketing Board could perform these tasks.

Organization

Improved organization could improve dramatically the way in which Chile:

- Services the importers,
- Services the retail trade,
- Coordinates supply and demand,
- Demonstrates size, stature, importance,
- Maximizes visibility and **presence** in each market

A new **organization** should have the following capabilities/functions:

- Tightly knit, *dedicated* resource for *Chilean* fruit
- Ongoing pan-European coverage
- EC liaison capability
- Handling importer and major trade relations directly
- Using outside consulting resources for Marketing Services and for Marketing Communications.

Source: Adapted from "Chilean Winter Fruit. A Marketing Plan for 1988/1989 and Beyond, Covering: West Germany, France and the United Kingdom," by The Marketing Unit, February 1988.

---

ineffective, because it is directed toward the consumer who doesn't see the brand; he sees only apples and grapes. Building a brand in the international fruit market is very costly, and large volumes are needed to absorb those expenses. Chiq-

uita, the famous brand of bananas, sells more than 120 million boxes all over the world. However, this is a brand for just one product shipped by one producer. No Chilean exporter has the volume to warrant such a huge investment. ∎

5-3   MEGA

Daniel Casselli, with Carlos Bernardez, summarized some of his concerns: "While we are thinking about an innovative project, clients are spending less money every day. I don't know if I am interested in clients whose purchases total $7. Therefore, perhaps we should refocus our target group, as $15 to $20 appears to be an acceptable sales average. Besides, it is necessary to create a good product mix and customer loyalty."

BACKGROUND

At the end of 1989, two corporations decided to join in order to generate a new commercial project for the city of Rosario. The Casselli family owned six Reina Elena and three La Reina supermarkets, low-price outlets of 500 to 2,500 meters, respectively. Gonzalez Hnos managed La Favorita during the last 92 years, a unique department store that continued operating in Argentina and was very well known in Rosario.

That year, the hyperinflation economic crisis, which had reached monthly levels of 450%, had shaken the country and caused the government to resign. Rosario was the center of attention where looting had taken place at the command of civic factions. With a population of 1 million inhabitants, it is one of the main cereal ports of the country and the center of a wide range of medium industries, but the acquisitive power of its people had been severely diminished. The upper-level people of Rosario frequently travel the 300-kilometer roadway which in two hours takes them to Buenos Aires, capital of the country and important cultural center. There they find a wide variety of commercial and gastronomic offerings including shows and entertainment. This physical and cultural nearness makes Buenos Aires the model of a wide sector of the Rosario population.

The retail situation was totally different in the remaining major cities of the country. The increasing trends to build large outlets versus small stores had strengthened in the decade of the 1980s with the expansion of Reina Elena and La Reina chains, and also their competitors—Tigre and La Gallega—with the consequent redefinition of the supplier-retailer power balance. However, numerous small retailers continued operating in the center as well as in the periphery of the city and there was no important purchase center. The economic crisis also impelled those who had lost their employment to open small stores in local neighborhoods. As they were very small and informal shops, they had the advantage of escaping tax controls.

In 1982, the first hypermarket of Rosario opened 12 blocks from the center of the city, but it closed some years later. Recently, citizens experienced business modernization with the opening of Olivia, a supermarket located in the periphery of the city, 5 km from the center toward the west. It targeted the high-middle class, of which 60% lived in the suburb of Fisherton. The location was a little far away for its customers. There were expectations for the announcements of three shopping center openings: Place Garden, Radar City, and Shopping del Siglo. These were promoted like commercial galleries consisting of ground and two or three floors with access through two streets, air conditioning, and a small food court.

This case was prepared by Assistant Professor John C. Whitney, Jr., as the basis for class discussion rather than to illustrate either effective or ineffective handling of an administrative situation.

THE CHALLENGE

La Favorita as well as La Reina and Reina Elena supermarkets had been pioneers in their businesses. The 25 years of supermarket management by the Casselli family added to Gonzalez Hnos' experience and client knowledge, and created a significant business volume and privileged negotiation conditions with local and foreign suppliers.

The management group considered that any proposal would be compared with what the people from Rosario saw in Buenos Aires. To define the project, they took advantage of the experiences of both organizations. Several trips to Europe and the United States allowed them to contact diverse alternatives. One of the most relevant was the development performed by El Corte Inglés from Spain with its chain of supermarkets, HiperCor.

However, the purchasing power of the Rosario people was weaker than that of the "porteños" (name given to the inhabitants of Buenos Aires). Also, their purchase habits were different according to what was reflected in the market research carried out by the marketing consultant firm managed by Carlos Bernardez (see Exhibit 1).

Therefore, the proposal should reflect the mood of Buenos Aires, but at a lower price. The first market surveys conducted among supermarket and store clients indicated they were satisfactory but incomplete. They tied the idea of "shopping" with expensive amusement not found in Rosario, and with family outings in Buenos Aires. Exhibit 1 shows more data on these surveys.

A commercial center with a wider range of products and new services could attract new clients, but it must provide services that make shopping easier and more enjoyable.

EXHIBIT 1   Market Research Conclusions

1700 interviews, ABC level

Preferences declared:

64.7%	Include their purchases in a family walk
44.8%	Buy everything in the same place
44.0%	Central not peripheral location
54.3%	Easy parking
64.3%	Prices equal to those of La Favorita or supermarkets
35.7%	Willing to pay a price difference in exchange for an offer of preferred products

Purchase Habits—Frequency	
Daily	27%
Weekly	43%
Fortnightly	16%
Monthly	14%

Source: Carlos Bartolomé y Asociados.

An increasing number of women in the work force with little leisure time was one factor that caused the larger concentration of shopping malls. Perhaps this situation will be exploited by external competitors belonging to local chains such as Disco or Norte Supermarkets and by foreign groups such as Jumbo or Carrefour hypermarkets. Market researchers also showed a high degree of nonsatisfaction with existing proposals.

Competitive space had to be filled in a hurry, because if some competitor settled down in advance, the possibility of generating a response is limited. Macro, a foreign wholesale chain, announced its plans to set up on Circunvalación Avenue, the previous site of a supermarket. Macro would sell to retailers and to the public, as it was already doing in Buenos Aires. Any of these companies had enough capacity for generating a sustained drop of prices, without a product offer much higher than that of the project partners. But there were several problems to be solved.

The financial limitations of the corporation made it difficult to consider a shopping center of great size like those in Buenos Aires or any modern city. Excessive promises were very dangerous for a public that would not forgive the frustration over another small offer that was presented to them. Notwithstanding, according to surveys, people were willing to pay more if they were gratified. An over estimated proposal with regard to expectations and market possibilities was undesirable—it not only added risk to a high investment but also incorporated a real estate and management effort with premises owned by third parties. On the other hand, if the proposal was confused with a supermarket, then it runs the risk of becoming invalidated because the population would not observe advantages, considering it as a large supermarket.

The corporation faced the risk of losing sales of current corporate outlets, because

Rosario is a highly concentrated city with a radius of no more than 10 km from the center, situated on the Paraná River. Exhibit 2 shows a map of the city with the location of La Reina and Reina Elena chain outlets and two possible sites where Mega could be established.

However, the first problem of the company arose within six months, when the partners from La Favorita decided to retire in order to attend to their own businesses. The Casselli family resolved to continue, assuming the operation risk on their own. They

EXHIBIT 2 Map of Rosario—Location of Stores

EXHIBIT 2 (cont.)

had an outlet in the center of the city, owned by Gonzalez Hnos, where a large supermarket that was closed several years ago had been operating. With some changes, it could expand to 5,000 square meters. Its front and back part looked out on two less important streets, but it was near Oroño Boulevard, the main artery that joined the city's north and south ends. If they succeeded in enthusing suppliers, they could obtain part of the necessary financing to start up the project.

THE PROJECT

The objective targeted the upper segment—ABC1—with an alternative that attracted a higher percentage of family consumers and loyal customers, but also increased the Reina Elena and La Reina chains' invoicing. To lose sales could be fatal for existing operations.

In the outlet area lived middle-class people; a second location toward the south of the city held a middle and middle-lower class district. The consultant believed it possible to appeal to a group of emulators willing to prove new proposals with more options.

One of the differentiation bases was product. They looked for an ideal mix of consumer products, including brands and presentations, as additional criteria to those of turnover and profitability. If a supermarket managed 5,000 to 10,000 products, then a hypermarket managed 12,000 to 15,000, and a department store about 25,000. How many products had to compose the Mega store's mix?

There was the possibility of incorporating exclusive suppliers, unusual for self-service stores, and importing brands directly from the United States, such as The Gap, Victoria Secrets, or The Limited, at clearinghouse prices. They could also add electronic and household products as decoration, design, and furniture. This strategy would involve a different proposal—a more time-demanding visit. It would then be necessary to analyze if customers would come alone or in a family group—such as in an outing—and to decide how buyers weigh the importance of each purchase, such as conventional food and cleaning items versus nonconventional items such as household decorations and electric household products. The furniture and space had to be consistent with goods and the price level.

In the self-service system, conventional products usually account for 70% of sales, but they have a significant lower margin. Although nonconventional products occupied more shelf space and turned over more slowly, if their sales could be increased, then the total margin would be improved. Exhibit 3 shows the space distribution of a supermarket

EXHIBIT 3 Hypermarket Layout

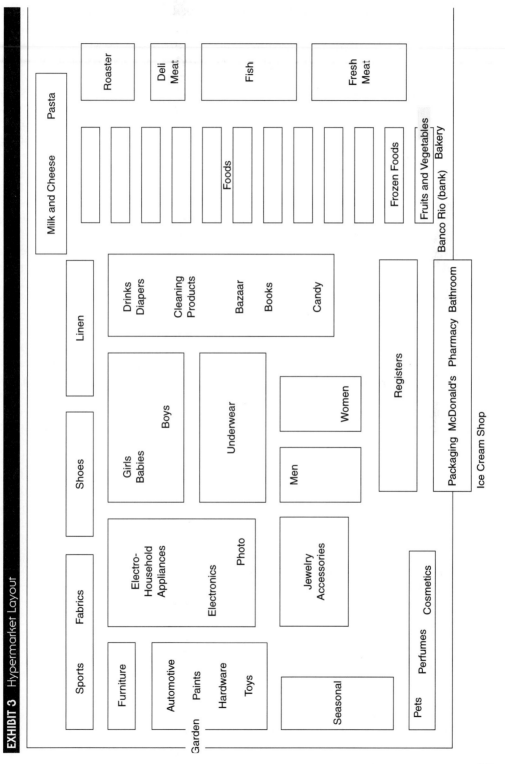

with the style of an American chain; but it would be necessary to adapt the experience of large stores (personalized attention and assisted sales, product displays, fitting rooms) to sell garments in a self-service outlet. Not all kind of garments would suit this type of display, besides the need of having to mix the fashion concept with the purchase of food.

To emphasize the idea of shopping, would it be enough to enlarge the product range, or will it be necessary to incorporate other aspects such as automatic pocket or on-line credit card authorization systems in check-out registers? The idea of placing a food court and other suggestions were part of the shopping proposal, but garment and cosmetic manufacturers of the popular brands did not accept their products exhibited in gondolas. Closed boutiques or open stands could be built and also some products introduced to increase client awareness.

Researcher and client knowledge showed a high price awareness, questioned a strategy of high prices, in accordance with the higher value of the proposal. On the other hand, the play of prices had to be managed between conventional products of scheduled purchase and those supplementary in the store, such as household and decoration.

Merchandising strategies focused on product price through promotional displays and advertising. Merchandisers had to decide whether to emphasize both conventional and supplementary products and the percentage each would take in the total advertising package. Regardless, price strategy had to be fair, but succeed in increasing average sales to $28–$30. Then the question is, would they be positioned above or below other corporate stores? La Favorita Hypermarket, a well-known company, could be a visible name for the store. And, if they searched for a competitive price image, would these products be placed as seasonal or exclusive, or for impulsive or planned purchase?

The communication strategy was also a factor in the product mix decision between using mass media advertising and in store promotions. One creative idea was to establish a Mega Game in the store, although retailers had to determine the kind and quantity of prizes. Some thought the prizes should range from products and free purchases to dinners to personal computers, to even cars and holiday trips. These prizes would be determined at the point of sale, and so turned communication emphasis more to the sales area than to a mass media campaign to attract an increasing number of clients.

Another key point involved the grand opening. The agency suggested a proposal that did not show the store, but only the motto: "Think on Big Things." The idea was to start with a mysterious concept and later reveal: "Think on Mega." In addition, the agency proposed to create a weekly publication which would inform consumers about new products, promotions, and news free of charge. They called it *New Mega Times.* Would the new market strategy work with clients of the surrounding area or instead attract customers from other districts?

Another issue involved how to balance demand, because during weekends demand for products rose sharply. This high demand created another problem—that of the number of registers. During weekend peaks, the store required a greater number of registers, which would then remain closed during the week. Likewise, home delivery could become a problem if clients came from a distance, adding operative costs.

LAST-MINUTE DECISIONS

Carlos Bernardez and Daniel Casselli met together.

> **DANIEL:** We have to decide not only the product mix but also its location in the store and the

space given to each category: household products, every-day-wear clothes, bookshop, bazaar, house linens. We have a warehouse in front of the supermarket that could be transformed into a store, moving part of promotions or placing the food court there or continuing to use it as a warehouse and make use of more space for the sales area on only one floor.

CARLOS: Speaking of space, how much will be available for parking? The lot in front of the store will have a capacity for 50 cars. If we want to increase the parking we will have to build an underground lot which could hold 300 cars.

DANIEL: The store setup allows several alternatives. One is to trace an internal street in the middle of the block and place the building transversely. In this way, it will look to its own street where the parking will be. Another option is to locate the store in the middle with the parking at both sides, or cover the building front with overhead garages. We could call it 'Vía Pueyrredón,' after its address, to make it easy for people to remember.

We are inventing a new format and we must explain it clearly to our customers for them to adequately make comparisons. Should we call it a superstore or hypermarket, or let people define it? The communication should be clearer, explaining the idea to the po-

tential clients who live in the area. The Rosario people do not like to move from one place to another, so television advertising is pointless.

CARLOS: I believe we could broaden our product mix with greater differentiation through more services: a kiosk, drugstore, perfumery, and candy or linen shops. These businesses should be within the main retail space. If they were outside the supermarket area, then they would be considered small, third-party stores. And, to maintain uniformity, perhaps it would be better to operate them with trained personnel.

DANIEL: A monthly billing of $3 million will place us within an acceptable profitability index. What will the looked purchase frequency be and which factors will we use to achieve it? What will be the role of services? We should try to create loyal clients, because suppliers think that promotions only serve to win merchandising spaces and achieve larger sales of their products.

CARLOS: We should generate a proposal that goes beyond a lineal negotiation, sale of special spaces, and ends— something that integrates their positioning and sales objectives with ours, instead of us requesting funds to support our promotion. In this manner, we would eliminate the promotional war and merge our mutual resources.

DANIEL: Finally, we have to plan the opening. Will there be a reception for suppliers and then we will open to the public or will we invite a large number of people with press media coverage?

CARLOS: We think it would be better to televise the event so the whole city gets to know us. ∎

CHAPTER

6 | COMMUNICATIONS

For a long time in this protected environment, product innovation was not a key issue: It was possible to continue selling the same product month after month. New product development was simply old products with cosmetic changes. In this regard, consumers felt manipulated or cheated. In the renewed competitive setting of Latin America, however, it is no longer possible to maintain weak products. Promotion and advertising now play the role of communicator between the company and the consumers.

The other fundamental change involves economic stability. In the former inflationary environment, it was complicated to measure results, because instability did not allow accurate measurements and certainly led to big mistakes. An incorrect price could be modified and disguised among inflationary movements: A low price could be increased with inflation; a high price could be maintained and allowed to wait for inflation to catch it. A deficient coverage was justified, because the delivery of goods with deferred payment meant a loss by exposure to inflation in that period, and therefore it was allocated in a minimal way.

THE PUBLIC IMAGE

Increased competitiveness encourages companies to find new market niches to help improve their image. The result involves two factors: money surpluses, which have appeared with economic stability, and state downsizing, which provides space to the private-sector companies for their management of culture. Companies realize that by contributing to the country's cultural development, they earn their customers' approval and improve their image as community benefactors. From this standpoint, a cultural investment is more beneficial for the public than an advertising campaign, and therefore the message and the image exert influence more easily than conventional advertising—even though culture and frivolity frequently are confused. Thus, it is sometimes easier to gain support for an important and high-cost megashow than for a fellowship program for students, artists, or scientists, even when the shows have a low residual effect.

The higher appraisal and recognition have increased patronage, although according to Mario O'Donnell, secretary of culture in Argentina: "Our rich people show no pride in visiting works of art. They prefer to be photographed with boats and cars. They do not like to be seen near collections of paintings or inside valuable libraries."

At Telecom de Argentina, the matter is evaluated from two angles. First is the responsibility they assume, to give back to the community part of what they received. The second is related to economic value. In the cultural field, where each company's prestige is at stake, investments in works of art achieve a better return than those in the stock exchange or in government bonds or securities. In addition, Argentine laws allow a 5% income tax discount for investments in cultural events.

THE VALUE OF COMMUNICATIONS

In a stable context, communications results can be measured. Executives must plan advertising and promotion activities with more detail, compare results with investments, and use the various tools to measure success. These concepts and tools were not familiar to the executives in the previous environment.

Advertising can no longer maintain outdated products in the market. Promotions at the point of sale produce immediate effects, but this bombardment of advertising will soon nullify consumer interest and thus weaken a brand's chance for longevity.

THE WAR OF COLAS

Which soft drink tastes better—Coke or Pepsi? This type of questioning cannot appear in the Latin American advertisements of the two large rivals, because comparative advertising is not allowed in many countries of the region. Another technique, which is used in less than 5% of advertisements in the United States, shows common persons tasting both soft drinks (with labels covered) who then declare their preference. This type is allowed in Argentina.

The situation is changing, however. In September 1995, after two years in court, Pepsi won the battle against Coca-Cola de Argentina to be able to advertise its "Pepsi Challenge." Pepsi held that as it had covered the name Coca-Cola in the ads, the campaign would have to be allowed. The verdict of the Argentine Supreme Court was that the injunction of its rival had infringed Pepsi's rights. This ruling follows the legislation recently proposed in the European Union that removes this advertising barrier, allowing the advertiser to mention the name of the rival product so long as the message is not deceptive or does not compare two different products. According to advertisers, these ads work better when they show a measurable advantage that can be expressed in figures.

This is a new chapter in the legend of the colas war. In 1987, Luis Suárez, president of Pepsi Cola Brazil, while addressing distributors of Sao Paulo, wore a combat uniform to relaunch Pepsi in that city, which would be the Normandy of Brazil in its own "D day." Later, Jorge Giganti, president of Coca-Cola, issued a symbolic check used to hire the best football clubs of Brazil, joining the campaign to a new national football championship. Even the president of Brazil, José Sarney, wore the Coca-Cola logo on the back of his suit.

With an annual consumption of 36 liters per person, Brazil is the third-world market of soft drinks, behind United States with 204 liters and Mexico with 92 liters. As Argentine people consume 45 liters, foreign markets become more important for North American multinationals as they are the new battlefields. If Pepsi succeeded in Brazil, it could become its beachhead for the rest of Latin America, where Coca-Cola dominates with the unique exception of Venezuela. Only the Brazilian soft-drink market accounted for $2 billion per year, which explains why it was among the five top markets for Pepsi, with Canada, Switzerland, the United Kingdom, and Japan. For Brazilians who enjoy all the sweet things impregnated with caffeine and who drink cola with meals, however, the generic term is "one Coke," which makes Pepsi's task of market saturation difficult.

For Coca-Cola, except in North Yemen, Kenya, Mauritius Islands, and Puerto Rico—and besides the United States—the war is not a factor because they dominate the market. In Brazil, where Coke entered in 1945, it had 45% of market share, based on 41% of Coke bottled in 76 plants from 30 licensees; Pepsi has 7% and only one distributor. In Chile, Pepsi is distributed by the CCU Corporation.

In 1985, Pepsi began its third attempt to enter Brazil. It had previously tried through Cisneros Group—its Venezuelan bottling plant—and tried again with the French group, Perrier. The result was an important market in the south of Brazil, where consumers thought that Pepsi was a local drink; but in both cases the distribution failed. The third attempt was arranged with Brahma, the largest beer bottling plant of Brazil, which has operated since 1904. This distribution network allowed it to cover more than 90% of retailer stores during the two weeks after launching. From the joint investment of $40 million for the launching in Sao Paulo, $7.5 million was allocated to advertising and marketing, $10 million to trucks, and the balance to packages, shelves, and personnel.

The Pepsi launching primarily encouraged the consumption of colas. Advertising, price discounts of both brands, and the fact that Pepsi's bottles do not require deposit made consumers change to cola drinks. Pepsi introduced the screw cap in the 1-liter bottle in a commercial made by J. Walter Thompson. The ad showed a funny family going through the situations that a screw cap can impose: It is difficult to remove and to keep the bottle shut, and the carbonate escapes. The ad showed that these problems do not occur with Pepsi.

Coca-Cola, which has already used screw caps, criticized Pepsi replying that, likewise, caps let the carbonate escape each time the bottle is open and Coke implied an additional cost for Brahma. Coke also rumored that the caps served as weapons for the guerrilla, and in another market Pepsi had ordered its personnel to go to supermarkets and open as many screw caps of Coke as possible.

Other sales tools were music and sports. A great part of Pepsi advertising produced in the United States included music addressed to "the new generation," with such singers as Tina Turner, Michael Jackson, David Bowie, and the Brazilian Evandro Mesquita. Pepsi targeted young people from 12 to 22 years old, which according to the company accounted for 70% of the cola market. The message was clear: Pepsi is for young people who do not wish to drink Coke—the drink of old persons. The reply was also clear: "Coke in Concert," with stimulating concerts in Rio de Janeiro and Sao Paulo.

In sports, Coke took the lead by contracting the main football clubs for $17.5 million during the "Uniao Cup." The players wore the Coke logo, which were also displayed on stadium panels and on 400 TV ads. Another $15 million were allocated to promotions and advertising, looking to double public exposure to its message and improving its relationship with points of sale through sales promotions and free external light placards. Coke also invested $150 million in new industrial equipment, as a "guarantee" that consumers would prefer Coke, adding that sum to $100 million in 1987 and $150 million of 1988. Its fleet of 400 trucks could distribute 200 million bottles of cola.

In 1987, both companies invested $4 million each in advertising campaigns and, as there were no promotions, a short-term consumption boom produced serious supply problems. The strong price reduction of 1988 set the price at $0.19 per liter, with no deposit for the bottle. Pepsi was gaining market advantage but Coke equalled prices to maintain position.

The resultant market size increase was estimated at 7% per year. Pepsi's share rose to 20% in Rio de Janeiro, 5% in Sao Paulo, and 17% of total market in 1988. Cola price remained low, then, because of the lengthy national peace talks underway.

CASES

6-1 DESORMEX, S.A. (A)

INTRODUCTION

At the end of 1983, Mexico was facing one of the most critical economic situations in its history. Inflation was beyond three digits and there was an obvious impairment in consumers' purchasing capacity. The National Gross Product was forecasted to decrease over 4% and consumer product demand could fall even lower.

In this uncertain environment, Mr. Julián Palma, brand manager for S-U, leading Desormex deodorant, had to submit a marketing strategy plan for the following years to the board of directors. Mr. Palma had only been with the company for a few months, so he decided to review all the information available to be able to design an adequate marketing plan.

BACKGROUND

Desormex, S.A., was a multinational company with extensive experience and reputation in several hygiene and beauty products. Its product lines covered the following categories:

• Shampoo
• Hair conditioner
• Hair dyes and tints
• Hair modeling products
• Makeup
• Deodorants

Desormex had leading products in some of these categories. It had several competitors in all of them, so it needed to carry out ongoing promotion campaigns at self-service and department stores. This effort was aided by continuous sales offerings and heavy advertising support.

The company had high profit margins. All product lines yielded 30% profitability. In deodorants, it had a 25% profit, in spite of the fact that its costs had grown due to the strong devaluations the country had experienced in the last few years. Some of the components, used as raw materials in the manufacturing process, were imported and the company had not been able to replace them with domestic ingredients. Fundamentally, the company was concerned with product quality and it had a very strict control policy regarding manufacture.

MARKET CONDITIONS

The deodorant market reached almost 20 million units in 1983. It had grown steadily for 25 years, but demand was expected to drop 4% in 1983. This contrasted with an annual average growth of 7.8% during the last 4 years. Exhibit 1 shows market evolution since 1981.

The deodorant market was divided in four segments:

• Spray
• Roll-on
• Stick
• Others

Exhibit 2 shows their relative significance and evolution in 1982 and 1983.

The spray segment accounted for more than half the market in terms of units and almost two-thirds in value. This was the most competitive sector and, although the leading brand, Inostral, which had 11% of the market, had positioned itself as a women's deodorant,

Alejandro Ortega, B.A., and Jorge Gutiérrez, M.B.A., prepared this case for the IPADE as the basis for class discussion rather than to illustrate the effective or ineffective handling of an administrative situation.

EXHIBIT 1 Deodorants–Market Evolution

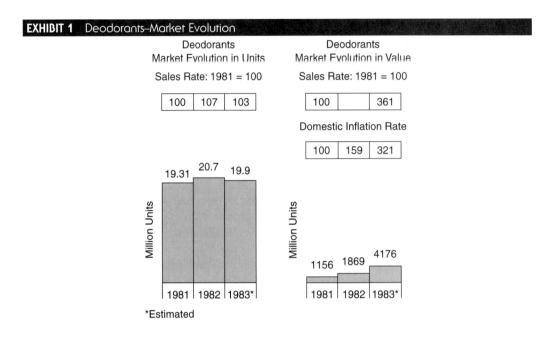

Deodorants
Market Evolution in Units
Sales Rate: 1981 = 100

100	107	103

Deodorants
Market Evolution in Value
Sales Rate: 1981 = 100

100		361

Domestic Inflation Rate

100	159	321

*Estimated

EXHIBIT 2 Deodorants—Market Sales Structure per Segment

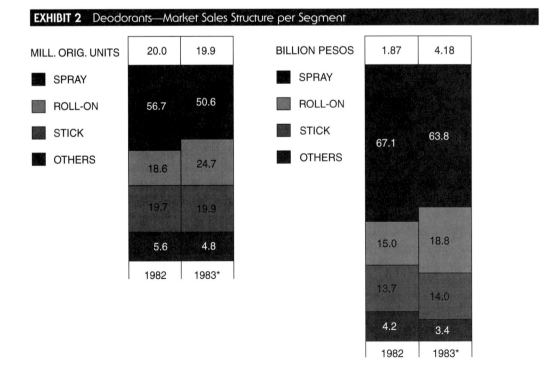

EXHIBIT 3 Spray Deodorant Market Share per Brand

	Million Units		Million Pesos	
	11.7	10.1	1.25	2.67
S-U	2.3	2.1	2.9	2.5
ZAZ	3.6	4.2	3.3	3.6
"32"	5.3	4.2	4.4	3.2
INOSTRAL	10.7	10.2	12.3	11.2
ODOR	2.0	2.4	1.6	1.6
BUENO	2.8	2.6	2.6	2.4
OTHER BRANDS	73.3	74.3	72.9	75.5
	1982	1983*	1982	1983*

the brand group selling family size units held most of the market (Odor, Bueno, Alerta and Guardián). This group was led by "32" (3%), Odor (2%), and Bueno (2%), all produced by other companies (see Exhibit 3). Desormex had competed in this segment with its brand S-U for three years and had a 2.5% share. Like Inostral, S-U targeted the women sector.

In the roll-on segment, the leading brand was ZAZ, which had a 30% market share and was considered the oldest brand, almost synonymous to roll-on brands since it had launched the "magic ball" concept in the 1970s. This segment was considered to be mainly feminine, even though ZAZ was also available for men. Inostral had a product in this market, but it only held an 8% share. Desormex's S-U also competed in this segment and had a 22% share (see Exhibit 4). The average price of a roll-on was 25% lower than the average deodorant and 40% cheaper than a spray.

In the stick segment, ZAZ was absolute leader with a 29.4% share, followed by two lotion brands which sold their scent in a stick deodorant (Exhibit 5). This was a male segment and Desormex did not participate in it. The stick was 30% cheaper than the deodorant average and 45% lower than spray.

Among the others, ZAZ had a deodorant cream and some talcum powders stressing their deodorant effect. Desormex did not compete in this sector, either. This was the segment bearing the lowest price range.

RECENT RESEARCH

Mr. Palma assessed some recent surveys which revealed that there was an average of 1.5 brands per home and that 80% of all households regularly used deodorants. Exhibits 6 and 7 show the consumers' profile for the four most important brands (S-U, ZAZ, Inostral, and Odor), taking into account socioeconomic level and age.

EXHIBIT 4   Deodorants Brand Market Share in Roll-Ons

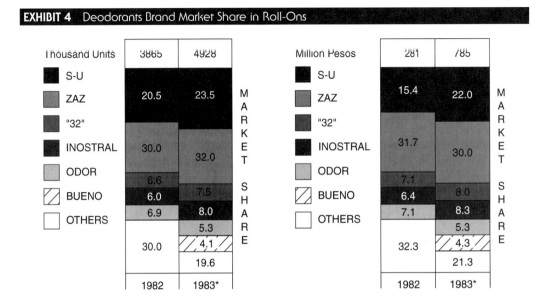

Thousand Units	3865	4928		Million Pesos	281	785	
S-U			M A R K E T S H A R E	S-U			M A R K E T S H A R E
ZAZ	20.5	23.5		ZAZ	15.4	22.0	
"32"				"32"			
INOSTRAL	30.0	32.0		INOSTRAL	31.7	30.0	
ODOR	6.6			ODOR	7.1		
BUENO	6.0	7.5		BUENO	6.4	8.0	
OTHERS	6.9	8.0		OTHERS	7.1	8.3	
		5.3				5.3	
	30.0	4.1			32.3	4.3	
		19.6				21.3	
	1982	1983*			1982	1983*	

EXHIBIT 5   Stick Deodorant

	Million Units				Million Pesos		
	4.1	4.0			256	585	
S-U			S H A R E				S H A R E
ZAZ	38.4	30.3			39.6	29.4	
"32"	3.9	2.3			2.3	1.3	
INOSTRAL	6.8	5.0			7.1	6.0	
ODOR	4.0	4.4			2.5	2.3	
BUENO	2.3	2.1			2.0	1.8	
OTHER BRANDS	44.6	55.9			46.5	59.2	
	1982	1983			1982	1983	

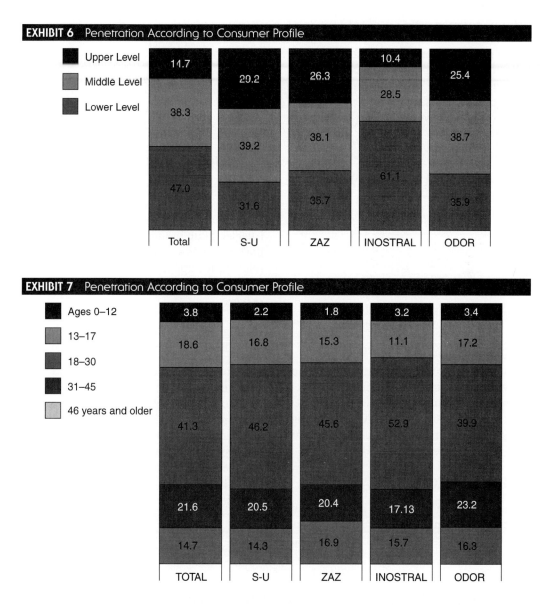

EXHIBIT 6 Penetration According to Consumer Profile

Upper Level
Middle Level
Lower Level

	Total	S-U	ZAZ	INOSTRAL	ODOR
Upper Level	14.7	20.2	26.3	10.4	25.4
Middle Level	38.3	39.2	38.1	28.5	38.7
Lower Level	47.0	31.6	35.7	61.1	35.9

EXHIBIT 7 Penetration According to Consumer Profile

Ages 0–12
13–17
18–30
31–45
46 years and older

	TOTAL	S-U	ZAZ	INOSTRAL	ODOR
Ages 0–12	3.8	2.2	1.8	3.2	3.4
13–17	18.6	16.8	15.3	11.1	17.2
18–30	41.3	46.2	45.6	52.9	39.9
31–45	21.6	20.5	20.4	17.13	23.2
46 years and older	14.7	14.3	16.9	15.7	16.3

Information regarding advertising investment showed that companies devoted at least 10% of their sales to advertising support. More than 90% of advertising was done on television.

Research on deodorant components indicated that all roll-on products contained triclosa, the active ingredient which prevents perspiration. Also, sizes and packaging were similar. However, not all of them contained alcohol. The scent was the differentiating component. S-U was considered to have a modern packaging with good visual impact (size impression), and it was alcohol free.

For spray deodorants, the active ingredient was aluminum hydroxychloride and not all brands contained alcohol. There were two sizes, 80 and 120 grams. S-U was available in the 80 gram size only (alcohol free).

The active element in stick deodorants was triclosan. S-U did not compete in this segment.

RETAIL DISTRIBUTION

These products were distributed directly to self-service and department stores and large drugstore chains. Small pharmacies were supplied by wholesalers.

Exhibit 8 shows deodorant distribution by the end of 1983.

Retail Prices

Retail prices at the end of 1983 were the following (pesos per equivalent unit).

Brand	Spray	Roll-on	Stick
ZAZ	290	160	150
S-U	272	120	–
Inostral	260	110	–
"32"	220	100	–
Odor	200	100	–

PROMOTIONAL ACTIVITIES

All deodorant companies carried out continuous sales campaigns, either engineered by the manufacturer or as discounts granted by the self-service stores. ZAZ had an aggressive demonstrator force constantly promoting sales at self-service stores.

TELEVISION COMMERCIALS

Upon analyzing television advertisement for the main competing brands, Mr. Palma found the following messages for each competitor:

Inostral: "Pretty women perfume" (scent)

ZAZ: "ZAZ stays with you" (protection)

Odor: "Odor does respond" (effective for the family)

"32": "All-day protection"

CONSUMER MOTIVATION

Several group surveys had shown that deodorant consumers primarily wanted protection and safety, which meant they should trust a certain brand. The scent was very important for lower income levels, but not as relevant for upper and middle classes.

ISSUES

Having reviewed all data, Mr. Palma pondered the following questions:

- How should the changes that have occurred in the deodorant market be interpreted?
- Would the relevant decrease in the spray segment be only temporary?
- Should he back the spray or the roll-on products? Should he enter the stick or the other segments?
- What are S-U's strengths and weaknesses as compared with its competitors? What should be the communication approach for television advertising? ■

EXHIBIT 8 Deodorant Sales by Store Type and Brand (percentage of stores distributing them)			
Brand Stores	*% Self-Service Stores*	*% Drugstores*	*% Department Stores*
ZAZ	100	98	85
Inostral	95	95	50
S-U	98	97	15
"32"	85	84	25
Odor	87	92	30

6-2 DESORMEX, S.A. (B)

After reviewing all the information, Mr. Palma made the following decisions:

1. To strongly support the S-U roll-on product, because it aimed at the segment with highest potential since spray was becoming more expensive daily. Also there was increasing environmentalist uproar regarding the ozone layer damage caused by sprays. Besides, the 20% market share in this segment gave it a solid basis to compete against ZAZ, while in the spray niche the product would have to compete against four large brands already settled.

2. Instead of following a low price strategy, he decided a 10% increase over the market leader. At that time it was considered somewhat risky, but the price increase was compensated with a strong change in communication strategy and a campaign including 30 demonstrators at main self-service stores. Desormex products had a very good quality image and this would boost the S-U deodorant.

3. After assessing ZAZ and Inostral advertising, Mr. Palma told the agency ZAZ already highlighted protection and Inostral enhanced its perfume. He believed it was important to sell the concept of protection more subtly, stressing personal satisfaction and self-assurance. Exhibit 1 shows a briefing of messages, support rationales, and

EXHIBIT 1   Desormex, S.A. (B)

Brand	Message	Support Rationale	Target

ZAZ	The deodorant supplies effective protection throughout the day.	• It is nonirritating.
		• It is alcohol free.
		• It has a youthful scent.
		• It lasts all day.
			Socioeconomic:
			  Women, ages 18–40, belonging to B/C segments
			Psychological:
			  Modern, practical women who like sports

Inostral	The deodorant with pretty women's perfume.	• It has an oriental fragrance.
		• It grants more protection.
			Socioeconomic:
			  Women, ages 20–30, belonging to B/C segments
			Psychological:
			  Feminine and confident women who like to be attractive

S-U	The deodorant that makes you look good.	• It makes you feel fresh and sure.
		• It is an antiperspirant.
		• It comes in three scents: dry, floral, and soft.
			Socioeconomic:
			  Women, ages 20–25, upper income level
			Psychological:
			  Sophisticated and independent women who care about their looks

targets addressed by the ads. The advertising agency developed a new concept: "A deodorant that makes you look good."

The outcome of these decisions is depicted on Exhibits 2, 3, and 4. ∎

EXHIBIT 2 Deodorants Market Growth in Units

100	107	103	109	125	141	141

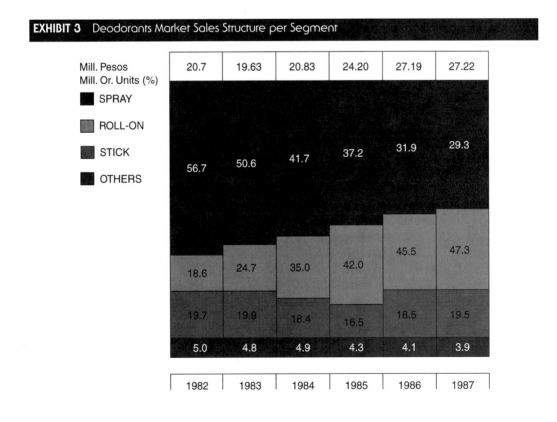

Million Original Units

19.31 · 20.72 · 19.97 · 20.83 · 24.20 · 27.19 · 27.22

1981 1982 1983 1984 1985 1986 1987*

EXHIBIT 3 Deodorants Market Sales Structure per Segment

Mill. Pesos Mill. Or. Units (%)	20.7	19.63	20.83	24.20	27.19	27.22
■ SPRAY	56.7	50.6	41.7	37.2	31.9	29.3
▨ ROLL-ON	18.6	24.7	35.0	42.0	45.5	47.3
▨ STICK	19.7	19.9	18.4	16.5	18.5	19.5
■ OTHERS	5.0	4.8	4.9	4.3	4.1	3.9
	1982	1983	1984	1985	1986	1987

EXHIBIT 4   Deodorants Brand Market Share—Roll-On Total

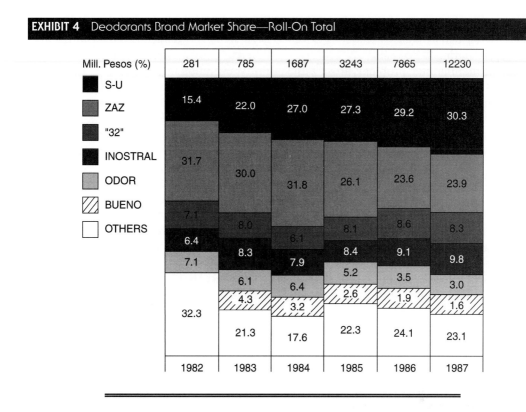

Mill. Pesos (%)	281	785	1687	3243	7865	12230
■ S-U						
■ ZAZ	15.4	22.0	27.0	27.3	29.2	30.3
■ "32"						
■ INOSTRAL	31.7	30.0	31.8	26.1	23.6	23.9
▨ ODOR						
▨ BUENO	7.1	8.0	6.1	8.1	8.6	8.3
□ OTHERS	6.4	8.3	7.9	8.4	9.1	9.8
	7.1	6.1	6.4	5.2	3.5	3.0
		4.3	3.2	2.6	1.9	1.6
	32.3	21.3	17.6	22.3	24.1	23.1
	1982	1983	1984	1985	1986	1987

6-3   PRITTY S.A.

In 1962, Carlos Sánchez and Marcelo Egea, successful businessmen of Córdoba, decided to merge their small family firms into a common project. Carlos Sánchez had reached a leadership position in the siphon soda market and supplied basically to retail grocers and home delivery. Instead, Marcelo Egea had achieved a similar development with his company, but distributed bottled soda to bars and restaurants.

The City of Córdoba—one of the 26 cities in the province—had at that time a population of 586,015 inhabitants, which represented 33.41% of the province.

Egea and Sánchez were well-known and respected persons, both in the city and in surrounding areas, due to their companies' backgrounds.

The new company, Pritty S.A., quickly became leader of the soda market in Córdoba and bordering areas. The fast growth encouraged its partners to enlarge their product line, and in 1964 they signed an agreement with Cunnington reps of Argentina for bottling and distribution of its products: Indian Tonic and Pomelo Neuss (grapefruit). With the marketing of these new soft drinks, the partners confirmed the quick growth that this market

This case was prepared by Research Assistant Andreés Terech under the supervision of Professor Guillermo D'Andrea, as a basis for class discussion rather than to illustrate effective or ineffective handling of a specific situation.

was experiencing was due to strong campaigns performed by industry leaders—Coke and Pepsi—during those years.

Some months later, problems arose with the Cunnington representative, with relation to the syrup delivery necessary to produce soft drinks. This hampered the operation and risked Pritty's image, due to delays in deliveries to retailers. These difficulties made Carlos and Marcelo analyze the possibility of developing their own soft drink line, not only for the purpose of overcoming supply problems but also to improve the contribution of different products to the company's end results.

After months of research, they launched a new product into the market, manufactured with natural juices, called Pritty. Both partners were convinced that the market still had room to grow. They developed a new product line based on the Pritty brand that included orange, lemon, grapefruit, lime-lemon, and double cola flavors. This new brand was introduced in the early 1970s with strong advertising support to the grapefruit flavor. The Córdoba people's reply was positive, as the slogan was, "It is a drink of Córdoba origin."

Due to the success achieved by the company with the launching of Pritty in 1972, the Seven-Up licensee for Argentina proposed to them to take exclusive charge of its operation throughout the province.

The partners and the company personnel became enthusiastic about the idea of bottling and distributing a leading brand and, as they had idle capacity in their bottling line, they decided to accept Seven-Up's proposal.

The relationship with Seven-Up allowed the company to consolidate and improve its performance from the process and distribution aspects, sharing best practices implemented by different licensees worldwide.

Because Seven-Up was a product that "sells itself," it was not necessary to put forth a great sales effort, and therefore, it quickly became the most important product of the company.

As consequence of this success and the need of funds to fulfill equipment and promotion requirements demanded by the licensee, Pritty evolution was neglected. Its market share with Pritty's full line fell to 3.2% in 1983 and produced a yield of –3%, with a product turnover of one case each 23 days.

To distribute merchandised products among the main population centers of the province, Pritty S.A. had 26 sales representatives and 22 third-party trucks. Each sales rep visited approximately 65 points of sale per day, with a periodicity of two to three times a week per point of sale. This aspect of the business which in its best moments attained a 50% coverage of the central market, became affected by the concentration of the supermarket channel and the consequent change in the relative importance that small stores represented for the company. This situation allowed Pritty only a 7% coverage of the central market in 1983.

THE COMPANY

Pritty S.A. was a family-owned company formed by the merger of two family firms involved in soda and mineral water manufacturing, sales, and distribution. The company employed 43 persons who worked at different tasks. Only some of the employees were college educated. Due to this fact and to the broad knowledge of the market that both partners had, important decisions were made with a minimal participation of sales and production people.

One advantage of this new company was its total backwards integration. It owned a natural water spring located about 20 km from Córdoba. This spring helped Pritty achieve market leadership, because soda and "cristal" mineral water quality was a factor appraised by clients at the time of buying. Others key factors for the company's success—which both Sánchez and Egea developed over the years—were its pleasant manner and relationship with the clients and the fulfillment of on-time deliveries. "In this city, where each one knows the other by his name, we can't fail a client, because he is more a friend than a client," observed Carlos in several meetings previous to the merger of both firms.

The results in terms of profitability and market penetration had been very good throughout the company's history, since its beginning in 1962. However, in 1983, Pritty S.A. only attained a sales volume equivalent to 66% of its production capacity, which was estimated at approximately 300,000 boxes per year.

The capital shortage and the absence of credit were at the same time a restriction and a way of performing an appropriate use of funds. In that respect, Marcelo Egea commented: "At the same time we made a good product, the fact of having been careful with the allocation of funds let us go ahead with the company without financial difficulties."

By the early 1980s, differences arose between the partners in regard to long-term strategies. These problems were aggravated by difficulties in company management and control, until 1982 when they decided to separate.

The physical structure of the company did not allow a simple division that let both partners continue in the business. Neither had enough money to buy the other partner's share. Finally, they reached an agreement by which Sánchez—who owned majority capital because he had furnished the water spring and his bottling plant to the company—kept the original business and Egea kept the rights on Seven-Up's license operation.

Facing the new challenge caused by the separation and the experience achieved through his development as soft drink manufacturer, Sánchez intended to study the relaunching of his own brand, Pritty. Notwithstanding the fact that the brand had attained an acceptable success in the past, at the time of their separation it was the product with less relative market share within Pritty S.A.'s product portfolio (Exhibit 1).

EXHIBIT 1 Product Portfolio Breakdown	
Cristal Soda	27.4%
Cristal Mineral Water	24.6%
Seven-Up	35.7%
Pritty	12.3%

In view of this possibility, Sánchez wondered what were his strengths? Was it convenient to relaunch his own brand or concentrate efforts in bottling for third parties? If he chose the first option, how should he carry out the campaign? What should be the product image? Which segment would it target? How would it be differentiated? What were differential product features in order to compete with major companies? Would he use comparative advertising? He knew that the company had no factory culture that let it become leader in costs, and therefore, he had to look for other valid alternatives to compete.

THE SOFT DRINK MARKET

The market of Córdoba province, where Pritty S.A. operates, consisted of a population that increased at an annual rate of 1.825% between 1960 and 1970, and at 1.609% between that last year and 1980 (see Exhibit 2). At the same time, population density increased two points—12.55 in 1970 and 14.56 in 1980—the concentration in urban areas went from 75.10% to 80.73%, respectively. The concentration in main cities of the province was also reflected in the variance of quantity of persons who lived in the capital city: 33.41%, 38.66%, and 41.24% in 1960s, 1970s, and 1980s, respectively.

The growth of the soft drink market had been quite important in the last years. This increase was mainly due to the soft drink boom produced at the end of the 1960s and to intensive advertising campaigns developed by different competitors.

EXHIBIT 2 Typical Population Pyramid of Argentina

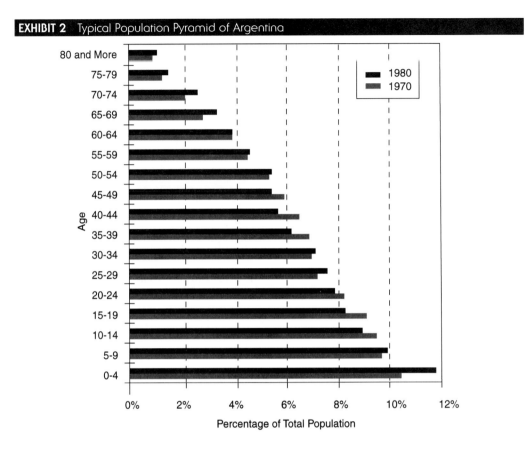

During the 1970s and early 1980s, a change took place in consumption habits as a consequence of the soft drink boom. From being a product consumed almost exclusively at home, it became a drink very demanded by young people in pubs and restaurants and, by the general public, in kiosks. These changes made the average consumption of soft drinks/person rise to 62 liters/year, in the 1980s.

The population of the whole Córdoba province had a rooted local feeling and considered the foreigner as an enemy. "To be from Córdoba" has an important and worthy value at the time of establishing commercial and personal links. Unlike what was happening in other zones of the country, diet drinks had not appeared in Córdoba, because the cultural change had not yet evolved.

When Sánchez kept Pritty S.A., the market had the following purchase intention:

- 90% colas, from which Pepsi only held 2.5%
- 5% lemon
- 5% others (lime-lemon and others)

Consumers looked for satisfying different needs at the time of drinking: colas were oriented to the pleasure of drinking, whereas water and lime-lemon or lemon-based drinks quenched the thirst.

The sales of Pritty S.A. during last years are shown in Exhibit 3.

EXHIBIT 3 Sales Evolution				
Product	*1981*	*1982*	*1983*	*1983 Budget*
Lemon	31.000	48.000	82.000	72.000
Orange	21.000	37.000	42.000	55.500
Grapefruit	13.000	17.000	20.000	25.500
Water with carbonation added	N/A	N/A	36.000	
Water without carbonation added	N/A	N/A	20.000	

The deviations produced in 1983 between estimated and real sales had complicated the supply of the different raw materials and packages as well as the production.

THE COMPETITION

In the 1980s, the company participated in the nonalcoholic drink market as part of the mineral water segment (where it was leader because of the quality of the water coming from the spring) and in the soft drink segment where its competence was a matter that worried partners. Several companies worked hard and invested strong budgets trying to conquer consumers.

There were different kinds of companies competing in the soft drink market in Córdoba:

- Local companies that marketed soda and mineral water, some of which had added other soft drinks to their product lines
- Multinational companies with local coverage that manufactured drinks, with a broad range of products and strong advertising campaigns
- Brewing companies that, although having certain alcoholic content in their products, had begun to participate in the soft drink market
- Other types of new companies with small market share, e.g., juices in large plastic or glass containers

Main companies dealing specifically in the soft drink market, where Pritty products competed, were as follows (also see Exhibit 4):

EXHIBIT 4 Soft Drinks Market Share, Córdoba, 1983	
Company	*Market Share %*
Coca Cola	70
Gini	14
7 UP	5
Pepsi	7
Crush	0.8
Pritty	3.2

Coca Cola

This multinational company occupied a leading position in terms of market share. It based its strategy in a strong advertising support and its product line consisted of Coca-Cola, Fanta (orange), Fanta (grapefruit), and Sprite (lime-lemon). It used a sales rep distribution system of salespeople who worked on a commission basis and who entered daily orders from the many points of sale and transmitted them to the bottler, which was in charge of immediate delivery.

The Coca-Cola bottling plant in Córdoba was owned by the Coca-Cola Company of Atlanta. Therefore, it was a plant that worked according to U.S. standards and received support from its parent company, including financial and technological resources, logistic design, know-how transfer, and experienced personnel for top management positions. Specifically in Córdoba, Coke invested 7% of its budget at the local level for advertising.

Gini

This smaller-size company based its strategy on low price and low quality. It had a very strong lime-lemon product and completed the line with grapefruit and mandarin orange. It held presence in peripheral zones and had recently launched a campaign of "1 1/4 liters at the price of 1." It sold directly, sending trucks to different points of sale that collected a commission of 15%. Its current market share was 14%.

Seven-Up

It was considered the leader in the lime-lemon segment with a market share of 5%. The head company was Embotelladora Mediterránea, whose plant was in Paraná, covering provinces of Córdoba, Mendoza, and Salta. It held a very good distribution and image, and was also considered a "healthy" product. Its sales were high in bars and pubs, which provided a high margin and a good place for promotion.

Crush

A subsidiary of Procter & Gamble, it did not receive much attention from its head company. The three stockholders who managed it were also owners of Gini. Its strategy was based on a single product of orange flavor.

Pepsi

The company that commercialized Pepsi was Embotelladora Mediterránea. It had a poor image as leader imitator in the colas segment, with a market share of 7%. It carried out a strong policy of channel promotion, having a second product of quality and image—a tonic water called *Paso de los Toros*—which served a relatively small market segment. One of Pepsi's main weaknesses in the Córdoba market was the bottler.

With regard to the competence in the mineral water market, there is no true data available about different brands, due to the existence of many small soda and water plants with zonal influence, particularly within Córdoba and generally in the whole province. It is forecasted that the brand commercialized by this company could reach a 40% market share.

THE PRODUCT

In May 1983, Carlos Sánchez and the sales manager of Pritty S.A., Pablo Budón, began to analyze the relaunching of Pritty. They decided to discontinue the Pritty lime-lemon and Pritty double-cola lines because of low acceptance in their markets. They also concluded that unique products of the Pritty line feasible to be commercialized were those of lemon, orange, and grapefruit flavor. Backwards integration and renowned quality of inputs—especially the water—with which different Pritty soft drinks were manufactured, constituted one of the company's main advantages.

Bottle size for the two product lines was one-liter standard, commercialized in six-bottle cases. Intending to improve its distribution logistics and redesign the original product packaging, the company was evaluating different materials for bottles, because glass was very fragile and heavy.

Changes in the product logo and packaging occurred every one to two years, approximately.

ADVERTISING

Soft drink business meant about $1 million per year at the beginning of the 1980s. Of that amount, 10% was invested in advertising at local as well as the regional level. The leader of this market, Coca-Cola, invested $50 million in advertising and promotion campaigns, at national and regional levels.

At the end of 1983, Sánchez contracted with a researcher to study values of Pritty's current and potential consumers. The market analysis carried out under the management of the consultant Leonardo Caden are shown in Exhibits 5, 6, and 7.

Communication media of Córdoba consisted of one morning newspaper and five major TV broadcastings. The latter had only two programs with high ratings in the morning and three during the afternoon time schedule (see Exhibit 8).

Advertising campaigns often involved games, such as with bottle caps, awarding such prizes as TV sets, videos, refrigerators, electronic products, and so forth.

Another method was to advertise using as much space as possible in the gondola's ends (Coca Cola held approximately 80% of this space).

PRICE

The gross margin of Pritty was 80%. Important components for producing Pritty were

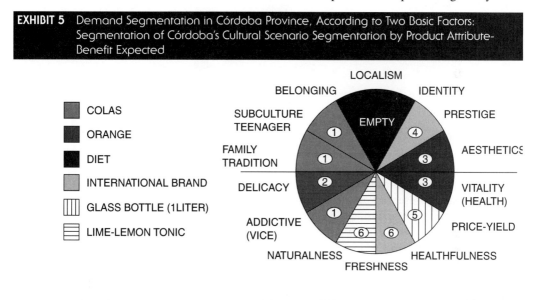

EXHIBIT 5 Demand Segmentation in Córdoba Province, According to Two Basic Factors: Segmentation of Córdoba's Cultural Scenario Segmentation by Product Attribute-Benefit Expected

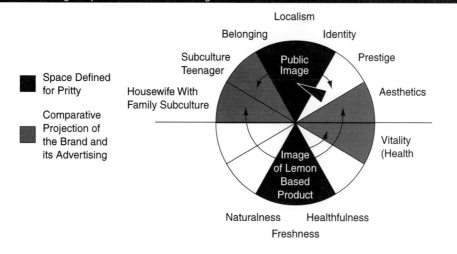

EXHIBIT 6 Strategic Operations of Positioning

EXHIBIT 7 Entailed Quantum Pre-segmentation of Soft Drink Consumer Market During the Last Week

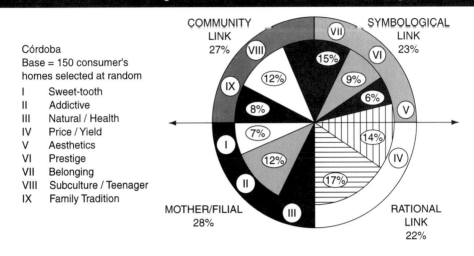

Córdoba
Base = 150 consumer's
homes selected at random

I   Sweet-tooth
II   Addictive
III Natural / Health
IV   Price / Yield
V   Aesthetics
VI   Prestige
VII Belonging
VIII Subculture / Teenager
IX   Family Tradition

THE DECISION

glass (returnable bottle), natural juice concentrate, and the bottling process. To this cost was added to the marketing cost (sales reps, warehouse and distribution) which was significant and represented about 25%.

Product prices were similar to those of the competition. The leading companies held the reference prices. Unlike others, Pritty S.A. had the advantage of not paying a 24% syrup tax, because Pritty was made with natural fruit juice.

Carlos Sánchez had to make an important decision. He believed he understood the advantages and disadvantages of relaunching his own brand, but he preferred to consult with an external specialist. Therefore, he decided to call in Alberto Wilensky and Alberto Bonis, directors of the Grupo Consultor Buenos Aires, who are specialists in marketing issues, and ask them for assistance and consulting to reanalyze the new venture and develop a growth strategy for new markets.

EXHIBIT 8 Mass Communication Schedules of Córdoba

Newspapers *rate per column centimeters*

La Voz del Interior
Monday to Saturday

Without location	135.000
Page 2	143.000
Page 3	181.000
Page 5	169.000

Sundays

Without location	162.000
Page 2	172.000
Page 3	217.000
Page 5	203.000

Diario Córdoba
Monday to Saturday

Without location	65.000
Page 3	85.000
Page 5	85.000
Page 7	85.000

Los Principios
Monday to Saturday

Without location	60.000
Page 3	80.000
Page 5	75.000

Sundays

Without location	72.000
Page 3	96.000
Page 5	90.000

Tiempo de Córdoba
Monday to Saturday

Without location	67.000
Page 3	87.000
Page 5	87.000
Page 7	87.000

Sundays

Without location	71.500
Page 3	97.500
Page 5	97.500
Page 7	97.500

Broadcasting: *7 am to 12 am*

Mitre

Sentence per word	7.800
Space per minute	$1'$: 159.000; $5'$: 152.000; $12'$: 145.000
Choice of program: additional 50%	
Newscast per minute	173.000

Continental

Word	50.000
Jingle per second	75.000

LV 26 Río Tercero

Word	2.300
Jingle per second	3.600

LW 1 Radio Universidad Córdoba

Word	20.000
Jingle per second	30.000
Newscast – 6 to 9 am (per	$5'$: 1.500.000; $15'$: 2.500.000

LV 2 Radio Belgrano (Córdoba.)

Word	5.900
Jingle per second	11.800
Newscast per word	8.850

Magazines *millions of pesos*

Gente y la actualidad

	4 colors	2 colors	1 color
1/2 page (10, 4 × 29)	56,40	43,30	35,30
1 column (5 × 29)		21,70	
1/2 column (5 × 14, 1)		11,60	

Chacra y campo moderno

	4 colors	2 colors	1 color
1/2 page (9 × 25,5)	12,50	9,70	8,30
1 column (6 × 25,5)		7,4	6,20
1/2 column (6 × 12,5		3,60	

El Gráfico

	4 colors	2 colors	1 color
1/2 page (9 × 24,7)	27,20	21,00	18,39
1 column (5,8 × 24,7)		12,50	

Television: *7 pm to 12 pm. $/per second*

	No choice of day	With choice of day
ATC	440.000	528.000
Channel 9	490.840	543.430
Channel 11	355.000	440.000
Channel 13	666.000	756.000
Channel 8 Córdoba	68.000	43.000
Channel 12 Córdoba	105.000	
Channel 13 Río Cuarto	21.000	28.000

7

MANAGING THE MARKETING MIX

The instability of the region's markets is one characteristic that has caused many executives to believe that planning is useless. The market environment will be the principal cause for most failures, and only those who take advantage of the changing scene will be successful. This attitude benefits short-term over long-term goals and makes flexibility an extremely important characteristic. When opportunism is a factor, it shifts the company's mission to that of simply trying to survive, and economic indicators must be carefully followed and analyzed to see which changes will affect the business. The growth and recession cycles are generally strong, making it difficult to follow through with plans. However, monitoring the macroeconomic variances will help to predict consumers problems and, therefore, guide product proposals in that direction.

POWDERED MILK IN PERU

The recession and social crisis in Peru led many investors to pack their bags and leave. However, the opposite is true of the Rodríguez Corporation. This company, in the evaporated milk business, showed excellent growth and became one of the most dynamic groups in the country. The company was willing to bet on the country's economy and yielded very good dividends. The Rodríguez Corporation, the country's main milk producer, added to its basic product—evaporated milk Gloria—ice cream, candy and sweets, milk, pharmaceuticals, and packaging products, reaching sales of $250 million in 1992 with a profit of $12 million.

Vito and Jorge Rodríguez were the sons of a small farmer and transport carrier in the Arequipa region of the country. While Vito was in charge of transports, Jorge was granted a fellowship by the British government to study milk production. From 1971 to 1973, he combined his studies at Leeds and Reading universities with practical work experience in Heinz, Alfa-Laval, and Cadbury.

In the mid-1970s, the company made a significant jump from being simple carriers to becoming important suppliers of cement, iron, steel, and other construction materials, increasing revenues to the $40 million mark in the 1980s. With these earnings they decided to penetrate the production stage, buying the Gloria evaporated milk company, a subsidiary of Nestlé. During this time, the economy was going through a turbulent period and the minority partner, the Berckemeyer family, decided to go out of business in 1986. The Rodríguez brothers gradually bought its 38% share, and when the Alan García government threatened with expropriation, Nestlé decided to follow the Bercke-meyer family and the Rodríguez brothers bought the block of shares.

Since then, expansion has pursued other courses. In 1990 they bought del Pacífico S.A., a subsidiary of Sterling Products and Kodak International, owners of brands such as Panadol and Sal de Frutas Andrew. Their experience in transportation and an initial investment of $1 million turned into sales of $15 million in 1992.

Their next acquisition was D'Onofrio, the ice cream leader in Peru, doubling, in two years, the 1990 sales of $29 million. Finally in 1992 they bought Centro Papelero, a supplier of cardboard packaging, with the idea that when the economy revitalized they would have good packaging for their exports. Their future plans included exporting evaporated milk, buying plants in Bolivia once they become privatized, and entering the stock exchange, possibly out of the country.

Foreseeing competition problems because of the globalization of the market and due to the stable political scenario, at least in the short term, they are currently trying to recover investment and lower the level of risk.

BUSES FROM BRAZIL

Recession hits all industries in the same way—no business can flourish when there is no money. But Camilo Cola has learned how to overcome this unstable environment with his company, Viaçao Itapemirim, the main interstate bus company of Brazil, and second only to Greyhound of the United States worldwide. Covering the entire country, it carries 18 million passengers per year, with a 25% share of the domestic market and a 33% share of the market in the Rio de Janiero–São Paulo section, the corridor with the highest bus traffic flow in the world. For Itapemirim, recession means growth, because people give up more expensive car and air travel and go by bus.

The best year for the company was 1990 which showed incomes of $650 million, but the hyperinflation that followed reduced that amount because, even though Cola has reinvested all his earnings, interest rates of 40% do not allow leasing.

The cost of each of the 2,000 buses in his fleet since 1980 is $125,000 a piece, saving costs by producing them at his own plant in Cachoeira, State of Espíritu Santo. A project with Cummins Engineers is being pursued to develop for Itapemirim their own engine which will replace the ones currently supplied by Mercedes-Benz.

Camilo Cola fought with the Brazilian troops in the Monte Cassino battle of World War II. With his savings from not smoking, drinking, or gambling for eight months, Cola bought his land route in 1947, after his return from Italy. In 1990, after trying unsuccessfully to buy a São Paulo airline (VASP), he decided to create his own company, Itapemirim Transportes Aéreos (ITA), devoted to parcel transport. The first express service in Brazil was established through Cola's ground network, connecting the Amazon and Northeast regions to São Paulo, from where Itapemirim buses and trucks from Transporte Rodoviario de Cargas—another Cola company—distribute deliveries.

Until 1993, air transportation was a protected industry in Brazil. International deliveries by such industry giants as DHL, Federal Express, and TNT could only arrive and depart from Rio de Janeiro, in order to protect the country's national postal service. That fact was used by Itapemirim to deliver shipments with its buses and trucks. Preparing for the deregulation by the government, in 1993 Cola inaugurated a new terminal in São Paulo and started buying aircrafts from bankrupt airlines, such as Pan Am and

Eastern, at a fraction of their normal cost (two Boeing 727s for $75 million), aimed at building a fleet of 10 planes by 1995 to launch his air offense.

The ground network has now begun to establish routes in Argentina, taking advantage of Mercosur growth, as it is still more profitable than ITA's aircraft, which must be subsidized for a few more years.

THE MARKETING PLAN

Planning requires formulating precise economic scenarios, foreseeing changes in the environment and their impact on competitive conditions, and analyzing their effect on consumers and their habits. Only then is it possible to begin to design feasible plans, whose fulfillment will have to be evaluated frequently to introduce corrections that would allow attainment of economic and market share objectives beyond changes in the environment. This evaluation will also permit an understanding of those biases usually introduced during the planning stages.

Developing markets are generally attracted by products coming from advanced countries, giving advantage to the multinational companies. However, local producers have often gone ahead and established market positions, from which even the multinationals with their highly renown products have difficulty removing them. The case of Cazalis-Leger in Argentina illustrates the difficulties Cinzano of Italy had in that market, competing against a very strong local producer, Gancia.

Courage Freres describes a textile company that grows, in spite of several years of economic instability and an Argentine recession. Throughout these bad times, however, company management remained true to their main objective: to serve its customers with specially designed textile products at affordable prices. The company focused on the condition of their customer segment and that of its channels. Recognizing trends that affect business progress, they focused on consumers' needs, the ones who will be buying their textile products. "I know that they will buy less, but of the little they buy, I want it to be my brand," says a company executive, pointing out the clear effort to carry its segment through the bad times.

Business design allows for a collaborative scheme among companies who are looking for ways to solve the problem of lack of capital to finance growth. Production agreements with supplies and franchising agreements with retailers help to speed growth, thus emphasizing their distinct competitiveness (design and sale) and leveraging the manufacturer's ability to produce, in addition to the retailers' interest in having a strong marketing scheme.

The marketing plan then, is a process that includes the following dimensions:

1. Situation analysis
2. Identification of opportunities and threats
3. Definition of objectives
4. Action plan
5. Definition of results and major risks
6. Planning process

1. Situation analysis focuses on external factors that exert influence in the business, analyzing two main groups of performers: consumers and competitors. The different segments of consumers, the trends of each segment, and their purchasing and consumption habits are identified. The description of competitors must be determined according to segments, products offered, its management of the distribution channel, management capability, financial situation, management objectives, and former successes and failures that condition their future actions. Situation analysis must build in the company's marketing framework a deep and permanent careful examination of the environment. Updating the information about the environment becomes a constant attitude and not a function fulfilled in a short period of the year only to meet a requirement.

2. Two analysis—external and internal—are carried out to identify problems and difficulties. External analysis studies those activities of competitors that can imply threats or opportunities. Internal analysis looks to identify organization capabilities, and strengths and weaknesses, but mainly tries to avoid using critical factor plans based on a weakness, which eventually may threaten success.

3. The objectives are defined by grouping them into two categories: primary (those addressed to the market) and secondary (the necessary actions to achieve the first objectives). Both must be defined precisely and with measurable goals in as many cases as possible. This will measure the degree of success achieved and will calibrate each action at the time of development. Objectives are obtainable in this way, and not mere statements without purpose. Primary objectives could include (1) to achieve the distribution of a new product (in the week 27), and (2) to increase brand awareness (from 35% to 60%). Examples of objectives are (1) hire a sales manager (in June), (2) select an advertising agency (in August), and (3) recruit 15 new salespeople (in December).

4. At this time, the action plan can be defined—its priorities, terms, and targets. From step 3, targets will measure the degree of success achieved, analyze deviations experienced, discover reasons for defects, and introduce the necessary changes to attain objectives, mainly those related to profitability, in spite of deviations.

5. The plan must clearly define expected results, such as sales volume and revenues, cost of sold goods and marketing expenses, and gross margin. Other aspects such as market share per segment and penetration of key accounts are also objects of specific definition.

6. Marketing planning is a process rather than a formal proceeding. As such, it integrates different functions, and promotes participation, general consensus, and communication. General consensus is an indispensable tool needed to face the tasks included in the planning stage. The planning must be frequently reviewed. Follow-up and adaptation create a workable marketing plan.

CASES

7-1 CAZALIS LEGER

"Till Monday, Mr. Martínez." The secretary said good-bye and as soon as she shut the door, Antonio Martínez, product manager of CIMBA S.A. (Compañía Internacional de Bebidas y Alimentos S.A., former Francesco Cinzano S.A.) began to review again the last details of a new product launch: Cazalis Leger.

The new appetizer implied a significant challenge for the company. Its future growth depended greatly on those results. The experience came preceded by successive failures with other products and the success of this new attempt was not clear.

This was not the first maneuver intended to face a slow but continuous sales slump, since early 1970.

SOFT DRINKS

It is a worldwide phenomenon. The studies carried out ascribe it to changes in consumption patterns. These changes are not only affecting appetizer market but also that of beverages in general and other foods.

The "light," "diet," "soft" trend—different names given to the change of consumer taste—is creating havoc among several kinds of products. At the same time, it is generating excellent opportunities for those who are adapting themselves to the new attitude of "a healthier lifestyle," taking care of their bodies, figures, and overall health.

The following table shows the evolution of consumer behavior in Argentina.

	1960s %	1970s %	1980s %
Red wines	74	50	26
White wines	17	24	54
Rosé wines	9	26	20

With regard to appetizer specifically, the trend shows a displacement toward consumption of white wines. In Argentina, this is evident in the sales growth of Gancia (Exhibit 1). This monoproduct company had to impose its product through an excellent distribution coverage and a sustained advertising campaign around a basic message: "Gancia, all a style." It appealed to desirable and amusing situations of high social level: "Gancia lifestyle."

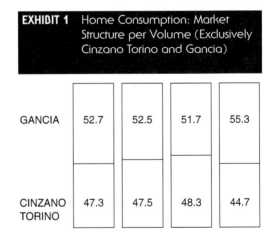

EXHIBIT 1 Home Consumption: Market Structure per Volume (Exclusively Cinzano Torino and Gancia)

GANCIA	52.7	52.5	51.7	55.3
CINZANO TORINO	47.3	47.5	48.3	44.7

VERMOUTH AND APPETIZER MARKET SHARE

Source: Nielsen.

This case has been prepared by Professor Guillermo D'Andrea as a basis for class discussion rather than to illustrate effective or ineffective handling of a specific situation.

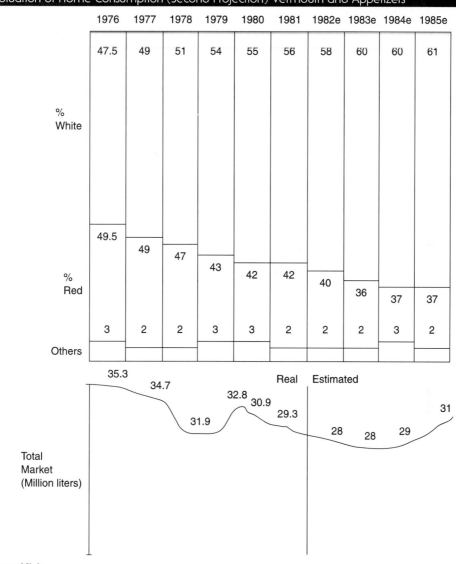

Evoluation of Home Consumption (Second Projection) Vermouth and Appetizers

	1976	1977	1978	1979	1980	1981	1982e	1983e	1984e	1985e
% White	47.5	49	51	54	55	56	58	60	60	61
% Red	49.5	49	47	43	42	42	40	36	37	37
Others	3	2	2	3	3	2	2	2	3	2

Real   Estimated

Total
Market
(Million liters)

35.3   34.7   31.9   32.8 30.9 29.3   28   28   29   31

Source: Nielsen.

COMPANY BACKGROUND

CIMBA, former Francesco Cinzano, produces and commercializes appetizers, leading "red" market with famous Cinzano Torino and Cinzano Rosso, that accounts for 90% of its sales. The company also has a cocktail line: Bitter Cinzano and Cinzano Amaro.

The reaction to an early perceived change of strategy, plus a strong policy of product diversification, led the company to attempt penetration into the "white" market that at the same time increased overall coverage of appetizer and vermouth markets.

However, the attempt was futile. Asti Cinzano, Cinzano Soda, Cinzano Rossé, and Cinzano Oro were successive alternatives tested from which only the last survived. But this, with Amaro and Bitter, only reached 10% of sales.

These facts were in Antonio Martinez's mind with the aggravating circumstance that company's present performance was not satisfactory. In 1982, sales amounted to $41 million and net profit accounted for 0.74% of sales, about 0.38% of its equity.

DISTRIBUTION

CIMBA and SAVA (Gancia) owned small sales organizations in the industry. Both companies serve only directly to wholesalers, supermarkets, and self-services, delegating to wholesalers the retailer coverage. The portfolio of direct clients accounts for 11%, that is, about 5,000. Both leading brands are locally distributed with a geographic coverage of 80% and a weighted coverage of 99%. Sales distribution evolved as follows:

Retailer	*1980* %	*1981* %
Bar, pubs, etc.	23	21
Small stores	48	42
Self-services and supermarkets	29	37

A NEW PRODUCT

Antonio began working on a new project—a good but necessary alternative. In his hands was the launch of Cazalis Leger.

THE FIRST STUDIES

In November 1980, the company carried out an attitudinal segmentation study to determine the composition of appetizer and vermouth markets and existing opportunities.

With relation to its composition, it was concluded that the Argentine overall market was distributed into four segments or consumer families, characterized by a homogeneous behavior or attitude toward a generic product and/or market brands.

The first two segments, which accounted for 50% of consumers, showed inclination toward appetizers (not wine based drinks) and particularly for Gancia.

The features of these segments are as follows:

Segment 1: Extroverted consumers, highly predisposed to buy Gancia, adherence to advertising, predominantly not home-loving, short seniority, and low consumption frequency.

Segment 2: Young consumers and "light users" with greater predisposition to Gancia than Segment 1. They considered the product color a key factor and have a high consumption frequency.

With relation to the two remaining segments, the features of Segment 3 were interesting for the company. It included "red" consumers that appraised the product's attributes—Cinzano Rosso was the most popular. Segment 4 was residual, predisposed to one or the other kind of product, mainly toward Gancia but did not disqualify the "red" (see a detailed report of these studies in Exhibit 2).

General conclusions were especially enriching and worrying:

- Cinzano does not attract new consumers, Gancia does.
- Cinzano decline has occurred over many years.
- Average age of Cinzano consumers is 10 years.
- Gancia penetrates more dynamically in the young segment, based on advertising strategy and consumer preference for the product color.

The study also identified the appetizer consumer profile, taking into account preferences pointed out by respondents with relation to Gancia.

EXHIBIT 2 Attitudinal Segmentation Study

Objective Find root causes of a constant but slight decrease of Cinzano's sales volume, capitalized by Americano Gancia.

Main Conclusions:

Habits	Attributes Valued	Segmentation	
• No difference from previous studies; Cinzano does not attract new consumers, Gancia does.	• Gancia exceeds Cinzano in these factors:	Attitudes of the four segments:	
• This deficit dates from many years ago.	• Activities and opportunities	• Segment 1: Extrovert consumers; advertising; consumption out of home; light user; recently began to consume it.	29%
• Cinzano consumers age is more than 10 years.	• Visual elements		
• Better dynamic penetration of the competitor; achieved with young people; focused in a better advertising communication.	• Mood	• Segment 2: Consumers by product feature: color, heavy users (three times Segment 1 consumers)	21%
• More active consumers; greater consumption out of home.	• Artificial/cocktail	• Segment 3: Cinzano Rosso valued by its attributes	25%
	• Greater possibilities of impact in brand choice	• Segment 4: Predisposition to Gancia without disqualifying Cinzano Rosso; attitudinally similar to Segment 3	25%
	• Product color, basic reason for Gancia preference		

(A & C, November 1980).

This profile characterized a consumer inclined to extracurricular activities (going to pubs, dances, vacations, parks) and informal contacts, who considers appetizer as a stimulant that causes happiness and pleasure or as the drink to relax with after an activity (sports).

In view of the sustainable decrease in sales and profitability, Antonio saw three possible alternatives.

1. Diversify by launching a "white"
2. Give full support to Cinzano Oro

3. Perform a commercial effort tending to reposition "red"

STUDIES OF A NEW PRODUCT

The implementation of either option 2 or 3 did not imply an important change in current activities. Option 1 was a less-known area; therefore, Antonio decided to investigate its possibilities.

He asked the research and development department to create a clear appetizer with

---

EXHIBIT 3

Conclusions of the test
- Tie between LV and 420.
- LV obtained more adhesions than 420 in younger and higher (middle-high and middle-middle) socioeconomic level segments.
- LV has a clear taste and color definition.
- Both alternatives were considered, in identified or unidentified bottles, as lighter, softer, and clearer than Gancia. LV had a slight advantage over 420.
- Alcoholic strength comparison between Gancia and LV/420 obtained the same above mentioned result.
- Packaging aspects were highly valued and were associated with the "light" concept.
- Origin and brand posed neither advantages nor disadvantages.
- LV taste appears as a new option.

Consequently, the scale turned to alternative LV

Product choice
Once conceptual product variances were defined and tested, it was necessary to verify the results through quantitative studies.
In October 1981, a product test was carried out and its objectives were:

- Test the two alternatives slected: LV and 420.
- Evaluate the winner packaging model in the qualitative studies.
- Analyze alternative concepts for a future product positioning.

The variances to be measured were:

- Tastes of LV and 420
- The concepts: light appetizer and low alcoholic strength
- The image: French origin, Cazalis Leger, Cazalis & Prats

Target consumers were defined as:

- Gancia consumers
- Age: 18 to 55 years
- Men and women

For this study 600 interviews were conducted in the Greater Buenos Aires. The interviewed population was divided into four subsamples. Product tests of 420/LV versus Gancia were performed in two particular conditions: a dressed and identified bottle on one side and a blind bottle on the other side (see results in Exhibit 4).

EXHIBIT 4 Comparison of LV and 420 Tastes

LV has a slight advantage in segments of higher potential as shown in the following data.

		LV %	420 %
Preferred to usual product	Blind test	41	50
	Complete test	61	52
	Average	54.3% (163 cases)	(50.6% cases)
Age:			
18 to 25 years		61%	45%
25 to 34 years		56%	57%
35 to 44 years*		43%	50%
45 to 55 years		58%	49%
Men		53%	47%
Women		55%	53%
Socioeconomic level:			
Middle high		51%	35%
Middle middle		54%	53%
Middle low		55%	52%

(*) Segment less disposed to accept a new product (only 45% preferred new products).

less alcohol and sugar in order to compete with Americano Gancia. This new strategy meant Antonio must switch from a "me too" product to one of innovation and with new direction.

More than seven different appetizers were manufactured with specified characteristics. A first evaluation eliminated most of them, leaving alternatives 420 and LV (Exhibits 3 and 4). However, there were many other product elements about which they had to make decisions.

During 1981, several motivational studies were conducted to test the receptiveness of the concept "light" on which the new product was based. *Light* means "without subsequent physical or psychological consequences foreseeable at the time of ingestion; it allows a person to live in pleasant and positive situations and therefore is feasible to be consumed freely, preferably in groups, at social gatherings."

To these studies a product test was added. Both research techniques showed highly positive results about receptiveness. The product concept met market expecta-

tions in several ways. The product was positioned as satisfying a demand (not explained until that moment) of a softer alcoholic appetizer that allowed the following:

- Provided nonconventional consumption, that is, as a "drink" without any other food, like Gancia appetizer. In this sense, it was considered only additionally as a drink.
- Because it was light, it could be consumed without soda or water to dilute it and it could be mixed with other beverages as a cocktail.
- Maintained attractive features of its alcoholic base, but eliminated guilty effects of a strong appetizer.
- Provided a product with a "young" and "dynamic" image based on its "light" attribute. Gancia had previously capitalized on its preference for attaining that image among consumers, although it was achieved exclusively through ad campaigns.

Another element of the product design was defining its origin. At this point, certain obstacles to using this brand were overshadowed by its "innovative" features.

Then, Francesco Cinzano refused to put his name on another "white," because he was still worried by former commercial failures. But the company had never launched a product without his name. They looked for another alternative and decided to create a fictitious brand support: Cazalis Leger from Casa Cazalis & Prats.

The French origin of the manufacturer and the fictitious brand support caused a triple effect in consumers' imaginations. First, it broke the origin "code" of appetizers associated with the "Italian" idea, therefore strengthening the image as an innovative product. Second, the French origin concept implicitly confirmed and supported in the consumers' minds its light characteristic, due to Italian products being assimilated as "thick" and "heavy." Third, the French origin brought prestigious connotations to Argentine consumers' imaginations—appraisal of the product itself (French wine quality) and a mythic halo that associates French with "elegance," "distinction," and "aristocracy." The term *French* was used only in implicit and indirect form (name, manufacturer, label colors), however, letting the consumer unconsciously associate such elements with the product.

The name Cazalis Leger was selected after a market survey. Other alternatives were Fussy and Soleil. Cazalis Leger was a name empty of content. *Cazalis* held a certain French sound, although without exact French phonetics. *Leger* emphasized foreign images and simultaneously referred to an intrinsic product feature: to be light.

Due to these innovative product connotations (product itself, origin, and name), they chose to anchor its institutional support (Cazalis Leger of Casa Cazalis & Prats), intentionally repeating the word *Cazalis* to strengthen its French reference and gain product appeal, similar to Cinzano of Francesco Cinzano and Gancia of Fratelli Gancia (see Exhibit 5).

EXHIBIT 5 Market Share (%)

	1980	1981	1982 Estimated
Cinzano	38	39	39
Gancia	50	45	44
Others	12	16	17

Advertising Investment (in million dollars)

	1980	1981	1982 Estimated
Cinzano	3.9	0.9	0.6
Gancia	4.6	1	0.7
Martini	0.3	0.1	0.1
TOTAL	8.8	2	1.4

PRODUCT TESTS

Product tests emphasized its quality and specifically its light feature, although taster expectations related to lightness were not explored. Antonio Martínez thought at this point that consumers' ideas regarding the product's "light" quality should be measured. Demand could then be based on the results of such a test.

Salable attributes as part of the promotional strategy should include the following:

- Softer than Gancia
- Particular pleasant taste
- Flavor
- Tested clear color

The quality of the tested product associated with brand, origin, and packaging was perceived as higher than those existing in the market. People's concepts of light and soft characteristics were linked to high quality. This point is important because appetizers are considered "artificial" in relation to other alcoholic beverages based on natural products such as wine (e.g., vermouth).

Regarding packaging, the essential decision was to communicate the same innovative and new image articulated with that produced by the other elements (product concept, name, origin). Qualitative as well as quantitative studies demonstrated that if the packaging broke traditional schemes, as they wished (Gancia and Cinzano were packed in 1-liter bottles of ordinary wine), then the differentiation would be easier. The packaging then was articulated with the other elements to outline the product as a clear and sharp innovation. In turn, the surprise component about the packaging awakened in the consumer a product assimilation to an appetizer of higher hierarchy, prestige, and exclusivity, allowing indirectly the reevaluation of the generic product: the appetizer. The risk was that the public did not perceive it as a vermouth substitute but as a different alcoholic drink.

The package label was key to transmitting the innovative product concept. They studied the possibility of introducing a dyed label that called consumer attention both to the label and to the product inside. Viewing the drink through the label would generate an irresistible wish to taste the product. This type of label would be perceived as "rational and technical," and thus contribute to the concept of strength and credibility. The question was, would consumers really perceive it?

Another element of the label balanced innovative connotations. In fact, the French flag colors were used to reaffirm indirectly the product's origin and name, but in turn it reproduced colors used by traditional appetizers Gancia and Cinzano. Would it be differentiated enough?

THE SITUATION IN DECEMBER 1981

With all this work performed, Antonio Martínez thought about several questions still unsolved:

- Is it convenient to launch? In which time?
- Which target segment should I attack?
- Would it be advisable to launch it at the local level or begin with a test market?
- Where would I set the price policy? Below or above Gancia's price?
- How should I act with the distribution channel?
- What are the communication objectives (target, message, style, etc.)?
- What are realistic sales objectives?
- On what terms could we achieve them?

Finally, there were two matters that deserved consideration:

- Could Cazalis Leger recover the company's handicap?
- Could Cazalis Leger face Gancia?

At 10:30 P.M. on Friday, Antonio sat alone in the darkness and silence of his office; the folders that he had reviewed many times were closed and sitting on his desk. He left the office and while walking to his car, realized that he had to organize his ideas during that weekend. ∎

7-2 COURAGE FRERES, SPORTSWEAR

"I want us to discuss a marketing plan of action that will keep us as secure as possible during this recession." With these words, Juan Valiente, president of Courage Freres, addressed the four-person meeting of the board of directors in his office. They were Francisco Mendez, production manager; Guillermo Klipsa, administration manager; Roberto Escudero, sales manager; and Andrés Valiente, brother of Juan and in charge of exports (Exhibit 1).

This case has been prepared by Professor Guillermo D'Andrea, as a basis for class discussion rather than to illustrate effective or ineffective handling of a specific situation.

EXHIBIT 1 Organization Chart of Courage Freres

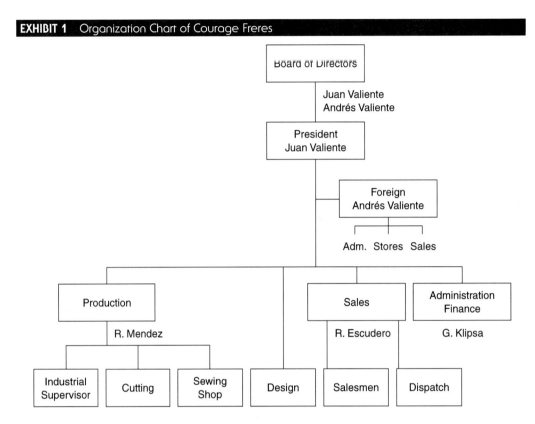

ANDRÉS: I wonder if we are not in the middle of a recession that seems longer than previous ones. This time it will not be two or three months like that of last year; 1990 appears to be a recessive year as a whole and the low activity level will possibly continue during 1991. I think the crisis of the country is terminal and until those measures considered essential by the government, such as privatization and public expenditure decrease, are implemented and show concrete results, it will not be possible to get out of this. Meanwhile, any recovery will have a limited length, like that of spring 1989, when activity grew during three months, falling again in summer to 25% from the previous season.

ROBERTO: However, I believe we should have to think about performing some promotional activities in order to stress the brand image or, I am afraid, we will have problems placing the winter collection.

JUAN: Is it a time to make promotions and spend money we do not know we will get back? Is it possible to encourage a completely depressed demand? Our policy never has been to make heavy investments in users' advertising. Are we going to do them now? Don't you see another way for supporting sales?

ROBERTO: I think they will buy from someone, and in such a case, I want them to buy from me and not the competition. On the other hand, we have never been in a first-line position like now. I wonder how long we can keep this position in the consumer's mind without strengthening it with advertising. Last winter we had a pre-sale as early as mid-summer, where retailers paid in advance and in cash for a collection we had not even shown them; but this winter was not very cold and, besides, hyper-inflation lasted all season. It is already known that this summer's sales were weak and the government froze term bank deposits, so retailers are decapitalized. How do I secure winter sales but encourage the market with advertising, strengthening in this way the channel trust? We are one month from summer's end and sales are very weak.

GUILLERMO: At the same time, we are in the middle of the export operation launch. We began exporting to Chile and Uruguay, neighboring countries with similar demand features to ours. In these markets we learned the procedure, but its size is not large enough to justify the positioning effort. For us, they are marginal volumes. Looking for a more significant and longer-term development, we began to penetrate the Italian market in 1989 and now we are in the middle of that venture, with an investment of about $450,000. The main part has already been set up: three business premises—two in Rome and one in San Remo—and a sales network that is starting operations. There we are not leaders as we are here, and we had two options: to compete with Korean products at a lower price or build the brand image and achieve a margin double that here. We chose the latter, but until that becomes a significant volume it will be necessary to wait three or four years, at annual expenses of $300,000 within the present structure and with plans of opening new premises . . . ! And here, the budget adjusted up to date is 30% of that forecasted in the five-year plan!

FRANCISCO: We have to search for an option of that kind. Industrialists depend on our ability to place volumes, and all they have decided to support is an ever-increasing volume, as occurred during the last five years. There are not only expectations but also important investments performed in that sense. That's why we cannot move back. In turn, we depend on them to grow, as they provide part of the working capital. And local market today does not accept these increasing volumes. But in normal periods, we would not be able to grow much more without saturating the market, with the risk of burning the brand.

MARKET TRENDS

To what extent do we have to continue supporting the brand? Do brands have a cycle like products? We seem to be entering into a new trend that goes farther than usual fashion changes from one year to the other. During the last 10 years, sports were in fashion, but this also seems to be changing. The last four years attitudes reflecting the "revival" fashion are increasingly in vogue. It was led by Ralph Lauren; Sisley tried to globalize it; and Chevignon created this fashion in our market. In 1988, young people dressed like 1940s pilots, then the "college" style of 1950, and now it reflects the 1960s. The trends of playing weekend sports and dressing like a sports player may be diminishing. People are, however, conscious of the benefits of exercise and will still want clothing to suit that lifestyle.

JUAN: Will it be possible to change this brand concept in the market, or will it be necessary to create a new one for this new less-active attitude, with more colors, cuts, textures, and codes? Is a different proposal credible under the same brand, Courage Freres?

ANDRÉS: The brand of New Man has made it! It has lowered its color tone, changed wornout denim to twill, emphasized corduroy fabric and wool, hid the jacket and showed a coat of modern cut, adding accessories . . . But it is not easy to sustain a brand in this market. If international companies such as Ellesse and Rossignol have dropped to a second level, could we think that we will maintain for many years? And that without mentioning those of local origin: Mac Alpine, White, Snoopy. Who remembers them nowadays? Argentine public is very fond of brands and this is a point we must not forget.

COMPANY BACKGROUND

Everybody knew the company's origin, but Andrés deemed it necessary to remind them. "When we began in 1975, we only had one assembly workshop and the ability learned from our father for manufacturing jackets. Until that moment, he manufactured raincoats and jackets for main stores of Buenos Aires. We decided to be specialists in jackets and use our own brand. We made 300 jackets for children and we did not sell one: sleeves were very short. The next year went well, the product was liked and sold satisfactorily. We contacted six independent salespeople in the provinces, the same as we still have today. Soon, the quality of our assembly stood out and, during winter or in ski places, users began to notice. Until recently, people came to the factory asking for "a model equal to this one that gave me such good results." Of course, at that time distribution was rather restricted, with 600 clients disseminated nationwide. The penetration was slow, as salespeople had their own rhythm, although Juan was enthusiastic about selling. Even when we managed the assembly, we found it difficult to create a new and dynamic fashion line for every season, but little by little we achieved it."

"In 1983, we decided to initiate our entry into Buenos Aires, although originally we were from there. It was the most attractive market, but also the most competitive. We had seen the rise and fall of so many brands with excellent proposals and many others that did not even reach light. That year, we began to elaborate alternative plans of growth. The Capital City implied an extra risk: uncertainty about the volume to be produced. In the provinces, clients planned purchases more often, because they don't have the possibility of buying during the season, like people from Buenos Aires. Here, they only plan purchases of important brands and the rest is padding; they buy either one or the other on a break at midday. By paying cash, they may complete any lack of product."

DIRECT COMPETENCE

In 1983, Ellesse was clearly leading the market. Its proposal had full international taste.

Associated with the image of Guillermo Vilas, its tennis line was unbeatable. It also had a ski line and a very well orchestrated and active promotion. Product exposure in ski centers, shop windows, point-of-sale posters, and some exclusive stores built a coherent image. However, only two years later Ellesse was sold to a textile corporate group that assumed a substantial debt accumulated during the last years. These quality people were production oriented but intimidated by the dangerous experience of their predecessors, devoted to doing what they knew: selling quality garments. Therefore, the active commercial presence began to disappear.

Then Dufour advanced, as Ellesse's immediate follower. The development of its line was local, based on the brand of windsurf boards. It also had a broad-range line of jackets, tennis and beach clothes, and specifically ski clothes. Later, they added less sporty casual clothes such as jeans, shirts, sweaters, and nautical moccasins. The Ellesse promotion team moved to Dufour and its promotions caused envy in the sector: Moscow, Transylvania, and Africa were scenarios for its line and it was impossible not to see its presence in ski centers and summer resorts. Company President Patrick Gilbert, a young man with suitable economic backing, knew how to generate a collection with a mix of good taste and innovation—without being explosive—that had much success among middle-high-class young people. Its communications were consistent with this proposal: very well done and without skimping either production or media resources. In a few years, their distribution became massive and then they generated a chain of stores. Many were located in places without active sales and thus did not work well; they also lacked attractiveness. Perhaps that was its first sign of decline. A year ago, Patrick was forced to sell part of the company affected by a high indebtedness and so left the management. Today, Dufour faces a second opportunity in the hands of a new director.

BRAND EVOLUTION

The image of Courage Freres in 1983, even though weak, was associated with skiing. "Then, we only manufactured jackets, especially ski ones. We overcame seasonality by making soft summer jackets for the brand Yves Saint-Laurent and collected a royalty per sold jacket. In summer 1984, we decided to begin working with our own brand, trying to change activity seasonality. We developed a line of shirts, bathing suits, and summer two-piece suits to be sold on the Atlantic Coast. We were not very convinced, because this was not our kind of product—it was very light. But a year later, we left behind the seasonality and began our collection that then continued growing" (Exhibit 2).

Those were difficult years because there was strong competition, with significant investments in advertising and material for the point of sale. Several brands were entering the market, some with great force and important advertising support, such as Benetton with a one-color page ad in the Sunday supplement of the first-class newspaper, *La Nación*, for two months. Others only consolidated their images, such as Legacy and Davor, through chains of their own shops, with little advertising effort. This restrained Courage Freres's progress, which still did not consolidate its image. It was subjected to the pressure of having to generate a completely renewed collection to pass the best again each season, which reduced strength for improving brand prices. The distribution in Buenos Aires was limited, because it was not easy to find place in the window shops for an unknown brand, and the problem became aggravated by the lack of investments in advertising. Retailers pretended to determine their conditions, especially those more interested in its shop's location that could give prestige to the brand they exhibited. Usually, these ones were less professional and more informal with relation to the fulfillment of its commitments.

"In 1984, when I just joined Courage Freres, we began to make promotions. How difficult it was to make them approve the budgets," remembers Roberto. "We had to adapt to the austere style of the company, but after two years, brand awareness was very extended. With a few things, they have achieved surprising results: to redesign the iso-logo, turning it more artistic and colorful, changing the reference "windsurf and ski" to another more generic: "It's not a look, it's an attitude." The motto was repeated on club posters and points of sale. It was present in squash, table tennis, and ski center tournaments; worn by instructors; and seen at summer beaches on flags, chairs and sunshades, windsurf sails, and sandals. The unique media action was a newscast in

EXHIBIT 2 Courage Freres Evolution of the Product Line, 1983–1990								
Item	*1983*	*1984*	*1985*	*1986*	*1987*	*1988*	*1989*	*1990*
Jackets	10,000	12,000	14,000	16,000	18,000	20,000	20,000	15,000
Shorts	2,000	5,000	9,000	15,000	18,000	20,000	25,000	30,000
Sandals		3,000	12,000	25,000	35,000	50,000	70,000	100,000
Slippers				5,000	15,000	8,000	10,000	20,000
T-shirts		3,000	12,000	25,000	40,000	55,000	70,000	110,000
Bags		500	1,000	1,500	2,000	2,000	3,000	5,000
Sweatsuits			5,000	12,000	30,000	50,000	75,000	100,000
Tennis suits				3,000	3,000	3,000	5,000	
Sweaters					2,000	9,000	15,000	30,000

a state-owned FM radio station from the ski trails in winter, during two seasons; and two ads in the fashion section of major newspapers. During the first year (1985) they spent $25,000—one dollar at a time. Nobody wanted to exceed the budget and the lack of experience made each step more prudent. The next year, with more self-confidence, they got excited and spent $70,000. Since then, they have maintained a good point-of-sale image. Posters, instead of drawings, turned out to be reproductions of excellent photos of garments made by a professional photographer, in such distant places as Australia. "The environment and models were just what we wanted to communicate with our clothes: youth, international level, funny. Canopies in the stores, elements for shop windows as hangers designed with our iso as head, shop window backgrounds, and curtains for fitting rooms were the tools for supporting the channel." Exhibit 3 shows regular promotion expenses of a typical year.

EXHIBIT 3	Promotion Expenses (in thousand dollars)
SUMMER 1987	
• Wind-surf championship	8,000
• Squash championship	3,000
• Posters, Development and Print	13,000
• Shopwindow background	2,000
• Stickers	2,000
• Sandals as a present	2,000
	30,000
WINTER 1988	
• Clothes hanger	25,000
• Posters	25,000
• Stickers	15,000
• Flags	3,000
• Curtain background	2,000
• Fashion Show	12,000
• Canopies	18,000
	100,000

Roberto's report, as of December 1987, described the following results:

- A sustainable growth of sales. The brand was well known, without systematic evaluation of its penetration. The product, its image, and its price were part of a coherent and tempting proposal.
- Distribution in Buenos Aires—Capital City and Greater Buenos Aires area (although there still was a deficient exhibition with regard to shop windows). New client policy had been selective, generating more than one resistance in the sales area, accustomed to a less strict policy. Up to that moment, clients were selected by solvency, which already meant rather strict exigencies. But criteria such as image, client collaboration, and display in shop windows were not easy to impose.
- A current and growing fashion collection. Enlarged each year, the collection achieved a wide line of quality clothes. Due to materials and assembly, design was always modern and pricey but not the highest in the market. To winter and summer jackets, besides those traditional for ski, they added sweaters and sweatsuits, shirts and polos, tennis and jogging two-piece suits, bathing suits for men and women, bags, slippers and sandals for the beach, socks, and accessories.
- New key products. Each collection introduced several "star" products that supported the rest. The sandal was a clear example. One innovative model, which was thick and had the foot sole printed on its surface and in bold colors, became an immediate success, being sold two times more than the most expensive sandal.

POSITIONING

The art of determining product positioning led to many discussions. Could an unknown brand without international backing compete with the largest brands of the market,

EXHIBIT 4 Income Statement Evolution (in thousand dollars)

	1983	1984	1985 winter	85/86 summer	1986 winter	86/87 summer
Incomes						
Own Sales	1000	1500	1500	300	1500	400
Sales through third parties				200		600
Royalties						
Export						
Cost of goods sold	450	700	700	100	750	140
Labor force	150	150	150	50	180	60
Marketing expenses						
Commissions	60	90	90	30	90	60
Representation	15	20	40	30	50	70
Advertising			25		70	30
Administrative expenses	60	100	190	100	190	190
Wages	180	260	130	130	150	150
Total Expenses	915	1320	1350	440	1480	700
Gross Margin	85	180	150	60	20	300
Investments						
Movable estate			30		50	
Real estate						

facing consumers who have strong tendencies toward brands? Regardless, who is the competition? On the sports side, brands such as Ellesse and Sergio Tacchini were supported by well-known sportstars worldwide. The largest shoe manufacturers— Adidas and New Balance, Topper which then incorporated Nike, Le Coq Sportif, Puma, Pony, and others—included all segments. All of them saturated their market niche. Some, like Topper and Adidas, led it clearly. On the other side were casual clothes. In this sector, New Man, Lacoste, Benetton, and Cacharel had consistent positions. "Who do we have to displace?" was the first question. The answer: anybody entirely. Courage Freres is a type of leisure garment. From todays casualwear to sportswear, the look is modern and updated, of quality, and with international designs adapted to the Argentine look—young, dynamic, and fun-loving people. The target clients were defined as young persons of both sex, between 17 and 28 years old, middle and middle-high class, active, who practice selective sports and enjoy leisure time. Clients follow fashion, take care of their images, and express and identify themselves through their clothes. After Ellesse slid to second place, only Dufour and Davor competed strongly in this segment. Dufour showed a more classic proposal and included more denim in its garments. Davor donned an active and colorful collection, sometimes getting ahead of local trends.

THE SCHEME OF COURAGE FRERES

Parallel to these developments, industrialists outlined a marketing scheme with others that would determine the current system.

1987 winter	87/88 summer	1988 winter	88/89 summer	1989 winter	89/90 summer	1990 winter e.	90/91 summer e.
1300	400	1300	600	1300	400	1000	400
300	700	500	900	600	600	800	900
	70	50	135	100	100	120	150
				200	100		300
600	150	650	200	650	150	500	
180	70	150	80	150	80	130	
96	66	408	42	63	33	54	
50	90	100	90	100	100	100	
100	50	100	80	100	100	50	
230	230	300	300	350	400	400	
200	200	250	250	300	350	350	
1456	856	1658	1042	1713	1213	1534	
154	314	202	593	537	−13	386	
50		40	40				
		150	250	150	100		

The sustainable growth was strong, not only in sales volume or quantity of garments, but also in its diversity in order to be able to create a real line. This obliged them to contact industrialists of different specialities. But financial requirements grew at the rhythm of new product incorporations. The solution was to offer industrialists certain associations that secured for them the sale of that part of their production they wanted, under the brand and design of Courage Freres, through a distribution system. The scheme was gradually incorporated in such a way that, in 1990, only jackets were of their own production. Courage Freres collaborated in the production planning and made the final quality control in its warehouse, before preparing deliveries to retailers, collected and sent periodically to the industrialists. For all these services, Courage Freres received a commission of 20%.

On the other side of the business channel, the appearance of Benetton brought to Buenos Aires the first coherent proposal of the new kind of retailing: higher quality at the time of purchasing, through its modern design stores and client attention. This accelerated the decision, postponed for a long time, of initiating a chain of exclusive stores. In 1987 the first store on Cabildo Avenue was opened, Belgrano City, with an intense traffic of young people, a middle-high-class zone that had grown considerably in the last 20 years, including plenty of luxury buildings. The person hired for the project was completely new to the organization. He was in charge of hiring the design, searching for a store site, selecting and training personnel, and setting its policies and administration systems. After one year, four additional stores were opened, plus six in different resort cities on the Atlantic Coast. In 1990, there were 20 stores in Buenos Aires and requests to open others in several Argentine cities. All stores received from Courages Freres a store's design, consulting to select its location when it was necessary, training for personnel, weekly service for the shop window, and assured restocking of products so that shortages were minimum. In return, Courage Freres collected a commission of 15% on sales.

THE SITUATION IN JANUARY 1990

JUAN: Last winter, garments from all collections were left over, so our benefits remained on the shelves. What quantity do we plan for this year? And especially, how can we be sure that salespeople place the collection following the curve and that they do not limit sales to clients? You must pay them more than two visits a season and you also must collaborate with them on the collection.

ROBERTO: I will have to think about this situation. The deal with the two salesmen from Buenos Aires is different from that with the eight salesmen in the provinces. They are independent, and collect only a commission that was reduced from 6% to 3% two years ago. That wasn't easy and now we ask them for additional effort. They will respond, "When potatoes burn, we appeal to them." I think there are other options besides supporting the brand. One is to lower prices so as to not lose sales. Will it be prejudicial for the positioning?

Anyway, taking into account the strong trend to change the fashion, we could begin just now to generate a new brand with a different proposal. I'm not sure that investment in promotion produces a yield that justifies it. And in any case, what would our target be? Intensive consumer advertising or support at the point of sale? Every day someone calls me to propose sponsorship for a tournament, a fashion show, or a party in a high school, and I don't know if I have to take it or reject it! Besides, media today offer facilities and discounts unthinkable one year ago! Imagine being on TV but paying through exchange! And they are salesmen too: Do I press them to push full collection sale? or Do I respect their relationship with clients? At the same time, we could extend our distribution with new clients through a broader coverage and by including more massive segments. Another alternative would be to limit the collection— with simpler models we would be able to make savings in production or mix with cheaper materials. I think with the image we already have, we could bear it without problems.

JUAN: That is just what supports us: the image of quality. To touch it now could be death. If we abandon it now, will we keep consumer's loyalty?

Juan turned toward the window, trying to be out of the discussion and concentrating on his own analysis. Again an alternative laid open the discussion of the company's strategy, with all the effort of the group he had seen sacrificing during the last five years to place it where it is now. Then, last season resulted in losses for the first time in 10 years, while in the middle of a growth stage. Would it be also necessary to review the expansion plans stated in the strategy? Juan turned his eyes and looked over his modern and comfortable office, although without luxury, and remembered the discussions with his brother about the investment made to expand and remodel the offices and factory warehouses. ■

7-3   GALLO RICE

In March 1992, Sig. Cesare Preve, managing director of F&P Gruppo, marketer of the Gallo brand of rice, was reviewing his company's current market position. Specifically, he was evaluating how to penetrate further the retail rice markets in three countries: Italy, where the Gallo brand had been present for over a century and held a 21% volume share; Argentina, where Gallo had been established in 1905 and held a 17.5% volume share; and Poland, where Gallo had been distributed in small quantities for three years and held less than a 1% volume share.

Sig. Preve wondered what experience, information, and insights gained in one market could be transferred to other markets and where to focus management time and effort. Should the company attempt to consolidate its position in large, mature, slow-growth markets, or should the newer high-growth potential markets receive a higher proportion of managerial time and marketing effort in the future? To assess the marketing requirements of each country and the potential sharing of experience across markets, Sig. Preve compiled a summary of the comparative country data (see Table A).

COMPANY BACKGROUND

Focused on the production of value-added rice, F&P Gruppo described itself as "the rice specialist" and was one of only a few companies in the world involved in the entire process, from growing and milling to the packaging and marketing of branded rice. The company added value through research and development of new and improved strains of high-quality rice, proprietary manufacturing processes, and packaging. Gallo had resisted the temptation to manufacture or market any food products other than rice. The goal of the company was to achieve market share leadership through bringing differentiated, higher-margin products to an

Research Associate Nathalie Laidler prepared this case under the supervision of John Quelch as the basis for class discussion rather than to illustrate either effective or ineffective handling of an administrative situation.

TABLE A Market Characteristics of Italy, Argentina, and Poland (1990)			
	Italy	*Argentina*	*Poland*
Population (millions)	57.7	32.3	38.4
Age distribution: 0–14, 15–59, 60+	18%, 63%, 19%	30%, 57%, 13%	26%, 60%, 14%
Percentage urban population	67%	85%	60%
Annual population growth	0.1%	1.0%	0.4%
GNP per capita (US$)	15,652	2,134	2,500
Per capita expenditures on food (US$)	2,170	465	256
GDP breakdown: agricultural, industrial, services	4%, 33%, 63%	13%, 41%, 45%	14%, 36%, 50%
Inflation rate	6.5%	17%[a]	600%
Cereal imports (tons)	6,699	4	1,550
Rice is a major crop	Yes	Yes	No
Television set penetration	1 per 3.9 persons	1 per 4 persons	1 per 3.9 persons
Radio penetration	1 per 3.9 persons	1 per person	1 per 3.6 persons
Literacy rate	98%	92%	98%
Advertising expenditures per capita (US$)	116	13	N/A
Advertising expenditures: percentage breakdown by medium	Print = 59% TV = 35% Radio = 2.5% Cinema = 0.2% Outdoor = 3.3%	Print = 45% TV = 31.3% Radio = 8.8% Cinema = 0.8% Outdoor = 14.1%	N/A
Number of consumers per retail food outlet	182	1,318	724
Distribution concentration: percentage of retail sales through supermarkets	56%	36%	15%

[a]Argentina inflation rate estimated for first quarter 1992, down from 3,000% in 1989.

increasingly segmented marketplace. A higher percentage of the resulting profits were, in turn, reinvested in research and development. It was a company objective to ensure that 35% to 40% of total gross margin was derived from products that were not in the product line five years before.

F&P Gruppo was a private, family-owned company dating back five generations. It owned production facilities in Italy, Germany, Argentina, and Uruguay and sold throughout Europe and South America. The group comprised wholly owned subsidiaries in the above four countries as well as Switzerland and Brazil, plus a joint venture in the United Kingdom.

The Gallo brand name and Gallo rooster logo were used consistently across geographic markets and product lines ("Gallo" meant rooster in both Spanish and Italian). In 1991, Gallo marketed white rice, parboiled (partly boiled) rice, and brown rice. The company had also recently introduced dehydrated, quick-cooking rice and dehydrated mixes in many of its more developed markets. These branded, top-of-the-line products delivered to the company as much as 50 times the profit margin achievable through the sale of the same quantity of bulk white rice.

THE RICE INDUSTRY

In 1991, world production of rice was around 500 million metric tons, and consumption, which varied significantly by geographic area, was around 350 million metric tons on a milled basis. Only 12 million tons were traded internationally.

There were two main strains of rice: Indica grains, long and thin, fluffy when cooked, and more popular in northern Europe; and Japonica grains, shorter and more absorbent, creamier when cooked, and more popular in southern Europe. In recent years, Spain and Italy had increased their production of Indica rice; as a result, imports of rice into Europe had decreased.

Rice reached the consumer in many forms:

- Paddy rice was the raw material harvested from the field, with only primary cleaning and drying.
- Cargo rice resulted from an initial milling process, whereby the hulls (accounting for 20% of the raw rice weight) were removed.
- White rice was the product of the final milling process and could be refined to varying degrees.
- Brown rice was similarly milled but the bran layer was retained on the kernel during the milling process.
- Parboiled rice was a response to the consumer's desire for more convenience. Its production involved a special milling process, whereby paddy rice was soaked in hot water, cooked with steam pressure and then dried. During this process, the starch was gelatinized such

that the vitamins migrated into the interior of the grain. This made the rice grains harder and almost impossible to overcook, resulting in a nonsticking final product. There were 40 steps in Gallo's parboiled rice production process.

- Precooked or quick-cooking rice was an increasingly popular niche product, processed by a freeze-thaw method. Regular milled rice was soaked in water to increase moisture content, boiled, cooled quickly with cold water, then allowed to freeze and thaw slowly. The end result was a rice kernel that absorbed water more readily, thereby reducing the necessary cooking time.

Exhibit 1 shows the breakdown of rice consumption by end use and type in both the United States and Italy. Domestic consumption, calculated from domestic production plus imports minus exports, included three primary use categories: processed food production (e.g., for breakfast cereals); beer production; and direct food use. Of direct food use volume, most was eaten at home after purchase through food retailers. It was in this channel that branding of rice played an important role. Most retail rice sales were of basic milled white rice, with parboiled white rice being the second most important sub-category.

Gallo-milled rice consistently earned the highest of six quality grades. In 1991, Gallo handled 200,000 tons of milled rice worldwide, valued at six times the average world crop price of cargo rice. In the 1980s, many other companies tried to enter the market for value-added, branded rice products. Although this caused some price pressure, price-insensitive consumer segments were identified for certain higher value products such as brown rice and dehydrated risotto mixes (rice mixed with dehydrated ingredients such as peppers, mushroom, chicken, and spices).

EXHIBIT 1 Distribution of Milled Rice Volume in the U.S.A. and Italy, 1992

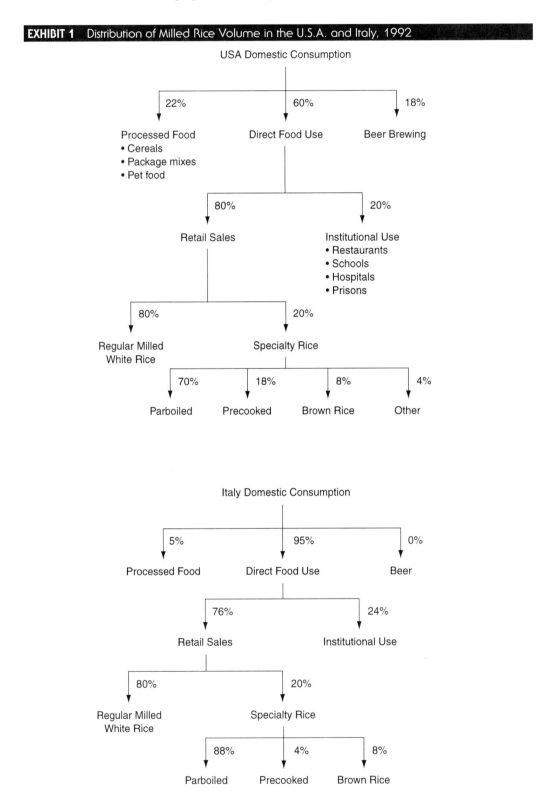

ITALY

Market Characteristics

Rice was a staple of the Italian diet. Used by 98% of the Italian population in 1991, per capita consumption averaged 5 kg[1] per annum. Some regional differences existed, with consumption being closer to 8 kg in the north (Italian rice production was concentrated in the Po valley, in the north of the country) and 3 kg in the south.

Of the 320,000 tons of rice sold in Italy in 1991, approximately 70,000 tons were sold through food service establishments, and 250,000 tons were sold through grocery stores. Retail sales in 1991 were 85% white rice and 15% parboiled by volume and 70% white rice and 30% parboiled by value. Sales of both parboiled rice and special rices (less than 5% of the market by value) were growing at 8% and 12% per annum respectively. White rice was losing share at 1% to 3% per annum.

Rice was seen as quick and easy to prepare, versatile, healthy, easily digested, and an alternative to pasta. Brand choices were based on quality, habit, availability, and packaging. Typically, rice was sold through stores in 1-kg cardboard boxes although a small percentage was sold from bulk bins and in 5-kg plastic bags. Legal restrictions in Italy required each variety of rice to be sold separately; the result was extended product lines since different rice varieties could not be mixed.

Gallo in Italy

Present in Italy since the nineteenth century as a rice miller, Gallo products accounted for 21% of Italian retail rice volume in 1991, 2% higher than in 1990. The Gallo logo, a cheerful rooster, was widely recognized and symbolized a trustworthy, good-quality, albeit somewhat traditional brand.

As the overall market share leader, Gallo offered three product lines:

- The basic *Riso Gran Gallo, white rice* line was offered in nine varieties (ranging from simple white rice to super-fine white rice), reflecting regional preferences and different recipe requirements. For example, Gallo Padano, popular in Milan, was used mainly in soups. Six of the nine varieties were long-grain, more absorbent rice suitable for risotto dishes.[2] In 1991, this line accounted for 64.4% of Gallo's total Italian sales volume and 51% of its total Lire sales. Gallo's volume share of white rice sales in Italy was 17.3% in 1991. (Product package illustrations appear in Exhibit 2.)
- The *Blond* line of parboiled rice included three parboiled nonstick products and one dehydrated, quick-cooking rice (also parboiled). The three parboiled products were (1) Orientale, white rice that cooked light and fluffy; (2) Risotti, a larger-grain rice suitable for risotto recipes; and (3) Integro, a "natural" brown rice that retained important ingredients and fiber sometimes depleted in the milling process. A dehydrated, quick-cooking product, Meta' Tempo (half time), was included in the line in 1990 and cooked in five to seven minutes. In 1991, this line accounted for 34.4% of Gallo's Italian volume sales and 48% of its Lire sales. Gallo's volume share of parboiled rice sales in Italy was 35.4% in 1991. (Product package illustrations appear in Exhibit 2.)
- The *Grandi Risi del Mondo* (great rices of the world) was a super-premium line introduced in 1989 in five varieties (Long and Wild, Bismati, Arborio, Carnaroli, and Patna). Although this line carried the familiar Gallo chicken

---

[1] 1 kg = 2.2 lbs., and 1 ton = 2,000 lbs.

[2] Risotto dishes were rice-based meals that included meat and/or vegetables.

EXHIBIT 2 Product Package Illustration for the Gallo Product Lines in Italy

logo on the front package panels, the line was marketed through a separate sales force and specialty store distribution. In 1991, this line accounted for just 1.2% of volume sales and 1.5% of Lire sales. (Product package illustrations appear in Exhibit 2.)

Most Gallo products were sold to retailers through a network of 60 agents and brokers, not by a company sales force. These agents carried other food products but no other rice brands. Due to its brand strength, Gallo received excellent push marketing efforts from its agents. A sales incentive program rewarded those who grew the Gallo business. In 1991, Gallo was carried in stores accounting for 80% of Italian grocery sales, more than any other brand. A typical supermarket carried two of Gallo's white rice varieties and three of the four parboiled items; the higher-priced Orientale was least widely distributed.

Competition

The Italian retail rice market was fragmented, with many local and regional millers selling under their own brand names. Grocery retailing was also fragmented but rapidly consolidating. In 1991, supermarkets and hypermarkets accounted for 60% of all rice value sales and 64% of Gallo's value sales, up from 57% and 59% in 1989. In 1991, private labels held a 17% share of rice retail sales volume, up from 13% in 1990. Gallo also competed against three major national brands:

- *Flora,* a subsidiary of BSN, the French food conglomerate, marketed only parboiled rice and competed directly with Gallo's Blond line.[3] Flora offered four varieties: Integral, Orientale, Risotti Blond, and Rapido. Combined, these items held a 41% volume and a 46% value share of the Italian parboiled market in 1991.

Flora television advertising was upbeat and depicted the lifestyles of four target segments, one for each item in the line. For example, the Integral commercial showed a health-conscious woman working out, while the Rapido commercial featured a successful business woman. The "lifestyle" commercials were modern, light, and appeared to be targeted at younger women. Flora also used five-minute television "infomercials" which included viewer call-in games to promote the brand. In 1990, Flora spent 20% more on advertising than did Gallo. A recent consulting study estimated that manufacturer gross margins on Flora were 30%, compared with Gallo's margins on the Blond line of 35%.

- *Curti-Buitoni* was acquired in 1985 by Nestle, the Swiss food company. The Nestle sales force provided the Curti brand with excellent distribution but the brand was not heavily advertised. Curti-Buitoni offered both basic white rice and parboiled products and held a 10.2% and 5.6% volume share of these markets respectively.
- *Scotti* was a family-owned, regional firm. Its product line was restricted to basic white rice. Scotti held a 7.5% volume share and had been approached by F&P Gruppo and others as a possible acquisition target.

Exhibit 3 summarizes market shares and brand awareness data for the four principal national brands in 1990–1991. Exhibits 4 and 5 compare Gallo and competitor market shares for white rice and parboiled rice and their relative retail prices.

Communication Strategy

Gallo's marketing expenditures had been increased from 13% of sales in 1988 to a planned 15% in 1992. (Actual promotional and advertising expenditures for 1991 and

[3]In Italy, BSN was also a strong player in branded pasta.

EXHIBIT 3   Market Shares and Brand Awareness Levels for Gallo and Competitors in Italy, 1990 and 1991

	Volume Market Shares (%)		1991 Awareness Levels (%)		
	1990	*1991*	*First Mention*	*Unaided*	*Aided*
Gallo	19.1	21.1	37	62	91
Flora	8.1	8.8	14	28	82
Curti-Buitoni	10.5	9.2	15	30	79
Scotti	5.9	6.1	8	14	64

EXHIBIT 4   White Rice in Italy: Gallo and Competitor Market Shares and Relative Retail Prices, 1990 and 1991

	Volume Market Shares (%)		Relative Retail Prices ($)	
	1990	*1991*	*1990*	*1991*
Riso-Gallo	16.4	17.3	1.00	1.00
Curti-Buitoni	11.1	10.2	0.98	0.97
Scotti	7.0	7.5	0.98	0.98
Private Label	15.5	17.3	0.78	0.78

EXHIBIT 5   Parboiled Rice in Italy: Gallo and Competitor Market Shares and Relative Retail Prices, 1990 and 1991

	Volume Market Shares (%)		Relative Retail Prices ($)	
	1990	*1991*	*1990*	*1991*
Riso-Gallo	31.3	35.4	1.00	1.00
Curti-Buitoni	7.8	5.6	1.03	0.98
Flora	43.3	40.9	1.05	1.04
Private Label	14.2	12.2	0.74	0.69

planned expenditures for 1992 are detailed in Exhibit 6.) In 1991, Gallo's television advertising was divided evenly between spot commercials and five-minute promotional infomercials. Television commercials for the Blond line depicted different consumers winning cooking competitions thanks to Gallo rice. Each commercial depicted a nervous individual holding a dish of rice, waiting in the wings, being called to the stage to receive an award, then being congratulated and applauded. The commercial cut back to the product, and an announcer explained that the award was won thanks to the Gallo brand of rice. Print advertisements in magazines often included a recipe, a photograph of the product, and detailed information on the differences of rice varieties. (Exhibit 7 shows a typical print advertisement, and Exhibits 8 and 9 show other Gallo magazine print advertisements.) Consumer promotions included in-store sampling and continuity programs, advertised on packages and in magazines, whereby consumers could redeem Gallo box tops for pottery and other merchandise. Gallo accounted for 33% of total category media advertising in 1991.

EXHIBIT 6 Gallo Advertising and Promotion Expenditures in Italy		
	Millions of Lira[a]	
	1991 (actual)	*1992 (planned)*
Media advertising:	9,466	9,210
TV ads for Blond		6,000
Gallo umbrella ads in magazines		1,150
Magazine ads for Blond Integro		200
Magazine ads for Blond Meta' Tempo		700
Supermarket magazines		180
Fees and production costs		980
Consumer promotion	3,039	2,300
Regional marketing	300	265
New product launch	789	350
Trade and sales force incentives	6,047	7,950
Total	19,641	20,075

Source: Company records and estimates.
[a]US$1 = 1,272 Lira.

In 1992, television advertising planned for the Blond line would focus on the non-stick benefit. Specific print advertising for Integro and Meta'Tempo products would communicate nutritional value and quick cooking time. An umbrella print advertising program, in both national and regional newspapers and magazines, would portray Gallo as serious and reliable and focus on the brand's tradition and culture.

Issues

In considering how to further penetrate the branded rice retail market, Preve was considering whether to create an entire new dehydrated line around the Meta'Tempo sub-brand. Consumers perceived Meta'Tempo to be superior to simple parboiled rice and some thought that the product could be the base of a whole new dehydrated product line, particularly since Gallo had a competitive advantage, being further down the learning curve in dehydrated technology than competitors. Sales of Meta'Tempo were growing rapidly, and dry rice mixes (such as risottos) were selling at three to four times the retail price of normal white rice.

Gallo's Naturis company produced dehydrated quick-cooking rice and supplied both BSN's Flora Rapido and Gallo's Blond Meta'Tempo. Flora's Rapido had been the only brand of quick-cooking rice on the market between 1988 and 1990. Gallo's Meta'Tempo was launched as a free-standing product in 1990, but had to be withdrawn due to poor sales and the high cost of promotional support. It was quickly repositioned within the Blond line and, by 1992, sales of Meta'Tempo equaled those of Rapido.

Preve also wrestled with several questions regarding the 1992 communications budget. First, he wondered if the competitive situation called for a substantially higher budget than in 1991. Second, he wondered whether Gallo should continue to put all its advertising behind the parboiled Blond line or allocate more support to the core white rice line.

There was also some concern that Gallo was not as strong as Flora in the growing supermarket/hypermarket retail segment. Actual retail trade margins were around 7% on Flora compared with 1% on Gallo's Blond line. Preve believed that the Gallo brand was often used as a traffic builder and that consumers who purchased Gallo branded rice were also more likely to purchase higher-value products, with greater retailer margins. In addition, Preve argued that Gallo products had a higher turnover than many other food products and that F&P Gruppo allowed retailers generous payment terms. Despite this, Preve was concerned that chains would be motivated to develop their own private label lines of rice products.

EXHIBIT 7 Gallo Italy: Typical Print Advertisement

LO SPECIALISTA DEL RISO

Il "riso bianco" non è tutto uguale. Comprende molte varietà che si differenziano tra loro per grandezza e forma del chicco, per trasparenza, contenuto in amido, tenuta in cottura, capacità di assorbimento dei condimenti. Conoscerle significa sfruttare al meglio le caratteristiche di ognuna per avere in cucina risultati eccezionali.

La gamma più completa presente sul mercato è firmata Riso Gallo che, con le due linee Gallo e Gran Gallo, propone nove varietà di riso bianco tra le quali troviamo: Gran Gallo Roma, con una grana lunga e grossa che assorbe molto bene i condimenti; dà grandi soddisfazioni se usato per risotti "ricchi" di ingredienti.

Gran Gallo Arborio, nato ad Arborio nel 1946 è il riso italiano con i chicchi più grandi e perfetti: ideale per i risotti più classici e raffinati.

Gran Gallo Baldo, è il riso con la struttura più cristallina e compatta, molto resistente in cottura, va benissimo per i risotti, ma è perfetto per le insalate di riso, i timballi, il riso in teglia.

Il segreto: per ogni piatto saper scegliere il riso bianco adatto e, con Riso Gallo, il migliore.

Ricettario

RISOTTO CON FUNGHI PORCINI E ANIMELLE

Ingredienti per 4 persone. 250 gr di Riso Gran Gallo Arborio - 200 gr di animelle 100 gr di funghi porcini - 1,2 l di brodo di pollo leggero - 25 gr di cipolla - 2 dl di scalogno - 2 dl di vino bianco - 1 cucchiaio di estratto di carne - 10 gr di dragoncello - 50 gr di burro 50 gr di parmigiano grattugiato - olio di semi sale e pepe q.b.

Lasciare spurgare le animelle per 5 ore

sotto acqua corrente fredda. Sbianchirle per 5 minuti in acqua bollente salata e asciarvele raffreddare. Una volta fredde sgranarle, liberandole dalla pellicina e spezzettarle. Pulire i funghi porcini e tagliarli a cubetti. Farli saltare, con 10 gr di burro, in una pentola antiaderente, salarli e peparli. Aggiungere e far dorare le animelle. A parte fare ridurre 2 dl di vino bianco con lo scalogno finemente tritato, l'estratto di carne e un po' di burro. Per il risotto far sudare la cipolla tritata con 10 gr di burro, aggiungere il riso e farlo tostare fino a quando non inizierà a scoppiettare. Bagnare con vino bianco, farlo evaporare e portare il riso a cottura bagnandolo a poco a poco con il brodo bollente. Togliere il riso dal fuoco e mantecarlo con burro e parmigiano grattugiato: disporlo sui piatti e guarnirlo con le animelle, i funghi porcini e il dragoncello tritato. Macchiare la

superficie del piatto con il fondo, di consistenza sciropposa, ottenuto con l'estratto di carne.

RISOTTO DEL DI' DI FESTA

Ingredienti per 4 persone: 250 gr di Riso Gran Gallo Roma - 1 litro di brodo - 1 cipolla - 2 peperoni gialli - 2 peperoni rossi - 1 ciuffo di basilico - 200 gr di pomodori pelati - 5 cosce di pollo - 1 bicchiere di vino bianco secco - prezzemolo tritato - olio, burro, sale q.b. - 1 foglia di alloro.

Rosolare la cipolla tagliata sottile e aggiungere le cosce di pollo tagliate in tre pezzi. Far colorire, aggiungere il vino bianco secco e lasciarlo evaporare. Mettere i peperoni tagliati a listarelle e i pelati, dopo 10 minuti versare il brodo bollente e cuocere per 50 minuti. Aggiungere il riso e finire di cuocere. Completare con prezzemolo e basilico tritati e una foglia di alloro.

EXHIBIT 8 Gallo Italy: Print Advertisement for the Grandi Risi del Mondo Line

TRACCE DI RISO.

GH CIEL

Quanta strada da fare in cucina, con "I grandi risi del mondo". Seguire le loro tracce, sarà un'avventura. Dall'India il Basmati, quasi una leggenda. In Thailandia è il Patna, l'orgoglio nazionale. Dal Nord America, il Long & Wild: chicco bianco e chicco nero. Dall'Italia infine il fiore. Fiore di Arborio per i risotti di grande tradizione, Fiore di Carnaroli, il re dei risi, per ricette d'autore. Sono loro "I grandi risi del mondo". L'avventura da portare a tavola. La ricetta per girare il mondo.

DA GALLO, LO SPECIALISTA DEL RISO.

EXHIBIT 9 Gallo Italy: Print Advertisement with Consumer Promotion—"Win a Car with Blond Rice"

LE SUE CLIENTI GIOCANO CON LINO BANFI. VINCONO CON RISO BLOND.

Si, la "febbre del quiz", con il successo della promosponsorizzazione Riso Blond ne "Il gioco dei giochi", sta ormai contagiando tutti: a cominciare dalle sue clienti. Dal 15 marzo, nessuno si sottrae all'appuntamento del venerdì alle 20.30 su Canale 5 con "lo Specialista del riso", l'unico che mette in palio, con il concorso Blond, fino al 7 giugno, ben 6 Spider Alfa Romeo, 7 Alfa 33 Station Wagon e 13000 litri di benzina Erg. Vincere è facile, ma per partecipare bisogna avere in casa almeno una confezione di Riso Blond Risotti, Metà tempo, Integro o Orientale. Rinforzi subito le scorte per soddisfare sempre nuove richieste, assicurate da questa spettacolare promosponsorizzazione che riconferma Gallo leader della tracizione del riso.

riso Gallo

Lo specialista del riso.

ARGENTINA

Market Characteristics

In 1991, an estimated 140,000 tons of rice were sold through retail stores and a further 40,000 tons through food service establishments. Per capita consumption approached 5 kg per annum, with 92% of Argentine households consuming rice at least once a week and 30% consuming rice at least three times a week. Sales of branded rice had decreased from 85,000 tons in 1990 to 81,000 tons in 1991, due to the increasing price of paddy rice relative to other food products such as meat. In July 1989, the retail price of 1 kg of meat was equal to the retail price of 5.4 kg of rice. By November 1991, the equivalent was only 2.7 kg of rice. Parboiled rice accounted for 18.2% retail

sales volume in 1991, compared with 16.1% in 1990; the remaining sales were of white rice, with brown rice accounting for an estimated 2% of sales volume. (Exhibit 10 gives an estimated breakdown of rice consumption by volume.)

During the 1980s, the Argentine economy had suffered from cycles of strong growth and consumption, followed by ever longer periods of recession. A new economic plan launched in 1991 aimed to tame inflation, initiate deregulation, privatize public enterprises, and liberalize trade restrictions and import duties. In 1992, inflation was estimated at 17%.

Rice was distributed primarily through supermarkets, which accounted for 63% of all retail rice sales in 1990; large, medium, and small stores accounted for 10%, 14%,

EXHIBIT 10 Distribution of Argentina Milled Rice Volume, 1991

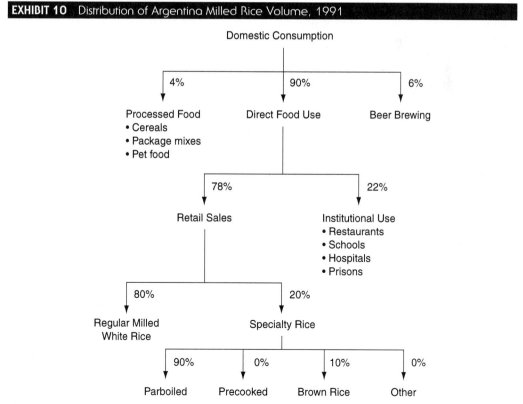

Source: USA Rice Council.

and 13% respectively. The volume of rice sold in different packages was 72% for plastic pillows, 19% for cardboard boxes, and 9% for triangle-shaped packages. Most packages were either 1 kg or 500 grams in weight.

Gallo in Argentina

The first rice mill in Argentina was established by Arrocera Argentina, a subsidiary of F&P Gruppo, in 1905. In 1991, the Arrocera Argentina mills were running at 85% capacity, milling rice grown in Argentina. All of the output was processed into Gallo-branded products. Sales of Gallo-branded rice were US$30 million in the fiscal year April 1991 to March 1992. In 1991, Gallo held a 17.5% volume share and a 23.7% value share of the total retail rice market, up from 15.7% and 22.8% respectively in 1990. In addition, Gallo held a 48% share in greater Buenos Aires, which accounted for 30% of the country's population. Solely focused on the rice market, Gallo was both the market share and product innovation leader.

The Gallo line included the following items:

- Gallo *Grano Largo Fino and Gallo Doble,* long-grain and European long-grain rice, were long, wide types of rice known as doble because each grain was double the length of an ordinary grain of rice. They were the original products in Gallo's Argentine product line and were targeted at traditional homemakers who enjoyed the art of cooking and described themselves as "knowing how to cook" and "using the brand that my mother used." Packaged in 1-kg and ½-kg cartons, this line accounted for 28% of Gallo's sales by volume in 1991, compared with 32% in 1989.
- *Gallo Oro,* long-grain and European long-grain parboiled rice, was positioned as a quality rice that did not stick

or overcook and was easy to prepare. The line was targeted at the modern, middle-income working consumer, aged 25 years and over, who wanted ease of preparation without sacrificing taste. The line included doble and boil-in-the-bag products in both 1-kg and ½-kg carton packages. The first parboiled product had been introduced in Argentina in 1963, and by 1991 this line accounted for 59% of Gallo's sales volume, compared with 62% in 1989.

- Gallo *Integral,* a long-grain parboiled brown rice, was positioned as a health and fitness product with a high nutritional value, levels of fiber, vitamins, and minerals. It was targeted at middle-income men and women, 18 years and older, who led a healthy, natural, and sporty lifestyle, and wanted a balanced diet without sacrificing good taste. It was sold in 500-gram and boil-in-the-bag formats as well as the standard 1-kg box. Sales of this product represented 5% of Gallo's volume in 1991, the same percentage as in 1989.
- Gallo *Risotto* dry mixes, made of European long-grain parboiled rice, came in four flavor varieties. The rice was mixed with dehydrated ingredients such as peppers, mushroom, chicken, and spices and was targeted at middle-income consumers aged 25 and over, seeking tasty, easy-to-prepare meals. Launched in 1984 and sold in 300-gram boxes, it represented 1% of Gallo's sales volume in 1991 as in 1989 and held an 87% share of the Argentine risotto market in 1991.

Exhibit 11 reports shipments, manufacturer gross margins, and package sizes for each item in the product line. Gallo was one of the only companies selling rice packaged in cardboard boxes (only two other minor competitors also packaged in boxes). Product packages for the four lines are depicted in Exhibit 12.

EXHIBIT 11	Arrocera Argentina Product Line, Shipments, Margins, and Package Sizes, 1991		
	Shipment (tons)	*Manufacturer Margin (%)*	*Package Sizes*
Gallo Grano Largo Fino (long-grain)	1,875	35	1 kg
Gallo Doble (European long-grain)	3,891	44	1 kg ½-kg pillow
Gallo Oro (long-grain parboiled):			
Regular	11,173	38	1 kg
Boil-in-bag	361	41	½ kg
Gallo Doble Oro (European long-grain parboiled)	761	45	1 kg
Gallo Integral (long-grain brown)	786	51	1 kg ½ kg boil-in-bag
Gallo Risotto (European long-grain parboiled dry mixes)	104	60	300 gm
Nobleza Gaucha:			
Long-grain	711	21	1 kg
European long-grain	256	35	
Long-grain parboiled	575	29	
Integral	44	43	

Three-quarters of Gallo's retail sales were through supermarkets. There was a trend toward consolidation in food retailing in Argentina, with the large supermarkets (of 350 square meters or more) increasing their market share from 34% in 1989 to 38% in 1991. Gallo was weaker in the medium and smaller stores, which represented 27% of retail volume rice sales but accounted for only 15% of Gallo's retail sales volume. Approximately 90% of sales were made through a company sales force, while 10% was sold through agents serving remote areas. In 1991, the Gallo line included 28 items and was present in stores representing 77% of the country's retail food sales with an average of 7 items per retail outlet. On average, large supermarkets carried between 5 and 7 different brands of rice.

Competition

The Argentine retail rice market was fragmented and regional. The four major national brands accounted for only 45% of total retail sales volume in 1991. Gallo faced one major and two minor competitors:

Molinos food products, a subsidiary of Bunge Corporation, a large Argentine conglomerate, held 10.1% of the rice retail market by volume in 1991, up from 8.8% in 1990. It seriously challenged Gallo in 1990 with its Maximo brand of parboiled long-grain rice.

Maximo, sold in triangle packages, held a 5.3% volume share of retail sales in 1990 and was the only Molinos brand that was not the market leader in its category. In 1991, Molinos spent twice as much as Gallo on advertising Maximo, despite the fact that the Argentine economy was depressed, promoting the brand as "oro puro of Molinos" on radio and television and in magazines. To gain market share, Maximo was priced 12% under equivalent Gallo products and, by the end of 1991, Maximo had increased its retail volume market share to 7.5%. Molinos had

EXHIBIT 12 Product Package Illustrations for the Gallo Product Lines in Argentina

Long Grain Rice   European Long Grain Rice

Dry mixes with European Long Grain Parboiled Rice
Four flavor varieties

Long Grain Parboiled Rice

European Long Grain
Parboiled Rice

Long Grain Brown Rice, in Boil-in-Bags
Quick cooking

difficulty achieving quality control on its doble and brown rice entries and these were marketed under the brand name *Condor.* Distribution coverage for Molinos was still lower than for Gallo, and the company was not particularly strong in any one region.

Gallo had responded to Maximo with a fighting brand called Nobleza Gaucha. Also sold in triangle-shaped packages, it came in four varieties: long grain, long grain parboiled, European long-grain, and Integral. In 1991, this line was priced around 25% below equivalent Gallo-branded products and around 12% below Maximo. Within one year the Nobleza Gaucha brand accounted for 7.7% of Gallo's sales volume and held a

1.3% share of total retail rice sales by volume in 1991. The brand was sold by Gallo sales force but supermarkets accounted for 65% of sales compared with the 75% for the Gallo brand.

Mocovi and Moneda were smaller, regional players in the long-grain and doble market segments, with shares of 4.2% and 4.4% respectively. Mocovi, a family-owned company, successfully fo-

cused on marketing its Mocovi Doble brand and was the leader in the doble market segment. Moneda's products included both the Moneda and Doble Moneda brands.

Exhibits 13 and 14 summarize overall market shares for the four brands from 1989 to 1991 and the volume and value shares of their specific product lines in 1991. Exhibit 15 compares the relative retail prices

EXHIBIT 13 Rice Brand Market Shares in Argentina, 1989–1991

	Percentage of Total Retail Volume		
	1989	*1990*	*1991*
Arrocera (Gallo and Nobleza Gaucha)	17.7%	15.7%	17.5%
Molinos (Maximo)	8.2	8.8	10.1
Moneda	4.3	4.7	4.4
Mocovi	7.2	5.4	74.2

EXHIBIT 14 Rice Brand Market Shares in Argentina by Product Line, 1991

	Percentage of Total Rice Market	
	Retail Volume Share	*Retail Value Share*
Dobles and Long-grain		
Arrocera:		
Gallo	5.2%	7.6%
Nobleza Gaucha	0.7	0.7
Molinos:		
Condor	2.6	3.3
Mocovi	4.2	6.9
Moneda	4.4	5.9
Parboiled		
Arrocera:		
Gallo	9.8	12.5
Nobleza Gaucha	0.4	0.4
Molinos:		
Maximo	7.5	10.3
Integral		
Arrocera:		
Gallo	1.2	2.0
Risottos		
Arrocera:		
Gallo	0.2	0.5

EXHIBIT 15   Relative Retail Prices and Distribution Penetration of Argentine Rice Brands, 1991

	Retail Price ($ per kg)	Index	% Distribution Penetration
Long-grain:			
Arrocera:			
Gallo Grano Largo Fino	$1.30	1.00	32%
Nobleza Gaucha long-grain	1.07	0.82	12
Molinos:			
Condor long-grain	1.26	0.95	35
Mocovi:			
Long-grain	0.98	0.75	10
Moneda:			
Long-grain	1.20	0.92	15
Doble:			
Arrocera:			
Gallo Doble	2.54	1.95	51
Nobleza Gaucha European long-grain	1.61	1.24	8
Molinos:			
Condor Doble	2.06	1.58	37
Mocovi:			
Doble	2.05	1.58	47
Moneda:			
Doble	1.82	1.40	29
Parboiled			
Arrocera:			
Gallo Oro	1.68	1.29	75
Gallo Doble	2.30	1.77	40
Nobleza Gaucha	1.30	1.00	26
Molinos:			
Maximo	1.48	1.14	59
Integral			
Arrocera:			
Gallo	2.16	1.66	45
Risottos			
Arrocera:			
Gallo	6.70	5.15	42

and percentage distribution penetration of thcsc brands in 1991.

Communication Strategy

Advertising expenditures on the Gallo brand in 1991 were the equivalent of US$562,000, only 50% that of Maximo, and were used exclusively to back Gallo Oro. Television commercials included demonstrations of how to prepare and serve rice (particularly boil-in-the-bag products) and "slice-of-life" depictions of family scenes. For example, one commercial showed children sneaking into a kitchen to eat the rice their mother just prepared, while a second depicted a daughter making the same dish for her mother that her mother used to make for her when she was a child. Other promotional programs in 1991 included consumer promotions and sales force incentives.

Exhibit 16 summarizes marketing expenditures for Arrocera Argentina in 1991 and planned expenditures for 1992. The budget for 1992 was $1.9 million, to be divided as follows: $762,000 on a new Gallo Oro television campaign; $400,000 on print advertising for the whole Gallo line; $220,000 on Gallo Oro radio advertising;

EXHIBIT 16	Advertising and Promotion Expenditures for Arrocera Argentina, 1991–1992	
	US$ (000s)	
	1991 (actual)	**1992 (budget)**
Media Advertising		
Television commercials:		
Gallo Oro	$342	$ 762
Doble Gallo		194
Risotto		
Others		84
Print advertising:		
Gallo Oro		
Doble Gallo		
Risotto		80
Others		320
Radio advertising:		
Gallo Oro		220
Doble Gallo		52
Promotions		
Consumer promotions:		
Gallo Oro	35	
Doble Gallo	25	26
Others	60	31
Trade promotions		25
Sales force incentives	100	173
Total	**$562**	**$1,967**

$57,000 on consumer promotions; and $173,000 on sales force incentives.

Competitive television commercials focused on displaying the cooked product in different forms. A typical Maximo television commercial stressed quality, price, and ease of preparation. The commercial was fast-paced with a musical background and depicted a number of meals that could be prepared with Maximo rice. A Moneda television commercial depicted a woman hosting a dinner party explaining that, when she used to cook rice, "nothing happened," but that now, with Moneda, she was able to serve flavorful meals. (Exhibits 17 and 18 show examples of Gallo print advertisements in Argentina, and Exhibit 19 gives an example of a Maximo print advertisement.)

Issues

First, Arrocera Argentina managers were debating how to respond to a market that was eroding due to a difficult economic climate and high product prices relative to other food products. Sig. Preve was hesitant, however, to implement price reductions on the high-end products despite a drop in raw material costs of approximately 63% between 1988 and 1991. Second, the issue as to whether Gallo should attempt to match Maximo's level of advertising was raised. Third, Gallo was committed to introducing new products and planned to launch Meta'Tempo quick-cooking rice under the brand name *Gallo Quick* in 1992. A key question was how the brand should be positioned and priced in the Argentine market, and what proportion of total marketing expenditures should be allocated to its launch.

Since it would be the first brand in the precooked segment of the Argentine market, Arrocera Argentina executives believed that Gallo Quick could be positioned to enhance Gallo's product leadership and market share. They suggested pricing the product at a 60% premium to Gallo Oro.

EXHIBIT 17 Gallo Argentina: Print Advertisement for the Risotto Line

Risottos Cremosos... Deliciosos...

Disfrute de los mejores risottos
con *Gallo Todo Resuelto.*
En cualquiera de sus 4 variedades: a la Normanda,
a la Piamontesa, a la Española y Primavera.
Su exquisito sabor proviene de la utilización
de verduras frescas deshidratadas de primera calidad
(sin el agregado de sustancias químicas ni conservantes)
y de la utilización del mejor arroz: Doble Gallo Oro.

EXHIBIT 18   Gallo Argentina: Two Separate Print Advertisements for Gallo Integro

EN 25 MINUTOS
USTED PUEDE MEJORAR SU VIDA.

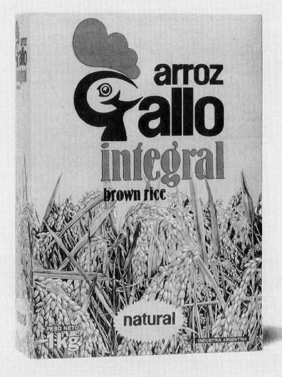

El tiempo en el que se cocina
Arroz Gallo Integral.
La elección más natural para su vida.
La base de una dieta equilibrada.
Sana. Rica.
25 minutos en punto.
Prepárese. Y mejore su vida.

• Retiene la película de salvado.
• No contiene colesterol.
• Bajo contenido de sodio.
• Sin preservantes ni ingredientes
  artificiales.
• Con vitaminas B1, B2, y E.
• Posee Calcio, Hierro y Fósforo.

ARROZ GALLO INTEGRAL. EL PUNTO DE PARTIDA DE UNA VIDA SANA.

EXHIBIT 18 (Continued)

Comer sano es el mejor camino para su cuerpo. Con Arroz Gallo Integral usted puede disfrutar de todo el sabor, a partir de una alimentación más equilibrada. Más natural. Más rica en todo sentido. Haga la prueba. Arroz Gallo Integral lo pondrá en carrera de una vida más saludable.

• Retiene la película de salvado.
• No contiene colesterol.
• Bajo contenido de sodio.
• Sin preservantes ni ingredientes artificiales.
• Con vitaminas B_1, B_2 y E.
• Posee Calcio. Hierro y Fósforo.

ARROZ GALLO INTEGRAL.
EL PUNTO DE PARTIDA DE UNA VIDA SANA:

arroz **Gallo** integral
brown rice

natural

EXHIBIT 19 Gallo Argentina: Print Advertisement for the Maximo Competitor Brand

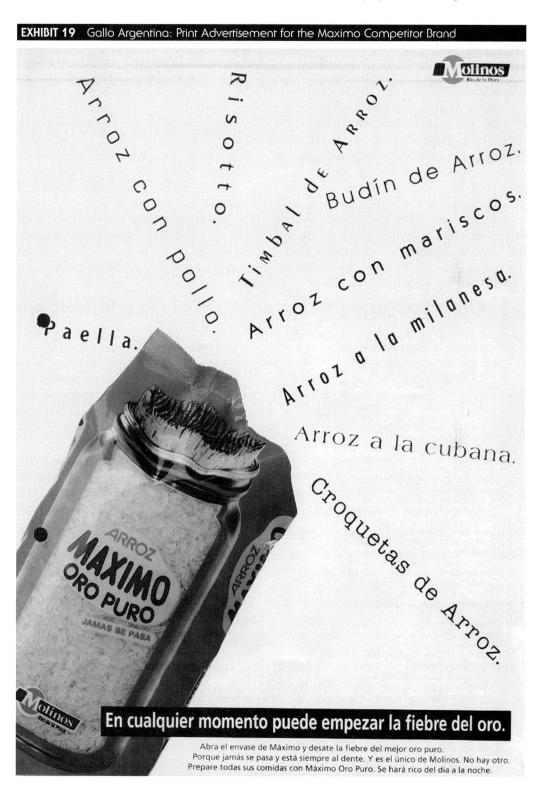

POLAND

Market Characteristics

With the demise of Communist control, Poland underwent rapid cultural and political change in the late 1980s. After 1989, Poland was flooded by imported goods of all kinds, mainly from Germany, Italy, and France. To deal with these imports, private wholesale and retail chains emerged in 1991 to replace the state-owned stores. Although in 1992 the Polish economy was still suffering from inflation and low wages, consumers were becoming increasingly sophisticated in the quality of products they demanded. With the advent of advertising and private companies, Poland was believed to be evolving from a market dominated by commodities to one where branding would become important.

Prior to 1989, rice had been imported in bulk by the state from Vietnam, Thailand, China, and Indonesia. It was of variable quality, often dirty and broken, and was sold in low-quality paper bags. Traditionally used as a substitute to potatoes, as a booster in soups, in cabbage rolls, or for rice pudding, rice had a low-quality image. Traditionally, imported food such as rice had been subsidized by the state. The end of these subsidies in 1989 resulted in price increases on imported food of around 1100%.

In the 1980s, distribution of branded Western products, including branded rice, had been controlled by a state-owned company called Pewex with a network of around 800 stores. Purchases could be made only in U.S. dollars. The stores enabled the state to obtain hard currency from consumers who received it from family members living outside Poland. In 1989, the Polish currency (the zloty) was tied to the U.S. dollar. An additional 800 private exchange stores and markets sprung up to distribute imported foods. Sales of such products by entrepreneurs through makeshift street stalls and open-air car-trunk markets also became common.

These were later organized into covered market halls. In 1991, private food retail outlets began to emerge although there were no dominant supermarket chains as yet. In 1992, 70% of retail food sales were made at open markets and market halls, 15% at supermarkets, and 15% at small grocery stores.

In 1988, total rice consumption in Poland was 64,000 tons or 1.5-kg per capita. By 1991, per capita consumption reached 2.3 kg per annum. Used by 65% of the population, 80,000 tons were sold through retail stores in 1991. Of this volume, 90% was standard white rice; parboiled rice was a novel product for Polish consumers. (Exhibit 20 shows the breakdown of rice volume in Poland in 1991.)

Gallo in Poland

In 1988, Arrocera Argentina started exporting to the Polish market through an agent who received a commission on sales to Pewex. Gallo rice was sold in 200 Pewex shops in packages with both Argentine and Polish labeling at an average retail price of $1 per kg. In 1991, with Pewex in decline, Arrocera's agent established a private distribution company, Argentyna Ltd., to import and distribute the products he had previously handled for Pewex. In addition to rice, Argentyna Ltd. imported and distributed tea, beverages, and soups. Argentyna did not handle other brands of rice.

Between March 1990 and January 1991, 59 tons of Gallo Oro (parboiled) and 9 tons of Gallo risottos, both imported from Argentina, were sold through Pewex. Initial package labels carried Spanish text to which a Polish sticker had been added; subsequent packages carried bilingual Spanish-Polish labeling. From February 1991 to February 1992, 70.5 tons of Gallo Oro parboiled white rice were imported exclusively through Argentyna Ltd. from Gallo's German factory, P&L Rickmers. Prior to 1991, P&L Rickmers had experienced excess capacity. These

EXHIBIT 20 Distribution of Milled Rice Volume in Poland, 1992

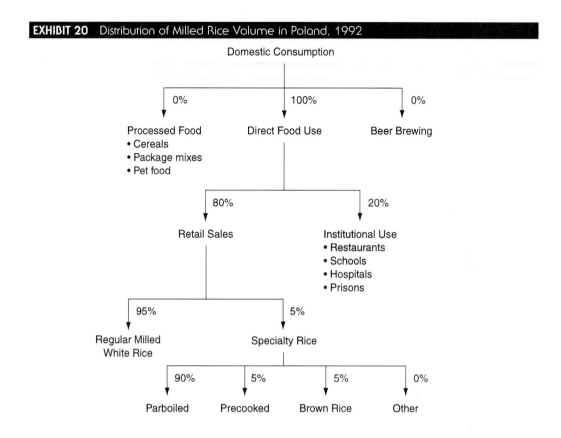

1-kg carton box packages carried the bilingual label. In 1992, Gallo expected to sell 100 tons of Gallo Oro in 1-kg cartons, less than one-quarter of 1% of the retail market volume.

In 1992, Argentyna Ltd. had a central warehouse in Warsaw and distributed 65% of Gallo's product volume directly to retailers in the Warsaw area. The remaining 35% of sales were made through four secondary distributors that served the major cities of Krakow, Sczeczin, Poznan, and Lodz. The Gallo brand was available in 200 supermarkets and upscale grocery stores, which accounted for 30% of all grocery sales volume in Warsaw and 5% in Poland. In 1992, Rickmers' gross margin averaged 21% of its selling price. The Argentyna Ltd. Margin averaged 40%, while secondary distributors made about 20% margin on Gallo products.

Retailer margins were 15%. Exhibit 21 shows photographs of three food stores, at the high, medium, and lower range, retailing rice in Poland in September 1992.

Competition

Gallo's main competitor was the Uncle Ben's brand owned by Mars Company, distributed in Poland since 1991. In addition, several German and Belgian brands of both white and parboiled rice had entered the market at lower price points. In mid-1992, it was estimated that 95% of the market was unbranded, white rice, packaged in paper bags, which retailed at an average price of 8,000 zlotys (US$0.58).

Uncle Ben's sold long-grain parboiled rice and brown rice in 1-kg cartons, ½-kg cartons, and boil-in-the-bag packages. In just over a year, Uncle Ben's had penetrated 90%

of the supermarket and grocery outlets in Warsaw. Initially, the company had supplied its products to retailers on credit and accepted returns of unsold product. The launch was supported with US$500,000 of expenditures on television commercials, print advertising, and point-of-sale displays.

Uncle Ben's used a North American television commercial translated into Polish. It depicted a rural picnic in the southern United States, where an African-American community was preparing to welcome home a young soldier. Considerable consumer confusion existed between the Gallo and Uncle Ben's brands; increased advertising by Uncle Ben's resulted in increase in sales for Gallo and other imported brands. In 1992, Uncle Ben's was expected to sell over 200 tons of rice. It was believed that Uncle Ben's was losing money in Poland but that the company's strategy was to increase brand awareness and build long-term market share.

Britta, Doris, and La Belle Caroline were other major foreign rice brands distributed in Poland. Usually priced lower than Uncle Ben's or Gallo, these brands were not advertised. (Exhibit 22 summarizes the relative prices of different brands in February 1992.)

Consumer Research

A consumer research study in September 1990 indicated that a basic meal in Poland consisted of meat, potatoes, and a vegetable. Rice was seen as an occasional substitute for potatoes. There was little knowledge of different types of rice and rice recipes, little understanding of nutrition, and little exposure to foreign foods. Homemakers were used to buying what was available, preparing meals every two or three days that could be stored in refrigerators; most Polish households had access to refrigerators in 1990.

In product trials of Gallo products, parboiled rice was enthusiastically received. Ease of cooking (aided by clear cooking instructions), taste, and ability to store once cooked, were cited as the main benefits of Gallo Oro. One drawback, however, was that consumers found the rice too firm for use in soups. Savory rice (with mushrooms added) was not well-received; it had an unfamiliar taste and smell, had to be watched when being prepared, and was higher in price. Brown rice was viewed negatively; most consumers felt that a good-quality rice should be long-grained and white and,

---

EXHIBIT 22 Relative Retail Prices of Major Rice Brands in Poland, February and September 1992

	February 1992		September 1992	
	US$/Kg.	*Index*	*US$/Kg.*	*Index*
Parboiled				
Gallo Oro	2.28	1.00	1.78	1.00
Uncle Ben's	3.50	1.54	2.24	1.26
Doris (Belgian)	1.27	0.56	1.23	0.69
White Rice				
Local brand (in plastic bags)	0.72	0.32	0.56	0.33
Local brand (instant rice flakes)	1.50	0.65	1.32	0.75
Britta (German)	1.50	0.65	1.31	0.73
La Belle Caroline (French)	NA	NA	1.23	0.69

lacking in nutritional awareness, were un-willing to pay a price premium. Consumers suspected the boil-in-the-bag concept because it involved cooking in plastic. Cartons were the preferred form of packaging and Polish labels were deemed necessary. Gallo managers wondered whether all these perceptions would continue or whether an investment in consumer education by Gallo and other foreign brands would change them.

Communication Strategy

Gallo's initial plan was to superimpose a Polish voice on an Argentine television commercial of a Chinese cook demonstrating how to prepare Gallo Oro. A variety of dishes that included rice were shown during the commercial, and the nonstick properties and taste of the rice were stressed. Testing revealed that the pace of the commercial was too quick and that the central message and product benefits were not well-understood. The commercial was never aired. In addition, television advertising was becoming increasingly expensive and radio was therefore considered as an alternative medium.

From February 1991 to February 1992, Gallo spent US$5,000 on promotional support and point-of-sale displays. In September 1992, $6,000 was spent on print advertising in women's magazines. A full-page advertisement, to be placed in one magazine for three consecutive months, pictured a Gallo Oro carton, and included a description of the product and a suggested cooking recipe. A total of US$20,000 was budgeted for 1992, and Exhibit 23 outlines the proposed breakdown of expenditures.

EXHIBIT 23	Proposed Gallo Communication Budget in Poland, 1992
	US$
Advertising	
Newspaper ads	4,000
Women's magazines	6,000
Promotion	
Point-of-purchase material	5,000
Three promotion reps	2,500
Other	2,500
Total	20,000

Gallo's agent believed increased advertising expenditures were essential. He explained:

> Gallo's product quality is better than the other cheaper brands, but consumers don't know this. We are caught between Uncle Ben's, perceived as a premium product, and brands such as Britta and Doris that compete on price. People do not know that Gallo is high quality and we need to create this perception of the brand.

Issues

Sig. Preve wondered how to establish the Gallo brand in Poland. Specifically, which lines should be introduced and in which order? How should the products be positioned and priced? What level and types of advertising and promotion would be needed? Could the Polish market be expected to evolve like Argentina and, subsequently, like Italy? If so, how rapidly would this evolution take place? To assess the potential transfer of products and expertise from one country to another, Sig. Preve reviewed the Gallo line in the three countries (see Exhibit 24). ∎

EXHIBIT 24   Gallo Product Line by Country

	Italy	*Argentina*	*Poland*
White Rice			
• Round, short grain	Riso Gallo Originario		
• Semi-long, "pearl"	Riso Gallo Padano		
• Round, fat grain	Riso Gallo Vialone Nano		
• Long-grain Italpatna	Riso Gran Gallo Europa		
• Long-grain	Riso Gran Gallo Ribe	Gallo Doble + Nobleza Gaucha	
• American long-grain	Riso Gran Gallo S. Andrea	Gallo Grano Largo Fino + Nobleza Gaucha	
• Semi-round Japanese	Riso Gran Gallo Roma		
• Crystalline	Riso Gran Gallo Baldo		
• Large grain Italian	Riso Gran Gallo Arborio		
• Brown		Gallo Integral + Nobleza Gaucha	
Parboiled			
• Long-grain	Blond Risotti	Gallo Oro + Nobleza Gaucha	Gallo Oro
• Long-grain brown	Blond Integro		
• Long-grain Patna	Blond Orientale	Gallo Doble Oro	
• Dehydrated long-grain	Blond Meta'Tempo	Gallo Quick	
Risottos			
• Parboiled dry mixes		Gallo Risotto	

CHAPTER

8 | MARKETING STRATEGY

Defining strategy is the basis for action in a marketing plan. Starting with a company's current position defines where it wants to go and how it will get there. Strategy provides the necessary long-term perspective and integrates the marketing strategy with the other functional strategies, defining the advantages a company wishes to gain over its competition. Marketing strategy encompasses the vision of a business and the company mission: What is the purpose of the company? What value will the company provide to its customers? The strategy defines why customers will choose to buy from that company rather than from its competitors.

Having a clear idea of a company's preferred customers is at the center of the strategy. Adequate development will help to define marketable products rather than defining the products and then seeking a market. The concept of marketing suggests that if we take care of the customer properly, all else will follow.

A first step in developing a strategy is to assess the competitive position. Is the company relying on its strengths, and is the market offering plenty of opportunities? Or is the market showing serious threats requiring a company to rely on its weaker or less-skilled activities? It is important to understand that most organizations don't position themselves for the changing market. Rather they weaken their competitive advantage because they are not aware of those changes.

Market definition is critical at this step. A definition that is too broad will lose focus, while a too narrow definition may miss opportunities. The art of segmentation—selecting the group of customers to be served—appears to be key. When the group is selected, defining a clear position in the market is not so difficult. Since markets evolve constantly, it is important to understand the dynamics of the market where we compete, its changing path, and how these dynamics relate to the wants and needs of customers. A clear understanding of the market and product life cycle is helpful in defining market share targets, and for timing of introducing new products and for withdrawing from the market.

A portfolio vision of the different components of the business arrays competitive position against market attractiveness, combining the concepts of market evolution with cost and share leverage. The growth-share matrix offers different generic strategies for growth, maintenance, or divesting before losses force more dramatic measures.

The constant evolution of markets makes competitive advantages temporary at best. Focusing on market evolution and competitors' activities and having a clear understanding of what is expected from the company are key strategic ingredients.

CASES

8-1
SUPERMERCADOS DISCO: REGIONAL STRATEGY

In 1997, the management of Banco Velox, an Argentinean banking group, was analyzing its strategy regarding its supermarket subsidiary, Supermercados Disco. It had been approached regarding a possible joint venture by Royal Ahold, the Dutch supermarket group, and at the same time there was the possibility of acquiring Santa Isabel, a Chilean supermarket chain. Disco needed to decide whether it would reinforce its existing operations in Argentina and Uruguay, or start moving towards expanding into the rest of Latin America and, in either case, whether to join a global retail group or attempt to grow by its own efforts. Stimulated by strong economic growth and deregulation in the 1990s, Argentina had become one of the most competitive food retailing markets in the world, attracting several of the largest global supermarket groups.

"We must be sure to catch the mood of the moment, for the rewards could be substantial. Perhaps we should even consider entering into other formats, like hypermarkets or hard discount," remarked Juan Peirano, president of

Bank Velox at the Disco shareholders' meeting.

Disco's basic strategy for growth had been to increase the profitability and market penetration of its stores. The company aimed to increase earnings by increasing sales and achieving greater operating efficiencies. During 1996 and 1997, selling space was increased by 56%, including remodeling of existing stores and the opening of 17 new stores, and another $140 million was planned for further expansion and upgrades over the following two years.

Disco had differentiated itself from the competition by offering quality products at competitive prices and a high level of customer service. The product mix was over 85% food (including 16% beverages) with a focus on the quality of perishables, including beef and produce. Using its information systems, the company could merchandise each store with an appropriate product mix and provide new services for the consumer.

DISCO BACKGROUND AND STRATEGY

Disco had commenced operations in 1961 when it opened its first store in the north of Argentina's capital, Buenos Aires. In 1991, the Velox Group acquired a controlling interest in the company and soon thereafter installed a new management team that developed a strategic plan designed to reduce

Silvina Romero Paz, Research Assistant at IAE, prepared this case under the supervision of Professor Guillermo D'Andrea of the Instituto de Altos Estudios Empresariales, Buenos Aires, Argentina, and Professor David Arnold of the Harvard Business School, as the basis for class discussion rather than to illustrate either effective or ineffective handling of an administrative situation.

costs, against the background of a rapidly changing macroeconomic environment in Argentina.

From September 30, 1991 to the fiscal year ended December 31, 1997, net sales increased by 220.3%, from US$358.1 million to US$1.147.1 million, while operating income increased from US$1.7 million to US$55.6 million, and net income recovered to a profit of $24.0 million from a loss of $29.3 million. (Exhibit 1 shows the company's financial performance.) Once productivity had been addressed, through closure of poorly performing stores and consolidation of systems, the new executive team pushed for growth through expansion of locations, primarily through acquisition. By 1997, Disco operated its supermarkets with one management team under five different brand names: Disco, Vea,

Su, Elefante, and La Gran Provisión. There were plans to gradually change the stores' names to Disco.

Gustavo Papini, chief operating officer, explained the company's operating strategy: "Our strategy is based on five pillars: location, assortment, perishables, service, and price."

Starting with location, in 1998, Disco operated 108 urban supermarkets with an average selling area of 1400 m^2[1] in five geographical regions throughout the country: Buenos Aires, Cuyo, Atlantic Coast, Northwest, and Cordoba (see Exhibit 2). The stores were designed to attract customers residing within five blocks of the stores who shopped on average twice weekly.

_____
[1] 1 square meter equals approximately 10 square feet.

Region	Number of Supermarkets	Net Sales (millions)	Net Sales as of Total Sales	Selling Space (in sq. m)	% of Total Disco Selling Space
Buenos Aires	58	910.6	56.7	62,688	43.5%
Atlantic coast	10	116.2	7.2	16,252	11.3
Córdoba	7	85.0	5.3	14,308	9.9
Northwest	7	114.9	7.2	14,210	9.9
Cuyo	27	380.2	23.7	36,638	25.4
Total	109	1606.9	100%	144,096	100.0%

The second pillar was the assortment of products, mainly foods, which included a private label program launched in 1994. Two-hundred-and-thirty premium quality products under the Bell's brand, mostly canned and dry groceries, were offered, representing approximately 2% of the company's total sales for the fiscal year 1997. The company intended to expand the Bell's line with additional items emphasizing the higher margin private label products, and engaged Daymon, a leading U.S. provider of private label products, as support for program development. A special laboratory was established to test new products and analyze microbiological conditions and hygiene. This laboratory also served as the control department, routinely checking quality and freshness of perishable goods.

Products were classified into four major categories: perishable goods, groceries, beverages, and nonfood items. Differentiation from its competitors was pursued by emphasizing the quality of the higher-margin perishable goods (the third pillar of the strategy).

Percentage Contribution to the Company's Net Income
(sales by product category—year ended December 31)

Product Category	1997	1996	1995
Perishable goods	46.80%	47.00%	46.00%
Groceries	19.10%	19.50%	20.70%
Beverages	15.50%	15.70%	15.70%
Nonfood items	18.60%	17.80%	17.60%
Total	100.00%	100.00%	100.00%

	1997	1996	1995	1994	1993
Consolidated Income Statement:					
Net sales	1147.1	844.4	804.6	791.8	696.2
Cost of sales	−831	−601.1	−598	−586.8	−516.0
Gross profit	316.1	234.3	206.6	205	180.1
Administrative expenses	−24.1	−18.9	−18.4	−20.6	−25.8
Selling expenses	−217.2	−164.3	−151.7	−153	−118.3
Depreciation and amortization	−25.4	−15.7	−11.7	−11	−8.8
Gain (loss) from equity investments	0.6	−0.1	0.2	0.2	0
Other operating income	5.6	2.9	2.4	2.7	1.9
Operating income	55.6	38.2	27.4	23.2	29.2
Financial expense, net	−20.8	−13.8	−13.2	−10.8	−23.4
Minority interest in subsidiaries	0	0	0	−0.1	0
Income before taxes	34.7	24.5	14.3	12.4	5.7
Asset and income taxes	−10.7	−3.5	−1.4	−2.3	−2.3
Net income	24	21	12.8	10.1	3.5
Net income per share	0.51	0.48	0.39	0.3	0.11
Consolidated Balance Sheet:					
Cash	25.2	13.6	10.9	13.3	10.3
Trade receivables	61.4	43.2	37.9	30.6	30
Inventories	109.3	53.2	41.7	48.9	45.1
Total current assets	214.6	120.9	103.7	104.3	95.6
Fixed assets	403.5	209.9	135.1	124.7	114.6
Total assets	868.7	343.1	251.4	244.7	222
Trade payables	252.8	138.4	104.2	98.4	80.3
Short-term debt	327.6	11.2	48.2	56.1	72.2
Total current liabilities	649	170.8	170.7	174.2	170.7
Total long-term loans	5.3	22.6	23.6	24.1	13.4
Total liabilities	702.6	200.5	196.9	200.5	185.7
Total shareholders equity	165.6	142.6	54.5	44.2	35.3
Total assets	844.6	327.9	239.4	230.6	208.2
Total shareholders equity	141.8	122	38.5	29.8	21.4
Other Financial Information:					
Gross margin	27.60%	27.80%	25.70%	25.90%	25.90%
Operating margin	4.80%	4.50%	3.45	2.90%	4.20%
net income margin	2.10%	2.50%	1.60%	1.30%	0.50%
Current ratio	0.3	0.7	0.6	0.6	0.6
Total debt/total capitalization	0.7	0.2	0.6	0.6	0.7
Solvency ratio	0.2	0.7	0.3	0.2	0.2
Illiquidity ratio	0.8	0.6	0.6	0.6	0.6
Profitability ratio	0.2	0.2	0.3	0.3	0.1
Consolidated fixed charge— Coverage ratio	6.4	6.3	3.2	3	1.9

EXHIBIT 1 (cont.)

	1997	1996	1995	1994	1993
Operating Information:					
Number of supermarkets (at period end)	109	60	52	52	52
Number of supermarkets substantially remodeled or expanded (during period)	6	11	3	3	1
Total selling space per supermarkets (in sq. m at period end)	144,096	75,246	58,183	56,947	52,506
Average selling space per supermarket (in square meters)	1284	1254	1113	1067	1010
Supermarket sales per square meter	12617	13372	13988	14512	13255
Increase (decrease) in same store sales	2.50%	−0.50%	−1.70%	13.40%	18.30%
Total number of equivalent employees (at period end)	11,225	6,405	5,339	5,611	5,310
Supermarket sales per equivalent employee	$152,054	150,479	155,409	154,622	136,816

Source: Disco S.A. Annual Report 1997.

The fourth pillar was to provide a high level of customer service. Unlike its principal competitors, Disco offered free same-day home delivery from each of its supermarkets in Buenos Aires and from some of its other locations. Other services included a frequent shopper program, Discoplus, which had 1,070,000 members by 1997. Purchases by Discoplus members represented 58% of sales in 1997. Also offered was a credit card, Discocard, with which the company's customers could purchase goods at the company's stores. By the end of 1997, 67,476 Discocards were issued, accounting for 5.4% of total sales. Other major credit cards were also accepted, with on-line authorization.

Discoflash was a special checkout counter where customers could leave their grocery carts to be checked out by store employees. The purchases were then delivered to the customers' homes for a fee of $3, usually within an hour. Banking services, including checking and savings account services, cash machines, and exchange of foreign currency were offered through Practibanco.

Through the Disque service, customers could phone in their purchases, which were normally delivered within an hour for a $3 fee. In 1996, Disco introduced 0-800-Disco, a 24-hour toll-free customer service telephone number for the company's customers. Customers could also purchase through Disco virtual, a CD-ROM, or through the Internet (http://www.disco.com.ar), the company's website designed to facilitate communications with its customers and the investment community. Since 1996, Disco and Elefante stores had interactive multimedia stands on the Worldwide Web with information regarding store services and hours of operations (Informidisco), and Discoplus account balance information for Discoplus shoppers.

EXHIBIT 2   Disco's Five Geographical Regions

Argentina

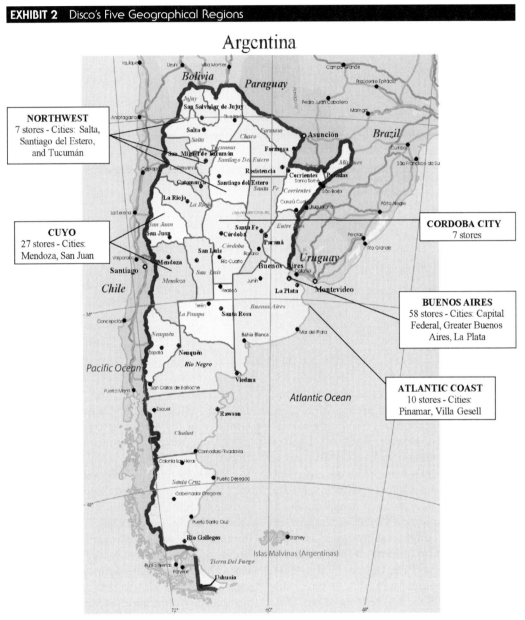

NORTHWEST
7 stores - Cities: Salta,
Santiago del Estero,
and Tucumán

CUYO
27 stores - Cities:
Mendoza, San Juan

CORDOBA CITY
7 stores

BUENOS AIRES
58 stores - Cities: Capital
Federal, Greater Buenos
Aires, La Plata

ATLANTIC COAST
10 stores - Cities:
Pinamar, Villa Gesell

Source: Disco Annual Report 1997.

Twenty-eight stores had childcare centers (Disquito) for parents shopping at the stores. They were run by highly professional staff and provided individual and differentiated services. Mordisco was an initiative of 1997, by which the company started leasing space to fast food operators, introducing fast food courts in five of its Buenos Aires supermarkets and one in Córdoba.

A magazine, *Entrecasa,* was published monthly, providing nutritional information, recipes, and information on promotions and sales at the company's stores as well as general interest articles. Its circulation of 450,000 was distributed at all the stores as well as inside *Clarín,* the nation's leading newspaper. In September 1997, the company introduced *Discochef,* a cookbook consisting of semimonthly circulars which contain recipes and cooking tips. The company also operated FM Disco, a closed-circuit radio station, in all of its store locations to broadcast promotions, weather announcements, music, information of general interest, and advertise specials. Additional services included film developing (Discofoto) through photo shops located within the company's stores, and Lavadisco, an environmentally friendly dry cleaning, laundry, and ironing service in three of the stores.

"The last pillar is price," explained Papini. "Prices are established regionally, based on store operating costs, the socioeconomic segment served, the level of special services offered, and the level of competition. Within limits set by central management, store managers have some flexibility with respect to the pricing of items."

In an effort to improve customer service and achieve operating efficiencies while projecting a consistent corporate image, the company began in 1992 to standardize its operating procedures. It maintained operating manuals at each outlet, as well as at the distribution facilities, warehouses, and central purchasing areas. These manuals outlined the company's procedures with respect to billing, purchase orders, storage and inventory, store upkeep and maintenance, payment of bills, and rules for cashiers. The company also developed architectural guidelines aimed at standardizing the layout of the stores, materials used for construction, and the equipment installed within and outside the store.

Products were purchased from over 1,000 suppliers, including the major local companies. The 10 largest suppliers accounted for 30.2%, 20.8%, and 22.7% of total products purchased in 1997, 1996, and 1995, respectively. A number of products were purchased directly, including meat and fresh produce. The company bought its own beef cattle, which were sent directly from slaughterhouses to the stores for cutting and final packaging. Fresh produce was purchased either directly from farmers located in the outskirts of the cities where the company operated or through regional markets.

Although the volume of purchases and product mix for each store was determined by the individual store manager, a centralized purchasing organization selected the company's product range and negotiated prices, promotions, discounts, and payment terms with individual suppliers. Besides managing the stores in his/her jurisdiction, each regional manager was assigned a category for which he/she was given companywide responsibility with regard to procurement. Categories were rotated every two years. Every year, the company discussed its strategy for the upcoming year at an annual suppliers convention. Information from the Discoplus database was shared with suppliers to jointly design special sales promotions and other sales events.

The company operated four distribution facilities. Two served the Disco stores in the Buenos Aires region, one for dry goods ($14,000 \, \text{m}^2$) and the other ($3,700 \, \text{m}^2$) for vegetables. One ($2,000 \, \text{m}^2$) served the Su stores and distributed both dry goods and vegetables; and the fourth, located in Mendoza, served the Vea stores ($5,500 \, \text{m}^2$).

LATIN AMERICA: THE CHANGES IN THE 1990S

Latin America represented a market of about 450 million people in 1997, compared to Western Europe's 380 million. The rate of population growth was slowing at 1.8%, but exceeded Western Europe's 0.3%, and was similar to that of the Asian Tiger economies. In the six largest countries (Argentina, Brazil, Chile, Colombia, Mexico, and Venezuela), the population was over 80% urban, and some 82 million people lived in the biggest 10 cities in the region.

The return of strong economic growth in the 1990s brought back confidence to consumers (Exhibit 3). There had been no sudden increase in wealth, but changes in attitudes had transformed the retail sector. In mid-1996, it was estimated that 92% of workers in Mexico were earning less than $330 monthly, and that 73% of urban households in Chile, the Latin tiger economy, had a monthly income of less than $1,000. With inflation pegged back, however, there had been an increase in the value of the money, particularly among these lower-income groups. Nowhere was this truer than in Brazil: more capital was available, and consumers and businesses alike had been able to plan their future, borrowing if necessary. This had led to a surge in confidence but had also changed shopping habits. Price comparison was now possible, and there was no pressure on consumers to hurry purchases as in the inflationary years of the 1980s.

In simple economic and demographic terms, Argentina and Brazil were the obvious destinations for retailers in the region; Argentina on the basis of its level of wealth, and Brazil on the size of its population and economic activity. Argentina was the richest country by far in terms of purchasing power per household and had the most even distribution of wealth. Brazil, Chile, Mexico, and Venezuela were roughly equal in terms of disposable income, but unequal distribution of wealth meant that up to 40% of these nations' populations were excluded from normal consumer activity.

Experts predicted that continuing growth beyond 2000 would produce a significant increase in the size of the working populations, in the number of working women, and in the ownership of cars and basic consumer goods. It was also likely that with the sustained foreign investment the region was attracting, improving communications and infrastructure, many medium-sized cities would grow disproportionately in size and wealth. These changes would provide opportunities for retailers. The only cloud on the horizon was the doubt that the economies would be able to absorb all the extra labor, resulting in high unemployment and depressed wage levels.

Latin American populations were highly urbanized. Despite their landmasses

EXHIBIT 3 Latin America—Population and GDP per Capita (1997)			
Country	*Population (in millions)*	*GDP Total (in $ billions)*	*GDP per capita ($)*
Argentina	35.2	231	6,570
Brazil	164.0	510	3,112
Chile	14.6	78	5,342
Ecuador	11.9	16	1,378
Mexico	94.7	411	4,343
Peru	24.3	54	2,206

Source: Adapted from data of World Bank and Inter American Development Bank.

and their dependence on agriculture, Argentina and Chile led the field, with higher urban rates than Germany's 83.3%, a large part of which was concentrated in a few mega-cities. Both Argentina and Chile offered large centers, Buenos Aires and Santiago, but had few other cities of size: Argentina had only two more cities of over one million inhabitants and Chile had none. The effect in Chile had been to force successful local hypermarket chains over the border into Argentina. Statistically, Colombia offered the most balanced spread of cities, with four centers of over one million, but its difficult geography had to be taken into account. Venezuela had only one city of over one million apart from the capital. Brazil and Mexico alone had a significant number of large centers.

Brazil had the world's sixth largest population (161 million) growing at over 2% annually. It was the world's major developing nation in terms of GDP; its economy centered on large agrarian, mining, and manufacturing sectors. Service employed 42% of the labor force, industry 27%, and agriculture 31%. Foreign investment was encouraged and there were no restrictions on involvement in the retail sector. Import tariffs were slowly coming down within the framework of the Mercosur agreement. Self-service food retailers commanded a high proportion of the total Brazilian market, but the sector was regional and fragmented. (See Exhibit 4.) Only the leading companies were technologically advanced.

The economy entered the 1990s with declining real growth, high inflation, and an unserviceable foreign debt of $122bn. Most infrastructure and utilities were owned and run by either the federal or state governments. Reform was initiated in 1990, state-owned enterprises were prepared for privatization, and in 1992–1993, most of the steel mills were sold, along with the chemical, petrochemical, shipping, and aircraft companies. Among other measures taken to

deregulate the economy, price controls were lifted in 1993. In 1994, the Plano Real was introduced. It reduced inflation by pegging the new currency—the Real—to the U.S. dollar. In the first year, inflation was reduced sharply to 31.1%. Under the new plan the government also sought to lower its spending and budget deficit and to reform the tax system. Brazil faced problems, including the second most unequal distribution of wealth in the world (after Botswana), poverty, and lack of education.

Credit remained a vital part of the retail equation in Brazil: most large stores and all home appliance chains offered some sort of credit scheme, which allowed the poorer members of society to buy not just consumer durables but also clothing and food. Consumer credit re-emerged as an engine of retail growth as the economy stabilized in the 1990s. There were various forms of lending. The most popular was the installment scheme whereby customers paid equal amounts monthly. Terms were reaching 24 months in 1996. Retailers generally operated their own schemes, and in 1996 Casas Bahia, one of the leading electrical goods chains, had 2.7 million active accounts. Other forms of lending were the postdated check and credit card.

Chile's economic policy resulted in very high growth rates from the mid-1980s and steady increases in income. In spite of strong efforts towards industrial diversification, exports of copper still represented 40% of the country's foreign sales. Chile adopted the free-market economic model earlier than any other Latin American country. The economy began to be opened up to competition in the late 1970s. Tariffs were cut from an average of 75% in 1975 to 15% in 1985. Chilean industry competed well and trade increased, and in 1991, the government felt confident enough to reduce tariffs to their current level of 11%. Some state industries were privatized, but some profitable ones, including the copper giant Codelco, were not.

EXHIBIT 4 Channel Importance in Latin America (%)

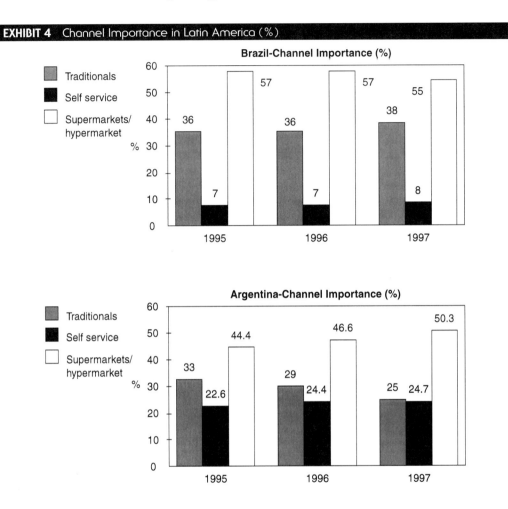

Foreign investment was encouraged, but restrictions on capital inflow were maintained to try to ensure that "fast money" stayed out. This included a 35% capital gains tax and a one-year lock-in period. The benefits of this policy were shown in the "tequila crisis," the aftermath of the Mexican peso crisis: whereas capital flight to the tune of $8.5bn threw Argentina into recession in 1995, Chile continued virtually unscathed, recording a GDP growth of 8.4%, and that year a record $3bn was invested in the country.

Another factor in Chile's progress had been its high level of savings, produced, in large part, by the government pension reforms. With the value of pension funds put at $22.5bn in 1994, the country—and business in particular—had not had to rely too heavily on international capital markets. Indeed, Chile had become an exporter of capital, being one of the major investors in Argentina, and its interest rates were low for the region.

Chile joined Mecosur as an associate member in 1996 and had agreements with Mexico, Venezuela, Colombia, and Bolivia. It was also a member of the Asia Pacific Economic Co-operation Forum (APEC) and sought access to the North American Free Trade Area (NAFTA). It had some of the simplest import regulations in the world, with a unified tariff of 11% on all imports, and import licenses were freely available

EXHIBIT 4 (cont.)

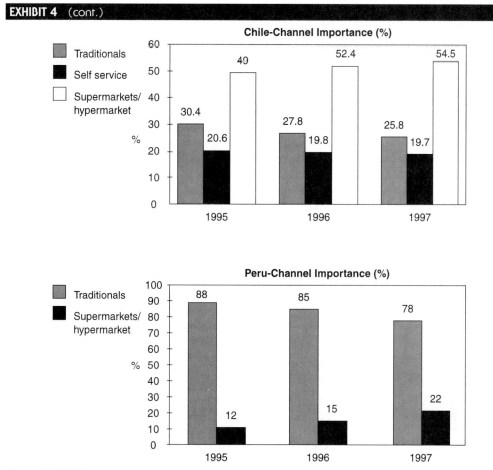

Source: AC Nielsen.

without quota restrictions. There were plans to reduce this to 4%, starting in 1997. Tariffs were lower for imports.

In the Chilean capital Santiago, the property market was extremely tight, with international retailers said to be waiting for availability in existing or new developments. Although institutional investors were keen to buy into new developments, there was a shortage of suitable sites. As a consequence, retail rents were comparatively high.

Retailing in Latin America

The world's biggest retailers had been investing heavily in Latin America, attracted by economic stability, growing populations with growing salaries, and the increasing affluence of its middle class. When Royal Ahold, the Dutch supermarket group, announced a joint venture in Brazil in 1996, it became the tenth of the world's top 20 retailers to enter the region. Of these 10, only 2 were present before 1991. Latin American governments had adopted free market policies which favored foreign investment and benefited the retail market, and as a result of these changes in the economic and political environment, the market was growing strongly. Argentina's economy grew nearly 35% between 1991 and 1994; Chile's grew

11% in one year, in 1992; and Peru managed 13.1% in 1994. The linguistic and cultural homogeneity of the region, compared to other emerging markets, also made it an attractive investment opportunity.

In general, incoming retailers focused first on the big metropolises with sizeable middle-class populations, such as Mexico, São Paulo, and Buenos Aires. The informal sector, comprising street fairs and pavement sellers, was still strong, particularly in Mexico and Peru. Though losing ground to the formal sector, small independent traditional retailers still held the lion's share of the market. It was only in food retailing, and only very recently, that self-service chains had begun to dominate.

In a region where personal contacts and influence were of paramount importance in business, incoming retailers generally tried to enter markets through joint ventures with local groups. The more forward-thinking Latin American chains prepared themselves for increased competition by improving their operations and cutting costs and by emphasizing growth. The first step for most was to invest in information technology, which had been prohibitively expensive before import duties started to fall. Electronic point-of-sales equipment was starting to be commonplace in chain stores, and stock levels and queues at checkouts were being reduced. A number of regional retailers raised capital through initial public offerings, including Electro of Mexico; Santa Isabel in Chile; Araupa, Makro, Globex Utilidades,

and the Pao de Acucar group in Brazil; and Disco in Argentina.

The first multinational retailer to arrive in Latin America was the Dutch group Makro in 1972, followed by the French Carrefour group in 1975, both in Brazil. In a difficult economic climate their growth was slow. Both moved into Argentina in 1982, but Makro waited six years before opening its first store there.

Partly as an effect of internationalization, retailing in Latin America had become more concentrated (see Exhibit 5). Whereas many of the foreign entrants were strategically committed to achieving economies of scale, many of the local retail groups also decided that the only way to defend themselves was to grow. This was most noticeable in the self-service food retailing sector and led to a spate of store openings and acquisitions.

In Chile, the top five supermarket groups had 34% of sales in 1994, but by 1996, a series of takeovers increased their share to 50%. In Argentina, the top five supermarket chains already had 58% of the market, but between them they planned to invest nearly $500m in 50 new stores in the coming years. Similarly, in Brazil, where the top 5 only had about 37% of the market, the process of consolidation was accelerating. Sector leader Carrefour was investing $300m in opening 6 new stores in 1997, on top of the 38 it already had, and number 2 Pao de Acucar planned to increase the number of its hypermarkets from 8 to 12. In Mexico, already a concentrated market, the lead-

EXHIBIT 5 Latin America Retailing—1997					
Country	*Stores*	*Sales Area ('000 sq. m)*	*# Checkouts*	*Sales (US$ millions)*	*Employees*
Brazil	5,200	8,000	60,000	32,000	400,000
Argentina	1,225	1,712	14,700	13,200	82,000
Chile	549	598	6,220	4,250	42,000
Mexico	1,079	4,156	15,800	1,650	116,000

Source: Adapted from Royal Ahold Annual Report 1997, and "1997 Retail Report," CCR/Information Resources Inc.

ing retailers' share would grow purely as a result of their joint venture arrangements (see Exhibit 6).

The hypermarket format, introduced by Carrefour, was the most dynamic vehicle for retail sales in Latin America in the 1990s. Carrefour was the leading retailer in Brazil, with only 38 outlets, while its nearest rival, the Pao de Acucar group, had 218 stores but its sales were some 21% less. In Argentina, the sixth largest chain was Jumbo, with sales of over $500m from just three stores. The format was being adopted by most of the leading supermarket chains across the region.

Most predictions for the future were based on the assumption that GDP per capita growth would continue. Margins would be forced down by increased competition, particularly from foreign entrants

with low-margin formats. The French group Promodes was in negotiations to acquire the Argentine Norte chain from Exxel Group and reinforce its existing Día hard discount chain, which was slowly growing. Franchise was predicted to be a growth sector, stimulated by shopping center development.

RETAILING IN ARGENTINA

The Argentine supermarket industry was considered the most dynamic in Latin America. Prior to 1990, food retailing was dominated by small family-owned "almacenes," convenience stores with $150 \, m^2$ to $350 \, m^2$, providing limited product selection of no more than 1000 SKUs. Their competitive advantage was to being close to the customers. The stabilization of the economy in

EXHIBIT 6 Some Joint Ventures in Retail in Latin America

Company	Country of Origin	Where in Latin America	Type of Operation	Details of Alliance
Amoco	USA	Mexico	Convenience stores	Femsa (Mexican service stations)
Auchan	France	Mexico	Hypermarkets	50/50 Mexicana
Carrefour	France	Mexico	Hypermarkets	50/50 Gigante
Dillars	USA	Mexico	Department stores	Cifra/ Wal-Mart
Ekono	Chile	Argentina	Hypermarkets	50/50 Casa Tia
Flemings	USA	Mexico	Supermarkets	Gigante
HVH	Netherlands	Brazil	Music stores	Conshopping
Kmart	USA	Mexico	Superstores	Liverpool
Makro	Netherlands	Colombia	Warehouse clubs	51/49 with a consortium of investors and retailers
Makro	Netherlands	Venezuela	Warehouse clubs	75/25 with Polar (food and brewing)
Price-Costco	USA	Mexico	Warehouse clubs	Mexicana
Radio Shack	USA	Mexico	Electronic Stores	Gigante
Sodimac	Chile	Colombia	Home centres	35/65 with Corona Group
Smart & Final	USA	Mexico	Discount warehouses	Calimax
Wal-Mart	USA	Mexico	Superstores and warehouse clubs	50/50 Cifra
Wal-Mart	USA	Brazil	Superstores and warehouse clubs	60/40 Lojas Americanas

Sources: Adapted from Royal Ahold Annual Report 1997, "The Economist" March 4, 1995, "Retailing in Latin America," MacDermot, "1997 Retail Report" CCR in addition with Information Resources Inc.

the 1990s created an environment that fostered the rapid development of the supermarket industry.

At first, competition was centered on lowering prices, with all chains heavily advertising their offers. By 1994, local supermarket chains were starting to differentiate themselves from the hypermarkets—mostly foreign companies—on the basis of convenience and customer knowledge.[2]

Supermarket chains generally competed on quality of products, service, product variety, and store conditions (see Exhibits 7 and 8). Among the local chains, Norte and Disco targeted the middle- and upper-class segments. Norte emphasized high-quality assortment, while Disco added service. Both forced another competitor, Hawai, to close. Coto based its strategy on high-quality beef, an important component of the Argentine diet, and low price. El Hogar Obrero, a successful cooperative targeting the low-income segments during the 1970s, and a pioneer in private label, could not keep pace with the volatile economy of the 1980s. Su Supermercado—later acquired by Disco—enjoyed popularity in the western part of Buenos Aires, where its fresh produce and beef won it business over the small local stores. Casa Tía repositioned itself as the Tía Express, a mix of food and personal care with low-priced apparel and other consumer products in less quantity than hypermarkets. Altogether the five leading firms were responsible for 68% of total sector sales. All were based in Buenos Aires and none could claim a full national presence, although Norte, Disco, and Tía had plans for entering in the smaller towns of the rest of the country.

The Chilean chain Jumbo opened the first hypermarket in Argentina in 1981. By mid-1996, Jumbo had four hypermarkets, all in greater Buenos Aires, reporting sales of US$548 pesos for 1995, and was expanding into D-I-Y hyperstores, with its Easy Home-centers attached to its stores.

The European entrants were led by Makro and Carrefour. The former bought land in 1982 but, owing to the economic and political uncertainty of the times, delayed opening until 1988. First targeted at supplying the small retailer, it later opened to general consumers but even with this broadened market it did not succeed over the other chains. By 1996, it not only had stopped growing, but it was considered that it needed a total redefinition of its business. Carrefour launched just after Jumbo, in 1982, but suffered six years of slow growth, and in 1988 it still had only three stores. By 1995, it had 12 and 2 more had been opened by September 1996.

The second wave of foreign retailers entered after 1990. Major new players were Unimark in 1991 and Ekono in 1992, both from Chile, and Wal-Mart in 1995. In December 1996, Supermercados Norte was bought by the international investment fund Exxel, in a deal worth $440m. This was one of the largest-ever purchases of a private company in Argentina. Wal-Mart opened its first superstore and Sam's Club in 1995, and grew to nine outlets in 1996. In 1996, it lost $10 million, tripling its losses from the previous year, and its Sam's Club concept suffered a fate similar to that of Makro.

Anticipating that the economy would emerge from recession in 1997, all the main food retailers announced significant investment plans for that year. Carrefour intended to open three new stores in the year, with an investment of $105m. Wal-Mart announced that it would invest $76m in four new supercenters. Having acquired Su and Vea—in Mendoza—and restructured and invested in IT, Disco announced a $145m investment in

---

[2]Supermarkets ranged up to 2,500 square meters, with an average 7,000 SKUs and an emphasis on perishables, beverages, and other foods. Hypermarkets ranged from 5,000–15,000 sq. meters, usually carried over 10,000 SKUs, and devoted a third of their space to nonfood items such as apparel, toys, and household appliances.

EXHIBIT 7 Importance of Supermarket Chains

ARGENTINA

Supermarkets Chains	Sales (in millions US$)	Stores	Selling Space (SQ.MT)
Carrefour	2,100	18	191,698
Disco-Ahold	1,700	109	148,179
Norte	1,200	22	91,125
Coto	1,200	44	99,077
Tía	650	58	97,182
Jumbo	600	9	78,592
Wal-Mart	460	9	89,791
Americanos	300	62	39,687
Hiperlibertad	440	67	53,512
Patagonia	300	50	45,246

BRAZIL

Supermarkets Chains	Sales (in millions US$)	Stores	Selling Space (SQ.MT)
Carrefour Com. Ind. Ltda.	3,721	44	450,525
Cia. Brasileira de Distribuicao	2,687	223	294,734
Casas Sendas Com. E Ind. S.A.	1,174	56	142,917
Bompreco S.A.	947	50	122,687
Paes Mendoca S.A.	767	35	138,345
Nacional Cda. Ltda.	528	65	82,713
Supermar Supermercados S.A.	499	51	102.004
Cia. Zaffari Comercio e Industria	446	18	51,323
Cia. Real de Distribucao	426	34	65,460
Eldorado S.A. Com. Ind. Imp.	379	8	57,968

CHILE

Supermarkets Chains	Sales (in millions US$)	Stores	Selling Space (SQ.MT)
D&S (Almac, Ekono, Lider)	384	30	37000
Santa Isabel (Multimarket)	374	52	42920
Unimarc	257	29	33100
Jumbo	170	2	25000
Las Brisas	121	14	15000

PERU

Supermarkets Chains	Sales (in millions US$)	Stores
Wong	195	12
Metro	85	2
Santa Isabel	175	14
Maxi Market	29	8
Top Market	29	5

Sources: Adapted from Royal Ahold Annual Report 1997, Deutsche Morgan Grenfell Estimates, 1997, Ranking ABRAS '97 Report, "Latin American Retail" by Morgan Stanley Dean Witter 1998, AC Nielsen Retail Report 1997.

opening 17 stores, but over a longer period. Other chains like Coto, Jumbo, Norte, and Tia all planned to spend between $40m and $80m each in new openings in the short term.

Despite the recession triggered by the tequila crisis, and a 3% rise in VAT, margins in food retailing remained high in Argentina in 1995. Disco claimed to have shared the burden of the VAT increase with suppliers, and showed a gross profit margin of 25.7%, only 0.2% less than in 1994 and 1993, and a net profit of 1.6%, compared to 0.5% in 1993 and 1.3% in 1994. The reason for the improved performance seemed to have been steady reduction of sales and administration expenses. Carrefour had a gross profit of 16.1% and a net profit of 3.2% in 1995.

Competition grew stronger, reflected in actions such as Carrefour's international thirty-fifth birthday sale, a month of aggressively promoted low prices in products like TV sets, bicycles, and microwave ovens. Wal-Mart reacted by adding to its Crazy Wednesdays—aggressive low prices on selected items for one day—its own celebration of its second year in Argentina with its Magic Birthday. Clients participated in a lottery for prizes ranging from appliances to lifetime vacations. Jumbo also organized a birthday celebration, competing on price for the first time, and also announced a weekly lottery for camping sets, bicycles and cars. Part of these promotional efforts were supported by the suppliers, who were asked to contribute 20 to 30% of their monthly sales to a chain.

RETAILING IN CHILE

Retailing was a well-developed and competitive sector in Chile, with total 1995 sales of $15.5bn, 35% of national GDP. Supermarkets and hypermarkets sold $2.73bn in 1995 and were expected to reach $3bn in 1996, 49% of which were made by the four leading chains, while the following six added 16%. Department store sales were estimated at $2bn and shopping centers at $1.37bn.

With no chain having national coverage, competition remained regional, based on location, price, service, product quality, and selection, as well as type and frequency of promotions. With an estimated penetration in 1997 of 64%, supermarkets were the primary retail distribution outlets of foodstuffs and other household items. From 1993 to 1997, sales grew 11.4% every year, exceeding the 7.7% GDP average annual growth over the same period (Exhibit 8).

EXHIBIT 8	Argentine Supermarkets	
Company	*Country*	*Market Share*
Disco	France	16%
Carrefour	Argentina–Netherlands	20%
Coto	Argentina	11%
Norte	Argentina	11%
Tia	Argentina	6%
Jumbo	Chile	6%
Wal-Mart	USA	4%
Others	Others	25%

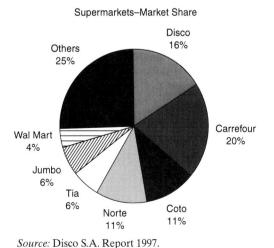

Source: Disco S.A. Report 1997.

Already having captured over 90% of food sales, the leading supermarket chains intended to increase market share either by opening hypermarkets or by acquiring smaller chains. Increased competition between new hypermarkets and existing supermarkets was leading to margin erosion, while smaller chains were being forced to be more innovative to maintain their share.

Five supermarket chains accounted for 48% of the supermarket sector ($1.3bn in 1995). Among these, three were stronger in the metropolitan region of Santiago and two, Santa Isabel and Las Brisas, were regional. Santiago represented 47% of the nation's sales. Only Santa Isabel was a public company in 1996, but Distribución y Servicios was preparing for an equity offering.

With the opening of hypermarkets, a trend began towards fewer stores and larger sales areas, at least in the capital, where from 1994 to 1995 the number of stores decreased 12%—from 189 to 176—whereas selling area increased nearly 13% to 265.000 m^2. With 17 stores, hypermarkets accounted for 32% of the industry sales. Two groups carried this development, D&S with its Líder chain and Jumbo who, with two well-placed stores, had 6.2% of the market. The Jumbo stores were located in the group's own shopping centers in middle-class areas of Santiago and had sales areas of 12.500 m^2, carrying 60,000 SKUs. Jumbo opened its third hypermarket in Santiago in December 1996, and also expanded into DIY through its Easy Homecenters, competing with Sodimac, the first entry into South America by The Home Depot. Despite its sales out of only two stores, further development could be restrained by the fact that outside Santiago there were only three or four cities that could sustain large developments of this kind. With Continente from Spain said to be building in Chile, and new stores being opened by existing groups, margins were likely to come under more pressure.

Lider's expansion had been more aggressive. Between 1995 and 1996, it opened four stores in Santiago and one in Viña del Mar. Some of these were recycled Ekono stores and some greenfield developments. The new stores were all 10,000–12,000 m^2 and were run on the lines of Wal-Mart's Supercenters, with nonfood being 50% of the product mix and limited store warehousing coordinating JIT delivery with its suppliers. Openings were accompanied by aggressive first-month promotion, including under lower-than-cost pricing for selected items, according to rivals. New Lider hypermarkets were planned for Concepción and the southeast of Santiago. Santa Isabel also announced plans to start building hypermarkets.

As they lost marketshare to the larger formats, some of the smaller operators were making purchasing alliances. One made in 1996 between Uriarte and Agas—each with 1.7% of the market—looked like being joined by Cosmos with 1.4%. Other small chains were also focusing on offering customers better and faster service from compact locations. Two of Cosmos's new stores, in Providencia and Recoleta, up-market suburbs of Santiago, were 900 sq. m and 1.300 sq. m and followed a super-express concept. Agas, Montecarlo, and Monserrat were following the same strategy.

Acquisitions seemed certain to lead to further consolidation in the supermarket sector. It was Santa Isabel's main vehicle for growth, with takeovers of the Multimarket chain in 1995 and of 70% of the bankrupt Marmentini-Letelier chain in 1996, adding 35 stores. The Marmentini stores would add over $60m to Santa Isabel's sales in 1996.

Information technology was quickly being adopted in Chilean food retailing, as the supermarket chains needed to cut costs to prepare for lower margins. In 1996, Santa Isabel was working to install bar code reading equipment to speed in-store reception of goods. More advanced in IT, D&S was considering EDI links and ECR.

ROYAL AHOLD

With more than 3,200 stores worldwide and sales of US$26 billion in 1997, the Netherlands-based Royal Ahold group was an international food retailer with leading supermarket chains in the United States, Europe, Latin America, and Asia. The company operated 830 stores in the United States, with sales of US$4.3 billion out of its Bi-Lo, Giant, Edwards, Tops Markets, Finast, and Stop & Shop chains. Sales in the Netherlands amounted to US$8.2 billion, operating six store chains with over 1,750 outlets including Gall & Gall (liquor stores), Etos (health and beauty care products), and Heijin supermarkets. Ahold had a 73% stake in Schuitema and owned an institutional food supply company and two production facilities. Exhibit 9 gives financial data.

Ahold intended to become the world's best supermarket company over the next few years, providing a superior shopping experience to the 20 million customers that visited the stores every week. Its strategy was aimed at strengthening and expanding its current position in the Netherlands and the United States, where it had built a strong position with a supermarket penetration of more than 50%. Decentralized decision-making was fundamental in this strategy.

New activities had been started in 17 growing markets, with joint ventures with strong local partners in 14 of them. Local market knowledge was complemented with Ahold's strengths in technology, logistics, and finance, benefiting with economies of scale and exchanging best practices throughout the group. Partnerships also included suppliers of branded and private labeled products.

Three Ahold Support Centers in Zaandam (Netherlands), Atlanta (U.S.A.), and Singapore provided the internal exchange of know-how, striving to be the best food provider through different formats in differ-

EXHIBIT 9 Royal Ahold—Consolidated Income Statement (amounts in thousands of US$)		
	For the Years Ended December 31,	
	1996	*1997*
Net sales	18,259,917	25,271,604
Cost of sales	14,298,046	19,501,413
Gross Profit	3,961,871	5,770,191
Selling expenses	2,937,397	4,198,498
General and administrative expenses	403,370	653,737
Operating Results	621,104	917,956
Income from unconsolidated subsidiaries and affiliates	3,116	3,133
Exchange rate differences	–	15,190
Interest income	24,564	47,221
Interest expenses	(186,825)	(302,355)
Net Financial Expenses		
Earnings before income taxes	461,959	681,145
Income taxes	(124,357)	(191,098)
Earnings after income taxes	337,602	490,047
Minority interests	(21,547)	(23,365)
Net Earnings	316,055	466,682

Source: Royal Ahold Annual Report 1997.

ent countries. Adaptation to local markets was facilitated by its ability to operate multiple formats: superstores, supermarkets, hypermarkets, specialty, and convenience stores.

In other European countries, it operated about 350 stores with sales of US$1.7 billion and was joint owner of Feira hypermarkets and Pingo Doce supermarket chains in Portugal. In the Czech Republic, the company operated with Mana supermarkets and Sesam discount stores, and was developing joint ventures for food retailing in Spain and Poland.

In the Asian Pacific region, it worked closely with local partners to develop Tops supermarket chains in China, Indonesia, Malaysia, Singapore, and Thailand, achieving sales of US$500 million out of almost 100 stores.

In Latin America, the company had been developing a strong presence in Brazil since 1996, where it was co-owner at 50% of Bromeco, a US$2 billion chain based in Recife, with over 100 stores in the northeast of the country.

Fritz Ahlqvist, a member of Ahold's corporate executive board, expressed its interest in joining Disco. "A partnership with Disco is fully in line with Ahold's corporate goal to become a leading global supermarket company. It broadens our international experience in this part of the world, where our aim is to grow our presence in the major markets of South America together with well-established local partners. Globally, our mindset is on geographic and format expansion, market leadership, and economies of scale. Locally, our product lines are flexible and adaptable to individual customer requirements, as are our store formats."

SANTA ISABEL

Santa Isabel was the second largest supermarket operator in Chile, Peru, and Paraguay in terms of net sales. In August 1997, it had also started operating in Ecuador.

Though the company had considered hypermarkets to be part of its overall supermarket competition in Chile, during 1997, it decided not to proceed with its previously announced plans to develop hypermarket format stores in Chile and Peru.

In January 1996, it completed its acquisition of 100% of Multimarket from Inversiones Insigne, increasing its number of stores in Chile by 75.8% to 58 supermarkets, and its total selling space by 69.4% to 70,742 m². In September 1996, the company acquired ten stores, thus becoming the second largest supermarket operator (see Exhibit 10).

In 1998, it operated 89 stores with a total selling area of 151,265 m²: 68 supermarkets in Chile, of which 47 were under the Santa Isabel name; 15 supermarkets in Peru, all located in the Lima metropolitan area; 6 in Asunción, Paraguay; four under the "$tock" name and two under "Santa Isabel"; and one Santa Isabel supermarket in Guayaquil, Ecuador.

In each market, the company tailored its product mix according to the particular consumer preferences. In recent years, consumers had shown an increasing preference for food stores that offered not only a wide variety of traditional food and nonfood items, but also an expanded assortment of prepared foods and produce. In response to this trend, the company continued to upgrade its existing departments with new selections, adding specialty service areas, such as full service bakeries, delicatessen and fresh meat, fresh seafood, and prepared food departments. A larger selection of nonfood items was also introduced.

A private-label program was launched in September 1996 under two brands: Elmi and 5 Continentes. Elmi was a price brand, positioned with a strong image as an alternative to the category leader. This strategy allowed the company to offer a unique selection of products in its stores at lower prices than national brands, while improving margins from these products. By year-end

EXHIBIT 10 Santa Isabel S.A. Consolidated Income Statement and Balance Sheet (in millions of US$)

| | As at and for the Year Ended December 31, | | | | |
	1997	1996	1995	1994	1993
INCOME STATEMENT DATA					
U.S. GAAP:					
Net sales	357,872.00	333,529.00	202,743.00	161,443.00	107,969.00
Cost of sales	−2,829,57.90	−2,633,02.50	−161,508.00	−128,465.00	−86,866.00
Gross profit	74,913.70	70,226.70	41,235.00	32,978.00	21,103.00
Administrative and selling expenses					
Operating income	7,092.70	13,531.00	8,684.00	8,052.00	2,933.00
Nonoperating income	5,8260	2,125.60	2,1200	589.00	452.00
Nonoperating expense	−7,682.10	−5,724.80	−1,868.00	−1,591.00	−1,25_.00
Price-level restatement (loss)	195.30	415,50	−384.70	−1,111.70	565.60
Income taxes	−1,851.90	−2,273.90	−2,474.00	−833.00	−734.00
Net income	3,580.00	8,073.40	6,078.00	5,105.00	1,966.00
Net income per share	9.37	33.21	27.36	17.43	16.84
BALANCE SHEET DATA					
total current assets	63,922.20	73,685.30	60,794.90	29,387.30	23,116.70
Property plant and equipment	96,670.80	74,954.00	44,279.80	30,546.70	26,51_.10
Total assets	191,033.60	177,768.10	114,786.40	63,168.20	52,840.30
Short-term debt	7,013.50	7,905.60	2,397.20	2,984.40	4,962.30
Long-term liabilities	54,031.20	46,162.90	10,555.60	10,290.90	5,767.70
Total shareholders equity	72,325.50	69,617.50	64,796.60	22,114.30	18,84_.80
Ratio of total shareholders equity to total capitalization	0.54	56.35	0.83	0.63	0.65
Chilean GAAP					
Total current assets	62,073.70	74,915.00	56,791.90	30,086.40	23,785.90
Property plant and equipment	102,961.50	82,164.90	48,877.40	35,935.00	30,387.40
Total assets	196,820.50	186,768.80	121,475.30	70,363.10	58,716.30
Short-term debt	7,013.50	7,905.60	2,397.20	2,984.40	4,962.30
Long-term liabilities	50,814.70	43,920.60	9,481.10	9,845.20	5,460.20
Total shareholders equity	83,573.60	84,175.90	76,303.60	31,355.80	28,505.20

Other Financial Information:

Capital expenditures	28,861.00	25,336.00	15,879.30	9,811.30	11,311.00
Depreciation and amortization	6,716.40	6,755.40	2,692.70	2,140.90	2,087.70
Financial ratios:	20.90%	21.30%	20.20%	20.00%	19.50%
Gross margin	2.40	4.30	4.40	4.50	2.90
Net margin	0.90	3.30	3.80	2.80	3.10
Current ratio	101.40	129.70	161.10	103.70	96.40
Total debt/shareholders equity	68.80	61.60	15.60	40.90	31.40

Operating Data:

Number of supermarkets (at period end)	89	80	44	38	32
Number of supermarkets remodeled or expanded (during period)	10	10	3	3	1
Total selling space of supermarkets (in square meters at period end)	150,225.0	114,692.0	59,298.0	50,022.0	40,104.0
Average selling space per supermarket (in square meters at period end)	1,711.0	1,408.0	1,348.0	1,316.0	1,253.0
Average sales per supermarket	4,820.6	5,124.3	4,881.2	4,450.1	3,741.0
Total number of employees (at period end)	12,261	12,125	7,220	5,983	5,148
Increase (decrease) in same store sales	−7.30%	5.95	12.40%	5.40%	1.70%
Sales per square meter (in thousands)	2,716.9	3,161.3	3,746.2	3,569.0	3,793.8
Sales per employee (in thousands)	29,522.9	30,088.7	31,559.4	30,244.4	30,357.4

Source: Santa Isabel S.A. Annual Report 1997.

1997, the company had 181 SKUs under its private label program, representing 2.4% of December 1997 net merchandise sales.

The company classified its sales into five main product categories: perishables, groceries, nonfood items, beverages, and health and beauty aids. The following table compares sales by category to the company's total net sales (not including supplier fees) in Chile for the years ended December 31, 1995, 1996, and 1997. Comparable information was not available as to sales at Multimarket stores for periods prior to the acquisition.

Percentage Contribution to the Company's Net Sales

(in Chile by product category—year ended December 31)

Product category	1995[a]	1996	1997
Perishable goods	38.2%	40.9%	40.2%
Groceries	34.0	25.0	23.7
Nonfood items	12.9	13.3	13.5
Beverages	7.9	12.6	14.3
Health and beauty aids	7.0	8.2	8.3
Total	100.0%	100.0%	100.0%

[a]Excludes Multimarket stores.

Product managers at the central purchasing office selected products for all its Chilean stores and negotiated price, promotions, and terms of payment with individual suppliers on a company-wide basis. Arrangements negotiated with each supplier averaged 42-day payment terms.

There were three purchasing and distribution schemes, under which products could be ordered by the central purchasing office for delivery to one of the three distribution centers, or by individual stores either to the central office or directly to suppliers, for direct delivery. In every case, payments were done at the central office.

The company operated with over 1,300 suppliers in Chile. The two largest were Nestle Chile S.A. and Lever Chile S.A., which accounted for 7.9% and 5.7% respectively of total purchases in 1997, and the ten largest suppliers accounted for 34.6% of total purchases. In 1996, it started to import products and intended to increase them over time. Imported goods accounted for 24.0% of total purchases in 1997.

During that year, plans were completed for building a new main distribution center of 45,500 m^2, dedicated to both perishables and nonperishables, which would serve all the geographic areas in Chile. This facility would be located on a site near the Santiago International Airport and was expected to be completed by October 1999.

Adaptation to each location included not only product selection, but advertising and promotions were also specifically tailored. For the Santa Isabel stores, the marketing emphasis was on offering value through a combination of high-quality service and wide assortment, and for the $tock stores the emphasis was on consistently low prices as well as product assortment.

During 1997, marketing efforts were oriented towards creating and increasing loyalty among existing clients through national and regional promotions. Primary advertising means were radio ads and magazine-type inserts distributed both door-to-door or as inserts in the major newspapers. TV would only be used to announce new store openings and certain promotional campaigns.

An ambitious MIS project was initiated in 1997 in order to support decision-making capabilities, incorporate industry best practices, and allow the decentralization of operations. The project included a financial and accounting system, an interactive human resources administration system to facilitate personnel management, and a commercial application.

The company had 8,147 employees in Chile in March 1998. Santa Isabel was the largest supermarket operator in Chile in terms of number of outlets and the second largest in terms of net sales. The competitors were D&S and Unimarc. Although there were no foreign supermarkets in Chile, Carrefour had begun the construction of its first hypermarket in Santiago.

FOREIGN OPERATIONS

Santa Isabel considered Peru, and especially the Lima metropolitan area, an attractive area for expansion of its supermarket business due to the recent stabilization of its economic and political systems, its potential for continued economic growth, and the current low penetration of supermarkets, reaching only 5% of trade.

The company started operations in 1993 through the acquisition of ten supermarket stores, of which seven were previously operated under the Scala trade name and three under the Mass brand. Seven were converted to the Santa Isabel format and three were closed. By early 1998, it operated 15 stores, all of them located in the Lima metropolitan area. The stores offered a wide range of food items, as well as nonfood. Through a joint venture with Farmacias Ahumada S.A., pharmacies were operated at 13 of the stores.

Store formats ranged between 1,000 m^2 and 2,000 m^2, carrying between 11,000 and 16,000 SKUs, operating around 15 hours daily, with flexible closing hours, according to each location's requirements. Product selection was adjusted at each store to consumers' preferences, but Santa Isabel approved products and negotiated with 540 suppliers on a centralized basis. Nestle was the largest supplier, accounting for 5% of total product purchases, with the following ten largest suppliers accounting for 29% of total purchases. The stores targeted the middle and higher income segments. Investments were made in optical scanning technology that would reduce labor costs associated with product pricing and check out, and in information systems that would facilitate

purchasing, receiving, accurate pricing, and management of inventory and accounts payable.

E. Wong, its main competitor, operated 12 stores in Lima, offering high levels of service and competitive prices. Doing business since 1980, E. Wong was Peru's oldest supermarket chain, and its share of supermarket sales had reached 47% in 1997, from an estimated 40% in the previous year. E. Wong also operated five Metro hypermarkets, and in this lower service segment it had doubled its share in 1997, reaching 24%. At the same time, another competitor, Maxi, had ceased operations, closing all of its eight stores in Lima.

In Asuncion, Paraguay, Santa Isabel started offering a wide range of foodstuff and household products, with two initial stores opened in 1995 that were followed by another two in 1996. These stores averaged 3,000 m^2. A fifth store of over 3,900 m^2 under the $tock brand was opened in 1997 and another was added in 1998. Products were imported from Argentina, Brazil, and Chile, with only a small proportion supplied locally.

A first store of 2,000 m^2 was opened in 1997 in Guayaquil, Ecuador's largest city, followed by a second in 1998, of 3,300 m^2. Competition came from two major chains: Mi Comisariato, with 26 stores, and Supermaxi, with 6 of its 24 stores in Guayaquil.

THE DECISION

"We are ready for increased competition and eager to grow with the economy throughout the region," said Eduardo Orteu, chief executive officer of Disco. "While the Argentine retail market is being attacked by international retailers, we have a solid franchise established in the market. I think we have an advantage through our emphasis on providing specialty services to our customers. After our investments in retail technology and information systems, we can handle operations up to double our current size. Given the high level of competition, success depends on innovation and the right product mix, and competition will become even harder with the new entrants that are looking at this market."

While there were opportunities for expanding regionally, management at Disco was not sure about the transferability of its model and whether this would add significant advantages to its new partners, while stretching on the scarce management resources. New countries meant not only transferring know-how, but also developing a regional management system at a time when the company needed to consolidate its growth in Argentina.

On the other hand, the chances for growing in the new countries provided by the acquisition of Santa Isabel were not so clear. Those who followed this line also pointed out that the real opportunities for growth remained in Brazil. Joining Ahold could provide new skills, but also preempt going into this attractive market.

"This decision will define our future profile. Either we remain local, joining Ahold's global network, or we take the challenge of becoming a regional player by our own means," said Juan Peirano. "It isn't a minor decision." ∎

8-2 IMPSAT

National frontiers will be lines drawn on the maps meanwhile the business and trade flow will run freely in a global digitalized economy.
John Naisbitt
Electronic networks form the key framework of XXI century and are critical for the business success and national economic development as the railways were in the Morse's age.

"We are generating a company in a hi-tech new business. I believe that we can achieve leadership in Argentina and that is why we should discuss the expansion plans next week. What kind of company should we develop?" asked Enrique Pescarmona, president of Pescarmona Group of Companies, of Ricardo Verdaguer and Roberto Vivo, president and vice president of IMPSAT. This company had been recently established to enter the satellite communication business. The three men were leaving the main central station, which monitored all IMPSAT services, at the South Dock of Buenos Aires port, a zone that was being recycled. The last rays of the afternoon sun colored the 84-meter tower and white screens of 11 m diameter faced the sky, each one toward one satellite.

"The possibilities offered at present by the satellite technology combine the economy of information transmission with the safety of using a reliable network, and the reduction of communication costs," said Ricardo Verdaguer. This is a powerful strategic tool to achieve business goals, such as increasing productivity and an accurate response to the market development. The benefits can reach not only our clients, but also their suppliers and even their own customers.

Roberto Vivo repeated the idea that had excited him years ago. We are in the

This case has been prepared by Professor Guillermo D'Andrea of the Instituto de Altos Estudios Empresariales, with the collaboration of Engineer Daniel Hourquescus, as a basis for class discussion rather than to illustrate effective or ineffective handling of any specific situation.

middle of a transcendental change. Many activities will become virtual, transforming physical activities into electronic ones and this, in turn, will also change the industries. Supplier-client relationships will be direct and continuous, bringing together both parts in the precise necessary moment. Products will become more and more personalized and provided at higher speed. Some governments are perceiving the enormous economical potential of modern communication infrastructures and promoting their development.

"We are going toward a global economy, so we should have a global system," said Enrique Pescarmona. The existence of commercial offices and operations of Pescarmona Group of Companies in different countries of Latin America, Southeast Asia, and the rest of the world provided the opportunity to study the feasibility of starting new businesses in those regions, similar to that in Argentina. Enrique Pescarmona was interested in repeating the experience of Argentina in other markets, as he wanted to export the technological and marketing know-how already developed.

At that moment, the company had 20 employees, most of them coming from a satellite project of the Argentine Air Force, the computer data transmission area or the radio-frequency sector. The country was leaving behind a hyperinflation period, during which it had reached a monthly rate of 200%, resulting in a deep social trace.

INDUSTRIAS METALÚRGICAS PESCARMONA (IMPSA)

Enrique Epaminondas Pescarmona arrived in Buenos Aires in 1906, from his native Torino, Italy. Since the age of 13 he had worked there with his father in his family casting shop, manufacturing parts for textile machinery, while studying at night at the technical high school. He went to Mendoza, a province located in midwest Argentine

over Los Andes mountains, an area famous for its wine and fruit production. In 1907, he had established his own business and later built the first grape mechanical milling machine and a miniturbine which used the hydraulic energy of the defrost channels. From there, he continued manufacturing equipment for the regional wine industry. Later, the 1930s crisis severely affected business development.

After the 1930s crisis, his son Luis Menotti Pescarmona graduated as master constructor at the Universidad Popular de Mendoza, and joined his father in their business recovery.

In 1946, he founded Construcciones Metalúrgicas Pescarmona S.R.L., later Industrias Metalúrgicas Pescarmona S.A.I.C.& F (IMPSA), which in 1970 made a major jump when it started to build big hydroelectrical centrals. In 1991, it earned $10.2 million from $198 million in sales, now under the direction of Enrique Menotti Pescarmona (the founder's grandson), an engineer with an MBA from IESE at Barcelona, Spain.

IMPSA was one of a handful of companies in the world that manufactured high-technology turbines, turnkey hydroelectrical centrals, and crane bridges for the U.S. Navy or the Malaysian port. Another $300 million in products were sold by different services companies engaged in activities related to loading transportation, waste collection, satellite transmissions, or wine production. Exhibit 1 shows the group's organization.

THE DEREGULATION OF COMMUNICATIONS

In 1990, interregional meetings of commercial blocks took place to discuss the rules which would give an equalitarian treatment to the different telecommunications carriers, and convince them to satisfy the growing demand for intelligent networks. In the

EXHIBIT 1 Corporación Impsa Organization Chart as of January 31, 1995

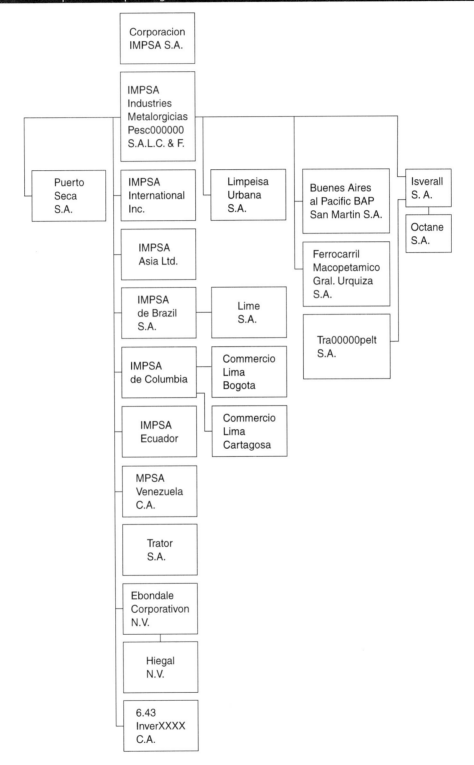

United Kingdom and United States, commercial clients used their influence to meet their own needs and therefore have the choice among different carriers. The elimination of voice service monopolies had been announced in Europe for 1988. Some of the formerly European closed markets, now liberalized, were the cable and air TV, the satellite data transmission services and those specialized for VSAT systems, and the intercompany or closed groups of clients and networks. Such countries as the UK, the Netherlands, France, and Germany were creating structures to grant licences for upward link satellite operators, with the risk of provoking a differentiated growth among the European Union members.

Increasing competition and smaller margins for the operating companies were expected due to the deregulation of the telecommunication markets through the elimination of monopolies and tariffs liberalization, especially for long-distance communications. Attracted by the possibility of expanding their operations internationally, domestic operators began to work on strategic alliances, showing an increasing interest in emerging markets. This was one of the most attractive areas of the business, with an annual growth of 17% in the last 10 years and more open to competition than the domestic markets of each country. Tariffs in the United States and Japan had decreased 50% in the last years.

Cable TV companies intended to enter the telephone market, and there was a growing use of cellular systems for personal communications. At the same time, national offices were formed to regulate domestic competition and the scope of company activities industry-wide.

By the end of the 1990s, low orbit satellite systems (LEO) were announced, such as Motorola's Iridium or Bill Gates and Craig MacCaw's Teledisc. Iridium was a project based in 66 satellites in 6 polar orbits at a height of 765 kilometers. It was intended to

offer bidirectional voice and data services among movable terminals in any place worldwide, as well as radiodetermination of position, search of personnel, facsimile, and local nets interconnection. The investment was estimated at $4 billion. Teledisc anticipated the installation of 840 satellites in 21 orbits, at a cost of $9 billion, offering voice, data, video, and multimedia services at the beginning of the twenty-first century.

This also reflected the increasing invasion of computers, which were expected to replace telephones and TV sets, as technology succeeded in placing more transistor circuits in smaller space, and the optic fiber offered an unlimited bandwidth capacity for communication transmission. In 1992, a fingernail-size chip held 20 million circuits, and it was expected that number would increase to 1 billion circuits by the year 2000, thus making their use more common and turning the focus of competition to additional services.

Anticipating a growing demand for connections and services, and aiming to attain an optimal and homogeneous quality of globally standardized services, the alliances between companies started to spring up. ATT formed World Partners with KDD and Singapore Telecom. France Telecom and Germany's DBP Telekom merged into Eunetcom at equal parts, to offer business and international services and information networks, and they were negotiating agreements with AT&T. British Telecom PLC joined MCI to form Concert, focusing on multinational corporations as clients. Telefónica de España formed Unisource, with its partners KPN, Telia, and PTT of Switzerland. The Spanish company entered into Chile, Venezuela, and Puerto Rico, setting up a company in Argentina with one of the big domestic economic groups, while France-Telecom joined Italy's STET with the same purpose.

Client evolution had a similar rhythm, led by main companies that avoided local suppliers, changed carrier or built their own networks, demanded better services and at a smaller cost, all conscious that alternatives were quickly evolving. Residential and small company markets were still being slightly exploited for interactive services, although cable TV and cellular telephones attained access to that market sector, offering not only entertainment and information, but also bank and shopping services, research, and access to libraries. Books, music, video, and movies were loaded into personal computers through communications, instead of being acquired in stores.

COMMUNICATIONS IN LATIN AMERICA

Meanwhile, in Latin America, the privatization and liberalization of the telecommunication markets were taking place at a much higher speed. During the 1980s, telephone companies in Chile, Mexico, and Venezuela were sold, producing a growth which in some cases duplicated the market size. The Chilean network was one of the first worldwide to adopt digital technology.

In Argentina, the Empresa Nacional de Telecomunicaciones (ENTEL) was privatized in 1990. At that moment, the number of lines was 8 per 100 inhabitants, and the buyers—Telefonica de España and the French Telecom consortium (STET)—announced a density of 20 lines per inhabitant scheduled for 1995.

Brazil, Bolivia, Ecuador, Colombia, Nicaragua, and Peru joined the process of liberalizing their telecommunications with different emphasis, preparing the political ground, studying proposals, or awarding companies. Turnkey contracts for building networks made those processes easier. Competition in long-distance private services was already implemented in Chile, Venezuela, and Colombia, including public services in the case of Chile.

Competitive networks of integrated services did not exist in Latin America. International carriers invested in basic telephone technology, with partial noninte-grated services, mostly in large urban centers. Moreover, the complexity of the Latin American market, with regulations, competition, and different development levels in each country, diminished their interest for assuming greater commitments.

In 1990, the perspective of regional blocks integration appeared more frequently. Meanwhile, the European Community turned into the European Union in 1992, and the NAFTA agreement was outlined in North America. In South America, the presidents of Brazil, Argentina, Uruguay, and Paraguay stated the bases for the organization of a free trade area: the Mercosur. Chile watched the evolution of its neighbors, from a path of progress on which it was a decade ahead.

The markets globalization was finally reaching Latin America, where domestic markets accelerated their evolution, generating interesting opportunity niches. The countries adopted development policies which allow them greater stability, with larger access to markets, and medium- and long-term international credit.

At that time, a worldwide increase of liquidity was observed entering into ventures, and making possible broader availability of medium- and long-term credits. International agencies showed greater interest in financing private businesses, those related to high technology with adequate profitability being the most attractive.

THE VSAT TECHNOLOGY AND ITS APPLICATION TO COMMUNICATIONS

In 1987, Mr. Roberto Vivo, born in Uruguay, had already spent many years managing his building company, specialized in public works. Due to the country's economic difficulties and looking for the diversification into new businesses, he had been studying telecommunications possibilities. He also made contacts with a group of Argentine scientists from the Comision Nacional de Investigaciones Espaciales (National Commission of Space Investigations), who had developed the projects for Argentina's domestic satellite together with the United States, France, and Germany. At that time, telephone communications were administered by a government monopoly, and data transmission was poorly supplied by the Arpac network, according to what Vivo personally verified through some interviews with client companies.

In turn, taking advantage of the fact that his father was the Uruguayan ambassador in Brazil, he decided to visit that country which had set in orbit its first two domestic satellites in 1986. He met Pedro Castello Branco, president of Embratel, who connected him with the two consulting companies that had developed the Brasilsat project. This relationship led him to read his first article about the VSAT technology, recently released from military to commercial use.

Through his relation as IMPSA supplier, he became acquainted with Ricardo Verdaguer, marketing manager, visiting him in 1987. He proposed to him to enter into the communications business, using the (VSAT) satellite technology with a "Shared Hub" concept. This was a new concept, as the initial success of this technology in the United States had been almost exclusively for large private networks.

During the meetings, where technological aspects were detailed and business possibilities were evaluated, Ricardo Verdaguer immediately understood the implications and potential of the project. Considering IMPSA's experience in the handling of huge projects and technology transfer agreements—both nuclear and capital goods—he decided to present and back up Vivo's project in the company.

Perceiving a decrease of public works, Enrique Pescarmona had already begun a process of diversification, and he decided to enter into the new business. On behalf of IMPSA Corporation, he appointed Verdaguer as responsible for the project.

During 1988, the initial group basically formed by Vivo and Verdaguer was applied to study technological, legal, and commercial aspects of the project. The two options were single channel per carrier (SCPC) or very small aperture terminal (VSAT) technologies.

The greatest possibilities of satellite communications appeared in the early 1980s, when technology allowed the building of smaller satellites but of greater power, which also permitted the utilization of smaller antennas. The launchings also were safer, reducing the failures of one in three, to only 5% of launchings and at a smaller cost.

European and American companies that wished to go abroad with their national networks were applying the VSAT technology. The Holiday Inn chain had hired MCI Communication Corp. for the installation and operation of 300 VSAT in Europe, anticipating its expansion to another 300 in Latin America by the end of the century. Three of the most advanced projects in Europe belonged to the automotive industry: Mercedes-Benz and Volkswagen of Germany, and Renault of France. These companies would connect their central inventory databases with their terminals, to organize their sendings and deliveries where their car models were required. However, the high cost of replacing current installations by hundreds of interactive terminals was one of the most important obstacles. The other one involved regulations, which restrained the possibilities of application to one-way communications in Europe. Regardless of ECC existence, the regulatory context reflected unequal rhythms in the different countries. Then, Spain and Italy kept stricter control over communications than northern countries of the continent.

The access to space was still being controlled, thus maintaining artificially high prices for satellite communications. Previously, satellite capacity in Europe could only be leased to Post, Telephones and Telegraphs (PTT) national companies, and users had to access the services of the state-owned corporation of the country where the upward linking was located. This prevented competition among suppliers of the space segments, as communications were from 3 to 10 times more expensive than in the United States. The market also grew at a 12% annual rate, which was less than half of American or Japanese evolution.

Xerox Ltd. spent three times more in Europe than in the United States for a similar volume of communications. The users of DBP Telekom of Germany could not refute overinvoicings, as the company could not issue a detailed call registry. Belgium has a 20-day waiting period for the installation of a new service, and in Italy regular communications were often cut off.

France, Germany, the Netherlands, and Great Britain were signing an agreement that would allow users of those countries to utilize Eutelsat's capacity from any of the other three signers. It would also grant VSAT licensees the rights to offer two-way services. The licensees could not be international carriers, although if French users could get connections between their own networks and the public ones, they would be able to use the hubs of American operators such as Panamasat and MCI.

The creation of a VSAT network required high investment to achieve a good cost-benefit ratio, but it also could yield cost savings. A study of Hughes Network System Inc., one of the two suppliers of VSAT technology, estimated that a 830 VSAT network covering several European countries would cost 25% less than the equivalent land network of packages commutation. Another users survey performed by the Utisat French Group indicated that a system of 5000 VSAT throughout Europe would cost one-third of the equivalent land network. AT&T had announced plans to invest $350 million in a pan-European network for commercial calls, threatening 20% of the $3000 million in sales of PTT in this segment.

The competition was oriented to the SCPC system, offering exclusive satellite links per client. After a deep analysis, they decided in favor of VSAT technology, which allowed share links between different clients without affecting the service rendered, that is, creating "exclusive virtual links." Then the problem was that only VSAT systems were operating in the "KU" band frequencies, and not in the "C" band, which was the unique satellite band available in Argentina at that time. The next step was to find a supplier of VSAT technology interested in developing the product to operate in "C" band. This certainly demanded meetings and negotiations with different suppliers and finally, after some months, Hughes Network Systems company agreed to develop the first VSAT system in "C" band for IMPSAT.

THE COMMUNICATION MARKET IN ARGENTINA

In 1987, the Argentine government issued a public service demonopolization decree which included telecommunications, making possible the granting of licenses for the rendering of data transmission services to private companies. The following year, IMPSAT achieved that authorization from the Secretaria de Telecomunicaciones, but in order to start operations it was necessary to modify what was established by the Telecommunication Law. By May 1989, through the decree 580 of the National Executive Branch, IMPSAT and the remainder competing companies were in legal condition to grant services. (Exhibit 2).

Within this framework, ENTEL's satellite capacity was contracted to offer satellite

EXHIBIT 2 Sales (%)						
	1989	*1990*	*1991*	*1992 (E)*	*1993 (E)*	*1994(E)*
Argentina	5.88	0.2	8.9	21	37.1	63.3
Exports					3.1	14.3
Total	**5.88**	**0.2**	**8.4**	**21**	**40.2**	**77.6**

communications. In fact, the Argentine communications market was monopolized by the Empresa Nacional de Telecomunicaciones (ENTEL) until 1990. This company operated the public telephone network and the Arpac national network of data transmission, available in main cities of the country. The system was essentially analogical, consisting of copper cables. The saturation and deterioration of the lines added to its scarcity and provided low reliability and service quality.

During that year, Argentine government faced an intensive plan for deregulation and economic openness, seeking to increase general industry competitiveness and to reduce the highly deficit fiscal cost in the telecommunication area. This would mean more efficient, inexpensive, and quality services and at the same time would generate competition, which ought to pull up the sector from the undevelopment in which it had been immersed by 40 years of state-controlled and deficitarian policies. Large investments would be required.

The Argentine market was becoming more and more demanding, although it did not know satellite technology and had little information about telecommunications in general. There was little development in communications matters, as they were based on an old centralized framework which had a highly inefficient image. Clients could wait years to get a telephone line or make illegal payments to officials in order to speed their negotiations, but with uncertain results. There was a relative data processing development, barely prepared for

long-distance data transmissions, and surviving segments with statist tendencies. Companies had difficulties setting up in proximity to their resources which were far away from their main markets. ENTEL rented satellite capacity to Intelsat, which practically went unused.

Given the deficit of traditional land systems and vast Argentine geography, with great distances between cities, satellite use appeared to be an excellent option for the land system. Its advantage was a better cost ration, and its higher quality increased the value of communications performed through this means. The available satellite capacity would be limited in the next two years.

The privatization of ENTEL took place in 1990, dividing it into two areas: north and south. Argentine southern networks were awarded to Telefonica de España (Spanish telephone company), while the Italian-French consortium, Telecom, had won the northern networks. Both companies had seven-year exclusivity in their respective areas until the later deregulation would permit the entrance of other competitors. That period could extend to 10 years, in case certain investment and service goals stated in the bidding conditions were fulfilled.

Three companies had obtained licenses for data transmission: Impsat, Satelnet, and Satelital. Satelnet had been set up by Dynamic Systems, a company engaged in communication equipments supply, then sold to the Argentine branch recently opened by the Banca Nazionale del Lavoro. Satelital, initially created by ALCATEL's Argentine branch, was then acquired by Comsat, a U.S.

signatory monopolist company of Intelsat, until its deregulation.

THE BEGINNING OF THE OPERATIONS

The IMPSAT concept was to apply VSAT technology, which until then was only implemented in company networks individually, to many companies that could share the same infrastructure and satellite capacity—a concept called "Shared Hub." That way clients would be permanently connected, but use the channels in a much more efficient way than if it were exclusive. A master station would act as a controller, receiving and redirectioning communications.

Until then, the configurations that were used connected factories and branches with the computer center at the head office, through point by point lines of the public network, that is, by means of copper cables.

The proposed satellite scheme entailed connecting client's central data processing equipment with the Teleport or main central station, through radiolink or optical fiber. The information from the client head office would be transmitted to the satellite from the Teleport, then retransmitted by satellite and would be received by little remote satellite stations (denominated VSAT) installed in the client's branches. This VSAT equipment was easily connected to the branch's computers; therefore, the communications would be established in real time and in both directions between clients' branches and the head office.

To connect clients with the main station, a network of optical fiber was installed, covering the center of Buenos Aires, 52 km in a 150-block area. This digitalized network provided reliability to the land communications of important information volumes in real time. The remote installations were rapidly made with small stations (1.8-m-diameter screens), or superior stations for high-capacity links.

An essential advantage, beyond the high reliability, availability, and confidentiality of the information, was the possibility of configuring point-multipoint networks, also called star, and the easiness of doing it through software. A simple software command installed in the master central station would allow the configuration of networks, increase their capacity, or interconnect clients among themselves.

A point to solve was the VSAT technology, which up to that moment had not been tested in shared networks, but it was used in corporative, non-shared nets. In addition, there was no experience on VSAT networks operating with satellites in "C" band all over the world.

A strong investment in equipment would be necessary, plus the need for highly specialized technicians who could continuously updated changing technologies. Today's solution could be obsolete tomorrow. Moreover, the changing rhythm of technology affected the supplier companies, which merged or disappeared at great speed.

After months of visits to suppliers, an agreement with Hughes would supply equipment at more suitable values as the volume increased. The initial investment had been forecasted by Vivo at $4 million, for a project of 100 remote entrances or down lines, but it was quickly increased to 500 remote entrances, to make the project more attractive. In spite of this, the estimates for the following years indicated the market would required investments of about $100 million. To raise these funds, it would be necessary to go to the capital market or associate with an important company. The project financing was then a critical aspect that had to be deeply analyzed.

PLANNING COMMERCIAL OPERATIONS

The entrance into the market showed two main alternatives: Attack the market aggressively, winning clients of all possible segments; or face a gradual growth, entering selectively and going along with it and competitor strategies, thus limiting the risks.

Part of the actions should be directed to attract investors who could finance the heavy investments. Fruit of the economic policies of the administration in course, which was controlling inflation and facing an aggressive program of economic modernization, the Argentine capital market was receiving a strong flow of international capitals, estimated at $20 trillion to that moment. Would it be enough to present the ambitious programs of Impsat, or would it be necessary to offer some other types of guarantees to investors who had abandoned the market early in the 1980s, due to the volatility of said period? Would it be necessary to establish some type of alliances, and in that case, with whom?

It was necessary to define the service level to be offered. There were possibilities to render a broad range of additional services, since fax, transmission of images, and data at an international level could be added to the data. Data transmission could be offered initially, and other services could be added gradually, which would allow additional charges for new future services, including 24-hour service.

When setting prices, the company must decide if they would be fixed to take into account distance or installation, and if the tariff level would be competitive with the other telephone companies or differential in relation to them. The base price could be set according to the utilization, similar to traditional telephone services, or a recurrent installment.

There was certain difficulty in the case of clients who managed great volumes of information, because they could saturate the channels. In these cases, the SCPC individual technology per client, with various channels of data, voice and fax, used by the competition, was more advantageous. It was also possible to offer the simultaneous diffusion of information, from a data center to a network of multiple recipients. Regional teleports would be necessary to offer better service in the whole territory, at the same time as clients and information volume increased. For that reason, the clients selection was carefully analyzed, along with the market coverage level.

The service was useful not only for companies who wanted to receive information about their stocks and link their local networks with its central computers, but it also allowed banks to connect with their cashiers networks, credit card companies could verify the purchases and enlarge their coverage, or hotel chains could check room availability in real time.

Conversely, implementing new technologies into daily tasks used to be a critical moment for organizations, especially in the case of great communication networks. Moreover, Argentine companies were quite backward in communications matters and its application possibilities.

Satelnet and Atelital had already begun their operations, selling equipment to industrial clients under SCPC technology. In their interviews with customers, they vaguely let them see disadvantages of the Impsat VSAT system. An alternative was to offer the equipment installation for Impsat's account and a service contract, instead of the sale or leasing.

These decisions would have consequences in Impsat positioning within the market. In order to enlarge the information in this sense and evaluate the situation, they undertook a market research (Exhibit 3).

Four main groups were identified. Of the respondents, 23% had more experience for managing long-distance data communications. Generally, they were banks and big companies with widespread activities around the country. Another 17%, also large companies and medium-size banks, held some culture and specialized advisers tried to find any

---

EXHIBIT 3 Impsat Market Research

Market Research Source: CIMAS
Methodology: Multivariable analysis
Sample: 200 first level companies

Objectives:

Telecommunication needs
Attitudinal framework toward new
    technologies
New services
Decision-making process
Sensitiveness to tariffs
Data processing equipment
Branches/activities layout

Conclusions:

High unsatisfaction with services
Inefficiencies impede companies growth
Telecommunications are not value appreciated
Increasing privatization consciousness
Backwardness in telecommunications
    countrywide
Good willingness to high-quality services

---

solution to their problems. A third group mainly included subsidiaries of multinational companies. Although their knowledge level was smaller than that of the first group, they had their own technicians, accounting for 28% of the respondents. The fourth group included pessimists—industries with low telecommunication culture, without personnel or advisers. There were doubts in the managing group about whether to attack all segments from the beginning and open the market aggressively, or address any segment in particular and gradually cover the market.

"They are generally very unsatisfied with the services offered," said Rafael Bustamante, from the research agency. "They considered them backward and their inefficiency impedes their own company's growth." In this framework, telecommunications are depreciated, claiming technical advice for the implementation of only high-quality new services. Companies were conditioned with

regard to investments, plus they did not have their own qualified personnel.

THE SITUATION IN 1990

At the end of that year, Impsat management met to discuss some aspects of the growth strategy and define the guidelines for the next years. Operations in Argentina seemed to be well aimed, as companies showed interest in Impsat services.

The trend toward deregulation and privatization seemed to progress quickly in Latin America. Impsat could make use of its advantage as a regional company, but it was necessary to advance fast. Operation organization in other countries implied investments—obtaining licenses and generating structures of technicians and managers (commercial and those related to the specific operation). See Exhibit 4.

Enrique Pescarmona: We must not forget that bases for the consolidation of Mercosur (common market among Argentina, Brazil, Uruguay, and Paraguay) are being signed. Many of our clients will extend their businesses to neighboring countries. In that case, we can also expand our operations abroad, taking advantage of the international structure of IMPSA. We have a contract for waste collection in Colombia, in addition to the metallurgical plant we operate in that country. It would be a good base to set up IMPSAT there.

Ricardo Verdaguer: Keep in mind that we have recently started operations in Argentina. Should we have to grow up internationally at the same time? If it is complex to have technical resources for first-operation growth, how are we going to generate others abroad? There is a risk of affecting negatively the growth in Argentina if we distract resources to other countries.

Although trends indicate we are moving toward a scenario of greater world liberalization in the telecommunications field, we do not forget Brazil is strongly regulated and

EXHIBIT 4   Venezuela Market Conditions

Summary

Venezuela is experiencing a new crisis, perhaps the deepest of its economic-financial history. Companies' fight to survive implies a strong need of technological updating; meanwhile it is estimated that the financial crash left 25% of circulating assets at the hands of clients who are uncertain about investment alternatives. The new Banking Law will allow the entrance of foreign banks, which has forced local banks to attract funds through aggressive commercial campaigns; however, some experts believe they are not prepared to absorb the foreseeable inflow of new clients, who will not be considered loyal. Therefore, they will have to face simultaneously strong investments in technology and communications.

If Venezuela succeeded in recovering itself after the crisis, it is possible the country will be able to face its entrance to a global economy. The telecommunication network is a key element to connect it with its more advanced neighbors of that area.

In the middle of this crisis, the investments required to install a Teleport with an antenna of 10 m diameter and a master central station would be about $50 million. The geographical position of this facility would allow communications access to the North Hemisphere.

Uruguay has a solid opposition to privatize its national telephone company, Antel. All of us have read the report about the difficult economic and political situation of Venezuela. The scenario is extremely complex. In addition to regulatory frameworks of each country, we must carefully choose the way and opportunity of expanding abroad.

Robert Vivo: The best available alternative of almost two or three years ago can be transformed today into a bad option. We should know this, and be current. Without research and change capacity, we would not be useful or we would even disappear. We must not forget that we only have developed experience in a very specific technology, but we cannot show background in data transmission, unlike our competitors. The doubt is if it would be necessary to get associated, and in that case, which kind of partner and which conditions: a local partner in each country or an international one for the whole region, or eventually both alternatives. In any case, it would be necessary to define the partner's capital participation.

Enrique: Don't you think we should think about far away markets? Like Europe, Asia, United States? Soon we could become one of the great world operators in shared networks.

All glances fixed on him and, for a moment, silence invaded the meeting room. ■

8-3 MIGUEL TORRES–CHILE (A)

At the end of March 1982, José Puig, general manager of Miguel Torres—Chile, subsidiary of Bodegas Torres from Spain, decided to stay back from the last grape harvest laborers and reflect alone at the foot of the majestic Cordillera of the Andes (magnificent mountain range), in the Curicó region. He wished to reminisce about what Torres—Chile had done since 1979, the date it began its operations.

Research Division, IESE, Barcelona. This case has been prepared by Professor Jon I. Martinez, DBA candidate, under the supervision of Prof. Jose M. Anzizu, on February 1987, as a basis for class discussion rather than to illustrate effective or ineffective handling of an specific situation.

The company had difficulties entering both the Chilean and export markets as the wines were produced in Chile. The first two years had closed with losses and future outlook did not show signs of recovery. The international economic crisis was just beginning, and Chile and Latin America, the two main markets of the company, began to sink into a severe recession.

Puig wondered if the strategy adopted at the beginning was right or if it had to be changed in light of results and coming events. He considered past advice from friends and the overall competitive market, and he knew he had to reevaluate his market strategy.

BODEGAS TORRES

Bodegas Torres, one of the most important producers of wines and brandies in Spain, was a family firm headquartered in Vilafranca del Penedés, 50 km to the southwest of Barcelona and 200 km from France. Viticultural tradition of the Torres family dated back to the seventeenth century; however, the export wine cellars were not founded until 1870.

The company owned 430 hectares of vineyard located in Pachs del Penedés, San Martí Sarroca, Pontons, and Poblet, all in the Penedés region of Cataluña. In 1981, total production reached 13 million bottles, including wines and brandies, which were sold in Spain and another 85 countries worldwide. Total sales of the Spanish company in that year were 2.743 million pesetas,[1] 27% of which accounted for exports (Exhibit 1).

Bodegas Torres's share in the Spanish market was estimated at 10%. It distributed its wines and brandies in Spain via 25 salespeople who served areas of higher consumption and 75 commission agents in less important regions, who also sold other wine and liquor brands. In short, Bodegas Torres reached approximately 35,000 outlets worldwide. Out of Spain, the company distributed through import agents on a firm purchase basis.

Bodegas Torres had several investments abroad. In the 1960s, the company established a commercial representation in London to import and distribute its wines in the

---

[1] In December 1981, the exchange rate was 97 pesetas per one US dollar (see Exhibit 1).

EXHIBIT 1 Evolution of Bodegas Torres, 1976-1981						
	1976	*1977*	*1978*	*1979*	*1980*	*1981*
Total sales (1)	694	1.085	1.834	2.062	2.335	2.743
Total output (2)	6.700	8.380	10.800	12.300	12.529	13.372
Exports (2)	2.308	2.932	3.587	3.192	2.720	3.847
Percentage of exports	34	35	33	26	22	29
Net profits (1)	16	24	46	50	81	130
Own resources (1)	323	386	475	463	490	813
Added Value (1)	70	180	247	293	380	422
Cash flow (1)	25	40	72	75	100	127
Number of employees (3)	189	184	175	168	160	173
Pesetas/US dollar Exchange rate as of 12/31	68	81	70	66	79	97

(1) Million of pesetas
(2) Thousand of 760 ml bottles
(3) As of December 31 of each year

Source: Fomento de la Producción magazine and company records.

United Kingdom. Then, in 1978, Torres Wines North America was created in the United States, as a base for distributing the wines in that country and Canada—two of its main markets abroad—where at the end of the 1960s it had already sold almost 1 million bottles. Later, the company established a commercial representation in Japan. In Chile, Bodegas Torres was owner of Sociedad Vinícola Miguel Torres Ltda., with 98 hectares of vineyards and a wine cellar, whose wines were traded at the local market and exported to several countries, mainly Latin American ones.

The company owner and president was Miguel Torres Carbó, fourth generation and heir of the viticultural family legacy. Company continuity rested upon his sons and daughter: Miguel Agustín, manager of Torres—Chile, famous enologist and well-known writer of books on wines; Juan María, manager of Torres Import S.A., an importer division of high-quality wines and liquors for the Spanish market; and his daughter Marimar, director of the United States branch.

Before the Spanish Civil War (1936–1939), the wine was sold and exported in bulk, not bottled, in Spain. After the war, which caused serious damages to company facilities, Miguel Torres Carbó took advantage of rebuilding tasks to relaunch Bodegas Torres with a new management vision. His travels through the United States and Europe convinced him to create a quality bottled wine with good brand image.

By 1982, Miguel Torres Carbó was 73 years old and full of energy. Although he used to delegate daily tasks to his sons and daughter, and a group of old and loyal collaborators, in order to engage only in strategic aspects of the business, Miguel liked to personally visit the most important customers of the company. He ate with them at selected restaurants of Barcelona and other cities, observing carefully which wines the customers ordered from the "maitre." Fre-

quently, he would wait on tables of friends and serve them Torres wine. In that respect, Miguel Torres Carbó commented:

> If a quality wine is served in the best restaurants to the most influential people, then it would be easier to sell it to consumers in the stores.

Miguel also promoted his wines and brandies in bars, restaurants, and food stores to explain how they were manufactured:

> At times during the week in Mallorca, I sold 100 boxes,[2] every day changing hotels and restaurants and always carrying a bottle under the arm, so the "maitre" could taste our wine. A British businessman established in Hong Kong once gave me important advice that I will never forget: 'Food and drink must be sold after people have tasted them...'

Between 1961 and 1971, Bodegas Torres undertook a strong technological development applied to enology. It began to implant experimental vineyards, introduced stainless steel vats, and controlled cold fermentation processes to preserve natural aromas and "bouquets" of the wines. Bodegas Torres's philosophy was to believe firmly in quality as the basis of success. Its strategy included the development of a strong brand image for high-quality wines, inside and outside Spain, to educate consumers about the appreciable difference so they would be willing to pay more for it.

This emphasis on the quality of its wines gave Bodegas Torres first prize in the Paris Wine Olympics, organized by critics Henri Gault and Christian Millau in October 1979, which included 800 wines from 33 countries. Among them were the famous French wines "Chateau Latour" and "Chateauneuf du Pape" (see Exhibit 2). In the nineteenth century, the company also obtained prizes

---

[2]Boxes of Torres wine, in Spain as well as in Chile, contained 12 bottles each of 750 ml.

EXHIBIT 2 Paris Wine Olympics

Gault/Millau

Oct. 79

RÉSULTATS DES OLYMPIADES
VINS ROUGES

Suite famille "Grands vins rouges diverse"

Pays	Dénomination	G.C.	Œ.-T.	Prix F
1er **Espagne**	Gran Coronas Reserva de Miguel Torres, Villafranca del Penedes, 1970	**15,5**	**14,6**	*29,00*
2e **France**	Château-Latour, 1er Grand Cru Classé, Pauillac, 1970	**16**	**11,8**	*150,70*
3e **France**	Château Pichon-Lalande 2e Grand Cru Classé, Pauillac, 1964	**12,5**	**13,2**	*83,50*
4e **France**	Château Mission Haut-Brion Cru Classé, Graves, 1961	**13,5**	**11**	*138,00*
5e **Chili**	Finissimo, Gran Viño José Canapa, sans mill.	**10,7**	**13,6**	*21,20*
6e **France**	Domaine de Mont-Redon Châteauneuf-du-Pape, 1955	**13,2**	**11**	
7e **Espagne**	Coronas, Miguel Torres, à Villafranca del Penedes, 1976	**8,7**	**12,8**	*7,00*

for the quality of its wines (Viena 1873, Philadelphia 1876, Paris 1878, and Barcelona 1888).

THE DECISION OF INVESTING IN CHILE

In the early 1970s, as a part of Bodegas Torres's expansion strategy, he considered producing wines in America. Miguel Torres Carbó commented at that time:

> When winegrowers in America produce enough quantity, they will shut the doors to European wine with protectionist barriers and high taxes; for that moment, having a good presence .in America will make our task easier than exporting from Europe.

California (US), Argentina, and Chile were the countries visited with the purpose of establishing a wine-maker subsidiary. Finally, the company decided to invest in the region of Curicó, Chile, about 200 km south of Santiago, at the foot of the Cordillera de los Andes (Exhibit 3).

Several reasons helped in the decision. Chile was a country with viticultural tradition since the conquerors' arrival in the sixteenth century. Later in the middle-nineteenth century, Chilean grape growers had brought from France vine shoots of the most selected varieties of the epoch: Cabernet Franc, Cabernet Sauvignon, Pinot Noir, Cot, Merlot, Sauvignon Blanc, and Semillon, which found excellent climatic and geological conditions in the Chilean valleys, and propagated rapidly.

The climate of the Central Valley of Chile presented ideal conditions for grapevine cultivation, due to a thermic difference of more than 20 degrees produced between day and night in summer. The soil and quality of Chilean vineyards made it possible to produce excellent wines (Exhibit 4).

The absence of grapevine diseases was another reason to establish production in Chile. Diseases are the result of fungus, bacteria, or virus, and especially an insect called Philoxera, which flogged all worldwide vineyards in the second half of the nineteenth century. The insect found in Chile an impassable barrier in the Cordillera de los Andes.

Also contributing were the favorable economic situation through which Chile was going during those years (Exhibit 5), its politic stability, and the fact that the country was a member of ALADI (Latin American Integration Association) which, as the European Common Market, established an area of free trade among some Latin American countries, including Mexico.

Finally and according to words of Miguel Agustín Torres Riera, who since the beginning was responsible of the strategic management of Torres—Chile:

> Also, it was of significant importance to have an old and great friend in Chile: Alejandro Parot Fernández, with whom I studied in France and nowadays is one of the most prestigious Chilean enologists and a notable expert on all wine-making regions of the country.

WINE SECTOR IN CHILE, 1981

The wine-making sector in Chile was characterized by the existence of vast agricultural properties devoted to the cultivation of grapevine (about 30,000) that equalled an area of 110,000 hectares. There were almost 420 wine makers/wine bottlers, 65% in the central zone of the country and producing 75% of the domestic total output. (See in Exhibit 6 a report from the Food and Agricultural Organization with regard to the wine sector in Chile.) Many of these wine makers/wine bottlers also marketed their own bottled wines (these companies were called *viñas*).

EXHIBIT 3 Maps of Penedes Region and Chile

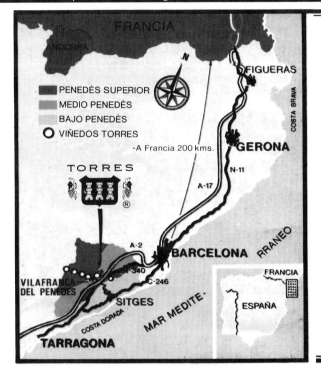

PENEDÈS SUPERIOR
MEDIO PENEDÈS
BAJO PENEDÈS
○ VIÑEDOS TORRES

Torres facilities are located in Spain in Vilafranca del Penedes surroundings, 50 km towards the west of Barcelona and 200 km from the frontier with France, in the heart of Cataluña. This Spanish region has a great variety of microclimates, from cold and continental conditions of Superior Penedes to those mild and typically mediterranean of Moral (Low Penedes).

The estate of MIGUEL TORRES-Chile is located in the region of Maule, province of Curico, at the foot of the amazing Andean cordillera, which peaks covered by eternal snows majestically contemplate the extraordinary beauty of fertile valleys.

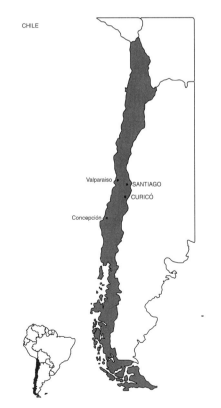

EXHIBIT 4   Abstract of the article "Vineyards and Wines of Chile," written by Miguel Agustín Torres in Meetings with the Wine Magazine

Professor Boubals from Montpellier University used to end many of his viticultural pathology classes with a full stop on referring to Chilean vineyards. He told us, students of the 1982–1983 course, that most insect, fungus, or virus plagues that lash worldwide viticulture are practically unknown in the trans-Andean country. "The vineyards of Chiio are the best of the world!" he used to declare enthusiastically.

However, in Europe and also in North America, Chilean wines are not well known. In many aspects, the country is unknown and people have difficulties associating Chile with some topic or natural detail. Its varied and beautiful geography, its habits and folklore, and its gastronomy are ignored. It is only known that Chile is very distant.

PARADISE OF THE VITICULTURE?

The foreign visitor who travels the Pan-American Roadway—the authentic dorsal spine of this country—will be able to observe that grapevine cultivation reaches a great importance along Chilean countrysides concretely, over 11,000 hectares, almost 55,000 of which are irrigated and situated in the Central Valley, and a total output that exceeds $6 million.

What are the reasons that explain why Chilean viticulture is considered privileged at this worldwide level? Let us examine them in detail.

1. First, the most feared vineyard plague—the Filoxera—is unknown here. In fact, this insect that razed European vineyards in the second half of the nineteenth century could never enter into Chilean lands, possibly due to the extraordinary natural protection provided to Chile by its peculiar geography: vast deserts to the north, Antarctic ice to the south, Cordillera de los Andes to the east, and the Pacific Ocean in the west make it possible to preserve the country from frequent plagues in all regions of the world.

Thereby, Vitis Vinifera grapevine can be planted in Chile without using grafts or American feet. Practical consequences of that are: sap circulation is totally fluid and the grapevine—in better physiologic state—provides 100 years of useful life compared with the 30 years in Europe or California, for example. In addition, French grapevines that were introduced here in the nineteenth century have a high grade of purity and can be advertised as the only ones in the world that descend directly from those existing in Europe before phylloxera invasion.

2. Most diseases or plagues of the grapevines due to fungus, bacteria or virus attack are unknown in Chile. For example, the Mildiu and the feared Botrylis (except in particular situations) are not import factors in Chilean vineyards.

3. Along a vast area of over 400 km between Santiago and Concepción are ideal soils and climate conditions for grapevine cultivation. It is also possible to produce abundant crops of 15,000 to 20,000 kg per hectare, where noble varieties maintain a good aromatic intensity and a great richness in coloring matter. Viticulture is not the only great benefit of these geological and climatic circumstances; the Chilean forest sector has experienced a huge development in the last decades and thousands of forest hectares have been planted, including the variety Pinus Insignis, which curiously reaches height in only 10 to 15 years that in northern Europe or in Canada would take 40 or 50 years.

EXHIBIT 4 (cont.)

4. The remarkable promiscuity that local flora acquire in certain microclimates of the Central Valley allow, for example, palms, pines, sallows, and poplars to grow in close proximity. In the case of grapevines, it is an incredible paradox that varieties so different in climate requirements, such as Riesling, Cabernet Sauvignon, or Sultanina, can grow super abundant in the same parcel and produce in each case harvest of good quality.

Well, I am persuaded that in the coming years, it will be possible to find within the vast territory of Chile, an optimal situation for each one of the Vitis Vineras and therefore to obtain aromas from varieties of even superior quality to those existing today, and at reduced production costs.

CLIMATE AND VITICULTURE

The temperatures of the Central Valley are rather high and during summer days are hot, with a thermal environment similar to that of the Mediterranean coast, in northern Spain. And, despite everything, aromatic rootstalks such as Riesling or Gewurztraminer produce aromas of great quality that are only available in the coldest regions of Europe. How is it possible?

Possibly, the main reason rests in the shorter length of the vegetative period of the grapevine in Chile and in higher growth due to brightness as there are few cloudy or rainy days during grapevine vegetal development and harvest ripeness phases.

In fact, whereas the grapevine in the Central Penedes, for example, begins its sprout at the end of March and is harvested at the end of September (total 6 months), the Central Valley of Chile's sprout begins by the middle of September and the crop is ripe at the end of February or early march (total 5½ months). Thus, with an integral of inferior thermic temperatures,* total brightness is of relative higher importance. And tody, we know that light—and not high temperatures—attains the variety of aromas and the anthocyanin or coloring matter.

Another factor in development may be thermal effect of night cooling in the Central Valley, due to the closeness of the tall Andean Cordillera peaks that are covered by snow year-round and make possible in night hours the large cold air masses that enter into lower layers of the Central Valley atmosphere. Therefore, daily temperatures of 30–35°C follow night temperatures of only 12–15°C. Also, today scientists appreciate the influence of these night-day thermic differences in the development of quality elements such as aromas and polyphenols (tannins and coloring matters) in the plant. Another factor contributing to these favorable circumstances is the cooling effect of the Humboldt current in the Pacific Ocean and the possibility of irrigating vineyards any time of the year, because the rivers and channels that carry the water from the Cordillera to the ocean are abundant, and so drought effects are unknown in the Central Valley.

As a whole and from a viticulture point of view, then, the Central Valley of Chile meets excellent conditions for a viticulture of great quality.

---

*Total temperatures experienced by the vineyards along the vegetative period.

EXHIBIT 4   (cont.)

GENERAL CHARACTERISTICS

Chilean viticulture that began in the nineteenth century resembles Bordeaux vineyards of the epoch. Even today, characteristics of that model viticulture persist in many parts of the Chilean region.

For example, a nineteenth-century practice, which is no longer used, mixed in the same parcel, so the "coupage" of the different varieties results are more intimate. Therefore, we will often see parcels where every two Sauvignon Blanc rootstalks are followed by one of Semillon, and so on. In the case of red wines, Cabernet Sauvignon is mixed with Cot or even Merlot.

The espalier or wire-support guides continue being predominant here. There is the traditional low espalier, similar to that of Bordeaux or the high espalier with posts that reach a height of less than 2 meters.

Outputs in these cases vary between 10,000 and 20,000 kg/hectare for noble varieties. And despite these high yields, quality is excellent due to a great quantity of favorable natural conditions.

Former plantation densities between 6,000 and 10,000 rootstalks/hectare have been regretfully spaced to 3,000 to 5,000 rootstalks/hectare, which is due to mechanization needs and modern Californian viticulture influence.

Over the last years, espalier has been replaced in many cases by the "parron" imported from Argentina, which provides enormous productions of 400 to 500 kg/hectare. In the "parron," grapevines grow to a roof of the wire support and then form a thick carpet of leaves. The clusters hang below and the works are quite simplified.

The innovative viticultural technicians who one day foresaw the introduction of parron, intended to demonstrate that it was possible to maintain quality of former espalier, multiplying quantity. Nothing is more false! Including noble varieties such as Cabernet Sauvignon, the effect of parron is clearly prejudicial to quality, and also in the case of Sauvignon Blanc, grapevine produces an unpleasant aroma of the herbaceus type. Today, the causes of these phenomena imputed to parron are known and also that the thick leaves carpet generates two microclimates with temperatures and humidities very different at the upper level of the leaves or at the cluster level. The physiologic plant disorders are responsible for the defects obtained in crop quality.

By 1978–1979, the Carbernet Sauvignon crops from espaliers or parrons brought the same price. Consequences were clearly harmful for quality and also caused several farmers to install the new system to reap the benefits promised. Fortunately, enologists soon understood that it was convenient to separate the Cabernet of espalier from the Cabernet of parron and today most cooperatives and makers foresee a tolva for parron grapevines of crop reception (which is paid at a lower price) and for espalier grapevine (which is paid at a higher price).

Grapevine varieties cultivated in Chile also reflect the Bordeaux influence with only a few exceptions. The most important is the grapevine called "pais," which descends directly from the "criolla" rootstalk, introduced by the first Spanish colonizers.

Regardless, the percentage of noble varieties such as Cabernet Sauvignon, Semillon, and Sauvignon Blanc is high—possibly the highest shown by any viticultural country of the world.

EXHIBIT 5   Chilean Economy Overview, 1977–1981

GEOGRAPHICAL BACKGROUND

Chile is located on the western side of South American, bordering at the north with Peru, at the east with Bolivia and Argentina, at the south with the South Pole when it extends into the Antarctic Continent, and at the west with the pacific Ocean. Pascua Island in Polynesia also belongs to Chile. Its surface consists of the following:

Continental Chile		756,626 km
Agricultural Surface	16,560	
Cattle Surface	129,300	
Forest Soil Surface	84,200	
Nonproductive Soil Surface	526,566	
Chilean Antarctic Region		1,250,000 km
TOTAL		**2,006,626 km**

DEMOGRAPHIC DATA, 1981

Population	11.3 million of inhabitants
Population growth	1.7% per year
Urban population	81.1%
Life expectancy	67 years old
Illiteracy rate	9.2%
Income per capital	2.582 US dollars

ANNUAL MACROECONOMIC FIGURES, 1977–1981

	1977	*1978*	*1979*	*1980*	*1981*
(percentages)					
GDP growth	9.9	8.2	8.3	7.5	5.3
Gross investment growth	15.4	17.4	16.8	22.4	15.5
Government Expenditure/GDP	25.8	23.8	24.6	27.2	n/a
Consumer price variance	63.5	30.3	38.9	31.2	9.5
Wholesale price variance	65.0	38.9	58.3	28.1	−3.9
Wage and salary variance	94.8	66.5	47.8	46.8	30.4
Unemployment rate	12.7	13.4	13.0	12.1	11.7
Real interest rate on 30 day loans	56.8	42.2	16.6	11.9	38.7
Real interest rate on 90-365 day loans	n/a	n/a	22.9	15.3	14.5
Shares index variance	n/a	97.6	15.7	85.2	n/a
(Thousand of dollars)					
FOB exports	2185	2460	3835	4705	3960
FOB imports	2151	2886	4190	5469	6558
Current account balance	−551	−1088	−1189	−1971	−4814
Income from foreign loans	556	1769	2014	2995	4393
Income from foreign investment	16	177	233	170	376
Balance of payments	13	712	1047	1244	70
Medium and long term external debt	4510	5923	7507	9413	12553
Peso/US Dollar Exchange rate	21.5	31.7	37.3	39.0	39.0

Source: Central Bank of Chile.

EXHIBIT 6 Abstract of FAO's report on the wine sector in Chile

Chile is traditionally a producer and small exporter of wine. For 40 years, the vini-industry of that country was subjected to a regime of strict control of plantations, prices, etc. It has only been permitted a very slow extension of the area planted with grapewines, mainly concentrated in small managements. A great part of the vineyard area is planted with varieties of European origin. As a consequence of that, more than half of the wine output corresponds to quality wine categories. Disregarding seasonal fluctuations of meteorological conditions, Chilean vinicultural output has shown a continuous upward trend, as a result of the gradual introduction of new improved techniques of cultivation. Production is domestic-market oriented, although Chile is also a small traditional exporter mainly of quality wines (3% to 5% of its output).

In 1979, a new legislation went into effect that considerably loosened the control over this industry and drastically broke some of the previous practices. The new law authorizes additional plantations not only of European varieties but also hibrid varieties in areas less appropriate for *Vitis vinifera*. It also permits commercialized wines with alcoholic strengths below 11-point grades, a mix of Chilean and imported wines, and the sale of consistent drinks in a mix of wine, grapes, and juice of other fruits.

These new resolutions probably have a light impact at the present time, because wine demand in Chile has become weakened due to economic stagnation and accumulation of unsold stock. However, this new policy could clear the way for the development of new possibilities of entrance to markets in the future. In such cases, large companies with an integrated output-commercialization focus will probably benefit more than small cultivators that face marketing difficulties. The latter have shown interest in table-grapewine production, because profits of this kind of cultivation have been higher. The surface dedicated to table-grapewine varieties has almost tripled, from 5,650 hectares in 1975 to 15,400 hectares in 1981.

OUTPUT

Viticultural surface is highly subdivided. There are around 30,000 properties, mainly small landholdings in northern and southern regions. Average surface has 2 hectares in the north, 8–9 hectares in the middle, and 2–3 hectares in the south of the country. Bigger vineyards are located in the central region: Curico, Talca, and Santiago generally belong to large producer companies, which at present are continually increasing their plantations. There are also 10 cooperatives that group 1,600 producers, representing 14% of the total country production.

Ordinary wines are offered to a great quantity of firms, while quality wines show an increasing concentration in a reduced number of companies. It is estimated that five or six of them together account for more than 60% of the market. The wine growers/wine makers offer 30% of the wine in bulk, cooperatives 15%, and the remaining 55% is processed by makers that buy the wine in bulk.

The number of large companies is reduced, which shows a high and increasing grade of integration (output—wine making—commercialization). Most significant companies in fine wine commercialization are now attending also to those wines of current consumption, based upon the prestigious image achieved by them. There are about 20 wine maker/bottlers, 65% are located at the central region and market 75% of the wine.

EXHIBIT 6 (cont.)

Year	Volume *thousand of hectoliters*
1970	4,020
1971	4.010
1972	5.250
1973	6.400
1974	4.365
1975	4.648
1976	5.143
1977	5.790
1978	5.612
1979	4.700
1980	5.920
1981	5.500

Source: National Association of Viticulturists, October 1979.

The storage capacity is 10 million hectoliters, 60% of which belongs to wine growers, 30% to wine makers, and 10% to cooperatives. Likewise, the industry has distilleries in the northern region for making "pisco" and in the central area for producing brandy. It also owns four facilities for concentration, located in the central region, with a total capacity of 25 million liters.

DOMESTIC CONSUMPTION

Domestic consumption fluctuates with annual production variances, which in recent years has oscillated between 47 and 52 liters per inhabitant. In the past, annual consumption in some exceptional years was considerably superior to 50 liters per person. The future remains to be seen what the popularity will be among consumers of less than 11-point wine, according to 1979 law. On the other hand, wine continues competing with other drinks which offer certain attractions to consumers.

EXPORTS

Chile has a long experience as a wine exporter. During the second half of the 1970s, the volume increased substantially. Broad annual fluctuations since 1976 arose from variances in commercial opportunities and difficulties found in the shipment to some markets of the region (e.g., Brazil, Ecuador, Venezuela).

In 1981, Chilean wine exports suffered a setback due to depreciation of Chilean money compared with other exporter countries' currencies. However, exports will be recovered during 1982 as Chilean prices become more competitive.

EXHIBIT 6   (cont.)

Exports of Wine, 1970–1981	
Year	Volume Thousand of Hectoliters
1970	67
1971	56
1972	60
1973	75
1974	69
1975	91
1976	246
1977	163
1978	127
1979	275
1980	220
1981	132

The product is exported as bottled fine wines and, fine and ordinary wines in bulk. As much as 10 years ago, larger volumes were exported in bulk, while at present more than 80% is sent bottled, which implies a higher profitability, besides the fact of divesting product image in different markets. Exporter companies are integrated as wine grower/wine makers, assuring quality and regular offer, and competitive prices with similar foreign products. Main buyers of wine in bulk are Japan, Switzerland, Belgium and West Germany; while, in bottled products, appear Brazil, Venezuela, Colombia, the United States, Ecuador, and Mexico.

Total Consumption of Wine and per Inhabitant			
Year	Population	Total Consumption (thousand of hectoliters)	Consumption/person (liters)
1970	9.369	3.794,4	40,5
1971	9.541	4,246,7	44,5
1972	9.714	5.303,8	54,6
1973	9.890	6.161,4	62,3
1974	10.070	4.698,5	46,7
1975	10.253	4.456,0	43,5
1976	10.441	4.995,0	47,8
1977	10.633	5.561,1	52,3
1978	10.830	5.536,3	51,1
1979	11.030	5.138,9	46,6
1980	11.235	5.349,4	47,6
1981	11.450	5.434,0	47,5

Source: Food and Agricultural Organization of the United Nations, FAO, Roma, 1984.

The number of large viñas was very small. The top five represented 80% of the market sales in 1981. Only an average of 10% of the viñas production came from its own vineyards, with which it made the best quality and best price wine to raise the brand prestige. The rest of the output used grapes bought from farmers or wine sold in bulk by other makers.

These great viñas, all public stock companies, presented the following results at the end of 1981.

	Sales ($ million)[a]	Market Share %	Exports (thousand boxes)[b]
Viña Concha y Toro[c]	3.330	31	506
Viña San Pedro	2.256	21	53
Viña Santa Carolina	1.719	16	52
Viña Santa Rita	752	7	62
Viña Undurraga	537	5	103
Other viñas	2.149	20	–
Total market	10.743	100	–

[a]Exchange rate was $39 per one US dollar, in December 1981.
[b]In Chile, one box of wine contained 12 bottles, which generally has a capacity of 700 ml.
[c]It did not include distributor branch incomes, which was a different kind of firm, not a stock company.

Source: Store Audit estimations performed by CADEM.

Overall production in 1981 was 550 million liters of wine. Consumption per capita reached 47.5% liters, for a population of 11.5 million inhabitants. Exports reached 13.2 million liters.

In spite of the fact that Chilean wine had well-known quality according to international experts, Chilean companies had never been able to export its wines on a large scale. Market observers stated the Chilean wine was unknown in the European market, which was dominated by France, Spain, and Italy; therefore, it was difficult to enter into it. Another important reason seemed to be the Chilean wine taste—generally it was not entirely liked by European consumers. The South American market also was very protected, specifically Venezuela, Brazil, and Colombia traditional buyers of Chilean wine. The two main country exporters, Concha y Toro and Undurraga, marketed a large portion of wines in the United States. For more than 10 years, they have exported to this market, where they invested many resources and devoted great efforts.

Even though the Chilean enology level was high, the technology used by the immense majority of viñas needed urgent modernization to update wine making and compete successfully at the international market. Chilean viñas were backward in technology due to lack of financial resources, not because of capacity or technology.

By 1981, only two viñas, Torres—Chile and Concha y Toro, used stainless steel vats, although the latter in small proportion. All others utilized 200,000-liter vats of reinforced concrete. The best-quality wines aged within wood casks, most of them being quite old.[3]

Popular-selling wines required a separate sales force grouped in branches, located in main cities of the country. These salespeople delivered wine to *botillerías*,[4] local supermarkets, bars, restaurants, and so forth. In regions and cities where the viñas had no

---

[3]Oak casks must not be used more than five years, so the wine did not get an unpleasant taste to old wood.
[4]*Botillerías* were little retailing stores that sold and made wines and liquors in Chile.

salespeople, distributors worked on a commission to serve the *botillerías* of their area.

With regard to distribution channels, in 1981, the breakdown of sales from viñas or marketing firms among the following channels was:

Botillerías	48%
Supermarkets	15%
Subdistributors*	27%
Others (hotel, restaurant, bar, etc.)	10%

*Subdistributors sold in turn to regional botillerías.
Source: Store Audit estimations performed by CADEM.

The botillerías and supermarkets exerted strong pressure against marketing firms. The first ones, even though they were many and small, demanded great discounts in prices and broad payment terms, profiting from the strong competence bore by large viñas. Moreover, they pressed in favor of an advertising support for a quick issue of their stocks, because it was difficult for small viñas, without large advertising budgets, to place products in the *botillerías*.

Large supermarket chains also have a great negotiation power resulting from their high sales volume. In Santiago, capital city of the country with nearly 4 million inhabitants, five large chains concentrated almost all supermarket sales.

About 80% of the wine consumed in Chile was of low price and sold in 1-liter bottles or demijohns. Most heavier wine consumers were middle- to low-income individuals (approximately 70% of the population), who shopped at the *botillerías* in large popular districts of Santiago and other cities. Middle- to high-income groups (30% of the population) consumed little wine during meals and social meetings. Young people drank little wine in Chile.

According to market observers' opinion, the business of large viñas was based more on its volume than on the profit margin. All offered a wide range of wines, but those of high price only helped to give prestige to their brands, although the margin was higher.

As it was a mass market, large viñas allocated strong advertising budgets to announce their products on television, which was the preferred and almost exclusive medium. The disadvantage was the cost, because Chilean legislation only allowed advertising of alcoholic drinks on television after 8:30 P.M., which was the most expensive time slot. On average, large viñas assigned to advertising 5% to 7% of annual sales, in 1981.

Few viñas were concentrated in middle-high and high segments. Some, such as Cánepa and Cousiño Macul, were well known by the consumer, even though they did not advertise on television. Cánepa had never used this medium, whereas Cousiño Macul used it up until a couple of years ago.

In 1981, the price of quality wines was 100 Chilean pesos per 0.7-liter bottle. Intermediate wines cost between 60 and 100 pesos. Cheaper wines cost less than 60 pesos per bottle.

The bottle was one factor of the product cost. Conversely, companies suffered major losses due to the breakage of bottles resulting from their bad handling.

A key aspect of large viñas was its storage capacity, which let them regulate market prices. Most of them stock piled product, either in third-party or their own warehouses, which equalled about 80% of estimated sales for the next year. In this way, if the harvest was abundant, the viñas would pay lower prices for the wine to other makers. If the harvest had been bad and prices rose, they usually resorted to the reserves already in storage.

TORRES—CHILE OPERATIONS

On February 2, 1979, Miguel Torres Carbó purchased old vineyards from the Ahrex family, founded in 1904. The property, bought by the Bankrupt Trusteeship[5] included 50 hectares of vineyards, a small wine cellar, and the family house. The total amount of the transaction was approximately $200,000. Later, in 1981, they purchased another 48 hectares of vineyards.

After February 1979, the company initiated deep reforms in operation infrastructure and technology. They installed 12 stainless steel vats with regulated temperature for wine fermentation (the first ones in the country), powerful refrigeration equipment, one discontinued horizontal press, and existing, recycled casks for wine production. With all reforms initiated, total investment in Chile as of March 1982 equalled $1 million.

Miguel Agustín Torres as manager was responsible for the strategic management of the recently created subsidiary, but his multiple activities in Spain impeded him from devoting much time to Torres—Chile; however, since 1979, he traveled to Chile three times a year.

In November 1979, the Torres family sent José Puig to Curicó. He traveled with his wife and children there to act as general manager of Torres—Chile. His former experience consisted of 25 years working in the Spanish hotel sector, with his own facilities, and then in Bodegas Torres, where he was in charge of exports to the Middle East for several years.

At the beginning, José Puig had to overcome several difficulties resulting from company start-up. Puig remembered:

We started from zero. The house was still not furnished for living so we stayed at a hotel. I began hiring four persons for the country. We paid two times more than regional farmers. In addition, we gave them a house, gas stove, and also taught them how to cook. However, one of the more difficult things was that they understand our policy: work hard, but talk with them and try to improve their social status. I think that, after 1981, they fully identified themselves with the company.

After overcoming problems related with the installation of stainless steel vats, in March 1980, the first grape crop began, but with a week delay because the wine press sent from Spain could not be installed on time. An enologist of the parent company, Félix Sabat, travelled especially to manage operations.

Various government and public services facilities provided assistance. José Puig remembered:

They received, listened, and helped us. Although our investment was small, we were well attended. I told them from the beginning: I am a foreign investor and that was enough. Universities also helped us, mainly due to new technology we have introduced in Chile.

In June 1980, the first 25,000 white wine units were bottled. The entire process was carried out at a manual plant. Puig showed marks that still remain on his hands. By 1982, the process was already semiautomated. From the beginning, all materials were very expensive to purchase in Chile, especially bottles. The company found it more convenient to bring from Spain a great part of the necessary inputs, including corks and labels, because the exchange rate and custom fees were low.

The first wines were made with the varieties already existing at the Ahrex's vineyard: a Sauvignon Blanc and a Cabernet Franc. The latter, red wine was aged 15 months in new American oak vats, recently imported by the company from the United States. Both wines were "Santa Digna" brand.

Once at the market, Miguel Torres—Chile's wines immediately awakened polemics

---

[5]Bankrupt Trusteeship was the official entity that determine bankruptcy of the companies and proceed to the auction or sale of its assets.

due to their different taste from wines traditionally produced in the country. The "fruited" taste of Torres—Chile wines was the product of modern technology, because slow must fermentation was performed at a controlled temperature in stainless steel vats. Instead, most Chilean wines were made according to traditional methods: its fermentation was quicker and at high temperatures, so they become quite "oxidized."[6] Other Chilean wines also maintained a wood taste because they were aged, after its elaboration, in old oak casks (especially red wines).

DOMESTIC MARKETING

Penetration into the Chilean market came via tasting tests in well-known restaurants of Santiago. This was the introduction technique used in Spain; however, at the beginning the task was very hard, as José Puig commented:

> One day I took white "Santa Digna" for tasting at a good restaurant in Santiago. I asked a waitress to taste the wine by one of the clients. He told her: 'If you say it is good, I will gladly taste it.' After tasting, the client stood up and reprimanded the young waitress for having annoyed in such a way an old client of the restaurant. Of course, I had to go in help of the innocent and explain to the furious client that our wines were of best quality, our company had a great reputation in Spain, and that was the taste prevailing nowadays at the international markets.

---

[6]The terms *oxidized* and *fruited* are opposites. A wine presented an oxidized taste when it was fermented in a short time and at high temperatures. On the contrary, it was fruited when it was fermented or aseptically processed under controlled temperature, avoiding its oxidation at every moment, preserving the best characteristics of its variety. This classification has nothing to do with the other: *sweet* or *dry,* also opposite terms and which are related with the total sugar grams contained in each liter.

Bodegas Torres was not well known in Chile before establishment in Curicó. Years ago, a Chilean importer brought Spanish Torres brandies to the country, but in small quantities. Since then, the name Torres was unfamiliar to retailers and less familiar to the common citizen.

In spite of these adverse results, José Puig continued trying to enter the prestigious gastronomic centers of Santiago. In 1981, it acquired approval from two of the best hotels, Holiday Inn Cordillera and Sheraton San Cristóbal, which agreed to include "Santa Digna" wines on their menus.

Wine distribution in the Santiago and Valparaíso areas, which held more than 40% of the country's population, began in June 1980 through a firm owned by a Spanish resident. This company was selected due to its broad distribution network in the *botillerías* of Santiago. Shortly after, however, they discovered that this firm distributed its own low-quality wine by the same channel. Wine was delivered by trucks and drivers performed the sale. They had no salespeople to position a wine like that of Torres. Later they hired several salespeople, but they were not experienced and did not perform as expected.

In October 1981, another local firm took charge of the distribution. Notwithstanding the change of distributor, things did not improve. José Puig lamented:

> They are not really wine salesmen, only "roll takers," accustomed to work with large vineyards already introduced in the market, like Concha y Toro and Santa Carolina . . . They arrive at a *botillería* and ask: 'Eh, you, How many boxes do you want . . .?' They sell more by friendship and from long business relationships with the *botillero.*[7] They do not know how to place a new wine, besides they are not interested in pushing a wine without advertising support.

---

[7]Man in charge of the *botillería.*

The distribution to other regions of the country also started in 1980 and continued growing the following year. Distributors that bought in-firm were appointed in Concepción and Tenuco for the southern area and in Iquique for the northern sector—just as it was done in the Capital City and Valparaíso. José Puig himself and other salespeople on commission served the Central Valley area, between Santiago and Talca. There still were extensive sectors without coverage, such as the northern sector from the south of Iquique to Valparaíso, south of Tenuco and the austral region (Exhibit 7).

José Puig estimated that Torres—Chile sales in 1981 will break through the following channels:

Restaurants and hotels	50%
Botillerías	35%
Individuals	15%

Retailing prices of Torres—Chile wines in *botillerías* were 115 Chilean pesos for both Sauvignon Blanc and red Cabernet Franc. These prices were comparable to those of its competitors in this same level: "Don Luis" from Cousiño Macul and "Casillero del Diablo" from Concha y Toro. From the beginning José Puig also decided to import some wines of Bodegas Torres to complete the product range. That is why they also sold "Sangre de Toro" for $150,

"San Medin" for $160, Torres five-year-brandy for $250 and ten-year for $280.

Miguel Torres—Chile did not advertise its wines. The president of the company, Miguel Torres Carbó, pointed out with regard to this subject:

I think in quality products. They have a name for themselves. That is the reason why we spend little in advertising. The best way of promoting our wines is through labels. Torres has differentiated itself from other brands without spending a lot of money on advertising. I firmly believe that a vineyard must produce quality wines, continually invest in the best technology available, and let their products speak for themselves. When the people tasted our wines, they bought them. We must not forget wine is a product whose qualities cannot be "felt" or "seen" by the consumer a priori. It is only appreciated by tasting and verifying its aroma. . . .

The company promoted its wines differently than its competitors. In November 1980, journalist Rosa Robinovitch took charge of public relations activities for the company. In early November, wines were introduced at the yearly FISA (International Fair of Santiago). On November 20, the wines were officially presented to the press

EXHIBIT 7 Evolution of Miguel Torres—Chile		
	1980	*1981*
Total sales (1)	5	16
Total output (2)	25	82
Exports (2)	17,5	24,6
Percentage of exports	70%	30%
Number of countries to which company exports	7	12
Number of employees as of December 31	18	22

(1) Million of pesetas
(2) Thousand of 750 ml bottles
Source: Records of Miguel Torres-Chile.

and television in the distinguished restaurant "La Enoteca" at Santiago.

By January 1981 they initiated the edition of an annual informative bulletin for all company customers, in which diverse activities performed during the former year were reported. Also, at the end of that year they officially presented in Santiago the international edition of the book, *Viñas and Vinos,* written by Miguel Agustín Torres.

EXPORTS FROM CHILE

Exports, one of the main reasons why Miguel Torres set up in Chile, was losing force as time passed. An article in *El Mercurio,* the main newspaper of the country, written after the wine presentation to the press in November 1980, said: "¡A New Wine is Born! Torres, a 'great' from Spain, buys vineyards in Curicó, adds to them European technology and makes wines to be exported to 46 countries. Low export taxes in Chile and quality of local vineyards, let Torres produce a competitive wine at international markets."

Miguel Agustín Torres and José Puig commented about this initial objective:

MIGUEL: Originally, we established in Chile for exporting wines produced in that country, especially to Latin America. But later we saw it was also convenient to penetrate the Chilean market.

JOSÉ: Our initial intention was to potentiate exports from Chile. However, soon we realized that a brand always has to become strong in its own country before beginning to export.

In spite of that fact, wine shipments to foreign countries, which began in August 1980 with destination to England, continued growing in 1981. Although the proportion to total sales of the company was substantially reduced (Exhibit 8). By the end of 1981, Torres—Chile exported to 12 countries, 9 of them from Latin America, besides the United States, the United Kingdom, and Germany.

International contacts for exports were made through Bodegas Torres for Europe and José Puig himself for Latin America. He explained:

> Many times we bartered. Torres—Chiles engaged to find new distributors in Latin American countries, where we sold Chilean and Spanish wine. On the other hand, the parent company returns the favor placing our products in Europe, where it is very difficult to introduce Chilean wine.

For these distributors from Latin American countries, Torres' Spanish wine complemented the Chilean wine line and, in turn, these wines complemented Spanish wines for many European distributors. Chilean wine, because of its rootstalks, soil, and climate, had a taste different from Spanish wine (although it was elaborated with the same technology and processes), and its main competitive advantage was its excellent quality/price ratio, which was appreciated by the European consumers once they tasted the wine. The difficult thing was to overcome that barrier . . . In certain countries, however, there were two separate distributors: one for the wine from Chile and another for that of Penedés.

THE DILEMMA

Shortly after finishing vintage tasks, at the end of March 1982, José Puig realized it was urgent to make a balance of the company progress. The sales of Torres—Chile failed to satisfy him and his expectations of export had not been achieved. The income statement for the first two years had ended with losses. The work up to that date had been very hard, without rest even on the weekends, and did not provide time for vacations. He was a little discouraged but he had promised himself not to draw back in the fight but to go on until the end.

His competitors and friends insisted numerous times that the taste of his wines would never be accepted by Chilean consumers, who preferred white "oxidized" wines and red wines with oak taste. Conversely, Torres—Chile offered two different wines: a "fruited" white and an aged red, but without oak taste, because the wood used was still young. José Puig wondered if he must continue going against the tide and if one day he would succeed in changing local consumer taste. His competitors could not compete with his company in frontier technology, but the relevant question was: Was it worthwhile to invest in sophisticated technology in order to obtain quality approval by the target market? How long would local consumers take to adapt his taste to the international market?

On the other hand, he realized most Chilean vineyards advertised their products through television, creating a strong brand image and enjoying main distribution channel support. However, Miguel Torres—Chile could not afford an expense of such magnitude, unless the head office allotted more resources to the Chilean subsidiary for a market penetration with advertising support. But this would go against company policy. He must analyze the pros and cons of this alternative or search for a new one that is compatible with the philosophy of the Torres family.

Another important problem was distribution. Torres had not yet found an adequate niche in which to sell in the Chilean market. Current distributors did not like him either, because they did not know how to sell a quality wine. They also gave constant administrative problems related with collection to retailers. He wondered if he ought to look for another distributor or try to sell on his own. However, it was not easy to control the two main markets, Santiago and Valparaiso, at a distance of 200 km.

Finally, he was worried about the worldwide economic recession that, in early 1982, showed its first symptoms. On one side, Chile was a country with an open economy that made it depend to a great extent on main international macroeconomic variable fluctuations.

Furthermore, the private sector of Chilean economy was very indebted, especially in dollars with foreign banking, because of lower international interest rates compared with domestic ones and, an artificially low pesos/dollar exchange rate (Exhibit 8). A big slowdown of local demand was predicted by market experts.

Latin America, the second main market of the company after Chile, presented no better perspectives. The external debt of these countries was also quite high and projections with regard to the wine market opened several queries (see in Exhibit 8 a study on wine consumption in Latin America conducted by FAO—Food and Agricultural Organization of the United Nations).

EXHIBIT 8 Abstract of FAO's report on wine economy in Latin America

SLOW GROWTH OF WINE PRODUCTION DURING LAST 10 YEARS

Grapevine cultivation began in Latin America with the Spanish colonization, but its commercial development dates from about a century ago. Latin America is the most important wine maker of the developing regions. The main part of its production is located at the south of the continent. Argentina, Chile, and meridional states of Brazil account for nearly one-half million hectares of vineyards, most of them irrigated. Likewise, there are limited areas planted with grapevines in Bolivia, Peru, Paraguay, Uruguay, and also in Venezuela, a country that made a small quantity of wine with grapevines from domestic cultivation and with imported concentrated musts.

In Central America, Mexico is an important grapevine grower, although only a small part of the crop is used for table-wine production, because almost all the wine obtained is distilled to make brandy. Also in Bolivia and Peru a substantial part of the wine produced is distilled for spirituous liquors (pisco, singani).

All vineyards of Argentina and Chile belong to *Vitis vinifera* varieties. In other countries, specially in areas of warmer and moister climates as Brazil, most plantations are of hybrid and American varieties. Usually, these varieties are more resistant and with higher yields. However, its musts are of worse quality and present a high grade of acidity and low alcoholic strength, which is why musts are enhanced by adding sugar in order to obtain wine with higher alcoholic strength. Over the last years, the trend has been towards white wine production instead of red wine.

It is difficult to obtain statistics of Latin America annual wine production. In several countries (e.g., Bolivia, Paraguya, Perú, Uruguay, and Venezuela), there are only general estimations. However, total production volume was estimated at 32.6 million hectoliters in 1972–1974 and 33.7 million hectoliters in 1980–1982. During the 1970s, the rhythm of output growth diminished considerably compared with the previous 10 years, when the production had increased 5.6 million hectoliters in 1962–1964 and 1972–1974. A great part of the recent increase corresponded to Argentina and Chile, with increments of one-half million hectoliters in each one of these countries.

Wine Production in Latin America (thousand of hectoliters)			
	Average 1971 to 1974	*Average 1979 to 1982*	*Change Percentage*
Argentina	23,247	23,712	+2.0
Bolivia	73	100	+37.0
Brazil	2,598	2,640	+1.6
Chile	5,438	5,988	+10.1
Mexico	123	150	+22.0
Paraguay	73	80	+9.6
Perú	80	80	—
Uruguay	910	860	−5.5
Venezuela	101	94	−7.0

EXHIBIT 8 (cont.)

LIMITED VOLUME OF WINE INTERNATIONAL TRADE

Intraregional trade volume is relatively small in Latin America as is the export level. Argentina and Chile are regular exporters, but annual volume has fluctuated considerably during past years. This consequence is partly due to scarce opportunities offered by the export market during some periods, because of temporary restrictions to imports in other regional markets, and partly due to unfavorable exchange rates, which had determined that exports of wine were not competitive or had acted as a unincentive for them.

Chile sends mainly bottled quality wines to other Latin American countries and the United States, whereas Argentina has important markets for bulk wine in Europe and Japan. Argentina's exports reached a higher position when URSS bought large quantities of ordinary wines in the period 1976–1978. In 1979 and 1980, the strong inflation and the foreign exchange policy of the government (peso overvaluation) led to an abrupt reduction of export sales. Wine exports began to recover slowly in 1981, owing to a more realistic foreign exchange policy. This trend continued to 1982 when, after many strong devaluations, total shipments increased to 230,000 hectoliters. Brazil is a small exporter in the region and sent its production mainly to neighboring areas of Paraguay and Uruguay.

There is also certain wine trade between Argentina and Chile. The latter country buys from Argentina small quantities of red wine necessary for the mix, because it increases the alcoholic strength and color of some Chilean ordinary wines. Instead, shipments of cheap Chilean wines are sometimes placed in the Argentine market.

Some Latin American countries import wine. The largest importer is Venezuela, with a volume of over 200,000 hectoliters. Most of its imports come from Chile and Argentina and, only a reduced part, from Europe. The sparkling wine also has an important position in Venezuela's wine imports, coming principally from France. While the imported wine of moderated price competes mainly with beer, quality wines and especially sparkling wines seem to compete with whisky, which is one of the most popular alcoholic drinks consumed in the country.

Wine Exports and Imports to Some Latin American Countries (in thousands of hectoliters)					
	1978	*1979*	*1980*	*1981*	*1982*
EXPORT					
Argentina	675	88	71	111	231
Brazil	7	47	30	11	8
Chile	127	275	220	132	85
IMPORT					
Brazil	89	97	60	45	50
Colombia	19	28	33	31	32
Ecuador	13	18	28	21	30
Paraguay	23	31	30	41	33
Venezuela	233	146	211	213	220
Mexico	39	112	119	229	180

EXHIBIT 8 (cont.)

The second major importer country is Mexico, whose import volume has quickly increased during last years, followed by Brazil, that imports mainly bottled quality wines. Chile is its main source of supply, but there are also significant imports from Portugal, especially of "vinho verde." In Brazil, wine imports are subjected to the licence system, very high import duties, and sometimes foreign exchange restrictions. All that causes important annual variances and recently, it has led to strong import volume decreases.

Colombia, Ecuador, and Paraguay regularly import small quantities of wine. All these countries apply great barriers to import, consistent of high custom duties or import quotas.

STAGNATION OF WINE CONSUMPTION

Wine consumption is a tradition, especially in southern vitivinicultural areas of the continent, mainly in Argentina, Chile, and Uruguay, and in less proportion Paraguay and Brazil. Domestic consumption varied with annual fluctuations of the crop but, during the past years, the economic recession has caused a decrease of the consumption per capita since 1970 and, in some countries, an additional reduction since 1975.

Wine Consumption in Some Latin American Countries (liters per capita)					
	1970	*1975*	*1978*	*1979*	*1980*
Argentina	90,3	83,2	83,3	77,6	76,3
Brazil	* 1,0 40,5	2,3	2,2	2,3	1,8
Chile	29,6 0,8	43,5	51,1	46,6	47,6
Paraguay	*	3,2	3,2	3,2	3,2
Uruguay	*	32,0	25,4	25,0	25,6
Venezuela	*	1,8	2,5	1,0	2,2

*1971

In most Latin American countries, wine consumption has decreased to less than a liter per person per year. Only Venezuela has a consumption of about 2 liters per person. Main factors limiting the wine demand are the poor knowledge about it, low income levels, commercial restrictions, relatively high prices, and the preference for traditional drinks such as beer and liquors.

MAIN PROBLEMS AND PERSPECTIVES

In Argentina and Chile, the main wine-producer countries, the output has a great social importance, because a large number of small wine growers are participants. However, in both countries, the sector is facing considerable difficulties due to a domestic demand decrease. Besides, surplus problems in Argentina are aggravated by the great production capacity of medium- and low-quality table-wines that exceeds present market possibilities. For both countries, exports play a secondary role and do not account for more than 5% of the production.

With regard to future perspectives, it seems slightly probable that factors limiting the wine consumption in other nonproducer markets of the Latin American region,

EXHIBIT 8 (cont.)

could be modified in a short or medium term. In those countries, the wine is a drink of only secondary importance. Traditional preferences for other drinks, low incomes, high-priced wine, and commercial barriers are factors that limit perspectives of the consumption growth. Therefore, prospects for an expansion of the regional import demand are not bright.

Out of the region, markets are also limited, especially in regard to ordinary table wines. Possible international markets for ordinary wines have shown to be very unstable and shipments can only be done at very low cost.

According to data gathered by the Inter-government Group on Wine and Other Grapewine Products in its fourth meeting, and especially taking into account limited possibilities of increasing remunerative marketing opportunities, it would seem that main producer countries should pay more attention to adjust the offer and to the fact that they need significant efforts to secure a reasonable equilibrium between offer and demand. In Argentina, it also would be necessary for certain restructuring and reconversion of vineyards, emphasizing the change of planted varieties by other of better quality for fine and table wines. This would improve the possibilities of a gradual expansion of wine exports and a certain diversification of the production oriented to direct consumption as table-grapes. In Chile, they have already developed a significant output of table-grape for export.

Minor producer countries such as Brazil and Uruguay have no problems of surplus, but wines made are of low quality. Ecological conditions in those countries are less favorable for grape growing and cultivation practices, and enological techniques are also less developed. In Brazil, it would be necessary to modify the composition as for varieties, reconvert old vineyard areas at Rio Grande do Sul State, and probably make a displacement towards more suitable zones for viticultural production. The main problem is to increase the participation of quality *Vitis vinifera* varieties to provide a better wine for consumers.

MAIN WINE IMPORTER COUNTRIES

Brazil Imports

Wine imports have been increasing gradually, although the imported volume has strong incidence of periodical foreign exchange restrictions, devaluations, and several procedures to be fulfilled. Imports are subject to licenses granted by CACEX (Foreign Trade Department) of the Banco de Brazil.

Brazil: Wine Imports by Types (in hectoliters)				
Type of wine	*1978*	*1979*	*1980*	*1981*
Total Wines	88.199	96.819	59.446	44.616
"Verde" table-wines	13.447	14.766	8.014	6.239
No table-wines	70.152	77.368	47.646	33.891
Liquor wines	3.507	3.569	2.926	810
Sparkling wines (Champagne)	520	278	137	155
Other sparkling	573	838	723	3.521

EXHIBIT 8 (cont.)

In all cases, wines are imported only bottled from different countries, mainly fine wines, plus a small volume of "verde" wine, proceeding almost exclusively from Portugal. Import duties to grape by-products vary according to features and country of origin. Amounts are 105% *ad valorem,* with a prime rate of 88% for imports coming from ALAC countries (Latin American Free Trade Association).

During last quinquennium, major imports from Chile account for 40% to 50% of the total. This country has increased exports to this market based on its price stability. It is followed by Portugal, with practically 20%, then Argentina with about 10%, and in small quantities: Germany, France, Italy, and Spain. Imports represented during the last years are only 2% to 3% of consumption. Estimating this figure will increase as economic conditions improve and quality wine consumption habits are developed.

Venezuela Imports

Within table-wine imports, during 1975–1980 period, those coming from Chile, Spain, France, Italy, Argentina, Portugal, and Germany have been prevailing.

As for fine wine imports, these are made up by different types, the cheapest ones are those of Chilean or Argentine origin, followed by Spanish and Portuguese, then Italian, and finally French. It must be pointed out that in relation to customs tariffs to imports, there is an agreement generally more favorable to Andean Pact countries (Colombia, Ecuador, Peru, and Bolivia), and secondly to ALAC countries (Argentina, Brazil, Chile, Uruguay, etc.) with regard to third-place countries (Italy, France, Spain, Germany, Portugal, etc.).

Venezuela: Production, Import and Consumption of Wine				
Year	*Production*	*Imports* *	*Total Consumption*	*Consumption per inhabitant*
	(in hectoliters)			*(in liters)*
1975	88.690	101.892	190.582	1,6
1976	99.030	165.563	264.593	2,1
1977	84.390	185.832	270.222	2,1
1978	95.000	231.940	326.940	2,5
1979	91.000	145.511	236.511	1,7
1980	** 95.000	207.570	302.570	2,2

*Imports of most are not included
** Estimated

Source: FAO (Food and Agricultural Organization of the United Nations), Rome, 1984.

Index